Race and Cultural Practice
in Popular Culture

Race and Cultural Practice in Popular Culture

EDITED BY DOMINO RENEE PEREZ AND
RACHEL GONZÁLEZ-MARTIN

Rutgers University Press

New Brunswick, Camden, and Newark, New Jersey, and London

Library of Congress Cataloging-in-Publication Data

Names: Perez, Domino Renee, 1967- editor. | Gonzalez, Rachel Valentina, editor.
Title: Race and cultural practice in popular culture / edited by Domino Renee Perez
    and Rachel Gonzalez-Martin.
Description: New Brunswick, New Jersey : Rutgers University Press, [2018] |
    Includes bibliographical references and index.
Identifiers: LCCN 2018006160| ISBN 9781978801318 (cloth) | ISBN 9781978801301
    (paperback)
Subjects: LCSH: Race in mass media. | Mass media and culture—United States. |
    Popular culture—United States.
Classification: LCC P96.R3152 U5575 2018 | DDC 305.8—dc23 LC record available
    at https://lccn.loc.gov/2018006160

A British Cataloging-in-Publication record for this book is available from the British Library.

⊖ The paper used in this publication meets the requirements of the American National
Standard for Information Sciences—Permanence of Paper for Printed Library Materials,
ANSI Z39.48-1992.

www.rutgersuniversitypress.org

Manufactured in the United States of America

For Maria Elsa Ortiz Perez

Contents

Part III   Racialization in Place

Foreword

Assembling an Intersectional Pop Cultura Analytical Lens

FREDERICK LUIS ALDAMA

I am a consummate consumer of all things pop culture. Late at night my laptop glows with blue phosphorescence; wrestling with insomnia I binge on televisual and silver-screen shows. My bed-stand lies buried under a wobbly stack of comics, currently topped off with indigenous-penned, smart and entertaining *Super Indian, Quarantine Zone, My Hero, Marvel 1602* along with *Bitch Planet Vol. 2* and some radical feminist Latinx zines. I wake to music playlists that variously include trip hop (Portishead, Tricky, Massive Attack), drum 'n' bass (Peter Tosh, The Fugeess, J-Malik), acid jazz (Jazzmatazz and Digible Planets), Drake, Luis Fonsi, Miguel, and Ana Tijoux. And I wipe the glaze of sleep from my eyes and brain through hours of my thinking, writing, and teaching about pop cultural matters. Morning lectures for signature courses such as "Intro. to Latinx Pop Culture" and "Film & Comics: Race, Gender, Sexuality, and Differently Abled" wake me to the world.

Don't get me wrong. I love my novels as much as the next. My shelves are filled with book spines etched with names like Julio Cortázar, Gabriel García Márquez, Junot Díaz, Elena Garro, Julia Alvarez, Salman Rushdie, Yasunari Kawabata, Carlos Fuentes, Luis Urrea, Dagoberto Gilb, Michael Nava, Ana Castillo, Denise Chávez, Carmen Machado Assis, among others. These same shelves include poetry collections of the most rarified sort (the maddening Apollinaire, for instance) along with some seriously self-reflexive, meta-critical Criterion Collection DVD films. I even have a Janson history of art tome that's gathering dust. And, I occasionally suit up to catch some high-brow live symphonic compositions.

Race, sexuality, gender, differently abled issues come alive mostly in and through my engagement with and thinking through pop culture, however. It's my primordial soup. I felt less different as a kid after having seen how much *fun* the Addam's family had together—an Othered family like mine in Sacramento. It was comic books that allowed me to soar far above my modest, single-parent Latinx tellurian confines—and expand my English vocabulary. It was an imaginary lightsaber that allowed me to slice-and-dice the Bros Ortiz, our neighborhood bullies.

I'm not alone. Many of us racialized and historically marginalized subjects can say the same. Sherman Alexie opens his *LA Times* reflection on the joys of writing and reading thus: "I learned to read with a Superman comic book." Comic book creator and scholar, John Jennings reflects: "Growing up black, poor, and Southern made sure of my imperceptibility to the mainstream. So, like most invisible people, I turned to stories in popular media to start to build some sense of self to reflect back to my burgeoning psyche" (*Latinx Superheroes* xi). And, creator of *El Muerto* and Latino Comics Expo cofounder Javier Hernandez reflects: "I don't remember the media itself (in-print comic, film, or TV show) when I first discovered Zorro, but I do recall imagining a character dressed in a fanciful black costume, riding atop a horse while brandishing swords and a gun. No matter his Spanish origin, I imagined myself, a Latino kid with Mexican ancestry, as this superhero" (*Latinx Superheroes* 183).

While I clearly think that pop culture matters in our everyday lives, scholarly inquiry, and knowledge dissemination, not all pop culture is made equally—especially when it comes to matters of race, sexuality, gender, and differently abled subjects and experiences. I had the great misfortune of sitting through Dax Shephard's silver-screen remake of the '70s show, *CHiPs* (2017). Unfortunate because Shephard as director and screenplay writer throws Latinx characterization back to the time of the Unenlightenment: Michael Peña stars as a Frank 'Ponch' Poncherello who is singularly defined by his sexual addiction (hand jerks or any convenient hole)—and sans any winks of irony or self-reflexivity. And, there's the hyperbolic histrionics of Sofia Vergara playing Gloria in *Modern Family* that continue to rankle. I can say the same of J-Lo's role as Marisa Ava Marie Ventura in the film *Maid in Manhattan* (2002) who is redeemed and made *good* (after being bad for supposedly stealing a fur coat) by association with aristocratic whiteness (Ralph Fienes as Christopher Marshall). Her role as Harlee Santos in the 2016-TV series *Shades of Blue* (2016–2017) isn't much better. The show's creator, Adi Hasak, characterizes her as a corrupted, double-crossing Latinx single mamá, playing into and reinforcing those age-old stereotypes of Latinas as malinches.

However, even these instances that lack a *will to style* (responsibility to representations of Latinx subjects both in form and in content) can reveal much about life for intersectional subjectivities in the United States. They can and do reveal the pernicious legacy of the EuroSpanish *casta* system that continues to privilege light-skinned Latinxs in the hemispheric Américas; they can and do reveal how Latinas are often depicted as bad and all bodied. They can and do shed light on how pop cultura *can* evince a great will to style. I think of how J-Lo turns the tables of whose peeping who, at least momentarily, on this saint vs. sinner, virgin vs. whore stereotyping in her music video "I Luh Ya Papí" (2014). And how corporate megalith Fox can create shows like *Brooklyn Nine-Nine* (2013–) that push Latinx complexity into the quotidian boob-tube lives of U.S. Americans; with Detective Rosa Diaz (Stephanie Beatriz) and Detective Amy Santiago (Melissa Fumero) the show's creators Dan Goor and Michael Schur serve up some of TV's smartest, wittiest, badass Latinxs on prime time.

Here and elsewhere we're seeing what Isabel Molina-Guzmán identifies as "color-conscious" TV programing that develops "characters with ethnic and racial cultural and experiential specificity and thereby more complexity" (*Latinas and Latinos on TV* 9). This color-conscious programming is happening on multiple perceptual levels, including the aural. As season 7 of *Orange Is the New Black* (2013–) unfolds, not only does the narrative move the voice and agency from the Anglo Piper Chapman (Taylor Schilling) to Latina leaders of the revolution, such as Dayanara Diaz (Dascha Polanco), but also there's an increased presence of a contrapuntal, English–Spanish bilingual linguisticscape heard between Maritza Ramos (Diane Guerrero) and Marisol "Flaca" Gonzales (Jackie Cruz). Spanish linguistic rhythms become as important an auditory shaper of the narrative as English in a show that radically reveals the deep truths about the racist, heterosexist neoliberalism that undergirds global capitalism.

There's a certain resplendence of intersectional representation that's happening in the mainstream. This provides the textured surfaces for viewers like myself to entangle identities and experiences with. It's more than just the token appearance of a Latinx character or soundscape. It's casting and writing shows like *I Love Dick* (2017), which features the Mexico-born, mixed Argentinian/Honduran Latinx lesbian actor Roberta Colindrez as the genderqueer Mexican-American, Devon. In a moment of passion, she commands their partner to "suck my cock." And in the twelve-webisode series, "Brujos," the creators use the *telenovela* and sitcom formula along with some *brujería* to make new perceptions of how racism, homophobia, and (straight, white male) colonization affect LGBTQ Latinx subjects. And in the Selena Gomez–produced *13 Reasons Why* (2017) the show's writers create a fully fleshed out Latinx gay character, Tony Padilla (Christian Navarro), with substantive screen time that reveals his complex struggle at home (a machista papá and Catholicism) and with his white boyfriend's Catholicism.

This isn't to say that pop culture gets it right all the time concerning intersectional assemblages of race, gender, sexuality identities and experiences. Throw a net into the pop culture flotsam and the detritus overwhelms. *Star Wars 8* continues to run with the Latinx actor Oscar Isaac as the central character, but it is color-blind to his Latinx identity; and this in sharp contrast to the writing for the character DJ (Benicio del Toro), whose Latinoness participates in a long history of misrepresenting Latinxs as linguistically inept and double-crossers. In a recent episode of *Z Nation* (Season 2, episode 15) Gina Gershwin appears in brownface as a Latina bruja (and leader of a pack of calavera-painted, machete-wielding Anglos) who imitates a stereotypical speech intonation of an East LA chola.

We need to have our eyes wide open to the continued gatekeeping practices that privilege white, male, and straight subjects. (Luis Fonsi and Daddy Yankee are talents in their own right, but it wasn't until Justin Bieber tried out his Spanish lyrics that "Despacito" became a huge hit.) And, we need to be especially vigilant in our everyday lives with the threat of U.S.–Mexico border walls going up, white supremacist attacks, along with deportations of our brothers and sisters.

Rachel, Domino, and the cadre of amazing scholars that make up this volume invite us to think deeply about everyday, living, breathing cultural phenomena that richly texture vital intersectional identities and experiences. They invite us to sharpen the analytic lens that sees race and racism, sexuality and heterosexism, gender and sexism as more than a set of binaries. In and through the analysis of *Breaking Bad, The Bridge, Orange Is the New Black, Shakira, Niki Manaj, Machete, Walking Dead, Sense8, Sicario*, and the bilingual, historically deep *Lucha Underground*, among many other pop cultural phenomena, we see how to construct sturdy yet elastic bridges between theory and praxis, between media studies and cultural studies, between genders and sexualities, between differently ethnoracialized communities; between creation and modes of circulation and reception. As this volume forcefully attests, until we truly live a postrace, postfeminist, postpost world a *pop cultura* intersectional analytic lens is necessary. It is urgent.

Works Cited

Aldama, Frederick Luis. *Latinx Superheroes in Mainstream Comics:* Tucson: U of Arizona P, 2017.

Alexie, Sherman. "The Joy of Reading and Writing: Superman and Me." *Los Angeles Times*. April 19, 1998. Web. Accessed December 21, 2017. https://www.google.com/url?sa=t&rct=j&q=&esrc=s&source=web&cd=3&ved=0ahUKEwjE_vOg8pvYAhVY82MKHYihBJoQFgg5MAI&url=http%3A%2F%2Fwww.u.arizona.edu%2F~freybaby%2FAlexie.doc&usg=AOvVaw38ZLomZj_RHqdZJ2ZEPrJ6.

Molina-Guzmán, Isabel. *Latinas and Latinos on TV.* Tucson: U of Arizona P, 2018.

Race and Cultural Practice in Popular Culture

Introduction

•••••••••••••••••••••

Re-imagining Critical Approaches to Folklore and Popular Culture

DOMINO RENEE PEREZ AND
RACHEL GONZÁLEZ-MARTIN

"To Be Alone," the fifth track of Irish singer, songwriter, and musician Hozi-er's 2014 self-titled debut album, opens with a bass chord laying down a heart-beat rhythm, which is then joined by the strains of a guitar mimicking a rattle and other percussive instruments. When the vocals finally begin, the singer keeps time with the heartbeat, often clipping words so that the song sounds like an American Indian–inspired chant without ever identifying itself as such. In the trailer for the film *Lowriders* (2017), directed by Ricardo de Montreuil, the extradiegetic narrator reflects on generational and community conflicts related to cultural practices and the movement in and out of physical, as well as spatial, geographies. Explicit value is placed on a particular kind of cultural practitioner (males) in this sonic, racialized, and classed community. The comedy-drama "Claws" premiered June 11, 2017, on TNT and stars Niecy Nash in a lead role as "Desna Simms," owner of "Florida's Artisan Nail Salon of Man-atee County." Desna uses her business to both adorn six-inch acrylic nails as well as launder money for a mob-owned pain meds clinic next door. Pairing nail art and extralegal entrepreneurship, the show features a cast of multi-racial women (African American, Asian American, Latina, and White), with complicated gendered subjectivities, as a community of practice that disrupts conventional expectations of race and sexuality. Taken together, these examples illustrate the intersection of racialized subjectivities in relation to cultural practices as represented, read, and circulated in popular imaginaries, which are of central importance to this collection.

Race and Cultural Practice in Popular Culture strategically addresses contemporary understandings of race and processes of social racialization. At the same time, it creates a contemporary body of scholarship that theorizes the concept of race as a social factor made concrete in popular forms, such as film, television, and music. As a shared conversation, this body of work pushes past the reaffirmation of static conceptions of identity, authenticity, or conventional interpretations of stereotypes. It actively bridges the intertextual gap between theories of community enactment and cultural representation. It also draws together distinct academic theories and methodologies (case studies, critical readings, and ethnographies, for example) in order to prioritize race as an ideological reality and a process that continues to impact lives, despite assertions that we live in a postracial America. Together, the contributors to this volume foreground examinations of the context and reception of cultural productions as critical spaces for reflecting upon the social politics of race. They demonstrate that popular cultural forms respond to, critique, and create racialized interventions in social life. These generative environments serve to reflect and remake popular conceptions of cultural practice and performance circulated globally. In doing so, they break with conventional studies of folkloric and popular forms. Such a break, even illustrated subtly, creates a spectrum on which texts, separately identified as popular culture and cultural practice (cultural forms, folklore), necessarily inform and complicate legacies of scholarly inquiry from both formal and contextual vantage points.

Contemporary critical readings of race, and to a lesser degree analyses of cultural practices, have been informed largely by Civil Rights era politics. Responses to, participation in, and ideological formations derived from this key historical moment have defined scholarly inquiry surrounding race, particularly in the field of ethnic studies, itself institutionalized in the wake of Civil Rights movements rooted in activist efforts on multiple fronts. The 2008 election of biracial president Barack Obama held powerful symbolic significance for academic and social discourses. Some believed his election instantiated racial parity, that Civil Rights measures had been effective, and announced a postracial era in which race no longer needed to be the focal point of cultural or political action. "Postrace" and "postracial" are contested terms not simply for their implied conditional posteriority but also because of the ongoing political realities communities of color face, from polluted water supplies and state violence to deportation and the rise of food deserts. Postrace rhetorics became a way to dismantle Civil Rights era policies and shore up (or in some cases reinstate) White male power. However, scholars such as Ramón Saldívar have argued for the utility of postrace as a critical paradigm that engages present and changing conceptions of race: "a new racial imaginary is required to account for the persistence of race as a key element of contemporary American social and cultural politics. What this suggests is not that we are beyond race; ... Rather, the term entails a conceptual shift to the question of what meaning the idea of 'race' carries in our own times," one not necessarily informed by Civil Rights' movement leadership or discourses (520). The book's contributors address these issues from multiple vantage points across texts and disciplines. Their considerations of race at the crossroads of folklore and popular culture highlight what Saldívar identifies as "racial symbolism," the ways in which "creative writers, filmmakers, musicians, and artists [for example] represent life experiences" (520). This collection offers critical and methodological strategies for reading and analyzing "life experiences" that are representative of and in conversation with other communities, cultural forms, and cultural practices. In other words, our contributors see race as a significant social factor, while also understanding that community practices are enacted in new racial contexts, with varying intersecting meanings linked to modes of circulation, and expanded multiracial audience reception, as well as unprecedented political environments.

Where the Folk and the Popular Meet

Folklore and popular culture are often seen as competing or discrete categories. However, cultural practices can represent sites where folklore and popular culture meet. Instead of seeing folklore as romantic, nostalgic, and salvaged, popular culture contexts make visible the ways that it is continuously being reformulated and reimagined. Such variations neither diminish nor devalue cultural forms that circulate in popular culture landscapes. This approach represents a shift away from early folkloristic methods that fail to directly engage with the interconnectedness of popular culture and lore. The erasure of intertextual connections between the two fields discounts the importance of the intersectionality of race, class, gender, sexuality, and citizenship in contemporary American folkloristics. Moreover, the entrenchment of popular culture in global markets requires that scholars of cultural practice evaluate the means by which cultural forms become cultural products as they are monetized in popular and mass media. Cultural practices mobilized by cultural entrepreneurs are *made* profitable by their circulation within mass cultural contexts.

This volume makes no distinctions between high and low culture. For our purposes, the consideration of public and private enactments of cultural practice allow for much more nuanced understandings of ontological frameworks on display. In other words, when what was once private is made public, cultural practices are rendered visible but also open to critique by both cultural insiders and outsiders. Such practice-based frameworks are then restaged within large-scale representative forms, for example, seeing cholos and goth girls in a music video based on a song from a British '80s New Wave duo. These platforms facilitate collective social receptions of particular forms creating "a terrain on which the 'politics of signification' are played out in an attempt to win readers [audiences] to particular ways of seeing the world" (qtd. in Storey 4). Popular culture is, therefore, a performative context in which reflections of distinct worldviews are signified through the representations of specific racialized cultural practices.

The field of folklore has continuously struggled since its inception to define solid boundaries for its proposed subject of study. This is especially true as folklore broke its disciplinary ties with anthropology to develop as its own independent field. "Folk-Lore," the term coined by William Thoms in 1846, while illustrating the spirit of the discipline's desire to identify emergent creative communicative practice, did not account for global social change that would reflect the complexities of social segmentation, class politics, technological advancement, or racial diversity. Conceptually, folklore is a metacultural category of informal interpersonal communication. Its contextual manifestations—jokes, slang, song, dance, narrative, ritual, et cetera—change based on relevance to current communities, and yet, despite modification, remain legible and identifiable across generations of practitioners. The use of such cultural forms furnishes, even inadvertently, a way in which people communicate relatedness and set sociocultural boundaries around notions of belonging in particular communities or self-ascribed folk groups.

Folklore creates a code for meaningful human interactions. Both material and verbal manifestations vary along intersectional axes taking into account experiences of race, class, gender, geography, and economics, just to name a few. Similarly, these forms become nested in mass media, in which audience impact transcends person-to-person or family-to-family communications, in favor of engaging larger publics. In this context, the intimacy audiences once valued is supplanted in favor of connections built from larger conceptualizations of nationhood and popular forms of global citizenship. Audiences, therefore, become re-categorized and disarticulated from the subjectivities produced in those of ethnoracial enclaves to those that can be more broadly claimed as "American." In such contexts, the complexities of what it is to live as a publically identified "minority" are obscured. Such loss occurs both when ethnoracial categories are exclusively used to judge individual experiences as more or less authentic and when ethnoracial categories are broadened to manipulate consumer-audiences into believing that national affiliations are race-blind. An examination of folklore, both as familiar, intimate modes of communication (folk speech, jokes, personal narratives, among other genres) and as those modeled en masse for global audiences (performing race and class in film and television, for example) allows scholars to assess interpretations of race, class, and gender politics as the material and verbal manifestations of personal expression as well as monetized consumer production.

Although the employment of variegated forms of cultural practices within global popular culture is interpretable as the embracing of cultural difference on its merits alone, we must not fail to recognize that appearing to value diversity in the twenty-first century is profitable. Industries that can supply diversity in different forms are sought after by both social institutions and communities of practitioners alike. Individuals who provide products, services, or specialized knowledge about enacting ritual practices or trade in the signifiers of race or ethnicity are cultural entrepreneurs. These professionals, operating in both formal and informal economies, provide material goods, services, or knowledge to signify or enact the traditions and practices of a cultural community. These culture brokers determine, produce, and reproduce culture by monetizing material goods used in ceremonies, performances, or other cultural practices. Thomas H. Aageson sees cultural entrepreneurs as "cultural change agents and resourceful visionaries who organize cultural, financial, social and human capital, to generate revenue from a cultural activity" (96). Often, they have significant, though unstable, economic power in the cultural marketplace because not only do they trade in the materiality of ethnicity and/or traditions but they must also compete with other knowledge brokers (who provide similar goods and services), as well as changing tastes and attitudes in the cultural economy. In the contemporary global marketplace, cultural entrepreneurs working in popular media reinforce industry identities as cultural enterprises that not only benefit from drawing in diverse audiences using familiar signifiers but also from influencing discourses of race-conscious ideologies in both micro- and macrosocial contexts in the United States. Forms of popular culture, such as film, music, and other mass media genres, serve as macrocultural contexts in which racialized social capital becomes a negotiation between enactment and expectation.

As such, folklore studies have the distinct capacity to speak to a middle ground, examining the ways in which personal creativity and communication draw on ethnoracial identities as well as understandings of nationalized subjectivities. However, the discipline has not been at the forefront of legible conversation on race, class, and gender formation in the United States. Focused more on objects of culture, whether verbal or material in form, the politics of representation and the awareness of authorial positionality lacks impact on a discipline that admirably promotes studies of individual artistry, but distances itself, by omission, from paradigms of contemporary interdisciplinary social and cultural theory.

This book contributes to the twenty-first-century canon in American folklore studies, reinterpreting the notions of "folklore" and "cultural forms" as texts that transcend verbal and material artistry of individuals, making the line that divides cultural forms (between the "folk" and the "popular") unproductive for truly understanding community-based creativity in the twenty-first century. Similar in title but not in scope, *The Folkloresque: Reframing Folklore in a Popular Culture World* (2015) by Michael Dylan Foster and Jeffery A. Tolbert, is a classical approach to folklore studies, in terms of both its content and its methodology and does not engage meaningfully with new media, race, or gender. The co-edited text implicitly reinforces the primacy of Euro-American and masculinist folklore traditions. Earlier comparative works, such as *Identity and Everyday Life: Essays in the Study of Folklore, Music, and Popular Culture* (2004) by Harris M. Berger and Giovanna P. Del Negro, which brings into conversation American folklore, British cultural studies, and French everyday life theory, are narrow in focus and often exclude critical engagement with race or ethnicity and, therefore, the social narratives of racialization that directly affect their collaborators' lives. Other books and studies focusing on folklore and popular culture are introductory or reference textbooks, *Folklore the Basics* (2016) or *Folklore, Cultural Performances, and Popular Entertainments* (1992); topic specific, *The Zombie Renaissance in Popular Culture* (2015) or *Lucifer Ascending: The Occult in Folklore and Popular Culture* (2004); anomalous or foreign practices in regional or hemispheric environments, *Welsh Mythology and Folklore in Popular Culture: Essays on Adaptations in Literature, Film, Television and Digital Media* (2011); or primarily concerned with fairytales, especially the Brothers Grimm, or concentrate on characters, genres, or specific motifs.

Beyond works that prioritize specific genres or methods when working on the popular or the folkloric, there are also collections that stand out for their desire to move scholarly conversations toward a deeper understanding of how ethnoracial solidarities, particularly those that amplify how personal artistic performances function collectively as sights of social resistance. *Performing the US Latina and Latino Borderlands* (2012), edited by Arturo Aldama, Chela Sandoval, and Peter Garcia, one example of such works, discusses how Latina/o communities use cultural practices, situated both physically and emotionally in U.S.–Mexican border spaces, as a mode of public self-fashioning. Particularly valuable is the blend of Latina/o studies scholars representing different generations of training and area specialties. However, their intellectual contributions implicitly prioritize an ethnically and racially specific view of Latinx racial formation in the United States.

In similar form, the recently published *The Routledge Companion to Latina/o Popular Culture* (2016) edited by Frederick Aldama builds and expands on a commitment to Latina/o perspectives and practices, while also actively engaging with a discourse of mass culture and its impact on larger national and global audiences. *Latina/o Popular Culture* creates space from which new levels of critical analysis, emerging from a wide range of Latina/o cultural studies scholars, who are positionally varied, represent various methodologies, and whose collective intellectual labor does not presume the monikers "Mexican American" and "Latina/o" to be synonymous. Much like the essays in *Performing the US Latina and Latino Borderlands*, authors in *Latina/o Popular Culture* seek to fill gaps in scholarship, where the presence of Latina/o cultural production is not only absent but actively erased. Collectively, this compilation and the topics of engagement represented precede necessary conversations about the construction of race in and of popular culture that are yet to be had, in particular explicitly comparative studies. Imagine—as Aldama, Sandoval, and Garcia do—a narrative of U.S. Latina/o cultural production representative of the materialization and intellectualizing of a Borderlands ethos through performance. In this context, a scholar would see culture in practice all along a public street in a cosmopolitan city like San Antonio, and choose to narrow her lens to include the elderly Tejano *paleta* vendor who sells his ice cream treats to locals and tourists alike, analyzing his performance as a cultural icon of endurance and resistance in an age of alienating technological advancement and toxic gentrification. Yet the forced relocation of domestic migrants from the ecological and economic impact of Hurricane Katrina in Louisiana created a cultural ripple effect, where the prominence of African American cultural communities in San Antonio has been increasingly made visible. So it would not be surprising if a block down from the *paletero* there was a group of young African American women turning double-dutch in plain view. While this narrowing of focus offers centrality to the *paletero* and his life story—a story often overlooked—it fails to help us answer multiple questions, such as, What can the overlapping of Latina/o and African American community space tell us about experiences of race in American cities? How are national perceptions of race and racialization customized to geographic spaces, and thus influence how cultural communities choose to perform identities in relation to practice? And finally, what is mass culture's role in defining or dismantling an understanding of shared processes of racialization at local, regional, and national levels? *Race and Cultural Practice in Popular Culture* strives for a complementary understanding of race and racialized cultural productions. The next frontier of critical analysis necessitates diversified collaborations across ethnoracial communities. Such collaborations must dialogue with more specialized narratives of race in order to advance a shared discourse of the realities of racialization as a lived experience in the contemporary United States.

The intersection between theories of cultural practice in American folklore and cultural studies and critical race theorizing in popular culture studies creates innovative articulations across fields differentially rooted in lived experiences of race and technologically mediated representations of race. A considerable body of work in cultural studies and American Indian studies has focused on these issues to varying degrees. The publication of Roy Harvey Pearce's *The Savages of America* (1953), later retitled *Savagism and Civilization: A Study of the Indian and the American Mind* (1965), for many scholars, initiates the critical study of literary and social representations of Native people. Since then, the analysis of American Indian representation has extended to include other popular and commercial forms, most notably film. With titles such as *Shadows of the Indian: Stereotypes in American Culture* (1982), *Celluloid Indians: Native Americans and Film* (1999), *Wiping the War Paint Off the Lens: Native American Film and Video* (2001), and *Making the White Man's Indian: Native Americans and Hollywood Movies* (2005), to name only a few, Native and non-Native scholars have brought historical, sociocultural, political, and generic questions to the analysis of Indians in film. Other representational studies focus on what images of American Indians do and how they are used. Inclusive of anthropology and cultural studies, *Dressing in Feathers: The Construction of the Indian in American Popular Culture* (1996), edited by S. Elizabeth Bird, considers how images of Indians created in film, photographs, advertising, and television are crucial to the narrative of White superiority and their myth of Manifest Destiny. *Selling the Indian: Commercializing & Appropriating Indian Cultures* (2001), edited by Cartier Jones Meyer and Diana Royer, takes as its focus how the circulation, via staging and marketing for non-Indians, of Indian lifeways, cultural practices, and cultural production represents a form of cultural imperialism. Philip Deloria's *Playing Indian* (1998) turns toward the long American history of White males dressing, appropriating, and sometimes inventing Indian customs or practices as a means of enacting a particular kind of nationalism, citizenship, and masculinity. Offering case studies that focus on violence, representation, athletics, technology, and music, Deloria's *Indians in Unexpected Places* (2004) examines disruptions or dislodgings, through Indian encounters with modernity, of static expectations about Native people in the U.S. imaginary. More recently, Pauline Strong in *American Indians and the American Imaginary: Cultural Representation across the Centuries* (2013) uses an ethnographic approach in order to "[employ] a theory of representational practice" that allows for a consideration of "the ways in which representations are significant parts of power-laden social and cultural processes" (1). While our collection does not focus on American Indians or Native peoples exclusively, our contributors engage with this rich intellectual history, which many have helped to build, in their readings of irony, metadiscourse, settler colonialism, nonnormative masculinity, and youth culture.

A focus on critical studies that prioritize cultural form and genre as their mode of entry into discussions of race and popular cultural practices leads to a different body of scholarship that speaks directly to disciplinary specialists. In *African American Music: An Introduction* (2006, 2015), Mellonee V. Burnim and Portia K. Maultsby's seminal work draws together a body of African

American music scholarship to narrate the field's complexity, documenting the social life of specific genres across time, implying a connection between historical moments and critical creativity, all under the umbrella of African American experiences of race in the United States. They include a section titled "Post–Civil Rights and Beyond (1960–) emphasizing the shift around and beyond this milestone period. They produce a critical discourse that is most legible to other specialists and students in training. A focus on social politics that prioritize form also leads to other discussions of race in musical production in *Sounding the Colorline: Music and Race in the Southern Imagination* (2003, 2015) by Erich Nunn. Drawing on different sources for the southern imagination, he uses literary texts, such as William Faulkner's *Sanctuary* and Jean Toomer's *Cane* to examine how cultural soundscapes become part of popular literary culture focused on race in specific regions. Nunn uses sound studies to analyze race in the South, drawing from American balladry to contemporary hip-hop, to develop a legacy that creates a throughline between folkloric forms and popular production. Music is a space where race is conceptualized as a product of intersectional experiences and a mode to create new collectively legible soundscapes across African American communities.

When examining music as a cultural practice that is race and class based very specifically in the United States, it becomes important to understand how ethnoracial communities use the genre to mediate racialized representations in the United States. In *Music and the Racial Imagination* (2000), editors Ronald Radano and Philip V. Bohlman, music scholars coming from African American and Jewish studies, respectively, draw together an impressive body of interdisciplinary scholarship on the intersection of musical forms and race in a global context. Their book narrates a link between musical forms considered non-Western (colonial formations) and those that have become consumer products (world music) and are not ethnoracially determined. Doing so reinforces the value of collaborative, cross-disciplinary conversations, highlighting an implicit connection between the folkloric and the popular that *Race and Culture Practice* seeks to emphasize. With a clear focus on music and race, *Music and the Racial Imagination* is a critical work in the field of ethnomusicology that serves as a model of collaborative cultural studies as it examines how the imagination of race has influenced musical production, reception, and scholarly analysis.

Toward New Critical Perspectives

Rather than an exclusive preoccupation with mimetic histories, *Race and Cultural Practice in Popular Culture* focuses on contemporary experiences of race and representational politics. As a result, the chapters that follow lay the foundation for new modes of inquiry that prioritize the impact of cultural practices in the present. These conversations are generative as they shift away from interrogative binaries that have influenced modes of inquiry, such as the use of Black–White racial dichotomies, assessments of visibility and absence, and static or dynamic appraisals that assign hierarchical value to cultural forms. This collection asserts the need for intersectional approaches to contemporary ideations of race in society sourced from scholars writing from myriad disciplinary homes and drawing on a variety of methodologies.

Race and Cultural Practice in Popular Culture reframes critical conversations linking folklore and popular culture studies, while moving away from ethnic nationalist discourse toward explicitly intersectional and multidisciplinary approaches. More practically, it emphasizes the ways scholars from distinct disciplinary frameworks and methodological standpoints rely on various discursive forms to implement analyses at the intersection of folklore and popular culture. *Race and Cultural Practice in Popular Culture* lays bare the often overlooked, shared conversation across American ethnic studies specializations to examine the politics of representation across multiple contemporary media platforms. By drawing together national and international approaches that innovate across fields and disciplines, these chapters create an accessible scholarly resource that builds on representational politics in a global cultural landscape. In this context, Eurocentric "Americanism" is replaced with multiple entry points constructed by diversely situated scholars, who embrace ambivalent theoretical intersections to enact and create critical cultural studies discourse. Contributors engage to varying degrees with questions of space, physical but also metadiscursive space, as represented in collaborative conversations of social, political, economic, and intellectual practices, particularly as they hold sway and work in the world. With its broad focus on cultural landscapes in the United States, place and context remain central to the work of many of our contributors. These ideas also frame the importance of public visibility and cross-cultural, spatial, and racial interpretations applicable to the larger United States.

Instead of affirming anthropological microcontexts of cultural performance, our volume creates connectivity across contexts of performance, drawing them together based on their common ground as cultural forms. The chapters assembled here offer critical insights, each from its own disciplinary discourse, facilitating dialogues between fields of inquiry and methodological approaches. For example, chapters that use formal textual analysis speak to others that feature first-person ethnographic observations. As such, we chose to create clear distinctions by thematically organizing chapters—creating sections that do not isolate studies by discipline, method, or rank. Instead, each section emphasizes theories of race and popular culture divided by forms generated by a particular ethnic community.

Race and Cultural Practice in Popular Culture narrates a story through a singular list of authors and titles with particularly strong offerings in Latino, American Indian, gender, and sound studies. Structurally divided into thematic sections and intertwining chapters oriented toward a variety of academic audiences, the book strategically addresses contemporary understandings of race and processes of social racialization. The cultural texts include, but are not limited to, physical adornment, ethnography, film, music, television, and public performance figured in local, regional, and transnational environments. Methodological variations for analyzing these texts are derived from the following disciplinary perspectives: American studies, Asian–Asian American diaspora studies, anthropology, Chicana/o studies, communication and rhetoric, comparative literature, cultural studies, English, folklore, gender and sexuality studies, history, Latina/o studies, Native American studies, and Spanish sociolinguistics. Grouped into three parts, across forms and genres, each section constitutes a conversation centered on form or theory that accounts for and includes multiple disciplinary perspectives and approaches.

Part I: Visualizing Race draws from American Indian and Mexican-themed films and television shows, such as *Orange Is the New Black* (Netflix), *The Bridge* (FX), and *Breaking Bad* (AMC), to consider how racialized and gendered subjects are formulated, and in some cases transformed, keeping in mind such factors as environment, kinship, and nation as they inform political geographies in popular imaginaries. The interrogations of transitional spaces, including prisons, tunnels, bridges, and even the imagined frontier, offer concrete settings for stagings and visualizations of race. Representations of borders and masculinities, for example, demarcate dynamic points of connection and points of separation that can reinforce the authority or morality of the state or nation in narrating racialized subjectivities.

Part II: Sounding Race collectively investigates cultural practices in sonic landscapes that emphasize the sounding of race in popular musical forms stretching across the hemispheric Americas with a focus on artists, including Hamac Caziim (Comc'ac from Sonora), Zak Tzevul (Tzotzil from Chiapas), Rafael Reyes and Dave Parley (rock-duo Prayers), Lila Downs, Astrid Hadad, and Shakira, in coexisting racialized systems, at times commercialized, performances. Sounding, separated but not independent from processes of visualizing race, examines racialized subjectivities from the vantage point of audible histories of colonial and neocolonial resistance, prioritizing examinations of discursive agency. These chapters rely on intersectional approaches to holistic sonic cultural practices to consider the embodiment of nation, gender, and race in subject formation.

Part III: Racialization in Place considers race in relation to intertextual performative geographies, inclusive of sites informed by aesthetics, culture, affect, gender, queerness, and politics. Inhabiting interstitial spaces, where subjects are equally likely to be unseen or surveilled, allows social agents to innovate expressions and formulations of race. Attending to analyses of location, both figurative and theoretical in traditional ethnographic narration, Robert Rodriguez's film *Machete* (2010), and the television program *The Walking Dead* (AMC), conceptualize how race is constituted or destabilized on stage and screen. Additionally, this section includes critical commentary on ethnographic practice, and a transparent collaborative dialogue creating contemporary folkloristic discourse predicated on the living relationship between artist and subject, as well as artist and scholar. Chapters in this section reveal the potentiality of cultural practices to make visible subversive reformulations of race in context and generate new theoretical paradigms that necessarily complicate the study of folklore and popular culture.

Across cultures, genres, methods, and nations, this collection engages with expressive forms and patterns of performance in distinct social, cultural, and political contexts, while also posing questions and mapping further areas of research. Drawing from the range of participating scholars of color, and those scholars devoted to advancing the study of race formations globally, *Race and Cultural Practice in Popular Culture* demonstrates the need to visit and revisit the realm of the popular as a public space for the mediation of foundational depictions of raced and classed experiences. We would like to thank our contributors for plotting new directions and bringing into conversation critical, theoretical, and interdisciplinary methodologies to open and inspire new sites of critical inquiry.

Works Cited

Aageson, Thomas H. "Cultural Entrepreneurs: Producing Cultural Value and Wealth." *The Cultural Economy*. Eds. Helmut K. Anheier and Yudhishthir Raj Isar. London: Sage, 2008. 92–107.

Saldívar, Ramón. "Speculative Realism and the Postrace Aesthetic in Contemporary Fiction." *A Companion to American Literary Studies*. Eds. Caroline F. Levander and Robert S. Levine. Oxford: Blackwell, 2011. 517–531.

Storey, John. *Cultural Theory and Popular Culture*. Abingdon: Routledge, 2015.

Strong, Pauline Turner. *American Indians and the American Imaginary: Cultural Representation Across the Centuries*. Boulder: Paradigm, 2013.

Part I

Visualizing Race

• •

1

A Thousand
"Lines of Flight"

• •

Collective Individuation and Racial Identity in Netflix's *Orange Is the New Black* and *Sense8*

RUTH Y. HSU

The problem of the twentieth century
is the problem of the color line, the
question of how far differences of
race—which show themselves chiefly in
the color of skin and the texture of the
hair—will hereafter be made the basis of
denying to over half the world the right
of sharing to their utmost ability the
opportunities and privileges of modern
civilization.
—(DuBois)

Context: The Past in the Present

The impact of the color line in the United States is as consequential in 2017 as it was when DuBois wrote and spoke the words above. One hundred and fourteen years after those words, in Ferguson, Missouri, on August 9, 2014, Darren Wilson, a white police officer, fired twelve rounds at eighteen-year-old, unarmed, African American, Michael Brown, killing him. "Ferguson" became an emblem almost immediately, reflecting the deep divisions in the United States on the matter of race. And the name of the town became instantly recognizable and representative of a moment when many more white citizens of the country realized, finally—as if a light in a room had been abruptly switched on—a reality that poor, black communities had long lived, which is that black lives do not matter, that many police have used for some time lethal force in predominantly black neighborhoods as the first rather than the last resort.[1] Yet, "Ferguson" did not become the irreversible tipping point of radical change for the better; while this chapter was being prepared, in what might prove to be a critical juncture for the whole of U.S. democracy, Heather Heyer, 32, was run over and killed by 20-year-old James Alex Fields, Jr., who drove into her and a group of counter-protestors demonstrating against a Unite the Right march on August 11–12, 2017, in Charlottesville, Virginia. The assault took place on the afternoon of August 12, 2017; nineteen other counter-protestors were injured, some critically.[2] The white supremacist terrorism in Charlottesville and President Trump's succor offered to the so-called alt-right at a press conference several days after the killing of Heather Heyer are clear signs of U.S. democracy in crisis, a crisis catalyzed once again by the issue of race.[3]

While the most evident forms of racism might be better understood today than fifty years ago, there continue to be deep divisions in the country over the less evident, systemic nature of racism. For example, there is very little comprehension of factors leading to racial groups being drawn to live in the same neighborhoods and perhaps to struggle with what sociologists and political scientists term environmental racism. Understanding is also lacking as to why one cannot "just move out" of those neighborhoods, or why there is no equivalency between the slogan "White Lives Matter" and the movement "Black Lives Matter." In addition, a pervasive viewpoint on racism is that its most pernicious forms have been destroyed or that it exists only in small pockets (read: black neighborhoods) of major cities. Barack Obama's election, for instance, briefly ignited the narrative that the United States had achieved a postracial state. The various, often conflicting, understandings on race are magnified by the lack of awareness about the imbrication of gender and racial identity and how both identity categories function to organize class hierarchy and economic inequalities.

One's awareness of how racial and gender identity intersect to bolster white supremacist, heteronormative divisions and oppressions in the United States stem from many factors, two of which are immediately germane to this examination of *Orange Is the New Black* (*OITNB*) and *Sense8*: (1) the extent to which race and gender matter—and the extent to which one apprehends how they matter—is a direct outcome of one's everyday lived reality, a reality that is distilled through one's body, its physical features, its half-life in time and space beyond the present moment; (2) in an age when social media, entertainment media, online culture, and so-called online news media constitute the vast majority of our daily lives, often, for many passive consumers of these popular cultural texts, what we are served becomes our reality. George Gerbner's "cultivation" theory seems to be applicable to this newer media environment (Morgan and Shanahan). The reporting on Charlottesville is the most recent example of this problem: the vast majority of news reports cast the "white supremacist" march to the statue of Robert E. Lee on the University of Virginia campus as a horrible event but nonetheless an aberration, a nostalgic throwback to the bygone era of the old Confederacy on the part of a small white minority. In sharp contrast, the discursive composition, throughout the history of this nation, of the "black" body and the African American presence has always already consisted of dehumanizing the individual and the whole group; this essentializing of blackness is frequently conveyed in popular cultural texts through images of criminality and black bodies as constitutionally incapable of self-discipline or incapable of knowing their proper place in the U.S. body politic. In short, white violence is an aberration, but violence is intrinsic to the African American, a supposition that is rationalized in a cruel circular (il)logic as located in the body's very blackness.

OITNB is particularly suited to an examination of the workings of intersectionality; the discursive framing of black and brown bodies as inherently out of control and violent (O'Sullivan); and the figuration of racial identity as a U.S. reformulation of traditional tribalism (a reformulation that both shows persistently transgress). *OITNB* and *Sense8* are important cultural texts, especially since the 2016 elections and recent events, and especially given the global entertainment hegemony of the company that funds, produces, and streams these two shows.[4] Both shows are important cultural texts also because they quickly garnered devoted fans as well as attracted favorable media reviews and, in the case of *OITNB*, scholarship. Moreover, both shows exhibit groundbreaking originality in terms of premise, scripting, and casting. Most important, they not only critique and deconstruct the ideology and apparatus of white supremacist heteronormativity they evince a radical rethinking of human-being, of the maturation of the individual-as-part-of-the-collective, and of the collective itself. This rethinking aims to undo the essentialist binary paradigm that structures prevailing identity constructs of race and gender.

Methodology and Collective Individuation

The argument of this chapter grew from several considerations: (1) a concern with the ways that otherwise incisive criticisms of racism and a racialist world-view in television studies fail to move beyond the dominant essentialist and binary concept of racial and gender identity. Most critiques of *OITNB* published in academic journals so far fall into this category (Caputi). This consideration is based on Paul Gilroy's trenchant argument "against race." Gilroy writes,

> It is impossible to deny that we are living through a profound transformation in the way the idea of "race" is understood and acted upon. Underlying it there is another possibly deeper, problem that arises from the changing mechanisms that govern how racial differences are seen, how they appear to us and prompt specific identities . . . . the creative acts involved in destroying raciology and transcending "race" are more than warranted by the goal of authentic democracy. . . . The first task is to suggest that the demise of "race" is not something to be feared. (11–12)

(2) The limitations of prevailing social science–based, empiricist methodology to measure the impact of televisual texts on the formation of race-d and gender-ed subjectivities; (3) the limitations of reading or interpreting televisual texts solely as if they are literature; (4) the emerging algorithmic calculus used by media giants such as Netflix, which upends current scholarship relying on tools that track viewership numbers and demography[5]; and (5) similar to item 2 in this list, viewership numbers and demographic data that cannot adequately explain the dynamic, fluid, unpredictable, and sometimes self-conflicting nature of subject formation, including the all-important impact of other cultural texts, discourses and interactions, the role of cognitive development, and the functions of memory and affect.

The goal of this chapter is not to diminish the invaluable antiracism work that has been accomplished in media studies; instead, I explore the capability of some of the ideas of Gilles Deleuze, Gilbert Simondon, and Rosi Braidotti to radically undo the binary paradigm structuring identity categories. Their ideas can open up a new vector of social science–based, cultural studies–centered analysis of the fictive media landscape. To Braidotti, "new figurations" or "alternative representations and social locations" are needed "for the kind of hybrid mix [in *Sense8*, for example] we are in the process of becoming" (2).

To be clear, *OITNB* and *Sense8* do not instantiate a postracial United States; instead aspects of scripting—in terms of plotting and choice of narrators—reveal a possible pathway beyond the prevailing essentialist racial paradigm. Both shows contain a radically alternative configuration of the individual as a process of becoming, not in the sense of becoming someone, that is, of achieving a somehow intuited or socially normative end point using innate essences—colloquially, who I really am or who I am meant to be. David Scott's monograph discusses Simondon's framing of the problem thus, "The ontological and epistemological privilege . . . granted to the individual by psychology, sociology, and other philosophical theories presumes a uniting of a metaphysic of substance with an underlying hylemorphism.[6] . . . . [but the problem is one of begging the question] the principle of individuation is made anterior to the process of individuation itself, thereby promoting the constituted and given individual as the only starting point" (31). Scott notes that, in contrast to a substantialist or hylemorphic schema of individuation, Simondon's conceptualization of living individuation consists of successive *and* simultaneous acts of social and psychological reformation . . . "ever partial, incomplete. . . . The living being is itself partially its own principle of individuation" (33). Furthermore, and this idea is crucial in Simondon's thought, "a living being exists as only always a becoming between individuation, not as a becoming after individuation" (37); a living being is "at once the individuating system and its partial result" (33). "System" does not denote a preestablished roadmap or routinized procedure, nor does it presuppose a transcendental, preexisting essence. Rather, "system" is derived from the living being existing as "only always a becoming between" phases of transformation that do not seek to rise to meet ideal, external forms or matter or to materialize from an internal essence, if indeed essence exists. Muriel Combes's metaphor of a rhizome may be useful, "like a crystal that from a very small seed grows in all directions within its aqueous solution wherein each molecular layer already constituted serves as a structuring base for the layer in the process of forming. Transduction expresses the processual sense of individuation" (6–7).[7] The ways in which the characters in *OITNB* and *Sense8* proliferate, to connect or merge or intertwine, unpredictably, in response to unanticipated occurrences is a figuration of a rhizomic becoming.

To critique and to criticize *OITNB* and *Sense8* in terms of racist and gender stereotypes is useful as a response to persistent racist tropes in the overall cultural cartography (Enck and Morrissey). However, this criticism does not remove the mechanics or the generative ground enabling the circulation and re-formations of racist and sexist discourse; to a disturbing degree, this type of criticism requires the existence of the offense, too often serves to harden the offensive trope in the collective imagination, and presupposes the existence of the ideal, the true, and an authentic essence of identity. In other words, this kind of anti-stereotype criticism, though still important to undertake, often derives from and reaffirms the prevailing paradigm. I shall discuss in more detail the issue of stereotypes and *OITNB* later in this chapter.

OITNB and *Sense8* transgress the predominant, conventional narrative plot and protagonist–antagonist structure of televisual texts to a degree that enables viewers to envision in these series radically different worldviews, whatever the intentions of their creators, respectively, Jeni Kohan and Lana and Lilly Wachowski and J. Michael Straczynski (*Sense8*, season 2 in its entirety was released in May 2017. Netflix has since canceled the series, citing the cost of supposedly $8 million per episode). First, writers have decentered the idea of a single protagonist, the essential character to whom viewers are sutured, are led to identify with, are induced to see themselves in, to compare themselves, or to pattern themselves after. The significance here can be grasped if we contextualize the conventional, single protagonist within a long, patriarchal and masculinist tradition dating back to Aristotle. That figuration of the male hero is typically dominating, aggressive, and frequently violent. Over the many centuries of the development of storytelling, the heroic, aristocratic, divine, or superhuman qualities of male protagonists have fallen away, most markedly with the advent of rationalist philosophy and thinkers like Locke and Spinoza. Fiction was to be about the quotidian experiences of representatives of many walks of life (Watt).

The multiple-protagonist scripting of *OITNB*, especially because the thematic purpose is about each inmate's backstory—gradually revealed—invites viewers to examine or to experience (1) the socioeconomic structures that are particularly unjust toward women of color; (2) the uniqueness of each featured inmate; (3) the sense that these women can change and in unpredictable ways; and (4) the profoundly transgressive nature of placing oneself no matter how briefly and partially in the world of another or, even, the other—the ability to sympathize or to feel compassion for another person, is imperative if humans are to survive current political conflicts and global environmental degradation (Kolbert; Klein). The criticism leveled against season 1, namely, that once again, this show will be about a white protagonist (Piper Chapman played by Taylor Schilling) derives from the concern that a minority group does not actually exist in a national cultural sphere if that group is underrepresented or not represented in popular cultural texts. Equally damaging, of course, is if a group is represented in racist or sexist stereotypes.

However, seasons 2 to 5 of *OITNB* switched narrative focus from Piper to other characters. Focal characters in *OITNB* are given biographical and psychological depth, and viewers are invited to comprehend why characters think and behave the way they do; a focal character becomes the main character of an episode, in other words, the protagonist of the character's own story. Pulling a character from the chorus into a leading role is effected through frequent use of medium or extreme close-ups that highlight a distinguishing physical feature (Nicky's long, curly hair, for instance) (Nicky Nichols played by Natasha Lyonne) and most importantly, on their facial expressions, particularly the expressions of their eyes and mouth, which both betray most clearly the emotions of the character at key moments. Focal characters are also developed through flashbacks to pivotal events in the character's past—often searing, painful, frightening moments of abuse and deprivation—that have had a defining impact on the character's psyche and worldview. Flashbacks also consist of happy moments, which can be equally defining and confining; these contrastive flashbacks round out the characters and work against viewers possibly stereotyping a character based on her sexuality or racial features.

The scripting, the acting, and the cinematography coax viewers to a closer proximity to the characters in *OITNB*, from where viewers might launch into strange and unfamiliar territory—lives very different from their own; this virtual journey is far from touristic, for the format of the show requires the audience to pay attention to dialogue and action, to subtle changes in the emotional experience of a focal character. Audience members are invited to suspend their biases and assumptions, their most cherished notions of the self, and to be open to understanding and experiencing Litchfield and the characters' pre-Litchfield worlds through their eyes. Viewers are invited to sympathize, to contemplate, to talk back, to imagine, that is, to engage with focal characters on psychic, intellectual, and emotional levels; in a significant departure from the extant corpus of prison films, the series actively works against the objectification of the women. In season 5, when the inmates instigate a riot and take over Litchfield, most viewers' sympathies, I believe, are with the inmates.

Returning to the issue of Piper, the "white protagonist," the writers have increased the number of focal characters to include other women and a handful of the correctional officers and administrators like Sam Healy (Michael Harney; counselor), Joe Caputo (Nick Sandow; administrator), and Natalie "Fig" Figueroa (Alysia Reiner; the Warden). The *OITNB* wiki lists the focal characters of each season.[8] In season 1, Piper is the focal character of eight of the thirteen total episodes; Red, Burset, Alex, Claudette, Diaz, Nichols, Watson, Tricia, and Pennsatucky were focal characters of at least one episode. Some episodes have more than one focal character. In season 2, Piper was the featured character of two of thirteen episodes; eleven other inmates were each featured in at least one episode (Alex, Taystee, Red, Suzanne, Morello, Gloria, Poussey, Black Cindy, Miss Rosa, Vee, and Ingalis). Piper was not the focal character of any episode in season 3 or 4; instead, each of the following sixteen women was the main character in at least one episode: Pennsatucky, Poussey, Sophia/Burset, Aleida, Nicky, Big Boo, Flaca, Chang, Norma, Alex, Leanne, Brook, Lorna, Janae, Gloria, and Black Cindy. In addition, the series began to foreground prison staff: Healy, Caputo, and John Bennet (guard who falls in love with and fathers a child with Diaz). In season 4, the focal characters were Ruiz, Brook, Healy (he checks into a psychiatric facility in the finale), Ramos, Whitehill, Flores, Warren, Bayley (inexperienced guard who suffocates Poussey), Berlin, and Poussey. In season 5, Piper is the focal character in one, the twelfth, episode. In the closing scene of the final and thirteenth episode of the season, "Storm-y

Weather," she is one of ten inmates holding hands waiting for their unknown fate; the riot has ended, some of the inmates are being transported elsewhere, others have escaped, and these ten will likely be punished as the ring leaders.[9]

This rewriting of the single-protagonist narrative structure into an individual-in-a-collective, multiple-protagonist narrative is the basis of the graphics of the beginning credits used in season 1 through 5, consisting of rapid jump shots of seventy-seven female faces, some of whom belong to actual inmates. Each frame in this sequence shows parts of a face—the nose, eyes to nose, lips, or whole face. The faces are distinctive with different skin colors, freckles, tattoos or piercings; the eyes are riveting in that they look directly into the camera, directly at the viewer to make an emotional connection. One is prompted to ask each face in the sequence, "Who are you? How did you end up in prison?" The theme song, "You've got time," opens with the lyrics, "the animals, the animals," lyrics that take on an increasingly ironical meaning when viewers begin to empathize with the focal characters and to realize that Litchfield's inmates are not animals even though they are caged and, at times, treated like they are animals (Spektor). If only through this opening montage, *OITNB* subverts the dominant signification of nonwhite bodies as inherently violent. Throughout the show, dialogue among the correctional staff frequently characterizes the nonwhite inmates as primitive, animalistic, dangerous, and needing to be constantly controlled (searched, told to line up, told when to sleep, eat, etc., and placed in solitary confinement for additional humiliation and punishment). However, the correctional staff are repeatedly shown to be lazy, mendacious, criminal, themselves quite in need of discipline and being disciplined. Viewers soon realize that a culture of constant fear is part of the punishment of prison, fear among inmates themselves and between inmates and the staff. Fear is used as a weapon of control and for self-survival, but it is also part of the ambient sound and vibration of Litchfield, determining interpersonal communications, relationships, and other aspects of everyday life. Litchfield is organized on a regime of fear that enslaves everyone.

The opening montage, therefore, means more than simply "multiracial diversity." Rather, a viewer might begin to see, after two or three seasons, each face as belonging to a unique individual, one of a collective of distinctive individuals. The women create this collective in the present, despite the burden of the past that threatens all hope of the future. In the first season, viewers might feel indifference toward the women whose faces constitute the opening sequence. But indifference becomes concern and empathy in the following seasons—what sorts of ill-treatment, indignities, self-inflicted wounds, and danger will these women go through? The brutalizing of the inmates becomes even more egregious after Litchfield gets privatized (in seasons 3 and 4). Prior to Management & Correction Corporation taking over the running of Litchfield, George

"Pornstache" Mendez (Pablo Schreiber) was the exception among the guards in terms of his predatory treatment of the inmates.

The character of Poussey Washington (Samira Wiley) can be articulated in thematic terms with the character of Piper. As the seasons advance, Piper recedes into the chorus, while Poussey becomes a main focus. The two characters have in common a middle-class upbringing, but the key, defining difference between the two is that Poussey was born with black skin. Her father's rank in the U.S. Army (major) and stable socioeconomic circumstances could not protect Poussey, who is traveled, speaks French and German, and loves to read. In prison, Poussey has few rights or avenues of redress, and she dies when Bayley, an inexperienced and fearful guard accidentally suffocates her ("Toast Can Never Be Bread Again," season 4, episode 13). She had a close relationship with her mother; when Poussey spirals into depression and alcoholism (season 3), it is difficult not to feel sympathy for this character.[10] Despite Poussey's desire for privacy and safety (the character seems most comfortable among the shelves of books in the prison library), she decides to stand up to Vee, the manipulative, criminal mastermind in season 2. Over the course of four seasons, from Poussey's decisions and perspectives, as well as from her memories of pivotal events, audience members might see the following tendencies in her personality: adventurous, fun-loving, open to taking risks, capable of deep passion, caring but at times impulsive, reserved, nonconfrontational, peace loving, and easygoing. Some of these qualities contradict others. And, as Muriel Combes puts it, "The source of all individuals, preindividual being, is not one. . . . it is not-one. Being is more than one . . . constitutively, immediately, a power of mutation"—Simondon's preferred term is metastability" (3). Being is a "power of mutation." Poussey's process of becoming involved the "resolution of a tension between potentials belonging to previously separated orders of magnitude" (Combes 4). Combes writes,

> A plant, for instance, establishes communication between a cosmic order (that to which the energy of light belongs) and an intramolecular order (that of mineral salts, oxygen . . .). But the individuation of a plant does not give birth only to the plant in question. In dephasing [changing, individuating], being always simultaneously gives birth to an individual mediating between two orders of magnitude and to a milieu . . . (the earth on which it is located and the immediate environment with which it interacts). . . . we may consider individuals as beings that come into existence as so many partial solutions to so many problems of incompatibility between separate levels of being. (4)

Over the course of four seasons, Poussey's character makes decisions that resolve her internal contradictions, or the "problems of incompatibility between separate levels of being," while Piper does not until season 5. In season 5, Piper learns to cross racial boundaries and to form an all-or-nothing alliance with the other inmates. In the final scene of the last episode, she stands with the other women, whatever their racial identity.

The first few frames in season 1, episode 1, showing Piper as a baby getting a bath, Piper with Larry in a bath, and Piper showering with Alexandra "Alex" Vause (Laura Prepon), serve the narrative purposes of thematic and character development. Piper, the daughter of privilege, will soon have to endure moldy, possibly dangerous showers at Litchfield that are controlled, she imagines, by predatory black gangs; the bathroom will no longer be her literal and figurative "happy place." In addition, Piper's love of cleanliness stands for her self-perception as someone who is innocent and unburdened by care, and someone for whom redemption is always an option and achievable. Her pre-Litchfield world promises a succession of baths, clean floor tiles, ample soap and water, and lovers. In prison, she is ambushed in the shower, not by the black inmates but by members of her nominal tribe; in fact, Taystee saves her life in season 1, episode 13 ("Can't Fix Crazy") when Piper is cornered by Pennsatucky and two of her gang.

If one frames *OITNB* as a conventional fraudenroman, Piper's terrible experiences at Litchfield will form the catalyst of a personal, internal maturation; and the conclusion of Piper's sojourn would be signaled by her leaving prison to reassume her normative role, as wife, domestic partner, mother, or some form of self-affirming occupation. Conventional bildungsroman and fraudenroman narrate the roadmap of normative assimilation. However, Piper's fraudenroman contains a subtly and profoundly transgressive reconstruction of the conventional narrative form—Piper's sojourn at the prison reminds one of a "circling of the drain," without an end in sight. Instead of Piper making ample progress through her life lessons, each season brings to light additional character flaws. More important, the tensions within Piper that arise from incompatible values and beliefs do not seem to be getting resolved.

In fact, no one from her past can help her; the codes and rules of interpersonal interaction and how to exert influence or strike a deal that govern Piper's pre-Litchfield milieu—earlier periods of individuation—are incompatible with prison life and serve to get her into trouble. In short, white upper-middle-class coded language is ineffectual in a place that privileges the unvarnished and brutally straightforward. Brutal honesty and, occasionally, even physical confrontations can increase one's chances of surviving in prison. In season 1, Piper is schooled by the African American women and by Pennsatucky Doggett (Taryn Manning) in the lesson that Piper has to be responsible for herself. Although Pennsatucky's characterization does not place her in the role of moral exemplar of the series, she shows Piper that the feelings and worldview of others matter—in life and death terms. In Piper's world, to refuse an invitation to

Bible study would be a trifling concern. For Pennsatucky, the refusal was a personal rejection. In the climactic scene, Piper reacts to the advancing Pennsatucky and her shank by pulling out her own (stolen) screwdriver; in that moment, the Piper Chapman of middle-class suburbia and privilege decided in favor of the most elemental and primitive of human desires, survival. Her college degree, Larry, her elevated social milieu could not protect her in prison, and, most remarkably, those semiotics of class identity could not obviate the most basic truth of human/animal being, the desire to survive in order "to perpetuate" oneself (Combes 4). In the most basic sense of being human, Piper is no different from the other "animals" in Litchfield.

The final episode of season 1 is an unrelenting counterpoint to the "my happy place" sequence in episode 1. Piper has been given the full measure of her imprisoned circumstances: her not having access to her happy place is the very least of her troubles. Instead of soap suds, Piper is baptized in her own and in Pennsatucky's blood. The temporal–spatial backdrop is significant in that this pivotal scene in which Piper loses her privileged innocence takes place outdoors, in white, pristine-looking snow, at Christmas, the celebration of the birth of Christ, the savior of humankind in the view of Christians; Pennsatucky, a fundamentalist Christian, is ironically dressed as an angel. Is the confrontation in the prison yard Piper's rite of passage? Where to?

As the seasons progress, viewers realize that Piper fails to apprehend that the fear that took over her mind during her confrontation with Pennsatucky is frequently the nucleus of the other inmates' worldview—a terrible place to be. Moreover, Piper's recidivism rate is high; the traditional fraudenroman functions poorly as a vehicle for this female protagonist's rehabilitation. And so, perhaps, the point of Piper's stalled maturation story serves to reveal to her and to the audience the limits of her habits of mind, of her worldview, of her assumptions about the women around her, of her middle-class sureties; the staples of the good life for women like her are illusory, have failed her, and will continue to fail her in Litchfield. The larger point is that the efficacy, the naturalness of the conventional fraudenroman itself—its assimilative epiphanies, its predetermined normalizing conclusions—must be met by viewers with deep skepticism.

It is in the characterization of Poussey that the bildungsroman most reveals its paucity and inherent bias. Poussey's story at Litchfield was never going to be about her undergoing epiphanies that would reintegrate her into society. The final scene has her, after death, in street clothes, wearing hoop earrings, gazing quietly out over the harbor at a section of the city lights of New York. She seems older than the Poussey in the flashback in which she is at the same place with a flock of Buddhist monks, who turn out to be not real monks but a performance troupe dressed as monks for the night. Everything that happened to Poussey that day—her phone is stolen, she is diverted to this dance club by hip drag queens, then the orange-robed monks on bicycles appear—symbolizes the sloughing off of aspects of her discursively prescribed identity. While at the faux monks' hangout, the cops arrive, and she is arrested for trespassing and posses- sion of marijuana. Her blackness resulted in an extended sentence in a peni- tentiary, her plan to start fresh in Amsterdam forever thwarted. Yet, what happened to her at Litchfield—while not to be read as fate or destiny—became inextricable from the individual she was in the finale of season 4. In Poussey's final scene, she looks at the city lights, then she turns around and breaks the fourth wall; she has a smile and an expression that implies openness, inno- cence, joyfulness, a bit wry. One interpretation is that Poussey could only find release and happiness in death. The unjust sociopolitical system would never treat someone like her fairly.

However, there is another interpretation of the ending and Poussey's jour- ney of becoming. Unlike Piper's way of dealing with situations, Poussey at Litchfield resolves most of the contradictions within her: she learned to con- trol her impulsive tendencies, and she expanded her definition of love from one that consisted of only her and her lover to ever larger circles. Poussey, like Piper, was not in her "natural" milieu at Litchfield. Yet, unlike Piper, she learned to care about the other inmates and to build relationships that were not exploit- ative. Poussey put her own life in danger when she opposed Vee. It was Poussey who acted as a character reference for the very lost and marginalized Brook Soso (Kimiko Glenn), and it was Poussey who inducted Soso into The Ghetto and possibly prevented another suicide attempt by the Asian American version of Piper. Piper's relationships fail to cross racial and sexual walls. Despite the dan- gerous situation in the cafeteria in the season finale, Poussey attempted to calm everyone down. The point here is that Poussey did not have to behave in the ways that she did. She headed in the direction of danger, whereas the audi- ence's last sight of Piper in season 4 was her and Alex running away from the rioting inmates because they did not want to get involved. Besides Galina "Red" Reznikov (Kate Mulgrew) and (in certain seasons) Alex, Piper has not appre- ciably extended her circle of friends. In season 5, however, Piper (and Alex) find that neutrality is not an option, that they have to do what is best for the larger community.

The Poussey character did not so much discover who she "really was," which requires the existence of a transcendental essence in the individual, as she became who she became in a process consisting of decisions—some in a split- second timeframe—in response to unexpected events, new circumstances, and emerging desires. Poussey unfolded through each lived event, each new inter- action with others and with her surroundings. Indeed, her backstory does not contain sufficient hints that her actions had a substantialist (essentialist, pre- formed) underpinning or were inexorably determined by the conventions of her upbringing. If Poussey had made other decisions, her process of individuation would have composed a different human being than the human being in season 4, episode 13.

The final scene with Poussey in season 4 contains a textual allusion—season 6, episode 15 ("The Quest") of *Northern Exposure* (1990–1995)—that can lend insight to Poussey's process of becoming, the singular events of her individuation. In *Northern Exposure,* Joel Fleischmann (Rob Morrow) believed that he had been indentured into serving the oddball residents of Cicily, Alaska. He pined for Manhattan. By season 6, Joel has become almost zen-like in his ability to take what comes, to adapt to changing circumstances, to accept others as they are and not what he wants them to be. In the final season, episode 15 ("The Quest"), he and Maggie (Janine Turner) set off to find the mythical Jeweled City of the North. They meet a gatekeeper, and Joel correctly answers a question from the gatekeeper about love. The gatekeeper lets them through, but Maggie decides to stay where she is instead of accompanying Joel. In the next scene, Joel finds himself on a ferry in New York harbor; he gazes at the nighttime Manhattan cityscape, which resembles the cityscape in Poussey's final scene. Later, Maggie receives a postcard from him. The postcard reads, "New York is a state of mind." Is this Maggie's fantasy? Is Joel dead or alive? Did he return to Manhattan only to find that the Manhattan he had been in love with during his exile in Cicily no longer existed? Such questions cannot be answered in realist terms and, what is more, they limit the interpretative possibilities of the ending. Instead, a response might be to ask if return is ever possible. Even as we head toward a future or as we back into a future, the past has irrevocably changed, turned into memory or rubble. Perhaps, the only avenue is to constitute the next event of becoming, part of a process of individuation that is ever partial, never complete. Combes's critique of individuation bears repeating here, as "the operation whereby a domain undergoes transformation . . . like a crystal that from a very small seed grows in all directions within its aqueous solution wherein each molecular layer already constituted serves as a structuring base for the layer in the process of forming" (6–7).

Sense8 and *OITNB* instantiate a Simondonian idea of an individual as "never exist[ing] alone; it is only ever relative to the milieu associated with its existing" (Scott 7). The "operation of individuation" is a "relational activity" between an individual and her milieu, that "requires their reciprocal codependency" (7). Simondon's conceptualization of a collective is discrete from the notion of community. Conventional communities, such as religious orders, experimental communes, a small gang in a school yard, or the imagined community of nation are constituted of beliefs, principles, or rules of behavior that determine membership and that police in-group behavior. What is more, community is rationalized by a mythology of origins; often, these subplots of the Volksgemeinschaft link to construct a narrative of teleology that crystallizes the so-called soul or lifeblood of the Volk in a mythological, legendary, or heroic figure. From this perspective, the multiple-protagonist structure of *Sense8* undercuts the traditional concept of community in several ways: each of the human-sensates is a hero (with superhuman abilities), yet each becomes more than she or he was as she or he gradually connects "telepathically" with one or more of the rest of the eight. In season 2, Wolfgang is contacted by a sensate from a different cluster; there are more clusters who have been hiding from BPO. Individually, each is beset by his or her oppressive socioeconomic structure, each is enduring in his or her community, locked in a straitjacket labeled national, class, racial, or gender identity. As the story clearly indicates, none, alone, has the means of achieving the next potential phase. Dephasing—change, resolving internal tensions or contradictions—has been stalled, because the nature of their process of individuation requires becoming part of and connecting with their collective, the August 8 Cluster. In the later episodes of season 1 and in season 2, the sensates realize that they have to trust and to seek help from sapiens. In the series finale—released on June 8, 2018—the Cluster 8 sensates connect with their sapien partners and allies to decisively defeat the evil BPO. The final minutes of the series finale consist of scenes—unapologetically filmed—of sensates and sapiens transcending temporal-spatial barriers and engaging in group sex. The series finale is titled, "Amor Vincit Omnia."

Under the traditional definition of community, the characters in *Sense8* (and *OITNB*) are imprisoned in their identitarian communities (Boston, Seoul, Berlin, and so on); social status turns out to be lockups that disappear the human being. Sun Bak (Doona Bae) reluctantly takes the blame for her brother's embezzlement because that is what her culture and father expect of her—to save her brother and heir to their father's corporate empire.[11] But gradually, she feels compelled to resolve the contradictory feelings that she harbors toward her father and brother. On the one hand, she wants to please her father, but she realizes that she is also helping her profligate brother to fail again and to damage, perhaps, irreparably next time, the company. Her process of individuation means that she has to decide how she wants to settle her internal struggle: she can truly revolt or she can accept the status quo. In season 2, she realizes that her brother tried to kill her in prison, and she decides to give up on the rules she had been taught by her family and culture. The character of Will Gorski (Brian J. Smith), humble beat cop in Chicago, is the earliest of the August 8 Cluster to become aware of his abilities. In season 1, episode 1, "Limbic Resonance," he gradually experiences the feelings of and hears what the other seven feel and hear. He sees Angelica's (his mother's) death in a vision. In "I Am Also a We" (episode 2), Will encounters Jonas, who tells him about his abilities and to expect to connect with others like him. Will is haunted by visions of Sarah Patrell, whose disappearance his father, also a cop, never solved. In season 1, the eight focal characters, during moments of stress and danger, begin to enter each other's world, which are continents apart: Will is in a life that is based in Chicago; Sun Bak is in Seoul, South Korea; Lito Rodriquez is a movie star living in Mexico City; Wolfgang Bogdanow (Max Riemelt) is a thief and safecracker in Berlin; Capheus "Van Damme" (Ami Ameen) drives a mini-bus in Nairobi, Kenya; Riley Blue (Tuppence Middleton) lives in Iceland and works as a DJ; Kala Dandekar (Tina Desai) lives in Mumbai and is a reluctant bride; the eighth of the August 8 Cluster is Nomi Marks (Jamie Clayton). In season 2, the sensates are able to "appear" at will in any of the other cities in which cluster members live: they give advice, they fight off gangs and, most important, Whisper and BPO.

In a thematically pivotal scene in episode 10 ("What Is Human?"), Wolfgang, in Berlin, is communicating with Jonas while Jonas is being held captive in a secret laboratory by Whispers (Terrence Mann), who leads the BPO. Jonas tells Wolfgang that sensates are biologically very similar to humans but more evolved in their "increased empathy," like birds or mushrooms that can communicate in a group. Most interesting is Jonas's thought sent to Will that the human species has evolved into the most successful killer on this planet, because we have evolved into individuals that are disconnected emotionally from each other and other creatures. Jonas's words imply that collective individuation need not have taken the route that it has so far and that the current trajectory can change. Thematically, then, *Sense8* echoes *OITNB*'s emphasis on the utmost importance of human beings developing sympathy and empathy, possibly as part of a process of planetary collective individuation.

This chapter concludes with a passage from Catherine Stimpson's article in the *Los Angeles Review of Books*, "In a contemporary idiom, growth demands a global multiculturalism with differing, but networked, perspectives that enrich each other," and Stimpson comments on the writings of Rosi Braidotti thus, "A responsibility of singularity is to recognize the singularity of others and each person's own voice. 'You cannot speak for me. I cannot speak for us,'" she [Braidotti] declares. "Yet, the claiming of an individual voice does not preclude acting with others, the building of a community and a politics. . . . because history is open-ended." Stimpson agrees with Braidotti regarding "Liberal humanism supports individualism, autonomy, responsibility, and self-determination." A more radical humanism promotes "solidarity, community-bonding, social justice and principles of equality."

Notes

1   Daniel Funke and Tina Susman writing in 2016 in the *Los Angeles Times* begin their column with a litany of other names preceding that of Michael Brown, "Amadou Diallo. Manuel Loggins Jr. Ronald Madison. Kendra James. Sean Bell.

Eric Garner. Michael Brown. Alton Sterling. Each was a black man or woman who died at the hands of police. Their names represent only a handful of such cases since 1999, when Diallo, an unarmed man standing in a New York City doorway, was gunned down by officers who erroneously thought he had a gun." Tamir Rice, shot and killed on November 12, 2014, was 12.

2   Unite the Right march consisted of neo-Nazis, white supremacists, and white nationalists, who were protesting the planned removal of General Robert E. Lee's statue, which was a response to the 2015 Charleston church mass shooting in which nine parishioners, gathered for a prayer meeting, were shot to death by Dylann Roof, 21 years old, who later told police that he had hoped to ignite a race war. Three other shooting victims survived their wounds.

3   U.S. attorney general Jeff Sessions declared the violence in Charlottesville on Saturday, "domestic terrorism." "Alt-right" has been used to refer to neo-Nazis, the Ku Klux Klan, white supremacists, and white nationalists. These groups are antifeminist, anti-Semitic, and anti-immigrant, and they believe in a white state. Some liberal and left-leaning groups refuse to use the term "alt-right" because they believe it is a term used to mask the ultraright and violent extremist goals of these groups. Liam Stack in the *New York Times* writes, "Both phrases [alt-right and alt-left] are part of a broad lexicon of far-right terminology." Stack continues, "Researchers who study extremist groups in the United States say that there is no such thing as the alt-left. Mark Pitcavage, an analyst at the Anti-Defamation League, said that the word [alt-left] had been made up [by far right groups] to create a false equivalency between the far right and 'anything vaguely left-seeming that they didn't like.'" Stack writes that "Antifa" stands for "antifascist groups," which can be traced to the early decades of the twentieth century; antifa is a group of individuals who expose white supremacists or neo-Nazis to their employers, neighbors, and so on (*New York Times*)

4   According to Netflix, "Netflix is the world's leading Internet television network with over 81 million members in over 190 countries enjoying more than 125 million hours of TV shows and movies per day, including original series, documentaries and feature films" (Netflix—https://ir.netflix.com/). In a March 2015 *Seattle Times* article regarding the worldwide top three streaming services, Netflix subscribers reportedly accounted for 36% of the number of households in the United States, while Amazon Video's percentage was 13% and Hulu Plus's share was 6.5%.

5   Data-driven research is inherently hampered by Netflix's revolutionary business model. Unlike traditional television broadcasters that use the demographic data of shows to sell advertising airtime to businesses, Netflix revenue is generated by the number of subscribers. In fact, Netflix refuses to release viewership numbers or demography at all. Most significant in terms of the future of scholarly research on global media corporations is the company's deployment of algorithms that can track and measure the minutest components of an episode that a viewer lingers over or fast forwards past or re-watches. Hallinan and Striphas explain that "new models of cultural identity [are] latent in the dataset" (123) and "that sex, age, race, and other broad classifications fail to capture the more subtle factors relevant to decisions people make about the cultural goods" (123). The implication is that an algorithm (devised and managed by a company) dataset is likely to be more accurate in tracking a viewer's likes and dislikes than a traditional research project using focus groups or targeted surveys. "Accuracy" here is unrelated to the

conventional demographical categories of race, age, gender, or class. Hallinan and Striphas refer also to John Cheney-Lippold's work on web analytics firms and his point about "algorithmic profiling systems" that "de-essentialize [identity] from its corporeal and societal forms and determinations while . . . also re-essentializ[ing] [identity] as a statistically related, largely market research-driven category" (Cheney-Lippold, 2011: 170; qtd. in Hallinan & Striphas). The impact of emerging "algorithm culture" on the evolution of extant identity categories is likely to be profound, as well as on our understanding of "culture" as, "particular modes of fostering human refinement, and their underlying frameworks of valuation and authority; patterns of social difference, commonality, and interaction; and the artifacts, particularly aesthetic objects, associated with specific groups of people" (Hallinan & Striphas 119). Prevailing theories that seek to resist racism or racialism would have to adapt to this new challenge beyond its current targets, such as stereotypes.

6 Muriel Combes's *Gilbert Simondon and the Philosophy of the Transindividual* (published in France in 1999) is the first monograph to introduce Gilbert Simondon's (1924–1989) thinking to a wider audience; previously Simondon's work, represented in three publications, had been known and admired by a small group of other philosophers, such as Gilles Deleuze, Maurice Merleau-Ponty, Isabelle Stenger, and Georges Canguilhem. Simondon was a philosopher whose ambitions lay in an in-depth renewal of ontology as a process of individuation—that is, how individuals come into being, persist, and transform (from the MIT Press website). Perhaps Simondon is best known for *Du mode d'existence des objets techniques* (1958) or *On the Mode of Existence of Technical Objects*, which is the first complete English-language translation by Cecile Malaspina and John Rogove.

7 Deleuze and Guatarri writing in *A Thousand Plateaus*, "A rhizome as subterranean stem is absolutely different from roots and radicles. Bulbs and tubers are rhizomes. Plants with roots or radicles may be rhizomorphic in other respects altogether: the question is whether plant life in its specificity is not entirely rhizomatic. Even some animals are, in their pack form. Rats are rhizomes. Burrows are too, in all of their functions . . . rhizomes (plants, crystals) grow unpredictably" (6–7).

8 *OITNB* wikia site: orange-is-the-new-black.wikia.com/

9 Netflix has renewed *OITNB* for another two seasons.

10 "Mother's Day" (season 3, episode 1).

11 *Sense8* wikia: http://sense8.wikia.com/wiki/

Works Cited

Braidotti, Rosi. *Metamorphoses: Towards a Materialist Theory of Becoming*. Cambridge, UK: Polity Press, 2002. Print.

Caputi, Jane. "The Color Orange? Social Justice Issues in the First Season of *Orange Is the New Black*." *Journal of Popular Culture* 48.6 (2015): 20. Print.

Cheney-Lippold, J. "A New Algorithmic Identity: Soft Politics and the Modulation of Control." *Theory, Culture & Society* 28.6 (2011): 164–181. Print.

Combes, Muriel. *Gilbert Simondon and the Philosophy of the Transindividual*. Trans. Thomas LaMarre. The Technologies of Lived Abstraction. Eds. Brian Massumi, Erin Manning. 5 vols. Cambridge, MA, and London, England: The MIT P, 2012. Print

Deleuze, Gilles and Felix Guattari. *A Thousand Plateaus. Capitalism and Schizophrenia. Mille Plateaux*, volume 2 of *Capitalisme et Schizophrenie*. Trans. Brian Massumi. 17th ed. Vol. 2. 2 vols. Minneapolis: U of Minnesota P, 2011. Print.

DuBois, W.E.B. "Address to the Nations of the World." Speech at the first Pan-African Congress, London, 1900.

Enck, Suzanne M. and Megan E. Morrissey. "If Orange Is the New Black, I Must Be Color Blind: Comic Framings of Post-Racism in the Prison-Industrial Complex." *Critical Studies in Media Communication* 32:5 (2015): 303–317. DOI: 10.1080/15295036.2015.1086489.

Funke, Daniel, and Tina Susman. "From Ferguson to Baton Rouge: Deaths of Black Men and Women at the Hands of Police." *Los Angeles Times* July 12, 2016, sec. Nation. Web.

Gerbner, George, Michael Morgan, and Sut Jhally. *The Electronic Storyteller: Television & the Cultivation of Values*. Northampton, MA: Media Education Foundation, 1997. VHS.

Gilroy, Paul. *Against Race. Imagining Political Culture beyond the Color Line*. Cambridge, MA: Harvard UP, 2000. Print.

Hallinan, Blake, and Ted Striphas. "Recommended for You: The Netflix Prize and the Production of Algorithmic Culture." *New Media & Society* 18.1 (2015): 117–137. Print.

Klein, Naomi. *This Changes Everything: Capitalism vs. the Climate*. New York: Simon and Schuster, 2015. Print.

Kolbert, Elizabeth. *The Sixth Extinction. An Unnatural History*. London, UK: Bloomsbury, 2014. Print.

Morgan, Michael, and James Shanahan. "The State of Cultivation." *Journal of Broadcasting & Electronic Media* 54.2 (2010): 337–355. Print.

Orange Is the New Black. Created by Jenji Kohan, 2013. Television.

O'Sullivan, Shannon. "Who Is Always Already Criminalized? an Intersectional Analysis of Criminality on *Orange Is the New Black*." *The Journal of American Culture* 39.4 (2016): 401–412. *Performing Arts Periodicals Database*, http://eres.library.manoa .hawaii.edu/login?url=https://search-proquest-com.eres.library.manoa.hawaii.edu /docview/1897714182?accountid=27140.

Scott, David. *Gilbert Simondon's Psychic and Collective Individuation. A Critical Introduction and Guide*. Edinburgh, UK: Edinburgh UP, 2014. Print.

Sense8. Created by Lana and Lilly Wachowski and Michael Straczynski, 2015. Television.

Simondon, Gilbert. *On the Mode of Existence of Technical Objects*. Trans. Cecile Malaspina and John Rogove. 1st edition. Minneapolis: Univocal Publishing, 2017.

———. *L'individuation Psychique et Collective: À la lumière des notions de forme, information, potentiel et métastabilité*. Aubier, 1989. Print.

Spektor, Regina. "You've Got Time." *Orange Is the New Black*.

Stack, Liam. "Alt-Right, Alt-Left, Antifa: A Glossary of Extremist Language." *New York Times* August 15, 2017, sec. Politics. Web.

Stimpson, Catherine R. "The Nomadic Humanities." *Los Angeles Review of Books* (2016). Web. July 13, 2016.

Watt, Ian. *The Rise of the Novel: Studies in Defoe, Richardson, and Fielding*. Berkeley: U of California P, 1964. Print.

Wikia. "Sense8 Wikia." (2015). Wikia. Web.

2

Performing Cherokee Masculinity in *The Doe Boy*

•••••••••••••••••••••

CHANNETTE ROMERO

Randy Redroad's feature film *The Doe Boy* (2001) explores masculinity in the Cherokee Nation. Through a coming-of-age story, *The Doe Boy* teaches non-Indigenous viewers about contemporary Cherokee culture. In addition, using predominantly visual clues, the film speaks directly to Cherokee viewers through subtler, pictorial references to historic tribal gender and kinship expectations. Historically, the primary responsibility of a Cherokee man was to hunt and provide meat, and the film uses deer hunting as a metaphor to highlight the differences between historical and contemporary Cherokee ideas of masculinity, differences it sees as leading to divisive views on identity and community. *The Doe Boy* contends that contemporary warfare, hunting practices, and assimilation of U.S. imperial views has led to a violent hypermasculinity in the Cherokee Nation. In contrast to Hollywood's image of the violent "Indian warrior," the film proposes returning to earlier tribal notions of masculinity. Doing so, it suggests, will help rectify the destructive and self-destructive relationships among contemporary Cherokees and restore the harmony and equilibrium so valued in Cherokee culture. Fascinatingly, the powerful agent capable of reinstating tribal gender and kinship obligations in the film is a protagonist that is able to cross genders. This interdisciplinary chapter employs methodologies from Indigenous, gender, queer, and film studies to explore the complex representations of gender in the film. By closely examining narrative and visual grammar, I demonstrate *The Doe Boy*'s efforts and, at times, failures to resist static understandings of Cherokee identity and community.

The subtlety of *The Doe Boy*'s visuals limits non-Cherokee viewers' understandings of the film's politics. The strategy is seemingly deliberate, as the film is set in 1977 and 1984 Tahlequah, Oklahoma, the capital of the Cherokee Nation, a place that the film's writer/director Randy Redroad says "means a lot to me spiritually and culturally" (Svenson). The plot features a half Cherokee–half Caucasian boy, who suffers from hemophilia, going on his first hunt and the hunt's later implications on his life. The boy, symbolically named Hunter, mistakenly shoots a doe on his first hunt as his father sleeps under a nearby tree. Much of the film is autobiographical. Like his protagonist Hunter, the filmmaker Redroad has a Cherokee mother and a Caucasian father and though he is not hemophilic, he has severe asthma that he says similarly "frustrates the outdoors kind of dad," who associates masculinity with outdoor activities like sports and hunting (Svenson). Redroad, too, accidentally shot a doe on his inaugural hunt while his father slept. He contends that he attached "mythic significance" to the hunt and that he created *The Doe Boy* to "attempt to resolve" emotional issues that arose from the event and from his family's understandings of gender (Redroad-Snapp, "Through" 117, 118). Despite the film's portrayal of an autobiographical incident and its exploration of Cherokee gender and kinship obligations, reviewers of the film critique it for lacking "any degree of cultural honesty" (Hall). One reviewer argues it "often seems as if its Cherokee story angle was tacked on to provide an exotic accessory. . . . Genuine understanding or appreciation of the Cherokee culture, either past or present, is absent in the film" (Hall). Another reviewer asserts, "the specifics of Cherokee culture are missing" (Schmidt); while a third reviewer claims, "I love N[ative]A[merican] movies but felt this one fell a little short on traditions and connection to the mother earth and its creatures" (Olsen). Primed to expect stereotypical representations of Indigenous "traditions," contemporary reviewers miss *The Doe Boy*'s portrayal, and keen interrogation, of Cherokee gender and kinship roles.

These reviewers are likely accustomed to Hollywood stereotypes that portray Indigenous men as either bloodthirsty savages or noble men living peacefully in nature (with "mother earth and its creatures"), removed entirely from settler cultures; in these films, settler cultures' encroachment is depicted as natural and inevitable, as is the dwindling of Indigenous peoples and cultures. This savage/noble dichotomy appears in wildly popular early and mid-twentieth- century Westerns, late-twentieth-century films like Michael Mann's *The Last of the Mohicans* (1992) and Kevin Costner's *Dances with Wolves* (1990), and contemporary neo-Westerns like James Cameron's *Avatar* (2009) and

Alejandro González Iñárritu's *The Revenant* (2015). Notably, these films feature a Caucasian protagonist as the viewers' point of identification; by learning tribal ways before Indigenous peoples' supposed "vanishing," the Caucasian protagonists, and by extension viewers, are projected as the rightful inheritors of Indigenous land and resources. These cinematic stereotypes work in the interest of imperialism. Because the films are critically acclaimed, award winning, and extremely popular and profitable, it is likely their stereotypical approach will continue to be copied.

The image of the always-already-dead savage/noble not only influences non-Indigenous viewers, it also affects Indigenous men's sense of identity. Paul Chaat Smith says, "The movies loom so large for Indians because they have defined our self-image as well as told the entire planet how we live, look, scream, and kill" (37). Indigenous men who do not fit Hollywood's projected image of the "Vanishing Indian" warrior often suffer from identity crises. Cherokee men, in particular, might feel this keenly since one of the most recognizable Indigenous performers in Hollywood is Cherokee actor Wes Studi, well known for playing the "savage" antagonist in roles like Magua in *The Last of the Mohicans* and Toughest Pawnee in *Dances with Wolves*, villains who are dramatically killed to bring about peace.[1] In contrast to Hollywood's long-haired, buckskin-clad warriors, filmmaker Randy Redroad calls himself a "half-Cherokee redneck with an Afro. I'm allergic to horses. I don't fit" (Marubbio 290). There are serious consequences when Indigenous men attempt to mimic inaccurate Hollywood portrayals; according to Redroad, "you are rendered a voyeur, an actor in your own life" (Marubbio 290). Indigenous men's externally scripted gender performances can reinforce the cinematic trope of their "vanishing" by rendering them and their cultures invisible. Redroad argues that rather than either adopting or rejecting Hollywood's stereotypes (and thus keeping them at the center of a narrative), Indigenous filmmakers should simply represent Indigenous people more accurately. He says, "Want to portray Indians differently? Then portray Indians differently" (Marubbio 299). His approach to filmmaking de-emphasizes Hollywood images in favor of a subtler, Cherokee-oriented portrayal of community and identity.

This does not mean, however, that *The Doe Boy* ignores cinematic stereotypes. Instead, the film seems to employ stereotypes to its advantage, first revealing them and then exposing their inapplicability as the main character chooses an alternative identity. Unfortunately, scholars can miss this subtle strategy. Houston Wood critiques *The Doe Boy* for "[a]ppealing too much to mainstream audiences," "lead[ing] to [a] loss of cultural specificity" (133). Allison Coke Hedge contends that "the film is heartbreakingly moving at times"; however, its pan-Indian cast, soundtrack full of flute and powwow music, and portrayals of deer hunting all lack realism (138, 133). Coke Hedge is especially critical of a scene (discussed later) where a character claims that "real hunters" use bows and arrows; she writes, "It's irksome that the Native filmmakers are trading in stereotypes for this scene" (136). *The Doe Boy* enlists these seeming stereotypes to draw in, and then prompt changes within, multiple audiences. Cherokee and non-Cherokee viewers alike are potentially less guarded watching an ostensibly familiar and nonthreatening coming-of-age story than when watching more didactic political films. Redroad also claims that many of the recurring images in his films, like cedar flute players, are autobiographical references to his own family members and are "more personal than stereotypical" (Marubbio 292). Angelica Lawson points out that the film is "subtly Native American" and "there are many moments in the film that express a Cherokee worldview . . . with no explanation, no translation" (217). Many of the "non-translated" moments in the film seek to address larger matters with a specifically Cherokee audience. Believing there is "something healing about an image," Redroad says he became a filmmaker after wishing he could videotape "my family at our worst moments in hopes that seeing ourselves in all our neurotic glory we would be collectively embarrassed into a life more ordinary" (Redroad-Snapp 115). *The Doe Boy* works to enact "something healing" by subtly revealing the "neurotic glory" of Redroad's family and the larger Cherokee community.[2]

Race, Imbalance, and Cultural Practice

Creating a protagonist who is a biracial hemophiliac might, at first glance, suggest that *The Doe Boy*'s central concern revolves around blood as a metaphoric racial marker; however, a closer examination of hemophilia's function in the film suggests that the blood disorder acts only as a convenient means for the film to begin a discussion regarding race that it soon complicates. Although the film's protagonist, Hunter, played by James Duvall, attempts to tie hemophilia to his Caucasian father—shouting (inaccurately) "It's probably your blood that ruined me. It's a goddamned white disease"—there is only a slightly higher rate of hemophilia in Caucasians than in other groups. More importantly, hemophilia is a genetic disorder that is tied to biological sex, transmitted solely through a mother's X chromosomes. Hemophilia is thus not passed from father to son, but from maternal grandfather to grandchild through carrier daughters. Critic Lee Schweninger questions whether Redroad "is aware of the biology involved" with hemophilia, though he does note that the "parallel of these blood characteristics carries weight in a film reflecting a society in which blood quantum or literal ancestry plays a role in one's political as well as one's cultural identity" (183). While a blood disorder does conveniently provide an initial means for the film to introduce issues associated with racial categories, hemophilia's function in the film is not simply to critique interracial mixing.[3] Rather, the film examines a disorder that is passed on from grandfathers to grandsons; it lies within Cherokee men themselves.

The Doe Boy knowingly enlists hemophilia's biological mode of transmission to examine the ways in which contemporary Cherokees hold tribal beliefs alongside internalized imperialism, particularly when it comes to imagining community. Redroad admits a fascination with "cowboys and Indians inhabiting the same body" (Redroad-Snapp 115). The film reveals the interpenetration of contemporary understandings of race and community in the Cherokee Nation in an effort to prompt Cherokees to abandon notions of identity and kinship influenced by settler cultures' views of race. Writing about Indigenous understandings of identity and community, Jace Weaver argues, "ultimately, racially based definitions are insufficient; what matters is one's social and cultural milieu, one's way of life" (6). *The Doe Boy* reminds contemporary Cherokee to explore understandings of self and kinship in far more complex ways than Hollywood or the U.S. government's categories of race. Through a voiceover that runs throughout the film to frame Hunter and other Cherokee males, Hunter's "full-blooded" grandfather Marvin (played by Gordon Tootoosis) describes Hunter as "a boy with bullets in his eyes and arrows in his chest." Hunter is portrayed as possessing both a violent gaze and an always-already-dying wound; he is both hunter and hunted. The film enlists Marvin as a familiar "wise elder" to teach Hunter and viewers tribal practices; however, the role does not discount the biological transmission of hemophilia. Instead, it usefully extends the issue beyond one particular family to encompass a greater problem running throughout the Cherokee Nation.

The Doe Boy enlists the historical Cherokee relationship between deer and disease to critique Cherokees' imbalanced relations with each other and the world. According to a Cherokee story, disease is introduced into the world as punishment for hunters failing to treat deer and other animals respectfully. In the story, as recounted by Robert Conley, Cherokees and animal peoples lived in peace until (historically male) hunters began to commodify them, overhunting and "slaughter[ing] the larger animals, birds, and fishes for their flesh or their skins ... without thought" (15). Deer and other animals punish the Cherokee for this objectification by sending them diseases. Read in a tribal context, Hunter's hemophilia can be viewed as a punishment by the animals for Cherokee males' greed. According to the Cherokee Nation's website, the story also reflects how the Cherokee were affected by colonialism: the "Cherokee story prophesied the impact of the deer trade on the Cherokees," as the Cherokees' hunger for settlers' goods led to their "exposure to new diseases, diseases to which they had no immunities" (Cherokee Nation). Assimilated Cherokee began to adopt imperial views of violence, commodification, and individualism. Theda Perdue notes that the deer trade introduced an economy based on commercial, not cooperative hunting and "made individualistic pursuits and triumphs not only acceptable but expected" (83–84). Because Cherokee hunters began to buy the goods and tools women in their households required, while also "acquir[ing] personal items that enhanced individual status," the deer skin trade led to the creation of gender and status/wealth hierarchies based on an "individualism [that] threatened the Cherokees' communitarian values" (Perdue 76, 84). According to the Cherokee Nation, with the assimilation of settler values, "The balance of their world was gone" (Cherokee Nation). Daniel Heath Justice asserts that "Balance is primary; if anything can be said to be a feature of contemporary and past Cherokee traditions, it is the quest for balance" (*Our Fire Survives* 37). *The Doe Boy* presents Cherokee viewers with a potential means for restoring balance.

The film seeks to intervene in the imbalance that arises when Cherokee men hold destructive tribal and imperialist thinking within themselves—"bullets in [their] eyes and arrows in their chest,"—particularly when linking community with issues of blood and race. The U.S. government relies upon blood quantum to determine membership in a federally recognized tribe. It issues identification cards that declare the percentage of an individual's ancestors listed on federal documents as "full-blooded" Indigenous peoples, a faulty process that is complicated by inaccurate historical recording, biased determinations of federal recognition, and a disregard for tribally based means of determining membership. For example, the Cherokee clan system is historically matrilineal; simply put, under the clan system a child is Cherokee if the child's mother is Cherokee, regardless of the father's background. Current Cherokee Nation citizenship is neither dependent on blood quantum nor on clan membership; instead, in Tahlequah, Oklahoma, the location of the Nation's capital, it is common to hear Cherokees adopt the U.S. legal term "lineal descendant." According to the Cherokee Nation website, "To be eligible for Cherokee Nation citizenship, individuals must provide documents connecting them to an enrolled direct ancestor who is listed on the Dawes Roll with a blood degree" (Cherokee Nation). Although the Cherokee Nation has seemingly eschewed blood quantum as a requirement for citizenship, Circe Sturm argues that it has "internalized ideas of race and then used them to their own political advantage in the process of nation building" (18). Redroad says his films resist the "the kinds of rigid identity criteria Indians impose on each other" (Marubbio 291). He says, "I'm not enrolled, so I'm not an Indian. I'm a half-breed, so I'm not an Indian. . . . If I take the Indian test, I fail. Who wins? The 'real' Indians? No. The colonizers? Probably. Because if I'm not an Indian, there is one less Indian and that is the point of extermination" (Marubbio 290). *The Doe Boy* critiques the internalization of settler cultures' imperialist preoccupations with race and blood and replaces them with a focus on maintaining respectful relations with the world. Marvin's opening voice-over declares, "Nobody cares how much blood runs through a deer. But everyone wants to know how much blood runs through an Indian." He proceeds to frame Hunter as "a boy who followed in a deer's footsteps instead of his father's." The film declares that what makes Hunter Cherokee is not his blood quantum but his kinship to the deer people, evidenced by performing actions that "followed in . . . a deer's footsteps."

The Doe Boy advocates a return to Cherokees' earlier notion of community; not dependent upon racial purity or "genetics," it calls for achieving balance in the world by actively maintaining and performing relational cultural practices. Justice asserts, "This isn't an issue of race. . . . at its core nationhood isn't about genetics; it's about kinship, our rights, responsibilities, and relationships as a people, about our sacred relationships to one another, to other peoples, and to all Creation" (*Our Fire Survives* 215). Cherokee identity, kinship, and community are not abstract concepts but require actions to sustain them. Indeed, according to Justice, "[Judith] Butler's argument that there are no identities apart from their performative expression offers interesting parallels to Indigenous models of context- and relationship-dependent identities" ("Notes" 218). Film, a medium that combines both performance and story, provides a useful means to show performances of cultural practices that can help maintain more balanced "relationship-dependent identities" and communities that "follow in a deer's footsteps instead of [a war-glorifying] father's." From its opening monologue, *The Doe Boy* insists on actions that uphold Cherokees' historical kinship obligations with each other and the deer, over and against settler cultures' divisive race and blood preoccupations.

Wounded Men

Redroad asserts, "in life there are coincidences and accidents. On film there are metaphors" (Redroad-Snapp 117). *The Doe Boy* uses Redroad's autobiographical "accident"—shooting a doe on his first hunt while his father slept under a nearby tree—as a larger metaphor for exploring both dominant U.S. and Cherokee understandings of gender and family. Redroad describes feeling emasculated by killing a doe; he felt he "kill[ed] in a wimpy way" and "was now walking around without my antlers, unable to look an Indian girl in the eye. As I got older I began to think of that original hunt as an emasculating event" (Redroad-Snapp 117). In *The Doe Boy*, Hunter's father, Hank, played by Kevin Anderson, asserts similar reductive views of masculinity. A constant watcher of war movies, Hank sees hunting as a way for his hemophiliac son to perform at least one of Hollywood's scripted expectations of a "man." He tells his Cherokee wife Maggie, "he ain't exactly a chip off the old block . . . can't play sports, can't work with tools. Damn sure never take him in the military." Hank's definition of masculinity, which the film implies is gleaned from mainstream media, requires tools and violence—contact sports, war, at the very least hunting. Hunter's hemophilia threatens this imperialist understanding of masculinity. Hank declares, "It ain't good. I'm afraid he's going to end up a nurse," Maggie's profession. Maggie, played by the talented Jeri Arredondo, retorts "Ain't nothing wrong with a boy taking after his mother." Hank symbolically loads his son's first hunting trip, seeing it as a public performance of Hunter's masculinity and also his genetic affiliation, a way to "see if he's got any of his old man in him." When Hunter shoots a doe instead of a buck, Hank feels shame at his son's inability to produce public evidence of "manhood"; he will not be able to "hang his antlers next to yours in the garage." Hank never asks his son to join him hunting again; instead Hank and other characters continually question Hunter's status as a "man" and his sexuality. Throughout the film, Hank verbally gay bashes and questions whether his son is gay.

Cherokee men's responses to the doe's killing extend *The Doe Boy*'s focus from simply father/son dynamics to a larger exploration of contemporary Cherokee masculinity. The film shows the immediate aftermath of the hunt through a fascinating visual and narrative lens. A blurry Hank and Hunter are shown in the background of a point of view shot loading the doe onto Hank's truck. They are filmed from the perspective of a Cherokee man, played by Gil Birmingham and symbolically named Manny, who watches through his truck's windshield. Manny's shotgun is wedged against the glass directly in front of the windshield, in the space typically occupied by windshield wipers. As Manny approaches the scene, the shotgun comes to occupy the center of the frame and visually overhangs not only Manny's sight, but also Hank and Hunter in the background. Literally framed by an instrument of violence, Manny nevertheless offers Hunter the only encouragement he will ever receive about the incident. Looking down at the doe from his side window (not occupied by his gun), Manny says, "She ain't much of a trophy, but she'll taste good. Way to go Hunter." Manny chooses to focus on the meat Hunter provides for his family, rather than the error. When not framed by his weapon, he expresses approval for Hunter fulfilling the historic responsibility of a Cherokee male. Although Manny privileges Hunter's providing of meat, he still objectifies the deer as a "trophy." In fact, we are first introduced to Manny through a shot that positions him in the background of an extreme close-up of buck antlers displayed prominently on the grill of his oversized truck. The shot's voice-over announces: "A buck with a broken or damaged rack is seen as inferior by other bucks. A strong buck won't hesitate to attack a weaker one and run him outta his territory." On the surface, the voice-over implies Manny will "attack" Hunter; however, the scene that follows this close-up instead reveals Manny's own "damaged rack." While Manny obviously prizes hunting and providing meat as upholding historic Cherokee masculinity, he himself is unable to fulfill the obligation. Since returning from the Vietnam War three years previous, Manny has failed to kill any deer. Manny's young son Junior, played by Kyle White, claims, "Mom says you're cursed. . . . Mom says the deer are holding a grudge against you because you hit too many with your truck." Manny's unnamed wife acknowledges the deer people's province and ability to punish hunters who fail to respect them as kin.

Manny's gender performance and disrespectful killing of deer is made iconographic by his overly large, antler- and shotgun-decorated truck that is also painted in U.S. military camouflage colors. He is costumed as constantly wearing U.S. Army–colored T-shirts with camouflage pants.[4] Manny's truck and actions (and name!) are explicitly gendered; he admits that he frequently hits does with his hypermasculine, war-decorated truck. His inability to successfully hunt is linked to disrespecting the deer and to U.S. warfare. In later scenes, his eighteen-year-old son Junior, played by Nathaniel Arcand, tells Hunter, "He said when he was in 'Nam and they'd get attacked, he'd just shoot in the direction where the bullets were coming from. Kinda hunts that way too." As Schweninger points out, Manny's portrayal "challenges the cliché of Indians as great hunters" and warriors found in many Hollywood films (179). However, *The Doe Boy* not only speaks back to mainstream cinema, it also addresses a specifically Cherokee audience. It warns that Manny's assimilation of settler ideologies, as reflected in his truck, costuming, and shotgun-framed sight has left him unable to fulfill his role as a Cherokee man. *The Doe Boy* suggests that Manny's and others' adoption of imperial worldviews has led to a reductive view of masculinity and an imbalanced mind. The film lauds Manny's affirming Cherokee men's responsibility to provide meat while simultaneously stressing that his objectification of deer as "trophies" is the result of a mind "diseased" by imperial settler culture.

Other Cherokee men in the film share Manny's imbalanced masculinity and complex response to the doe's shooting. After the hunt, the film fast-forwards seven years. This time frame is significant; Cherokee viewers are prompted to see the allusion to the seven Cherokee clans and juxtapose the characters' actions against clan notions of community. Seven years after the hunt, Manny's son Junior and their childhood friend Cheekie, played by Robert Guthrie, still publicly laugh at Hunter and call him Doe Boy. Junior's girlfriend Bird, played by Alex Rice, questions the "Doe Boy" label: "Maybe we shouldn't call him 'Doe Boy' on his birthday?" Taking a long drag on his asthma inhaler, Cheekie responds: "He loves it." This scene visually links divisive behavior with disease. Soon after, Junior and Cheekie join the U.S. Marine Corps, making even more explicit the links among disease, imperial warfare, and violence against one's kin and community. The men mark their enlistment by getting matching "USMC" tattoos from a tattoo artist sporting his own large tattoo of a personified Death raising a scythe. Schweninger notes how the artist's tattoo, along with a close-up of blood from the tattoo needle and Cheekie's resulting wince of pain "emphasize the death and destruction rather than glory and heroism associated with the military" (178). Marking his birthday with Junior and Cheekie at a Tahlequah bar, Hunter responds to their insults by mimicking their divisiveness and picking fights with other men. Tommy Deer in Water, played by James Smith Jr., steps forward; he is a man Marvin calls "a real hunter," the epitome of tribal masculinity because he hunts with a handmade bow and one arrow. Tommy tells Hunter, "You have a funny way of celebrating," implying there is nothing celebratory about excess violence and disrespect of one's community. The double play of "funny" here reveals that Junior, Cheekie, and Hunter's violent masculine expression is both bizarre and, ironically, nonhumorous when seen from a tribal point of view.

The way imperial violence gets horrifyingly turned against one's community is made even more explicit when Manny later kills Hank in a hunting accident. In the scene, Manny wears a camouflage hat, shirt, and pants, and he carries an extra cartridge belt slung across his chest. He is hunting with a fellow Cherokee named Bear, played by Norman Brown, who wears camouflage pants, aviator sunglasses associated with the Vietnam War, and a camouflage shirt around his waist. They spray the forest with a barrage of bullets without hitting any deer, reminding viewers of Junior's linking his father's failed hunts both to disrespecting deer and participating in the Vietnam War. Multiple close-ups are used in this scene to emphasize how these men's internalized imperial violence not only fails to provide sustenance for others but also kills a member of their community. The film harshly critiques Cherokee men's imbalanced expressions of masculinity; its narrative and visuals stress that internalizing imperial ideologies leads to violence against one's kin and community.

The Doe Boy presents Hunter as a corrective means of restoring balance to the Cherokee community through gender ambiguity. The longtime nickname "Doe Boy" not only refers to Hunter shooting the doe, it also codes him as gender ambiguous. Because he never hunts after the event, he is both "boy" and "doe," both male and female. When Hunter and Hank return home after the symbolic hunt, Hank and Marvin are filmed outdoors discussing it while Hunter is positioned in the kitchen with his mother who gives him an injection of hemophilia medication. The medication is not only linked to his mother and her female role as caregiver; because it must be refrigerated, it is also associated throughout the film with the kitchen, a feminized domestic space, and with the life-sustaining food typically found in a refrigerator. The characters' settings following the hunting trip visually references historic Cherokee gender roles where men hunt and women nurture by preparing food. To further reinforce the gendered division of labor, this scene cuts from an extreme close-up of Maggie's face to an extreme close-up of Hunter's face seven years later while he injects himself with the hemophilia medication, visually implying that over time Hunter has taken over his nurse mother's role as a healer and nurturer. The visual links between Hunter's anomalous blood and gender ambiguity are deliberate and are some of many nontranslated metaphors the film uses to speak directly to a Cherokee audience. Theda Perdue describes early

Cherokees' highly gendered division of labor, and she claims "any intrusion, any crossing of boundaries, involved a certain amount of danger" as it could upset the harmony and equilibrium so valued in Cherokee culture (17). However, anything able to cross boundaries between genders or bodies is also considered extremely powerful. "Anomalies," writes Perdue, "were the source of both great peril and amazing power" (29). Blood was considered the most potent of all boundary crossers as it belongs inside the body but can be emitted through hunting, warfare, and menstruation. Menstruating women's continuously flowing blood is considered the greatest "spiritual power"; "the power to bring about change . . . change in the family and in the community" (Purdue 35, 34). Hunter is both male and doe through his actions, but also through his hemophilia, a boy who routinely sheds flowing blood.

Closer analysis of Cherokee gender roles and views of blood demonstrates the great power Hunter possesses to bring about change in his community. Hunter is a powerful figure; the film tells viewers he is the only living Indigenous hemophiliac in Oklahoma and the only one of his extended Cherokee relatives, according to his grandfather, capable of passing on cultural practices. What he attempts to pass on to his community are more balanced gender expectations. After Hank is killed, a victim of his own and Cherokee men's hypermasculinity, we watch Hunter begin to perform historical Cherokee female expression, learning to cook and to verbally express his emotions. Interestingly, Maggie declares that the tomato soup Hunter cooks for her following Hank's death "looks like afterbirth." Hunter births his own female self, reinforcing the gender balance he performs. Reading Hunter's anomalous body and behavior in historical context reveals that his rebirth seeks to prompt larger tribal renewal. Justice notes that in pre-Christian southeastern tribes "the anomalous body . . . functions as both a personal and communal 'interpretive occasion,' placing into an ever-contextualized relationship all that we assume to be 'traditional,' 'human,' 'other-than-human,' and 'natural'" ("Notes" 221). The anomalous body (in a community or in a feature film) is to be viewed and interpreted through its relations to other bodies. "In other words," asserts Justice, "the anomaly is constitutive of the norm, not outside or insignificant to it" ("Notes" 221). Situating Hunter within a tribally specific context reveals that rather than being "insignificant" to his community, his actions help to constitute it. His performative gender balance is necessary for the Cherokee Nation to re-achieve balance, and his actions, particularly in regard to gender and kinship, are intended to be both interpretive and generative.

Transgressive Gender and Ritual Performance

Hunter's expression of both masculine and feminine genders seeks to repair an unbalanced hypermasculinity in the contemporary Cherokee Nation;

unfortunately, his seeming gender balance is created at the expense of women. While the film effectively critiques a masculinity associated with imperial violence, its use of the feminine to promote gender balance is at times problematic. Women in the film are not three-dimensional characters in their own right; they are limited to acting as foils for Hunter's representation and embrace of the feminine. One area of limitation is the curtailment of female speech; as Hunter learns to express himself more verbally, powerful women characters lose their voice, shifting from being outspoken, emotive advocates for themselves and their loved ones to being silent or having only muted speech. For example, after Hank is killed, Maggie's grief is presented entirely in silence. Maggie never speaks in the scene where she learns of her husband's death, and her silence is paired with a change in how she is filmed. In the scene, Maggie is filmed with a medium shot and two close-ups where she is centered in the frame. The scene's final shot shifts from a close-up to a wide, tilt-angle shot that highlights her powerlessness in the face of her husband's death. The scene's shot editing and her silence powerfully reinforce the emotional storyline. Less understandable, though, is that Maggie continues to be similarly filmed and silenced for the remainder of the movie. In the montage of mourning that follows, three medium shots film Maggie from behind and off-center in the frame as she cries silently. A fourth medium shot depicts her left of center, silently sleeping as Hunter, positioned in the center of the frame, covers her with a blanket. Similar shot editing is used in the remainder of the film. By filming Maggie and other women off-center in the frame, *The Doe Boy*'s visuals suggest that women's stories and emotional and gender expression are not at its center. Yet the female characters function as catalysts to better position Hunter's feminine gender performance. After watching a silent Maggie in four subsequent shots, the film includes a shot of Hunter, now also filmed off-center in the frame, voicing emotions to his grandfather; he declares, "I should have been there granddaddy. I should have been with him. . . . Maybe it was supposed to be me." Rather than insulting and picking fights with others as he did throughout the film, Hunter gradually learns to communicate his feelings directly and nonviolently. It comes with a temporary shift in camera angles that visually symbolize his embrace of "feminine" caretaking roles, performing domestic acts and using speech to care for the emotional well-being of his family. Unfortunately, Hunter's embrace of the feminine comes with a reduction in the speech of female characters, such as Maggie and Hunter's neighbor Geri; in the remainder of the film both characters' earlier verbal sparring is exchanged for silence or notably muted speech.

Hunter's gender balance is created through the gradual silencing of Indigenous women's voices and also through their objectification and sexualization. Though the film portrays Hunter as performing both male and female gender expressions, it proclaims his heterosexism. The second scene we are shown of an adult Hunter reveals his unrequited desire for his female friend Bird, who is also filmed off-center. We are then shown his immediate transference of desire to his female neighbor Geri, played by Judy Herrera. We first meet Geri in a tilt-down angle shot where the camera and Hunter gaze down at her from a balcony two stories above her. Her low positioning and off-center framing visually suggest her lesser power, as does Hunter's dialogue; upon meeting her, Hunter laughingly admits he would like to see Geri topless. While this frank remark elicits spunky flirting from Geri, "I *bet* you would," the film shows Hunter kissing a topless Geri soon afterward. It is significant that their foreplay takes place shortly after Hunter has learned that he has possibly acquired HIV/AIDS through his blood transfusions. In line with the film's 1984 setting when limited knowledge was available, Hunter initially thinks AIDS is a "gay disease." The film shows Hunter getting tested at his doctor's office, and then taking Geri out on a date that leads to intimate kissing. Through the specter of HIV/AIDS and Hank's homophobic taunting of Hunter, the film briefly raises questions about Hunter's sexuality. *The Doe Boy* positions Geri more as a placeholder than as a three-dimensional character to refute the issues surrounding same-sex desire that it raises. Geri functions in the film not only to assert Hunter's heterosexuality but also to further facilitate his embrace of his dual-gendered identity. She urges him to help launder her clothes and to verbally voice his emotions. She says, "Don't just run away Hunter. Hunter, talk to me." Once Hunter begins to express his feelings, the film further sexualizes Geri. After leaving her a note where he confesses his hemophilia by giving her his medical bracelet, Hunter drives by an imaginary road sign. Depicting a topless, sexualized Indigenous woman with long black hair draped suggestively over her bare shoulder, the sign reads "soft shoulder." The sign signifies Geri's position as both a sexual object and a comforting soft shoulder to cry on. While Hunter is positioned as a powerful figure, capable of bringing tremendous change to his community, women in the film are relegated solely to supporting roles. Although viewers learn that Hunter and other male characters need to embrace the feminine to restore gender balance in the Cherokee Nation, we never learn what female characters need to change to grow. Women are an absent presence in the film, serving to signify the feminine that Hunter more effectively embodies.

While it is possible to read Hunter's relationships with women in the film as a product of sexism learned from his father, the film's visual language reinforces its biased narrative. As noted, female actors are filmed differently than male actors. Not only are they usually filmed off-center in the frame, while males occupy centered positions, they are not filmed through straight angles. Never staring directly into the camera, the women characters are all positioned as objects, not subjects, of the camera's gaze. None of the film's actors look directly at the camera; all keep the illusion of the fourth wall where an actor does not acknowledge the audience. However, the male actors are frequently portrayed with straight-angle shots and filmed staring almost directly at the camera, visually representing their status as the film's subjects. Aside from being typically framed off-center, occasionally through tilt-down angles, the female characters are always filmed with their eyes and faces turned or significantly slanted toward the male characters. They are not filmed as full-fledged subjects in their own right, but as figures to be understood through their relations to the males in the film. While it could be argued that the female actors' averted gaze is a gesture of respect in keeping with historic Cherokee culture, the fact that the male actors stare directly at each other and almost directly at the camera during intense moments of connection and intimacy suggests that males are visually coded as subjects and females as objects of the film's and the male characters' gaze. The film is likely signaling its primary focus and audience of Cherokee males; however, its narrative and visuals ultimately uphold the gender imbalance it critiques.

Gender and sexual expressions are historically linked in Cherokee culture, and the film seems cognizant that individuals with the strength to cross gender expectations might also possess the power to desire freely as well. Hunter's anger over Hank's frequent homophobic comments, and his refusal to make any himself when he discovers his blood transfusions potentially contain HIV antibodies, make clear that Hunter neither shares Hank's homophobia nor feels insecure enough in his own heterosexuality to feel threatened by others' same-sex desire. One might ask then why the film briefly mentions and then drops same-sex desire and AIDS at all, and why HIV/AIDS is utilized as a catalyst (along with Hank's death) for changing Hunter's self-identity. When hundreds of gay men in the United States were first medically documented with and began dying of severe immune deficiency in the early 1980s, their deaths were largely ignored by policy makers, who saw HIV/AIDS as a disease that affected lesbian, gay, bisexual, transgender, and queer (LGBTQ) individuals and poor, nonwhite drug users. When Ryan White, a Caucasian hemophilic boy who acquired HIV/AIDS from his blood-clotting transfusions, gained national media attention after being expelled from his Indiana middle school in 1984, White and other hemophiliacs functioned as public advocates for challenging the negative and prejudicial perception of individuals who acquire HIV/AIDS. White and others made great strides in raising public interest, awareness, and funding to support HIV/AIDS care.[5] *The Doe Boy*'s 1984 setting follows this proven media strategy, enlisting hemophilia as a means of raising and then displacing prejudicial views regarding race, same-sex desire, and disease. The film metaphorically (and visually) moves from the poorly lit doctor's office where Hunter first learns he has possibly acquired HIV/AIDS, to its final scene of a triumphant Hunter in a brightly lit, sun-filled meadow after he learns to accept himself and reunites with Geri.

Unfortunately, this symbolic movement from darkness and fear into bright, internal insight and external validation is not extended to queerness in the film, which remains metaphorically and literally shadowed. Though Hunter refuses to engage in homophobia, no characters in the film openly express same-sex desire. The audience does not even hear of queer individuals in the Cherokee Nation; they exist symbolically far away in "a neighborhood in Dallas," Hank says in a mocking, higher-pitched voice. *The Doe Boy* echoes a phenomenon found in other well-known Indigenous American films. Though LGBTQ characters appear in early, influential films like *Johnny Greyeyes* (2002) and *The Business of Fancydancing* (2002), Lisa Tatonetti notes that these films' protagonists leave their same-sex lovers off-reservation and the cinematography of their returns home emphasize empty landscapes and solitude. Tatonetti demonstrates how the literal and figurative "boundaries of nation in indigenous contexts are constructed and maintained by a heteronormative gaze" (158). Unfortunately, *The Doe Boy* repeats this narrative and visual closeting. Conceivably the closeting is an effort to stave off alienating Cherokee viewers. Christianity continues to be the most popular religion for contemporary Cherokees and, likely reflecting dominant Christian beliefs, the Cherokee Nation refuses to legally recognize same-sex marriages.[6] Attempting to appeal to a predominantly Christian Cherokee audience, *The Doe Boy*'s erasure of queer characters in Tahlequah notably limits the film's politics. Craig Womack asserts, "the queer world is as necessary toward the all-important function of balance as the normal world" (245). While *The Doe Boy* seeks to create communal balance, it narratively and visually reinforces imbalance. The film misses an opportunity to portray all peoples that constitute the Cherokee Nation.

Raising the issue of same-sex desire, then immediately asserting heterosexism, is another instance of *The Doe Boy* enlisting historic Cherokee culture while simultaneously constraining it. When Hank and others collapse metaphoric gender crossing with same-sex desire, the film subtly draws upon Cherokee historical practices while carefully limiting their present-day application. While not much is known about early Cherokees who expressed genders alternative to their biological sex, these individuals were historically associated with same-sex desire. Sarah Hill, Qwo-Li Driskill, and Theda Perdue all provide evidence of Cherokees during the colonial era whose gender expression differed from settlers' perceptions of their biological sex. Perdue notes, "some evidence suggests that a kind of sexual reclassification occurred for men who preferred to farm and that these men functioned sexually as well as socially as women" (37). Perdue claims that biologically female-sexed individuals expressing masculinity "acquired considerable prestige," but she contends that biologically male-sexed individuals expressing femininity likely became the butt of jokes (39). She admits, "Joking does not necessarily imply scorn," but could function "to recognize deviant behavior and incorporate it into the repertoire of acknowledged behaviors" (39, 38). In the film, the contemporary Cherokee community's jokes about Hunter's deer hunt and his hemophilic flowing blood might be a rhetorical performance that incorporates him into preexisting Cherokee understandings of the world. Further, Qwo-Li Driskill notes that Perdue bases her assumptions on European colonists' accounts, and their cultural prejudices likely misinterpreted the positions of male-sexed individuals expressing femininity and left unrecorded possible "blood rites existing for male-embodied Two-Spirits via ritual scratching, tattooing, or other kinds of activities" (132).[7] Gregory Smithers argues that because Cherokees who expressed anomalous genders and sexualities often held important positions in rituals, "the guarding of such knowledge helps explain the gaps in colonial archives" (645). He writes, "Cherokees might have felt no need to identify two-spirit people to missionaries, traders, and ethnographers because their physical appearance was incidental to the special spiritual gifts that they possessed and the ritual roles that they served. Moreover, refusing to give non-Cherokees access to, and knowledge of (and thus over), the most sacred details of ceremonial life may have protected Cherokee two spirits from the often disruptive colonial gaze of government agents, missionaries, and ethnographers" (Smithers 647–648). *The Doe Boy* continues not only to reflect the importance of this ceremonial position but also to guard the knowledge from non-Cherokees by failing to translate its visual references to historic gender and ceremonial performances.

Privileged Sight

The film's visual language contextualizes *The Doe Boy* within historic Cherokee understandings of the ritual roles of both blood and anomalous gender expression, and affirms that Hunter's simultaneous "boy" and "doe" gender is indicative of his potential spiritual function. Looking more closely at the film's shot editing reveals that when Hunter shoots a doe instead of a buck as a child, it is because the deer play a trick on him, not because of a personal error. When Hunter first sees the doe, viewers are shown a wide-angle shot from Hunter's point of view that makes the deer appear to have antlers; however, two subsequent medium side angle shots reveal that to viewers and anyone other than Hunter, the animal has no antlers and is a doe. Hunter's privileged sight in this scene and the way the event prompts him to critique his community's hunting and warfare practices suggest that Hunter functions as a tool for the animals to restore balance.[8] This role is reinforced through additional shot editing when Hank and Hunter follow a literal blood trail to discover the deer is a doe. In an extremely low angle shot the deer and its suffering are in focus in the foreground, with Hunter and Hank blurred in the background. Because the camera tilts up from the earth to frame the deer, it visually asserts the deer's power over Hunter and Hank. The doe's eyes are filmed in the center of the frame with a blurry Hunter immediately behind. The film cuts from the doe's eyes to a close-up shot from Hunter's point of view of the doe's ears. It then cuts to extreme close-ups of Hunter's eyes, Hank's eyes, and then Hunter's eyes again before cutting to a modified version of the low-angle shot. This time deep focus is used to highlight the deer's impact on Hunter and Hank, and while the deer is still in the foreground, Hunter is now in the center of the frame, positioned directly in line again with the deer's ears. The film's visuals highlight the importance of accurately using sight/insight to first see and then hear the deer's call for balance. Twice highlighting Hunter's eyes and gradually centering him in the frame signals his growing ability to see, hear, and learn from the deer.

Following this hunt, Hunter tries to teach his community the importance of hunting in a way that honors the deer; he tells community members, "There's a difference between hunting and killing." To "hunt" a man must use handmade bows and arrows, rather than guns (which are associated with imperial war and "killing"), and he must chase the deer, not deceive them by shining flashlights in their eyes or wearing camouflage to "look like a tree." Hunter literally followed the deer's blood trail to this insight. Hunter's flowing blood and decision to "follow in a deer's footsteps [and blood] instead of his father's," associates his later acts with Cherokee blood rituals. Thus Hunter's ability to express both genders through actions and flowing blood reveal his ability to bridge the familiar and unfamiliar, the mundane and sacred.

The shot editing used later in the film emphasizes Hunter's powerful, changed position, moving him from the background to an equal position in straight, objective angle shots that include him and deer. In the film's climax, Hunter enacts a ritual he first saw in a visionary dream. He receives the dream just as the dawn sun comes over the horizon, a liminal time when night and day are in balance. In the dream, Hunter stalks a buck wearing a string of beads that is rumored to have been placed on the buck's neck by Tommy Deer in Water, the "real hunter" who chooses to honor rather than kill deer. Two wide-angle shots show viewers the bead-wearing buck nudging Hunter's leg as he sleeps in the back of his El Camino after a fight with his father. The buck then stares directly at him. Shot editing leaves ambiguous whether the buck is part of Hunter's dream or exists in real-time events while Hunter sleeps. Both scenes are shot in sharp focus and contain wide-angle shots that locate the deer and Hunter in the landscape, along with an equivalent number of medium and close-up shots of the deer and Hunter. Robert Conley says that in Cherokee belief, "to dream of a deer looking directly at you is good luck;" alternately, "it may not be a dream at all . . . [but] a shape-shifter trying to pull something on you" (72). In *The Doe Boy*, the visionary dream and potential real-time shots of the buck looking directly at Hunter as he sleeps signal both luck *and* a benign trick the deer play to prompt Hunter on a path to restore communal balance.

Notably, the vision dream ends when the sleeping Hunter hears a real-world bullet shot by a nearby hunter; visions of balance sent from the animals are narratively positioned as being at odds with gunfire. Hunter's initial (and faulty) response is to immediately wake and point his father's gun, before finding that the beaded/honored deer has disappeared. Hunter's subsequent yell "Jesus H Christ" expresses his frustration and also subtly alludes to the collusion between settler culture's Christianity and guns. Despite Hank's claim that there are no "magic beads and magic hunters" in Tahlequah, the film visually signals that "magic" or at least visions distinct from Christianity are available to those able to recognize the messages sent from the deer. In fact, Hank's earlier comment, "There ain't no magic around here Marvin. It's just real life" is ironically illustrative. The film's visual grammar reinforces the point. Visions and kinship with the deer are *not* "magic"; they are filmed exactly the same as any other part of its portrayal of contemporary Cherokees' "real life."

The colors red and white are also used in nontranslated ways to signal that Hunter's actions are for the Cherokee community and not just for himself individually. Leaving home after being struck by his father, Hunter receives the visionary dream while sleeping on a red and white blanket in the back of his El Camino.[9] Schweninger sees this red and white blanket as "something that looks very much like an American flag," linking Hank's violence with larger U.S. military violence (178). Schweninger's argument that "*Doe Boy* does indeed talk back to Hollywood" portrayals of military glory upholds the film's critique of the U.S.'s violent imperialism (174). However, the argument ignores the film's efforts also to speak to a Cherokee audience. *The Doe Boy*'s director Redroad says, "I find 'talking back' to be a slippery slope. . . . We have to be careful or we can end up dignifying what we're battling because we aren't imagining ourselves out of it" (Marubbio 298). Instead of interpreting the red and white blanket Hunter lies on during his visionary dream as a response to a broken U.S. flag, a tribally specific reading of the film's use of red and white offers a more complex understanding of the film's politics. Red and white appear together numerous times in the film: Hunter tries to take Maggie's red and white pow-wow chair when he moves out on his own; instead, she gives Hunter red and white bed linens. Hunter also wears a red and white shirt when he begins to embrace "the feminine" by cooking soup for his mother, and he again lies on the red and white blanket in the scene that leads to a reconciliation with his father. Reading the red and white framing within a tribal context demonstrates the subtle way the film reinforces its narrative focus on balance with visuals that would potentially be understood by a Cherokee audience. Historically Cherokee sociopolitics were based on a balance between red/war/resistance and white/peace/negotiation. According to Justice, a balance between the red and white paths is essential to maintaining a balanced community, and this "has in fact persisted to the present day, albeit in altered forms" (*Our Fire Survives* 30). The purpose of Hunter's performance of gender balance becomes clear after he receives his visionary dream from the deer people; like historic Cherokee who blurred the balance between genders and biological sexes, Hunter is expected to play an important role in ritual, in this case, the ritual hunt he sees in the dream.

Only after he learns to embrace the feminine following his father's death does Hunter perform the ritual hunt. In preparation, Hunter first prays, receives a smudging from his mother, and wears the specific face paint and clothing he saw in the dream, both red and black, the Cherokee colors for war and death according to Mooney (342). Hunter carries a handmade bow with one arrow. Once he enters the woods at the start of his "hunt," a sudden windstorm replaces the previously peaceful day, blowing debris into Hunter's face and leading to numerous visible scratches. Several Cherokee male purification rites involve bloodletting, and the scratches Hunter receives provide visual evidence that Hunter is participating in a ritual. The visuals offer a cultural reason for why Hunter must leave behind settler cultures' blood-clotting medicine before beginning his hunt. Despite the physical difficulty of moving forward, Hunter continues and, through the trees, spots the beaded buck from his dream looking directly at him. He chases the deer, "giving it a chance" before tripping, falling, and further scratching himself. His honorable hunt and bloodletting are rewarded when the buck suddenly appears in extreme close-up, gazing at Hunter and viewers. Hunter draws an arrow and the camera cuts between extreme close-ups of Hunter's eyes, the buck's eyes, and Hunter's wounds dripping blood. Schweninger asserts, "the filmic convention of shot/ reverse-shot editing in this scene suggests that Hunter and the deer are in some sort of conversation" (182). As dialogic subjects, they are not objects of the camera and each other's gaze. The extreme close-ups of the drawn arrow and Hunter's rapidly flowing, nonclotting blood visually assert that both Hunter's and the deer's lives are simultaneously threatened. Their physical danger signals a deeper, more significant danger if Cherokee men continue to ignore their kinship relations to the deer. Hunter's flowing blood in the scene allows him to blur not only gender boundaries but also the boundary between the deer and himself; it allows him to fully identify with the deer and recognize their shared position. Close-ups are paired with a twice-repeated wide, straight-angle shot where the camera visually positions Hunter and the buck as equals, filming them at a similar eye-level height, in a similar position gazing intensely at each other, and both possessing weapons, a bow and extremely large antlers. The buck lowers his head and antlers, and in response Hunter "followed in [the] deer's footsteps instead of his father's" by lowering his arrow and head. Hunter recognizes and honors his kinship with the deer and chooses not to kill unnecessarily. His personal sense of masculinity no longer depends upon his mastery of deer; instead it relies upon his understanding of their shared kinship.

The scenes that follow the film's climax include additional visuals that reinforce Hunter's performance as a ritual to achieve balance. Immediately after Hunter chooses not to shoot his arrow, the buck disappears. Hunter then walks through a field of goldenrod, a plant that Cherokees, both in their homeland Appalachia and in the Cherokee Nation's new lands in Oklahoma, have long used to effectively clean wounds and stop bleeding. The field is strategically placed next to a flowing river where Hunter washes the remaining blood off his hands. The wound seems to clot on its own following a ritual that includes scratching, goldenrod, and a flowing river. Washing blood off a character's hands is a common performance metaphor.[10] In *The Doe Boy* it also alludes to, without directly showing, bloodletting rites that at times precede "going to water." The Cherokee Nation's website describes going to water as "a cleansing ritual that was performed at the river in running water"; ritual rinsing "washed away impurities or bad deeds and started a new life" (Cherokee Nation). Notably, this is the first time that running water is shown in the film. *The Doe Boy* suggests that learning more respectful, balanced notions of kinship will lead to personal and communal cleansing. Robert Conley says going to water is "perhaps the single most important of all Cherokee rituals" (70). It is a "quiet, low key, straightforward" ritual, Conley writes, "Anyone looking for feathers, chanting, and dance . . . would almost certainly go away from a genuine Cherokee ritual disappointed. It's not a show. It just gets the job done" (70). While *The Doe Boy* includes a hunter with face paint and a feather in his hair, and a well-timed eagle's cry is heard at the start of the ritual hunt, the film otherwise seeks to "get the job done," to assert respectful notions of masculinity to all its viewers, while sending nontranslated visual messages to Cherokees. The nontranslated visual allusions to rituals perhaps explain why reviewers and even some film scholars fail to see the Cherokee content of *The Doe Boy*. Through the use of seeming stereotypes, the film ensures that gestures toward the sacred are not entirely missed by all its viewers. Indeed, when Hunter pulls his hand from the flowing river he finds the beads the buck has worn for years and immediately wraps the beads around his now healing hand, visually reinforcing that a ritual healing has occurred.

Notably, the film's gendered visuals change in the next and penultimate scene of the film, shifting back to the cinematography viewers briefly saw during the mourning montage when Hunter is shot differently as he begins to embrace the feminine following his father's death. Cutting away from an extreme long shot of the flowing river, viewers see an extreme close-up of Hunter's hand knocking on Geri's door; his hand is wrapped in a white bandage, the color white symbolically signaling that a peaceful healing has occurred and Hunter is returning to the world cleansed. With the exception of the mourning montage, the film meticulously reflects a highly gendered visual grammar, filming male and female characters differently. However, after the ritual hunt, Hunter's view of masculinity is no longer dependent upon mastery of the deer and others, and this difference is signified in the cinematography used in the penultimate scene. We watch Hunter knock on Geri's door, and when she answers, the actor playing Geri looks almost directly at the camera, a first for the film. Though Geri has a gender ambiguous name, she is always filmed like the other female characters, with eyes downcast or significantly slanted toward the male characters. However, in the penultimate scene, she is positioned as the subject of the gaze, shown looking almost straight at the camera. Surprisingly, Hunter assumes the film's "feminine" visual language; he looks down and away from Geri's and the camera's straight-angle gaze. The film's grammar in the scene reflects a restoration of gender balance. Potentially, it implies that in order for men to embrace the feminine, women must embrace the masculine. Geri quickly resumes the role of a feminine caretaker; she worriedly asks, "Are you OK?" Rather than using the voice Hunter asserts throughout the film, he sobs silently, much like his mother. Hunter's balancing of masculinity and femininity seems like an apt solution to overcoming the hypermasculinity the film sees plaguing the contemporary Cherokee Nation; however, its portrayal of gender balance apparently requires the silencing of those performing femininity. The switching of gender in this scene continues to render one character the subject and another the object of the gaze. The film's penultimate shot offers a glimmer of hope, as the shot/reaction shots shift to a wide objective angle shot of Geri and Hunter tightly embracing while he cries, seemingly signaling a restoration of gender balance. The balance is reflected narratively in their reunion and visually. The 5'9" actor playing Hunter, James Duval, leans down and significantly bends his knees to hug the shorter 5'3" actor playing Geri, Judy Herrera, who stands on her toes; the actors' physical manipulations make the characters appear to be of equal height, visually symbolizing the equal importance of both genders to heal the Cherokee Nation.

Unfortunately, the restoration of balance is undercut with the reassertion of individualism displayed in the final scene. The film's darkly lit penultimate shot of Geri and Hunter's embrace cuts to a sunshine-filled wide-angle shot of a young Hunter, played by Andrew Ferchland, in the woods and wearing the same camouflage he wore on his inaugural hunt in 1977, except he now clutches adult 1984 Hunter's homemade bow and quiver. The film uses Cherokee understandings of time here, displaying how ritual enables the past to actively affect the present, thereby allowing young Hunter to wear his 1977 costume while holding adult Hunter's 1984 bow/quiver. Walking toward the camera, young Hunter's stoic face breaks into a large grin and he raises the bow in triumph, accompanied by another well-timed eagle's cry, before the film cuts to black and the credits. The film's final shot visually signals the accomplishment of a successful hunt—for masculinity, a more complex understanding of kinship, and a sexy girlfriend—but it again suggests that this accomplishment is for individual males alone. The final shot celebrates a revised understanding of gender that balances historic and contemporary Cherokee understandings of masculinity; nevertheless, its focus on individual accomplishment over and against communal change is problematic.[11] The film comes full circle in the final shot by alluding to its opening scene, the only other time we watch Hunter raise his hands in triumph. Young Hunter celebrates winning a foot race against his friends Junior and Cheekie after running through a similarly sunlit wood. The absence of Junior and Cheekie in the final scene is a missed opportunity where the film could demonstrate that Hunter's ritual is part of communal Cherokee male blood rites to further reinforce tribal views of masculinity over and against settler culture's individualism.

In addition, the final shot also reasserts heteronormativity. Because of the historic link between Cherokee ritual and individuals who cross genders, it is possible to read the 1977/1984 temporal aberrance as reflecting both ritual and queer temporalities. Mark Rifkin contends that queer Indigenous temporalities can use tribal cosmologies to work against heteronormative understandings of linear history. As discussed, Hollywood has long colluded with imperial narratives, rewriting history with so-called progress doctrines where settler cultures' advancement is portrayed as permanently replacing "vanished" Indigenous peoples and cultures. Rifkin suggests the possibility of a "rupturing of the present by the unexpected (re)appearance of what had been thought gone" in ways that "might unsettle existing social arrangements" and "open the past and one's relation to it so as to feel one's way toward alternative ways of being in the present" (138). It is possible to read Hunter's nonlinear 1977/1984 triumph as the queer reappearance of historic Cherokee beliefs regarding kinship, where family includes animals and one's clan, not necessarily nonclan tribal members. While this might explain Junior and Cheekie's absence, it does not explain the absence of Maggie and other female clan members, nor does it explain why Hunter is alone. By the time this scene occurs, Hunter has healed (at least temporarily) the nonclotting blood that provided access to the blood ritual and blurred gender boundaries. It is a solely male and individualized Hunter that triumphs at the film's end. While the film seeks to promote a restoration of balance, at times it narratively and visually limits the very changes it seeks to enact.

The Doe Boy raises an expectation of gender balance that it repeatedly fails to deliver. If the film seeks to assert a historic Cherokee balancing of genders, it could have briefly shown female characters engaged in separate activities with equivalent responsibilities. While we are told that Maggie works as a nurse, the only time we watch her working is a few establishing shots showing her happily and silently walking through a clinic's hall immediately before Manny and Bear appear to inform her of Hank's death. Her silence in this and later scenes, as well as the fact that she is set only in domestic settings prior to and after this scene limits the film's portrayal of women's work. Maggie's nursing labor is echoed in Geri's portrayal as well. While Geri has a gender-neutral name— "You have a boy's name," Hunter exclaims upon meeting her—she is not presented as gender ambiguous. Instead, Geri, like Maggie, is fully associated with feminine activities of caretaking. She is going to school "to work with people who have speech impediments because of strokes and head injuries." Though she is of "Pueblo, Navajo, Mexican, and Spanish" descent, she is somewhat gendered like a historic Cherokee woman, thoroughly associated with caretaking and the home. Unlike Hunter's sterile, empty apartment, her apartment is filled with floral linens and organic wreaths made into heart and butterfly shapes. While creating such art would have been a historic Cherokee female activity (Perdue 22), the film does not position Geri as a creator, reserving that position alone for male characters. Hunter and his grandfather Marvin are shown to be accomplished woodworkers while Geri is a consumer of premade, low-cost goods; Hunter first meets her after she returns from a shopping trip at TJ Maxx. Despite Geri's gender-ambiguous name, Hunter alone is in a position of power, a creator who promotes community change by expressing both genders simultaneously and more effectively than any other male and female characters in the film.

Redroad claims, "there could be something healing about an image" and he writes/directs *The Doe Boy* in an effort to heal from the hypermasculinity he and others were raised with in the Cherokee Nation. Unfortunately, Hunter and Redroad's "healing" seems to depend upon the silencing and objectifying of those positioned as female or queer. Writing about Redroad's earlier film *High Horse* (1994), Beverly Singer claims, "The cultural perception of freedom projected in the film by Redroad is akin to letting go of the need to be in control and dominating other people, places, and animals" (83). While *The Doe Boy* displays a similar antidomination concept of freedom, it does so by visually and narratively controlling and containing representations of women and by omitting Indigenous queer characters entirely. The film misses an opportunity to examine masculinity in a larger context where female characters and LGBTQ characters of multiple genders are presented and filmed (even in supporting roles) as three-dimensional subjects with their own fears, desires, and abilities.

While the film's portrayal of women and closeting of LGBTQ individuals is problematic, the very fact that it raises these expectations at all suggests the film's power to prompt a reexamination of Cherokee culture in the eyes of both Cherokee and non-Cherokee viewers. Weaver argues, "language and narrative have tremendous power to create community" (40). The story Indigenous people tell, according to Weaver, "both reflects and shapes contemporary Native identity and community" (ix). *The Doe Boy* actively seeks to critique and reshape contemporary Cherokee ideas of masculinity as a means of strengthening Cherokee community. The film also seeks to bring about a cinematic reimagining of Cherokee culture by resisting Hollywood stereotypes of Indigenous men as always-already-dead noble/savages. Much like the bead-wearing buck that gives Hunter a visionary dream, viewers are presented here with an alternative Tahlequah where Cherokee men live and refrain from divisive violence adopted from settler culture, instead returning to more balanced recognitions of their larger kinship with each other and the world. *The Doe Boy* calls upon all viewers to recognize historical Cherokee expectations of balance in the world and to begin actively to perform behaviors that resist destructive imperialist ideologies. To achieve balance and begin to heal its audience, however, *The Doe Boy* would have been better served by representing all genders and beings that constitute the historic and contemporary Cherokee Nation.

Notes

1   Will Rogers is likely the best-known Cherokee actor; however, many mainstream viewers are unaware of his Indigenous heritage.

2   In this way, *The Doe Boy* seems to anticipate Paul Chaat Smith's advice to Indigenous filmmakers not to emphasize Hollywood images but instead to "embrace the extraordinary complexities of Indian life" by portraying "both the ugliness and the beauty of our circumstances" (41).

3   Melanie Benson argues that hemophilia "converts biological fact into a metaphor for acute cultural crisis"; Hunter's "uncontrollable blood loss becomes an urgent, evocative sign of both biological and cultural erasure" (264). In a recent essay, Redroad openly critiques the way "the cold mathematics of genocide has left a void," but he asserts, "All attempts to terminate our membership have failed" (Redroad-Snapp 113, 114). *The Doe Boy* intervenes in "cultural erasure" by calling upon Cherokees to use historical tribal practices actively to resist imperialist ideologies.

4   The only scene where Manny is costumed differently occurs after he accidentally kills Hank; wearing overalls, Manny is shown digging Hank's grave. Manny's costuming and enacting of historical Cherokee men's obligation to dig graves visually suggests that his gender expression might be changing. We learn in a later scene that Manny sent Maggie food after Hank's death, further suggesting he might return to tribal gender obligations. However, because Manny is never again shown, the film holds open the possibility without confirming it; it refuses to let Cherokee viewers believe that fictional characters have accomplished vicariously the hard work of social change for them.

5   In fact, in the 2017 U.S. federal budget, the Ryan White HIV/AIDS Program (created after his death in 1990) remains the largest HIV-specific grant and the third largest federal funding source for HIV care after Medicaid and Medicare.

6   "Declar[ing] that an emergency exists," in 2004 the Cherokee Nation Council unanimously amended its Marriage and Family Protection Act to "define Marriage as one man and one woman to protect the traditional definition of Marriage in the Cherokee Nation" (Cherokee Nation Legislative Act 26-04). The Nation's definition of "traditional" is debatable. In an affidavit by academic Brian Gilley submitted to the Cherokee Nation Supreme Court in an appeal of the Act, Gilley declares, "there is overwhelming evidence for the historic and cultural presence of multiple gender roles and same-sex relations among most if not all Native North

Americans, including the Cherokee, and that they historically shared in the institution of marriage" (Gilley). Justice contends "the simplistic formula of one man + one woman = traditional marriage is, quite simply, historical revisionism" that is "more than a little bit queer and anomalous in . . . the broad sweep of Cherokee history, nationhood, and social identity" ("Notes" 223).

7   Driskill uses the umbrella term "Two-Spirit" after acknowledging "not all of us use this term for ourselves any more than all of us use any of the other terms available to us in English. All of these terms and ideas are slippery and complicated, but 'Two-Spirit' carries with it a particular commitment to decolonization and Indigenous histories and identities that is at the center of this particular telling" (121).

8   While Angelica Lawson similarly argues that *The Doe Boy* is "a film about balance and ethics," she sees the hunt as the result of a personal error, "Hunter's mistake of killing the doe throws everything out of balance" (218, 219). I believe the editing of the scene's point of view shot complicates the issue of responsibility.

9   The car's make is also significant, as "El Camino" means "the way" in Spanish.

10 Lady Macbeth immediately comes to mind.

11 The final shot also alludes to Hunter's first hunt with his father, Hank, but Hank is missing from the scene as well. According to the Cherokee Nation website, many "Traditional Cherokees . . . believe that after a person dies, his soul often continues to live on" and that souls possess the ability "to materialize where some, but not all people, can see them" (Cherokee Nation). The film uses historical Cherokee beliefs throughout, so it seems a deliberate choice not to include Hank when asserting wider views of kinship. Perhaps doing so would confuse non-Indigenous viewers—Is young Hunter dead now?—or it might signal that the film's revised version of masculinity is solely for Cherokee men. Regardless, his absence reinforces Hunter's individualism.

Works Cited

Benson, Melanie. "The Native Screen: American Indians in Contemporary Southern Film," *American Cinema and the Southern Imaginary*. Eds. Deborah Barker and Kathryn McKee. Athens: U of Georgia P, 2011. 253–276. Print.

Cherokee Nation website. July 26, 2016. http://www.cherokee.org/Culture/ Web.

Cherokee Nation Legislative Act 26-04, "An Act Amending Title 44 of the Cherokee Nation Marriage and Family Act," Council of the Cherokee Nation website. July 23, 2016. https://cherokee.legistar.com/LegislationDetail.aspx?ID=267141&GUID=CCCC7596 -00D0-4E39-BE7B-217F65670783&Options=&Search=&FullText=1 Web.

Coke Hedge, Allison. "The Doe Boy," *Seeing Red: Hollywood's Pixeled Skins*. Eds. LeAnne Howe, Harvey Markowitz, and Denise Cummings. East Lansing: Michigan State UP, 2013. 133–138. Print.

Conley, Robert. *Cherokee Medicine Man*. Norman: U of Oklahoma P, 2005. Print.

Driskill, Qwo-Li. "Shaking Our Shells: Cherokee Two-Spirits Rebalancing the World." *Beyond Masculinity: Essays by Queer Men on Gender and Politics*. Accessed June 5, 2016. http://www.beyondmasculinity.com Web.

Gilley, Brian J. "Gender Diversity and the Cultural Crossfire," Affidavit submitted in Cherokee Nation Supreme Court Case Number 05-11, *Baker et al. v McKinley et al.* November 20, 2005. Print.

Hall, Phil. Review of *The Doe Boy*. Originally published Daily-Reviews.com. Accessed October 26, 2010. http://www.imdb.com/reviews/329/32929.html Web.

Hill, Sarah. *Weaving New Worlds: Southeastern Cherokee Women and Their Basketry.* Chapel Hill: U of North Carolina P, 1997. Print.

Justice, Daniel Heath. "Notes Toward a Theory of Anomaly," *GLQ: A Journal of Lesbian and Gay Studies*, special issue "Sexuality, Nationality, Indigeneity" 16.1–2 (2010): 207–242.

———. *Our Fire Survives the Storm*. Minneapolis: U of Minnesota P, 2006. Print.

Lawson, Angelica. "Teaching Native American Filmmakers: Osawa, Eyre, and Redroad," *Native Americans on Film: Conversations, Teaching, and Theory*. Ed. M. Elise Marubbio and Eric Buffalohead. Lexington: UP of Kentucky, 2013. 202–222. Print.

Marubbio, M. Elise. "Wrestling the Greased Pig: An Interview with Randy Redroad," *Native Americans on Film: Conversations, Teaching, and Theory*. Lexington, KY: UP of Kentucky, 2013. 288–302. Print.

Mooney, James. *The Sacred Formulas of the Cherokee*. Washington, DC: Government Printing Office, 1891.

Olsen, A. Review of *The Doe Boy*. March 26, 2008. Posted on Amazon.com Reviews. Accessed October 26, 2010. http://www.amazon.com/Doe-Boy-Kevin-Anderson /productreviews/B00006FD9Z/ref=dp_top_cm_cr_acr_txt?ie=UTF8&show Viewpoints=1 Web.

Perdue, Theda. *Cherokee Women: Gender and Cultural Change, 1700–1835*. Lincoln: U of Nebraska P, 1998. Print.

Redroad, Randy, dir. *The Doe Boy*. Curb Entertainment, 2001.

Redroad-Snapp, Randy. "Through a Mythic Lens," *Screenwriting for a Global Market: Selling Your Scripts from Hollywood to Hong Kong*. Eds. Andrew Horton and Bernard Gordon. Berkeley and Los Angeles: U of California P, 2004. 113–118. Print.

Rifkin, Mark. "Queering Indigenous Pasts, or Temporalities of Tradition and Settlement," *The Oxford Handbook of Indigenous American Literature*. Eds. James Cox and Daniel Heath Justice. Oxford: Oxford UP, 2014. 137–151. Print.

Schmidt, Rob. "Newspaper Rock: Where Native America Meets Pop Culture," Review of *The Doe Boy*. October 14, 2007. Accessed October 26, 2010. http://newspaperrock .bluecorncomics.com/2007/10/review-of-doe-boy.html Web.

Schweninger, Lee. *Imagic Moments: Indigenous North American Film*. Athens: U of Georgia P, 2013. Print.

Singer, Beverly. *Wiping the War Paint Off the Lens: Native American Film and Video*. Minneapolis: U of Minnesota P, 2001. Print.

Smith, Paul Chaat. *Everything You Know about Indians Is Wrong*. Minneapolis: U of Minnesota P, 2009. Print.

Smithers, Gregory. "Cherokee 'Two Spirits': Gender, Ritual, and Spirituality in the Native South." *Early American Studies* 12.3 (Fall 2014): 626–651. Print.

Sturm, Circe. *Blood Politics: Race, Culture, and Identity in the Cherokee Nation of Oklahoma*. Berkeley: U of California P, 2002. Print.

Svenson, Michelle. Interview with Randy Redroad. April 2001. Accessed October 30, 2010. http://www.nativenetworks.si.edu/eng/rose/redroad_r_interview.htm Web.

Tatonetti, Lisa. "Visible Sexualities or Invisible Nations," *GLQ: A Journal of Lesbian and Gay Studies*, special issue "Sexuality, Nationality, Indigeneity" 16.1–2 (2010): 157–181.

Weaver, Jace. *That the People Might Live: Native American Literatures and Native American Community*. New York: Oxford UP, 1997. Print.

Womack, Craig. *Red on Red: Native American Literary Separatism*. Minneapolis: U of Minnesota P, 1999. Print.

Wood, Houston. *Native Features: Indigenous Films from around the World*. New York: Continuum International Pub., 2008. Print.

3

Truth, Justice, and the Mexican Way

• • • • • • • • • • • • • • • • • • •

Lucha Libre, Film, and Nationalism in Mexico

JAMES WILKEY

A hooded vigilante strikes. His face is shrouded by shadows and the hood. In the gritty darkness of an abandoned building he roughly confronts three criminal types. The vigilante moves like a trained fighter, but there is something unpolished about the way he fights. Before long the outnumbered vigilante is on the defensive when help suddenly arrives. The newcomer, despite his blue jeans and green button-down shirt, is unmistakably heroic. With his colorful mask on proud display, the newcomer is also unmistakably a Mexican professional wrestler: a *luchador*. Even in such casual clothing, the *luchador* displaying the familiar moves of one of Mexico's most iconic pop-culture displays, quickly chases off the hooded vigilante's attackers. With the criminal types defeated, he sits the younger, rougher vigilante down and begins to speak: "We need to talk; about the seven tribes of our ancestors, about the warriors who built the Aztec empire, and about the legacy they left behind. What do you know about Lucha Libre?" ("Welcome to the Temple").

This is the opening of the 2014 show *Lucha Underground*. While the roots of wrestling in Mexico are more transnational than this monologue suggests, the first moments of the show offer an intriguing distillation of the way that

Lucha Libre in its various formats, but especially crystalized on film, has become a space of both Mexican identity construction and performance. Produced in the United States, *Lucha Underground* sought to expand the tradition of Lucha Libre by creating a show that broadcasted in Spanish and English, slightly re-imagining the sport into a rougher performance with more modern, cartelesque villains. The show's chief producer, British-born Mark Burnett, partnered with director Robert Rodriguez's El Rey Network and the top wrestling league in Mexico, Lucha Libre AAA, to launch the weekly one-hour program (de Moraes). The show is produced outside of Mexico, yet taps into a long cinematic and live-performance Mexican tradition in order to strike a chord with Mexicans abroad, while simultaneously presenting a kind of Mexican national identity to a wider audience through its English-language broadcast. *Lucha Underground* even maintains the same canon of wrestlers that have long been familiar to Mexican fans, while inviting new viewers into the history of the sport.

Yet, before it was being exported weekly as a transnational product based on Mexican culture, Lucha Libre cinema was just one iconic part of Mexico's grand history of film; one of modern Mexico's chief nation-building mediums. This chapter explores how Lucha Libre performs an image of Mexican identity while simultaneously examining the place of the sport's genre-infused cine-matic representation in the larger history of Mexican nation building on film.

Charles Ramírez Berg, in his influential critical study of Mexican film *Cin-ema of Solitude*, presents the images produced for the screen as a particular kind of construction: one that contains contradictory images and themes that com-pete for the title of Mexicanidad, Mexican identity. The cinematic version of Lucha Libre (the medium, as we shall see, being a critical part of the message) never shirks from this contradictory bent. These films embrace the oversight of contradiction as part of the essential Mexican-ness crystalized and constructed on film. In its open embrace of absurd, yet somehow internally logical, narratives, Lucha Libre creates in the background of its heroes a Mexico in which the many histories of the country (the preconquest, the colo-nial, the revolutionary, the modern, and the frustrated-modern) can all exist simultaneously.

Meanwhile the *luchador* character exists beyond the reach of concepts like race, class, or creed when on screen. He is simply Mexican in the most com-plete, state-sanctioned, culturally in-tune and racially-ambiguous way. Further, because he is a product for consumption, he is shamelessly adaptable on the outside, even if his core values are fixed. He is macho and monk, Aztec warrior and modern intellectual: concerns over contradiction need not apply in the un-real reality of film. However, like all good heroes the subtleties behind *luchador* performance must first be understood through their "secret origin" story, and for that we turn to the end of the nineteenth century and the motion picture camera's grand entrance into the complex cultural and political scene of turn-of-the-century Mexico.

Storyboarding a Nation: The Birth and Rebirth of Nationalist Mexican Cinema

In 1890, Mexico, viewed from without, was prosperous, politically stable, and a member in good political standing with the nations of Europe. Viewed internally, this stability and prosperity largely came from the iron grip and aggressive positivism of Porfirio Díaz, as well as heavy foreign investment that helped endear Mexico to Europe. Regardless of its cause, however, the "modernity" of Mexico meant that when the first films and projectors were invented by Louis and Auguste Lumiére, they appeared in Mexico shortly after almost immediately. Just after the projectors became popular in Europe (Mora 3).

It is difficult to chart the history of film produced in Mexico during the silent film era because most films produced domestically between 1897 and the 1920s have been lost (Mora 3). The origins of filmmaking in Mexico can be traced to Salvador Toscano Barragán, an engineering student who opened Mexico's first movie salon. He would make films of real-life events, and in 1898, he created the country's first fiction film, *Don Juan Tenorio*.[1] In 1898 the United States manufactured the veriscope, a projector unsubstantially touted to be superior to the Lumiére device, which was imported and set up in the Grand National Theatre. By 1900, cinema's popularity was solidly established and enjoyed a viewership of thousands.

For all that remains unclear about the silent-film era in Mexico, what is clear is that Porfirio Díaz quickly grasped the value of a visual medium in the promotion of his state and rule. In fact, some comment that Díaz was Mexican cinema's first star (Noble 72). When film arrived in Mexico in 1895, the *Porfiriato*, the regime of Mexican President Porfirio Diaz, used the medium in a way that offered a shared, state-sanctioned view of the larger country. In essence, the way Mexicans *saw* Mexico and Mexican society could now be controlled (Noble 50–51).

Circumstances changed as technology improved, and with the outbreak of the Mexican Revolution in 1910 came an unprecedented freedom of filmmaking and film content. Politically and visually prominent *caudillos,* military and political leaders vying for control of the state, all saw the same potential for film. Emiliano Zapata Salazar, Pancho Villa, Venustiano Carranza, and Álvaro Obregón Salido among others envisioned the mediumas a means of presenting their alternative visions of Mexico—which Díaz saw in promoting his authority. Villa is especially noteworthy. After signing an exclusive contract with North American Mutual Film Company, Villa arranged battles and hangings by the light of day to maximize their camera friendliness (Noble 51–52).

Despite the prominence of revolutionaries in the advancement of film in Mexico, the Revolution was decidedly ignored on cinema screens once Carranza rose to power in 1917. In order to promote stability and social calm, the new post-Revolution ruling elite actively prevented any film footage from being shown in cinemas that might stir the masses to take up arms. There was a tacit understanding that the Revolution should be ignored for the sake of peace (Noble 52–53). Yet peace was far from the characterization of Mexico in the decades following the Revolution's conclusion.

Mexico by 1910 was more a collection of fragments than a coherent whole. The country gave birth to a bitter and fractional revolutionary conflict. Carranza and Obregón were seen as the embodiment of conservative, middle-class Constitutionalists. The men were perceived as emerging victorious over the *campesino* radicals embodied by Villa and Zapata; tensions were high at the Revolution's close. Consequently, the Revolution had to be retrospectively represented as both coherent and propelled by a social and political revolutionary agenda (Noble 52–53). This aggressive project of nation building and memory shaping was intended to generate a sense of continuity and connectivity among Mexican people who, until the Revolution, predominantly held the local at the center of their lives. By supplanting the local with the national, the Mexican government would more easily be able to express its authority over its "new" citizens (Anderson).

By 1930, it was clear that the postrevolutionary state had opted to neglect the relatively new technology of film. The state did not see the potential for mass outreach in the medium that Porfirio Díaz had seen. Instead, the new state chose to pursue muralism as a national art form to promote Mexican nationality. The state's distrust of film can be partially attributed to the medium's origins as a foreign import. Consequently, the Mexican government viewed film, as with all foreign imports, as a threat to revolutionary potential. Further, the frequent outbursts of violence between 1920 and 1930, including the *Cristero* rebellion of 1926–29, promoted a sort of willful amnesia among filmmakers working within the young industry and seeking to block out traumatic memories of the past (Noble 54–55).

The Revolution did finally begin to appear on screen in the 1930s with Fernando de Fuentes's revolutionary trilogy: *El compadre Mendoza* (*Godfather Mendoza*, 1933), *El Prisionero trece* (*Prisoner 13*, 1933), and *¡Vamonos con Pancho Villa!* (*Let's Go with Pancho Villa!*, 1935).[2] It is striking that the films in De Fuentes's trilogy, despite their traditional melodramatic genre trappings, feature an overt disenchantment with the shortcomings of the Revolution. This disenchantment is expressed through human relationships that form the core of each film and ultimately conclude with betrayal (Noble 55). Such overt criticism is startling on the tail of a decade of silence. This critical voice was short lived, however, as the 1940s saw a return of more aggressive censorship and government involvement in the film industry.

The 1940s also brought the end of the *longue durée* of the Revolution in Mexico (Knight). Lázaro Cárdenas's presidency from 1934 to 1940 could easily be taken as the pinnacle of the fulfillment of decades-old revolutionary goals through land redistribution programs and nationalization of petroleum. This pseudovictory was brief, and the political winds of Mexico changed yet again with Manuel Avila Camacho (1940–1946) and Miguel Alemán (1946–1952) rising to power. Further, the Second World War brought on the "economic miracle" of an increasingly urban and consumer-oriented Mexican middle class (Noble 56–57). Thus the relationship between the memory of the Revolution and the state grew more complicated as the state shifted away from revolutionary ideas, even as the Revolution itself slowly transitioned into a legitimate foundational myth for the country, complete with its own pantheon of heroes (Noble 56–57).

Remaking the Imagination: Discourses of State and Nationalism in the Golden Age of Mexican Cinema

The violence and chaos of the Mexican Revolution caused a slump in film production in the 1920s due to a lack of official industry support by the government, which at this point still failed to see the ideological potential of the medium. This continued until the invention of sound in the 1930s. Sound drastically altered the way film reached out to its audiences, but the technology to dub films into other languages had not yet been invented. Thus Hollywood-based studios seeking to reach foreign-language audiences were left unsure how to proceed. The solution chosen was the creation of the ill-fated "Hispanic films," studio reproductions recycled out of English-language films already in production (Noble 30–31).

The cultural insensitivity and homogenization present in these Spanish-language remakes failed to find an audience in Mexico, and that Hollywood misstep created minor footing for the establishment of a more prominent Mexican film industry, including early steps in the return of state support for the medium. Hollywood recovered quickly, but the small industrial base that Mexican film managed to establish was critical to the development of Mexican cinematic experimentation and the creation of a number of key genres and films that formed the foundation of Mexican cinema's Golden Age (31).

This Golden Age lasted from roughly 1930 until 1954, and its history charts a complicated relationship between the Mexican state, Mexican perception of nationalism, and the Mexican film industry. Indeed, the tight relationship between industry and government has been a particularly popular subject with regard to Golden Age discourse and discussions of the portrayal of Mexico in Mexican films. It is easy to assume that cinematic expression during Mexico's Golden Age demonstrates direct control of the government through the financial dependence the industry had on the state. However, such relationships are common in major metropolitan film industries, including in the United States, Germany, and France, which have fiscally rescued or influenced their respective industries several times over the past century. Thus, although this relationship should not be ignored, overanalysis is equally perilous in determining how best to break down the discourses of Mexican film (Chavéz 115–116).

Daniel Chavéz suggests circumventing some of the interpretive shortfalls that have plagued the study of Mexican cinema by changing the point of view through which Mexican cinematic discourse is typically explored. Chavéz breaks with the tendency that "seeks to establish when and how the state fosters or controls the production of images." Instead, Chavéz, in "The Eagle and the Serpent on the Screen," analyzes the varieties and evolution of cinematic representations of the state in film. That is, rather than focus on what took place behind the scenes of Mexican cinema, Chavéz examines Mexican film discourse based on the content of the films themselves and the way in which they illustrate the state (116). Using this methodology, Chavéz identifies four constitutive discourses used to visually represent the Mexican state. As Lucha Libre is a kind of state–nation performance, understanding these discourses is helpful in situating the content of *luchador* films within Mexico's larger domestic dialogue over what Mexico *looks* like. These discourses are organized by the time of their respective emergence, but Chavéz stresses that once created, each form of state imagery can then reappear at any future point in Mexican history, should the discourse have acquired a residual character that has allowed it to coexist with emerging ones (116).

The first of these discourses is the mystifying-*indigenista*, in which images reproduce the aesthetic principles supported and promoted by government institutions. These images were frequently in tune with the main tenets of the ideological apparatus of the revolutionary state from 1920 to 1940. Hence films in this period include dogmatic deployment of national narratives based on principles of *indigenismo* and *mestizaje*. That is to say, the official narrative of the Mexican state after 1920 affirms that the deepest roots of the nation are found in the indigenous past that Spain destroyed. The true Mexican identity, then, emerges from hybridizing Mexico's Spanish and indigenous roots into a mestizo people. In this narrative, the mestizo people of Mexico have crafted their own history through synthesis and the ongoing struggles for liberation and affirmation (Chavez 116–117).

It is this image of Mexico that preoccupies the lenses of the mystifying-*indigenista* discourse, and consequently films of the era incorporated elements of the 1920 to 1930 visual rhetoric of Mexican muralists Diego Rivera, David

Alfaro Siqueiros, and José Clemente Orozco. Muralism was, after all, the state-chosen form of artistic expression for the early Revolution. Consequently, it was logical to adapt those visual tropes to a more nationalized cinema. In particular, the mystifying-*indigenista* is marked by a cinematic romanticization of the past and the present agrarian indigenous cultures, as well as depictions of the revolutionary struggle for their paternalist redemption (117).

It is somewhat ironic that Fernando de Fuentes, who crafted the first critical images of the Revolution on screen, also created a film that not only is held by many to be the inception of the Golden Age but also thoroughly establishes the tropes of its period. *Alla en el rancho grande* (*Out on the Big Ranch*, 1936) was a hugely popular, even phenomenal, *comedia ranchera* released in 1936; a genre best described as a musical comedy in a rural setting (Noble 31).

Alla en el rancho grande is the story of two young men, one the son of a ranch owner, the other the son of his ranch manager. Both boys grow up to inherit their fathers' respective stations and unknowingly fall in love with the same girl. They each vie for her affection, but ultimately Cruz, the girl, reveals to the young ranch owner that she is in love with Francisco, the ranch manager. The revelation of Cruz's love and the camaraderie between ranch owner Felipe and the people who work for him overpowers any ill sentiments, and a happy ending arrives for all, complete with a double wedding. *Alla en el rancho grande* was part of a trend of nostalgic films depicting the "good old days" of Porfirio Díaz's regime known as *añoranza porfiriana*. Hence the *comedia ranchera*'s rural setting harks back to the feudal, prerevolutionary days with wistful longing.[3] The film is a mixture of an idealized Mexican past, a message of fraternal unity, and contemporary Mexican popular music that hit a special spot in the hearts of Mexican audiences longing to see their culture on screen (Paranaguá 153–162).

When the Golden Age of Mexican cinema began its decline in the early 1950s through the 1960s, Chavéz asserts that a second discourse of cinematic representations of the state began. Through a series of generic conventions and script formulas, the picaresque-folklorizing discourse dealt indirectly with the shortcomings and the gradual erosion of the revolutionary legacy (Chavéz 117). The films of this era are marked by extensive complacency toward the increasingly authoritarian and paternalistic practices of the government and its "modern" institutions (117). In particular, witty, fast-talking comedies like those of internationally renown comedy actors Cantinflas or Tin-Tan were the genre of choice, riddled with repeated jokes and winking references to government corruption without ever formulating a clearly expressed critique (*Si yo fuera diputado*; *Hay muertos que no hacen ruido*). The *ranchera* comedy also remained popular, but even when films of this second discourse mirrored the genres and settings of the prior discourse, it was with a slightly sharper, more parodic edge (117). If the Golden Age was overt in its embrace of the state and nostalgia, the films of the 1950s and '60s were covert in their subversive criticism: establishing camp as a relatively safe space in which to criticize or postulate on the success and failures of a divisive Mexico's past, present, and future.

Chavéz's third discourse emerged by the mid-1970s in part as a reaction to the tumultuous events of the 1968 massacre (Zolov). The massacre, along with a crisis at the box office, provoked a change in the mode of film production and the tone and reach of state representations. According to Chavéz, this third twist in cinematic discourse coexists with the previous ones but challenges the outdated melodramatic and comic repertoire that Chavéz describes as denunciatory realism (117–118). Settings and characters were grittier and reflected a growing disappointment that large swathes of the public felt toward Mexican society in general and the government of the Partido Revolucionario Institucional.

Chavéz concludes with his forth discourse beginning at the end of the 1990s, which he refers to as demystifying realism. Demystifying-realist discourse playfully, and sometimes sarcastically, recasts previous conventions and discourses with deconstructive or parodic intentions (Chavéz 118).

While helpful for grasping the history of state depiction on Mexican screens, Chavéz's discourses overlook a major section of Mexican filmography, the visually inventive and popular horror genre that began to emerge as Mexico's cinematic Golden Age came to an end. The popularity of exploitative Mexican horror has done little to aid the genre's critical and academic consideration as more than a low-culture appendix to serious cinematic discourse. That many of these horror movies mix with other low-culture genres like science fiction and the eminently popular Mexican pseudosport of Lucha Libre to create a kind of "Mexploitation" genre does even less to earn these films respect as part of any meaningful discourse or representation of Mexican nationalism and state on film. Even Charles Ramírez Berg, for all that he does extensively explore about Mexican film and horror, never touches extensively on the eventual infusion of Lucha Libre into genre pictures except as a symptom of larger trends. Yet the wrestler at the heart of each of these movies is what elevates the genre beyond other depictions of nationalism, identity, or state power: the Lucha Libre film creates a dialogue for establishing a kind of fantasy ideal for the Mexican self that other genres lacked.

Like the American science-fiction films of the 1950s and 1970s that are lauded today for their insightful, metaphorically masked discussions, representations, and counterrepresentations of critical questions surrounding cultural and societal norms, Mexploitation is *not* a vapid genre. Rather, Mexploitation represents a critical fifth discourse in depicting Mexico on screen, beginning roughly in 1957 and lasting until 1977 (Greene 1). This Mexploitation discourse synthesizes elements of the mystifying-*indigenista* and picaresque with surreal or fantasy stylings visually reminiscent of the Spanish exile and visually arresting surrealist director Luis Buñuel, whose critical success and prolific work within Mexico informed a generation of Mexican filmmakers (Turrent 202–205).

Although decidedly less serious than Buñuel's work, Mexploitation cinema operates in the same surreal, multitonal space that Buñuel helped to establish in Mexico's cinematic language. The result of Mexploitation's syntheses and tendency toward nationalistic metaphors is a parallel discourse to denunciatory realism that, especially when mixed with Lucha Libre, offers an inverted filmic image of Mexico in which state representations are respected and nearly infallible, and the only threats Mexico faces come from outside an otherwise idyllic nation. Further, Mexploitation firmly establishes in Mexican filmography the country's ideal nationalistic representation in the *luchador*.

Sunset Bulevar: The End of the Golden Age and the Rise of Mexploitation

The earliest origin of horror films in Mexico is rooted in the "Hispanic films" of the 1930s, despite their critical and financial failure. During the classic era of U.S. horror dominated by Universal Studios, props, sets, and storylines from hit English-language horror pictures were recycled and repurposed into Spanish-language versions of the same films. For example, when Tod Browning directed his 1931 version of *Dracula*, a Spanish-language version was directed simultaneously by George Medford for Latin American audiences.[4] The Hispanic film rendition of *Dracula* featured Mexican actors and crews who used Browning's sets at night to make the double production faster and cheaper (Greene 7–8).

Horror films were also produced domestically in Mexico throughout the 1930s and 1940s. Film historian Gary D. Rhodes suggests these domestic horror films reflect not only the deep influence of Hollywood-produced horror pictures but also cultural conflicts between science and religion expressed through metaphorical emphasis on monsters and mad scientists (Greene 7–8). This reading is especially compelling from a historical point of view, as the 1930s through 1940s contained not only the violence of the *Cristero* rebellion but broader conflicts between the Catholic Church and a modernizing, increasingly secular state.

In 1957, the seminal Mexican horror film *El vampiro* (*The Vampire*, 1957), directed by Fernando Méndez, premiered in Mexico. The film was produced by Abel Salazar, written by Ramón Obón, and starred Germán Robles in the titular role. All eventually proved influential figures in the development of Mexploitation. The film was the genre's first major commercial and critical success. As a result of *El vampiro*'s popularity, audience demand for more Mexploitation films skyrocketed and firmly established the genre in Mexican cinemas.

Lucha Libre's incorporation into Mexploitation cinema helped "Mexicanize" the genre by tying its horror and science fiction tropes to Mexico's immensely popular professional wrestling spectacle. Like film, professional wrestling was imported to Mexico from abroad, despite the sport's popular modern associations with ancient indigenous Mexican societies. Charles Wilson traces professional wrestling to a style called "collar and elbow" that developed in Vermont in the early nineteenth century. The name refers to the wrestler's starting position, in which each wrestler grasps the other elbow with one hand and the collar with the other. Vermont soldiers brought collar and elbow wrestling to the barracks of the Civil War, where it became a popular pastime among Union soldiers. Following the end of the war, collar and elbow wrestling moved from the barracks to saloons in New York City, where matches were promoted to draw customers (Levi 6–7).

As the twentieth century approached, P.T. Barnum instituted wrestling as a circus "spectacular." The transition from the barroom to the circus brought about important changes to the relationship between sport and audience. Initially, Barnum's wrestlers would fight matches against untrained marks from the audience. By 1890, the tradition of fixed fights was instituted. Trained shills were planted in the audience in advance. By establishing the fixed fight, Barnum's rendition of wrestling changed from an actual contest to the representation of a contest, establishing the performative roots of Lucha Libre (Levi 7).

By the first decade of the twentieth century these exhibition-style matches had grown popular at city and country fairs, eventually spawning a system of intercity wrestling circuits in 1908. By the 1920s, exhibition wrestling was referred to as "professional" wrestling and was enjoying its peak popularity in the United States and Europe (Levi 7). During this period, wrestlers began adopting theatrical gimmicks to their wrestling performance to mark themselves as memorable characters. These personas usually involved stressing some kind of ethnic background to which a wrestler belonged. The 1920s also marked the establishment of several other conventions that govern professional wrestling today, including the creation of the basic units of both amateur and professional wrestling, the match and the fall (7). In Lucha Libre, a match is referred to as a *función* (show) or *programa* (program) consisting of five matches played out over roughly two hours (8).

In Mexico, during the *Porfiriato*, sports were primarily a pastime of the elite but were introduced to the working class in some degree by paternalist programs in British- and U.S.-owned factories, mining camps, and plantations. After the Revolution, the state took over the role of introducing sports, including wrestling, to the masses as part of the post-Revolution government's nation-building reform programs (Levi 11). Beyond a few exhibition matches around the turn of the century, professional wrestling did not begin to develop in Mexico until 1933. Exhibition wrestling was then brought to Mexico by a promoter named Salvador Lutteroth. On September 21, 1933, Lutteroth and his partner Francisco Ahumado sponsored their first wrestling event in Arena Nacional. The arena owner chose not to make the arena available to Lutteroth and his part-ner for the entire year, so the pair bought and renovated an arena nearby. Lut-teroth renamed the arena "Arena Mexico," and Lutteroth and his partner incorporated themselves as the Empresa Mexicana de Lucha Libre (22).

In the years that followed, local wrestling talent emerged and fan bases grew. Innovations in costuming, character, and technique helped further Mexicanize the increasingly performative pseudosport. Characters, and the masks that identified them, grew particularly important to the Lucha Libre genre, sepa-rating the wrestlers from their human selves when they were performing. According to Heather Levi in her insightful ethnography *The World of Lucha Libre: Secrets, Revelations, and Mexican National Identity* (2008), wrestling characters are constructed along two axes: costume-persona and ethical role. In the actual sport, rather than its film incarnations, some wrestlers play only one role, but others change sides during the course of their career: "From the point of view of the audience, a wrestler's moral stance is changeable, but his or her character is fixed. A wrestler is not thought to 'play' a character so much as to 'be' that character. Likewise, wrestlers never say that they play a given char-acter, but that the character is their *nombre de batalla*" (65).

Despite Lucha Libre's dubious position as a pseudosport, certain basic nationalist concepts of team formation, fandom, respect for authority, and structure are all present within the performance of a live wrestling match. That these characters and their intertwined dramas drew such strong fan bases only added to the nationalist value of wrestling. Further, given Mexico's complicated past, the backstories of *luchador* characters were appealingly unidentifiable beyond the mask. These heroes, at least during a performance, could be any-one, could be pretending to be anything, but were almost certainly Mexican under the costume, whatever that might mean. The effect was, literally, phe-nomenal. In the 1930s, the fact that the wrestlers of Lucha Libre steadily began to outperform wrestlers from the United States became a point of nationalist pride for fans (Levi 67).

The range of character categories in Lucha Libre is a critical difference between professional wrestling in the United States and Mexico. According to Levi, professional wrestling, in both contexts, is a drama about conflict and domination. Wrestling is a model of how people have power over one another. Consequently, the pseudosport makes an implicit argument about how social action happens, and what kind of historical agents are effective in the world (Levi 77). In short, the performance of Lucha Libre represents, through a par-ticular character type's short- and long-term victory, the values and character-istics that make a "winner" in a Mexican context.

Lucha Libre characters inhabit a fixed moral binary consisting of "*rudos*" and "*técnicos*." In simple, melodramatic terms, the *rudo* acts as the villain and the *técnico* as the hero (Levi 81–82). *Técnicos* are graceful; they are expected to enter the ring elegantly and follow the sport's rules. *Rudos* move closer to the ground, are clumsier, and fail miserably when coordinating as a team. Although *luchadores* see themselves as athletes, they are, in a sense, also actors within the performances of Lucha Libre's arranged matches. For all intents and purposes, Lucha Libre is sport in the mode of melodrama. That is to say, melodrama has come to describe performances that present a polarized worldview in which moral struggle is made visible to the audience. Narrative conflict in melodrama, as in examples of the early films of the Golden Age of Mexican cinema, is always acted out between two characters; it is never presented as internal drama (81). Read in this way, Lucha Libre's binary morality and dueling conflict between ethical standards very clearly epitomizes melodrama's core tropes. Further, that a particular side of the moral binary is considered "good" and is aligned with authority, while the other is labeled "bad" and aligned with corruption and dishonesty helps to form a clear connection between the drama of Lucha Libre and its value in telling simple, nation-affirming morality plays.

Yet the presence of a live audience and the need to keep that audience entertained, as well as the responsibility of maintaining the drama between characters while ensuring that popular characters remain in constant circulation, makes reading Lucha Libre as a nationalist melodrama slightly problematic. Sometimes in the arena, for the sake of drama, evil can win (sometimes a fall, sometimes the entire match). Further, while most of the public favor *técnicos*, *rudos* usually have their own vocal supporters. Lastly, and perhaps most critically, wrestlers can change their moral role over the course of their career, the result of a character's performer seeking to expand his character's appeal rather than maintain his symbolic significance relative to the state. In the interest of generating ongoing drama, then, Lucha Libre is perhaps too *much* a sport, even as a fixed sport, to be completely considered a nationalist performance.

Yet, as Lucha Libre grew in popularity, so too did cinema. When the Golden Age of Mexican film entered its decline in the 1950s, Mexploitation producers looking for cheap genres to convert into movies quickly saw the potential in Lucha Libre's heroic *técnicos* as combatants to face off against the grotesque monsters of Mexican horror. It was from this fusion that Mexploitation developed a new language that incorporated the nationalist binary of Lucha Libre while elevating the pseudosport beyond the limitations of its live performance into a simple, yet effective, form of nationalist state metaphor in which a masked hero is never *not* a masked hero, immune to concerns like race, class, and creed unless also embraced by the state. That is to say that in the cinematic version of Lucha Libre the *técnico* is beyond the certain critical aspects of the human experience, consequently allowing such issues to be logically (if irresponsibly) ignored. The filmic *luchador* is the idea of Mexico (including the state) given a persona and human form, but not given any authentic *humanity*.

A Silver Mask on a Silver Screen: Mexploitation, El Santo, and Lucha Libre's Emergence on Film

Studios began producing wrestling movies in the early 1950s. Faced with a crisis of rising costs and collapsing foreign markets, Mexican producers focused on crafting formulaic, low-budget Mexploitation films in huge numbers. Between 1952 and 1983, roughly 300 films in the genre were released (Levi 187). Among the first four films in the cinematic Lucha Libre canon, *El enmascarado de plata* (*The Man in the Silver Mask*, 1952) stands out for establishing most of the genre's conventions in a single film. Yet the movie is also significant for its title, which indirectly alludes to one of Mexico's most popular *luchadores*, El Santo, el Enmascarado de Plata. Santo's popularity in Mexico was so great that of the 300 movies produced during this period, fifty featured the silver-masked *técnico*. Curiously, however, Santo does not appear in the film *El enmascarado de plata*. Although the film was intended as Santo's cinematic debut, the wrestler backed out, and the film's name was passed on to its villain (Levi 187).

El Santo's actual film debut came in 1958, when he starred in *Santo contra cerebero del mal* (*Santo versus the Evil Brain*, 1958) and *Santo contra los hombres infernales* (*Santo versus the Infernal Men*, 1961). Interestingly, the movies were actually filmed in Cuba because the budget could not afford Mexican union wages (Levi 188). The first film, *Santo contra cerebero del mal*, features Santo teaming up with fellow wrestler El Incognito to battle a mad scientist. The latter film, *Santo contra los hombres infernales*, features Santo assisting an undercover agent in bringing down Cuban drug smugglers.

The formula of a Santo film usually consists of at least one wrestling match, typically a prelude to Santo receiving his mission. Additionally, in the tradition of melodrama and *ranchera* comedy before it, Santo movies also typically contain a song and dance number. *El Santo vs el estrangulador* (*Santo versus the Strangler*, 1965) in particular features nine musical numbers lasting several minutes each, only a handful of which actually feature any connection to the plot. Even as the tone of El Santo's pictures shifted through darker visuals aided by improving horror makeup in the 1970s, most of the genre's tropes remained intact.[5]

Consistently, El Santo faces off against enemies who represent counternationalist threats, either from outside Mexico in the present—foreign mad scientists, alien invaders—or internal threats from Mexico's precolonial past—Aztec mummies, ancient werewolves. Note that these ancient threats are threats only because they take a form that precedes their *mesticization* into a part of Mexico's history. In Santo's world, Mexico is a specific product of Mexico's indigenous past, Spanish conquest, and modern development. If one of these elements presents itself without the other two, it becomes a plausible threat to the overall balance. Even the less fantastical foes, such as el

Estrangulador, who is simply a sociopath, are usually antisocial entities who threaten nationalism by undermining the promotion of fraternity. Additionally, in the various gratuitous wrestling matches that sprinkle Santo's film, the characters he faces in the ring are almost never named and are frequently without masks.

Who Santo fights is critical to understanding how film changed the way Lucha Libre represented nationalism. The live rendition of the pseudosport presented limited nationalistic imagery in the simple ethics of its moral binary and the way the sport reinforced respect for authority. Yet the dynamics of live entertainment, the need to keep the show interesting because of the ongoing overall narrative of the Lucha Libre organization, necessitates that sometimes nationalistic victory must be postponed for shock value. Unlike live Lucha Libre, a film is a self-contained story. Regardless of the outcomes of individual matches, there is an end, and with that end comes the victory of El Santo and the nationalist representation of strength, rationality (for Santo is an excellent scientist and detective), and moral righteousness (as Santo is a *técnico*.)[6]

Most importantly, in film the wrestler's position relative to the moral binary of Lucha Libre remains static. In the cinematic world of Lucha Libre, there are no true *rudo* wrestlers. Their place is usurped by foreign and supernatural threats, or else they cameo briefly in one of the film's peripheral wrestling matches.[7] Thus, in cinematic form, *luchadores* are always *técnicos*, and because the lens controls the framing of the narrative, even an audience member who sees a film for love of the villains must tacitly agree by way of experiencing the story's structure to root for the movie's *técnico* hero.

Film also changed the wrestler's relationship to mask and character. In live Lucha Libre it is implicitly understood that characters have other identities and faces, and sometimes those faces are revealed, or those lives impact the portrayals of characters and their position on the moral binary. Eventually a wrestler might die and be succeeded, might retire, or become a *rudo*. In short, there is an understanding that what is playing out in the ring is performance. In its film incarnation the narrative encourages audiences to accept the reality of the fictional Lucha Libre world to an extent that live wrestling does not. Consequently, the El Santo of Mexican cinema has no secret identity that could undermine the legend. The film Santo is *always* Santo. When he is not expressing the dominance of *técnico* values in the ring, he is defeating counternationalist threats to defend Mexico.

Even Santo's romantic life in the film world is conducted in character, in the mask. Santo is accompanied by a number of beautiful Mexican women throughout his career. He is a respectful gentleman with all of them, and they are all deeply in love with him, although the relationships are decidedly nonsexual. It would not be unreasonable to suggest that the magical realism of the world of Lucha Libre on film allows for the seemingly contradictory notion of El Santo as both the embodiment of *machismo* and the embodiment of gentlemanliness, thus wholly embodying the dual interpretations of state masculinity.

By turning Lucha Libre into a world separated into self-contained narratives, film removed the problematic aspects of the live rendition of the pseudosport. The filmic version of Lucha Libre made the moral alignment of its heroes static, eliminated the undermining-other of the wrestler behind the mask, freely promoted dual concepts of masculinity in a seemingly noncontradictory way, and assigned all villain roles to counternationalist monsters (human or nonhuman). Thus, despite the camp style and low-budget quality of Lucha Libre, the transformation the genre underwent during its 1960s transition to film constructed a form of nationalist media that, while not critically respected, deserves historical recognition for the way it translates Mexican conceptualizations of nationhood, power, and strength to the screen.

Lucha Legacy: Lucha Libre's Place in the Discourses of Mexican Film

The remaining question, then, is where to place the Lucha Libre movie within the larger history of Mexican film. Lucha Libre–infused Mexploitation comes chronologically after denunciatory realism and Luis Buñuel's appearance on the Mexican screen. Certainly, the visual darkness and grit that appeared in horror as well as the influence of Buñuel's surrealist, anything-is-possible worlds can be seen in the visual style of El Santo's more monster-centric films. However, the drama in Lucha Libre films is of a particularly melodramatic flavor that connects wrestling films with the genre legacy of the demystifying-*indigenista* discourse of the 1930s. The coded nationalist discourse on display within Lucha Libre's genre-mashing style also begs comparisons to the coded critical language of the picaresque discourse of the 1940s, but in method, not content. Finally, the simple morality plays and general positivity of the Lucha Libre genre exclude it from the denunciatory realist discourse of the 1970s and 1980s.

It is more accurate to consider the Mexploitation drama broadly, and the Lucha Libre subgenre specifically, as its own discourse. Lucha Libre films represent an eclectic mix of genres, tropes, styles, and plots from across the cinematic spectrum, assembling these disparate elements into a form of expression that is uniquely Mexican. The discourse these films form exists parallel to denunciatory realism, but in dialogue with the gritty critical representation of the state. Lucha Libre presents a colorful alternative to the Mexico of denunciatory realism by presenting a unified state defended by an ideal, modern man; a representative of the ideals of progress and order. The discourse of Lucha Libre, then, is one of state fantasy, in which the project of nation building has been completed and perfected, and in this world El Santo passes his time in the ring until his next opportunity to defend truth, justice, and the Mexican way.

Notes

1 Mora 4–5. Barragán went on to document many events of the revolution that would ultimately be used by his daughter, Carmen Toscano, to form the documentary Carmen Toscano, *Memorias de un Mexicano*, Archive Salvador Toscano, 1950.

2 Fernando de Fuentes, *El Compadre Mendoza* (*Godfather Mendoza*), Internamericana Films and N.A. Reichlin, 1933; Fernando de Fuentes, *El Prisionero Trece* (*Prisoner 13*), Compañía Nacional Productora de Películas, 1933; Fernando de Fuentes, ¡*Vamonos con Pacho Villa!* (*Let's Go with Pancho Villa*), Cinematografica Latino Americana S.A. (C.L.A.S.A.), 1935.

3 Not unlike the depiction of the rural South in the American imagination as classically embodied in *Gone with the Wind*; Noble, *Mexican National Cinema*. 31–32.

4 Tod Browning, *Dracula*, Universal Pictures, 1931; I have not included a citation for George Medford's *Dracula* because, as far as I can tell, there are no available copies of the movie.

5 For the example of this style of Santo film, see Rubén Galindo and Jaime Jiménez Pons, *Santo vs. Las Lobas* (*Santo versus the She-Wolves*).

6 Several films, including Cardon, *Santo vs. El Estrangulador* (*Santo versus the Strangler*) feature Santo's variety of gadgets, sports cars, and sophisticated laboratory that complement his muscles and wrestling skill.

7 Examples of some of Santo's most counternational threats can be found in Alfredo B. Crevanna, *Santo el enmascarado de plata vs. "la invasión de los Marcianos"* (*Santo the Man in the Silver Mask versus "the Invasion of the Martians"*), Producciones Cinematográficas S.A., 1967; Federico Curiel, *La momias de Guanajuato* (*The Mummies of Guanajuato*), Películas Latinoamericanas S.A. and Películas Rodríguez, 1972. In the former, Santo fights against invading Martians, in the latter, Santo fights against ancient mummies from Mexico's precolonial past.

Works Cited

Anderson, Benedict R. *Imagined Communities: Reflections on the Origin and Spread of Nationalism*. Rev. ed. New York: Verso, 2006. Print.

Browning, Tod, dir. *Dracula*. Universal Pictures, 1931. Film.

Cardona, René. *El enmascarado de plata* (*The Man in the Silver Mask*). Filmex, 1952. Film.

———. *Santo vs. el estrangulador* (*Santo versus the Strangler*). Cinematográfica Norte, 1965. Film.

Chavéz, Daniel. "The Eagle and the Serpent on the Screen: The State as Spectacle in Mexican Cinema." *Latin American Research Review* 45.3 (2010): 115–141. Print.

Crevanna, Alfredo B., dir. *Santo el enmascarado de plata vs. "la invasión de los marcianos"* (*Santo the Man in the Silver Mask versus "the Invasion of the Martians"*). Producciones Cinematográficas S.A., 1967. Film.

Curiel, Federico, dir. *La momias de Guanajuato* (*The Mummies of Guanajuato*). Películas Latinoamericanas S.A. and Películas Rodríguez, 1972. Film.

De Fuentes, Fernando, dir. *Allá en el rancho grande* (*Out on the Big Ranch*). Lombardo Film, 1936. Film.

———. *El compadre Mendoza* (*Godfather Mendoza*). Interamericana Films and N.A. Reichlin, 1933. Film.

———. *El prisoner 13* (*Prisoner 13*). Compañía Nacional Productora de Películas, 1933.

———. *¡Vamonos con Pancho Villa!* (*Let's Go with Pancho Villa*). Cinematografica Latino Americana S.A. (C.L.A.S.A.), 1935.

Greene, Doyle. *Mexploitation Cinema: A Critical History of Mexican Vampire, Wrestler, Ape-Man, and Similar Films, 1957–1977.* Jefferson, NC: McFarland, 2005. Print.

Knight, Alan. "The Mexican Revolution: Bourgeois? Nationalist? Or Just a 'Great Rebellion?'" *Bulletin of Latin American Research* 4.2 (1985): 1–37. Print.

Landero, Humberto Gómez, dir. *Hay muertos que no hacen ruido* (*There Are the Dead Who Make No Sound*). AS Films S.A. and Producciónes Grovas, 1946. Film.

Levi, Heather. *The World of Lucha Libre: Secrets, Revelations, and Mexican National Identity.* American Enounters/Global Interactions. Durham: Duke UP, 2008. Print.

Méndez, Fernando, dir. *El vampiro* (*The Vampire*). Cinematográfica ABSA, 1957. Film.

Mora, Carl J. *Mexican Cinema: Reflections of a Society, 1896–2004.* 3rd ed. Jefferson, NC: McFarland, 2012. Print.

Moraes, Lisa de. "TCA: Mark Burnett to Launch Lucha Libre AAA League in U.S. with El Rey Network; 'From Dusk Till Dawn' to Premiere in March" *Deadline: Hollywood.* Penske Business Media. January 12, 2014. Web. 1 May 2016. http://deadline.com/2014 /01/tca-mark-burnett-to-launch-lucha-libre-aaa-league-in-u-s-with-el-rey-network -662728/.

Noble, Andrea. *Mexican National Cinema.* New York: Routledge, 2005. Print.

Paranaguá, Paulo Antonio, ed. *Mexican Cinema.* London: British Film Institute, 1995. Print.

Pons, Rubén Galindo and Jaime Jiménez, dir. *Santo vs. las lobas* (*Santo versus the She-Wolves*). Producciones Jiménez Pons Hermanos, 1976. Film.

Ramírez Berg, Charles. *Cinema of Solitude.* Austin: U of Texas P, 1992. E-Book.

Rodríguez, Joselito, dir. *Santo contra cerebero del mal* (*Santo versus the Evil Brain*). Columbia Pictures, 1958. Film.

———. *Santo contra los hombres infernales* (*Santo versus the Infernal Men*). Columbia Pictures, 1961. Film.

Toscano, Carmen, dir. *Memorias de un Mexicano.* Archive Salvador Toscano, 1950. Film.

Turrent, Tomás Pérez. "Luis Buñuel in Mexico." *Mexican Cinema.* Ed. Paulo Paranguá. London: British Film Institute, 1995. 202–208. Print.

"Welcome to the Temple." *Lucha Underground.* Prod. Matthew Stollman, et al. El Rey Network. October 24, 2014. Television.

Zolov, Eric. "Introduction: Latin America in the Global Sixties." *The Americas* 70.3 (2014): 349–362. Print.

4

Native American Irony

• •

Survivance and the
Subversion of Ethnography

GERALD VIZENOR

Native American Indians and Jews were unmissable monitors of gossip theory and cultural survivance. Natives were once nominated in churchy hearsay as the descendants of the Lost Tribes of Israel. Jews and natives were revealed as an ancestral union of tradition and torment, removal and murder, the outsiders in the discovery, crusades, and crude missions of Christianity.

Thomas Thorowgood proclaimed in *Jewes in America, or Probabilities That the Americans Are Jewes*, that the "Indians do themselves relate things of their Ancestors, suteable to what we read of the Jewes in the Bible, and elsewhere. . . . The rites, fashions, ceremonies, and opinions of the Americans are in many ways agreeable to the custome of the Jewes, not onely prophane and common usages, but such as be called solemn and sacred" (3, 6). Hallelujah, and three centuries later the gossip theory of a spiritual and cultural union continues, but with a greater potentiality for survivance stories with a sense of ancestral irony.

Tailors and Moccasins

Woody Allen wrote in *The Insanity Defense* that

> Rabbi Yekel of Zans, who had the best diction in the world until a Gentile stole his resonant underwear, dreamed three nights running that if he would only journey to Vorki he would find a great treasure there. Bidding his wife and children goodbye, he set out on a trip, saying he would return in ten days. Two years later, he was found wandering the Urals and emotionally involved with a Panda. Cold and starving the Rev was taken back to his home, where he was revived with steaming soup and flanken. Following that, he was given something to eat. After dinner, he told this story: Three days out of Zans, he was set upon by wild nomads. When they learned he was a Jew, they forced him to alter all their sports jackets and take in their trousers. (46–47)

Some forty years ago a professor of history at the University of Minnesota kindly invited me to a faculty dinner at his home. He promptly escorted me into a side room where he handed over a pair of stained leather moccasins. I was ready with an ironic comment, but the historian was serious and expected me to convey the name of the culture, and provide some footsy provenance of a surly warrior. The warrior walked silently in the forests, was my first ironic tease, but the historian was focused more directly on the ethnographic features of the sacred footwear than the cultural irony.

I closely examined the beaded decorations, blue beads, first acquired in the fur trade with the French. Deer hide, and the soles were thin, more house worn than from game runs in the forest. I then sniffed each moccasin and handed them back to the historian. He waited for my innate cultural analysis. My voice was resonant, of course, suitable for a discourse on the irony of ancient moccasins: "Norwegian man, early 1930s, stinky feet, and he walks with a twisted foot."

Ironic Disruptions

"Dissembler," and "simulated ignorance" are the original sources of the meaning of irony, according to the *Oxford English Dictionary*. More precisely "irony" is defined as the "expression of meaning using language that normally expresses the opposite," especially "the humorous or sarcastic use of praise to imply condemnation or contempt." Figuratively, irony is the discrepancy "between the expected and actual state of affairs," and the "use of language with one meaning for a privileged audience and another for those addressed or concerned," and those excluded in certain cultural situations (Brown). More so native ironic stories can be perceived as a tease, the converse of simulations, and the fake, feign, and guile of language.

The Native American Indian potentiality for irony could be observed more critically as a condition embedded in the notes of discovery, in the documents of cultural dominion, historical archives, ethnographic monographs, the politics of blood quantum identities, and the scenes that were told and translated as traditional stories. These specific sources of irony are actually inside, at the heart of the narratives, at the core of monographs and archives of native discovery, and not a coy imposition or outsource of irony. These heavy situations eventually provide untold ironic stories and clearly provoke mockery.

The most outrageous trickster stories, gambling songs, dream songs, and creation stories were outright ironies, and the most memorable storiers understood that the confidence of any story was wisely deferred to other situations and versions of the story. The cultural traces and diction of oral stories were original, of course, and imitation or mockery was ticklish. The variations of stories, or the actual creative teases of sense and native substance were never owned by a single storier; consequently the stories were mutable and ironic. The essence of an oral story was not absolute or universal by definition, but deferred, and with respect to the creative vision of another native storier. Some ceremonial and dream songs, however, were considered personal and repeated with respect for the original singer.

Native stories, creation and otherwise, were seldom delivered as a catechism or liturgy. The many translations and transcriptions of native songs and stories established an archive of comparative narratives, an ironic departure from the cultural scenes, and many ethnographic interpretations undermined the creative irony and cultural traces of oral stories.

The ethnographic interpretations, however, now provide the potentiality of an unintended source of native irony. Clearly the irony is embedded, even implied, in the actual methods of transcription; in the general notions of structural analyses, thick or thin; and in the heavy sway of academic advisers and editors.

The moccasin game song about "bad moccasins," for instance, was translated and misinterpreted as the lament of a poor native, and with unintended irony. That translation of the song must now be delivered as an ironic story. The actual gestures in the moccasin game song were about the chance of losing the game, not poverty.

The translated song, a love charm, by a native woman who said she was as beautiful as the roses, was actually an ironic song created by a native woman who understood she was not beautiful. Frances Densmore noted in *Chippewa Music* that the singer was "a woman about sixty years of age and was the most dirty and unattractive woman with whom the writer has come in contact" (88). The woman, in a thin and nasal voice, sang in translation, "What are you saying to me? I am arrayed like the roses, and beautiful as they" (89). I would favor a more concise and poetic tease in translation, "I am as beautiful as the roses."[1]

The pictomyth or song picture shows a heart in a figure surrounded by four roses. A singer who lived on a nearby reservation recognized the pictomyth and sang the same song, and was not likely aware of the irony of the love charm.

The ancillary sources of native irony, then, are implied in the translations and ethnographic interpretations of oral stories, songs, and narratives by and about natives. The unintended ironies are not derived from outside the native stories or transcriptions; they are actually embedded in the medley of ethnographic methods and expositions, in the social science models and simulations of natives, and in the archives of historical documents. Many original native songs and stories, however, were published as literal translations with no recognition of irony, intended or not.

The scientific methods of ethnographic interpretations are obviously not the actual documents or histories of native cultures. The archives, the collections of documents, and the outcome of academic authority over cultures on federal reservations have become the obvious sources of unintended irony.

Surely the creation and unstudied play of native irony is more memorable than the deconstruction of discovery narratives and ethnographic simulations as sources of irony, but the strategy of *différance* and the deferred sense of irony is a necessary direction of academic discourse.

I was present at a memorable scene of tragic and situational irony. The scene was posed as tragic, and the situation of the query and cultural concern was obviously not intentional irony. Roger Jourdain, the late elected leader of the Red Lake Reservation in Minnesota, met a group of professional women from the city who had arrived by bus to tour the remote reservation. Jourdain welcomed visitors as they exited the bus. One woman paused and said in a very serious tone of voice, "I have been waiting a long time for an answer to my question: what do Indian women do when they can't nurse their children?" The query revealed traces of cultural and racial separatism that was structured in the language about natives, but unintended in the absurd and heartfelt concern of the tourist. Jourdain was prepared to provide a concise and ironic comeback. He kindly told the woman, "Those children were nursed by porcupines."

Ted Mahto, a native philosopher, invited me to trade stories many years ago at Hello Dolly's in Minneapolis. The notorious native bar was sour and sticky that late summer afternoon. At the end of the bar three young natives were boasting about their scars from a Sun Dance Ceremony. The boasting was contemptible, and my friend excused himself, calmly walked over to the three young men, who were much taller, smiled, slowly unbuttoned his shirt, and pointed to the scars on his chest. Ted said, "Do you see those scars?" The young men leaned closer and examined the prominent scars. Ted shouted, "Chicken pox, 1940," and then he turned away, buttoned his shirt, and we continued our stories.

Clyde Kluckholn, the cultural anthropologist, was teased as the man who pissed too much on the reservation. Hitchhikers on the Navajo Nation told stories about the notorious scholar and his ostensible weak urinary bladder. The Pisser asked hitchhikers about native witchcraft, and probably reasoned that natives would more readily reveal scenes and secrets of witches and skinwalkers in motion on the road. He listened to witchery rumors and hearsay but could only recollect about thirty minutes of stories. So he frequently stopped and pretended to piss, but he only walked behind a shrub or tree to quickly transcribe in a notebook what he had heard in motion. The natives were no doubt eager to remain in motion, especially at night and in bad weather, and told whatever stories of witchery that might have come to mind (Vizenor, "Native Tease" 79–80).

Kluckhohn published *Navaho Witchcraft* in 1944, and the stories of his witchcraft queries and unintended irony continue with great pleasure. One scholarly reviewer pointed out that the anthropologist had described his methods with care, but he did not provide specific information about the "informants."[2] Surely many of his informants were hitchhikers because natives in ordinary situations would rarely mention skinwalkers or the ghastly practices of witchery. Other reviewers commended his "method of presentation" (Parsons 566). The monograph on witchcraft was primarily a collection of simulations that were derived from hearsay and gossip theory.

The American Indian Movement carried weapons for the first time in preparation for an armed confrontation with state-licensed anglers on the opening day of fishing in 1972 on the Leech Lake Reservation in Minnesota. The urban militants were heavily armed and determined to fight for native hunting and fishing rights on the reservation, but they were not prepared for an ironic war. The militants were not aware that the treaty rights had been decided in favor of the reservation by the federal court.

Dennis Banks, who wore a fur trade mountain man costume, and a dozen other armed leaders were invited to a meeting in an elementary school on the first day they arrived on the reservation. The militants slowly meandered into the classroom and reluctantly sat on tiny chairs, their knees tucked under their chins.

Simon Howard, the president of the Minnesota Chippewa Tribe, was the last person to enter the classroom. He sat on a tiny chair at the head of the circle and twirled his thumbs over a heavy stomach. Howard was at home, at ease, and wearing a bowling jacket and a floral print porkpie hat, cocked back on his head. The militants were decorated with pantribal war vestments and carried new weapons. Howard called the meeting to maintain peace between the local residents, the fishermen, and the militants. The strategy to invite the fierce urban warriors to sit on tiny elementary school chairs was shrewd and marvelous.

"Stand up and introduce yourself," said Howard. One shy warrior stood in front of a tiny chair. He was dressed in a wide black hat, leather jacket, dark green glasses, and two bandoliers of heavy ammunition that did not match the bore of his rifle, with a bayonet and revolver on his waist. "We came here to die," he said and returned to the tiny chair (Vizenor, *Literary Chance* 80).[3]

The sound of heavy rifle fire broke the silence one night on a country road near the Episcopal Church Camp. The new warriors had been invited to stay in the camp cabins for the duration of the war against white fishermen. Federal marshals conducted a speedy investigation of the rifle fire and revealed that several militants had decided to shine for deer late that night. Seeing what they thought were the bright eyes of a huge deer, the warrior hunters opened fire with advanced weapons. The animal in the dark was a milk cow owned by a local farmer. The farmer fired back at the warriors, but there were no casualties, not even the cow. The warriors were rather new at riflery. An armed warrior seated on a tiny chair was a strategic parody, and the late night deer hunt was an inadvertent irony.

Native Deconstruction

Jacques Derrida, the French philosopher, introduced the contentious strategy of "deconstruction" to reveal the instability and *différance*, the difference and dissimilarity, or the disparity of meaning in language. Stuart Sim pointed out in *Derrida and the End of History* (1999) that deconstruction was a "tactical exercise designed to demonstrate the instability of language and the shaky foundations on which most of our theories rest" (71). The ethnographic gossip theory about natives would surely demonstrate the instability of language and provide the potentiality of irony.

Derrida demonstrated in *différance* the chance and change of meaning, the mutability of language, which, as he puts it, "is always both 'differed' and 'deferred.' Deconstruction, as a movement of thought, is concerned above all to draw the fact of linguistic instability to our attention" (Sim 33). Moreover, the concept of *différance*, "the manifestation of that instability, is to be found, Derrida argues, everywhere in our discourse, serving to disrupt our conventional conception of language as a stable medium for the communication of meaning between individuals" (33).

The ethnographic methods of interpretation, therefore, are not stable conceptions, and are questionable in the ordinary conferences about natives and others. The social science methods, simulations, and models of so many dissertations, endorsed by learned scholars in the academy, are not reliable, or the deductions are mutable, and by *différance* and deferred sense and meaning the sources of ironic disruptions.

Derrida argued in *Marges de la philosophie* (*Margins of Philosophy*) (1972) that *différance* "governs nothing, reigns over nothing, and nowhere exercises any authority.... Not only is there no kingdom of *différance*, but *différance* instigates the subversion of every kingdom. Which makes it obviously threatening and infallibly dreaded by everything within us that desires a kingdom, the past or present of a kingdom" (74). Rather, he continues, "*différance* maintains our relationship with that which we necessarily misconstrue, and which exceeds the alternative of presence and absence" (73). Finally, "*différance* remains a metaphysical name, and all the names that it receives in our language are still, as names, metaphysical" (75).

Consider, for instance, the cultural theories and erudite narratives that have circumscribed natives for centuries, and the simulations and *différance* of just a few words: "Indian," "Red Skin," "vanishing race," "squaw," "tribe," "tradition," "blood quantum," "reservation," "shaman," "powwow." The meaning of these words is unstable in any discourse, and surely in the simulations of gossip theory and ethnology. Then consider the thousands of federal agency reports, discovery notes, museum objects, translated stories, demographic estimates of early native populations, and grasp that every historical document must be ironic, and sometimes with unintended irony and shared humor, because of the chance and mutability of language. The *différance* is conveyed in the deferred meaning of language in translations, transcriptions, ethnographic narratives, and gossip theory. The *différance* and mutability of language and disruptions of misconstrued discourse over natives could be perceived as unintended irony, if only to reach beyond the racial metaphors of cultural separatism and tease the absence of natives in continental literature and history.

The "object of ethnology," declared Clifford Geertz in *The Interpretation of Cultures* (1973), is a "stratified hierarchy of meaningful structures in terms of which twitches, winks, fake-winks, parodies, rehearsals of parodies are produced, perceived and interpreted" (7). Moreover, culture, "this acted document, thus is public, like a burlesqued wink or a mock sheep raid. Though ideational, it does not exist in someone's head; though unphysical it is not an occult entity" (10).

Geertz noted that the "ethnographer 'inscribes' social discourse; *he writes it down*. In so doing, he turns it from a passing event, which exists only in its own moment of occurrence, into an account, which exists in its inscriptions and can be reconsulted" (19).

The "concept of culture" is "essentially a semiotic one," observed Geertz (5). Consequently, the interpretations, or simulations by translation, are reductive systems of linguistic signs, symbols, and representations. The closure of meaning by cultural representation, however thick, and despite the social science models and gossip theory, provides the potentiality of native teases, parody, mockery, and irony.

The literary play of *différance*, or subversion and irony, in the language of cultural evidence is a chance fusion of situational irony rather than a methodology. Derrida might have turned to natives and elaborated his creative discourse of *différance* to include the tease and irony of federal treaties, the trace of unnamable visionary totems, the extravagant legacy of the fur trade, casino envy, gossip theory, and the misconception of racial and cultural victimry in the history and literature about Native American Indians.

Fate and Irony

The *Urban Dictionary*, a "crowdsourced" online dictionary of common words and phrases, notes that the word "irony" is "One of the most misused words in the entire English Language," and then goes on to list five common situations of irony:

Socratic Irony: "When someone pretends to be naive about a certain subject, and uses his questions about it to point out a flaw in the established belief."

Sarcasm: "Understatement, mocking overstatement, or heavy-handed irony (stating the flat opposite of the truth) where both parties are aware of the difference between what's said and what's actually happening."

Situational Irony: "The irony that most people think of. A difference between what you expect to happen (in a story, for example) and what actually happens."

Irony of Fate: "The concept that the Gods, Fates . . . are toying with humans for amusement by using irony. Beethoven's loss of hearing is a famous example; one would expect a composer to be able to hear his compositions, but fate denied him that ability."

Tragic or Dramatic Irony: "When the audience knows something that some of the characters don't know," as in a play, movie, or novel (*Urban Dictionary*).

Selected native stories and scenes in contemporary native literature reveal the practices, aspects, and situations of these five discussions of irony. Native tricksters and creative figures in stories, for instance, might pretend to be naive about the cosmopolitan turns of the world. Poses of silence, overstated traditions and sexuality, and artistic and literary mockery were once common native situations, especially as responses to federal agents and policies, ethnographic studies, and now the secretive operation of reservation casinos. Situational irony could be a designer mongrel on the reservation, convertible sports car at a breadline, organic wild rice, rubber moccasins, plastic bear claw necklaces, porcupine wet nurse, or the Stars and Stripes beaded on a powwow vest. The irony of fate, however, is a complicated situation because chance is a more common sense of native futurity. Missionaries pronounced the godly irony of fate, and the situation of fate is at least doubled by the traces of chance in more traditional creation stories. The native trickster in the familiar earthdiver stories, for instance, creates a new world with bits of sand in the paws and claws of birds and animals.

Tragic irony is situational, actors who played natives in movies, the victimry themes of romance novels, and specific responses of native audiences to movies such as *Cheyenne Autumn* directed by John Ford in 1964. The Cheyenne were speaking Navajo, a great source of native humor in movie theaters, and others in the audience could not appreciate the tragic or dramatic irony. Consider Jeff Chandler who played Cochise in *Broken Arrow*, directed by Delmer Daves in 1950. The movie was filled with delightful, unintended irony. In one scene, a peace treaty is being negotiated as a naive native woman watches with wonder as James Stewart, a very good white man with a mirror, shaves his face in the great outdoors.

Mortal Vocabularies

Mockery is intentional, but situational irony is both intended and unintended, and that condition would be present in every narrative, not only the obvious poses and stories. Consider, for instance, the millions of books in libraries, many about natives, that await readers with the experience and capacity to deconstruct the narrative and then to perceive the irony. The style, the artistic and descriptive language, and the meaning of the words have changed, but the books remain the same, as memorials of unintended irony. The irony is unintended because most authors could not have anticipated the deferred meaning and *différance* of language.

Richard Rorty pointed out in *Contingency, Irony, and Solidarity* (1989), the words of our lives are a "final vocabulary," or the learned language that becomes an essential border. "All human beings carry about a set of words which they employ to justify their actions, their beliefs, and their lives. These are the words in which we formulate praise of our friends and contempt for our enemies. . . . I shall call these words a person's 'final vocabulary'" (73). Rorty observed that the common sense of final vocabularies is the opposite of the doubt and renunciations of ironies. The ironist "thinks nothing has an intrinsic nature, a real essence" (74).[4]

Jonathan Lear, in *A Case for Irony* (2011), considered the actual insecurity of irony and distinguished the "experience of irony from the development of a capacity for irony" (9). The experience was essential and personal, and the "experience of irony thus seems to be a peculiar species of uncanniness—in the sense that something that has been familiar returns to me as strange and unfamiliar" (15).

The dominance of discovery, sway of social sciences narratives, power of archives, and authority of government documents created a simulated sense of the familiar, a final ethnographic vocabulary about natives, and the necessary deconstruction of the familiar was irony. Lear named this experience an "ironic disruption" because what was once "taken as familiar" has "suddenly become unfamiliar" (19). There was "something about my practical identity that breaks my practical identity apart: it seems larger than, disruptive of, itself" (21).

Merde Manners

Victor Barnouw recorded hundreds of trickster stories and published them in *Wisconsin Chippewa Myths & Tales* (1977). From "these stories," he observed, "we can learn something about the belief systems of the people who told and listened to them." Barnouw declared that the trickster "was a real person whom they respected although they also laughed at his antics" (4). The trickster as "a real person" is gossip theory, an ethnographic concoction of unintended irony.

Tom Badger, an ethnographic name, told trickster creation stories that were recorded at Lac du Flambeau in Wisconsin and published in the early 1940s. Julia Badger, his wife, was the interpreter. Badger told about the trickster Wenebojo, or Nanabozho, who was standing on the top of the tree in a creation story:

> He had his head back, and the water was up to his mouth. Pretty soon Wenebojo felt that he wanted to defecate. He couldn't hold it. The shit floated up to the top of the water and floated around his mouth. After a while Wenebojo noticed that there was an animal in the water. This animal was playing around. Wenebojo couldn't see the animal, but he knew that it was there. He tried to look around. Then he saw several animals—beaver, muskrat, and otter. Wenebojo spoke to the otter first, "Brother," he said, "could you go down and get some earth? If you do that, I will make an earth for you and me to live on." (Barnouw 38)

Barnouw evaluated the ironic trickster stories of creation with putative psychoanalytic theories that ruined the moment of the stories, but the interpretation and publication of the stories contributed to an incredible source of unintended irony, a source of much humor in a more secure native academic world seventy years later.

Barnouw observed that "Tom Badger was a reserved, intelligent, mild-mannered man in his seventies. . . . I gave him a Rorschach Test and collected two Draw-a-Person drawings. . . . The man's head was drawn very large in relation to the rest of the body, and there was a strong emphasis on the mouth, while the arms were weakly depicted. Moreover, although Tom said that the man was naked, he was given no sexual organs" (Barnouw 60–61).

Werner Wolff, a psychologist, "suggested that Tom Badger was probably a passive, dreamy person, with sexual inhibitions and that perhaps the frustration in the sexual sphere resulted in a transfer to the oral region" (61). Pauline Vorhaus analyzed the Rorschach record, and "remarked that there was evidence of emotional dependency and also some confusion about sex, since Tom's form level was good except for the sexual responses. The two interpretations suggest the existence of repression, which is also suggested by the origin myth, with its avoidance of women and sex and its recurrent oral and anal themes" (61).

Dennis Tedlock, the literary scholar and anthropologist, considered native stories as art, not a clinical or comparative subject, and wrote that storiers were "not merely repeating memorized words" or presenting a "concert reading," but rather an art performance, and "we are getting the *criticism* at the same time and from the same person. The interpreter does not merely play the parts, but is the narrator and commentator as well" (15).[5]

Barnouw pointed out that there "seems to be more emphasis on the anal zone in the folklore," and "Freudians find an explanation for the 'anal character' in severe early toilet training, but one would not expect to find strict toilet training in a 'nomadic' tribal culture" (240, 241). Perhaps "we should not see the presence of anal motifs as something surprising or pathological. After all, an interest in feces is natural and understandable" (242).

Barnouw noted that Alan Dundes, folklorist at the University of California, Berkeley, "suggested that the earthdiver motif is a male fantasy of creation stemming from male envy of female pregnancy and an assumed cloacal theory." Moreover, this "may seem an extravagant hypothesis, but it would be in keeping with the Chippewa myth with its exclusion of women and its striking anal themes" (Barnouw 54).

"Despite the lack of a great number of actual excremental myths," observed Dundes, "the existence of any at all would appear to lend support to the hypothesis that men do think of creativity in anal terms, and further that this conception is projected into mythical cosmogenic terms." The concept of coprophilia, the abnormal pleasure of feces, was based on the "existence of a cloacal theory of birth, and the existence of pregnancy envy on the part of males" (Dundes 278).

Fecal Psychobabble

The trickster stories of an earthdiver creation have clearly captured the cloacal discourse of several serious academics. The earthdiver stories were obviously ironic, and in translation these stories continue to be delightful literary parody, but not psychodrama or psychographic. The gossip theory of *merde* manners and cloacal speculation has become a great source of unintended irony. The winter trickster earthdiver stories were weather diversions, and the scenes were more urgent on a cold night with the insistence of a bowel movement, and at the very moment a new island world was about to be constructed with a forepaw of sand and mire. The cloacal psychobabble has become a collection of academic earthdiver stories with the untold excreta of unintended irony. The monographs of ethnographic gossip theory about natives have ultimately provided an enormous source of unintended irony and the promise of mockery. Thousands of academic dissertations and conference papers on native cultures and stories await the deconstruction and ironic disruptions of final academic vocabularies.

Victor Barnouw and Alan Dundes, if they were alive today, would surely commence a cloacal critique of the current exhibition of weighty fecal specimens and mucky stories at the National Poo Museum on the Isle of Wight, the first comparative and formal *merde* exhibition in the world: "The museum, which officially opened to the public on the Isle of Wight, was created by the Eccleston George artist collective using animal and human droppings donated by members of the public and the Isle of Wight Zoo and Dinosaur Isle Museum" (Hooper). This new tease of fecal creation stories is a marvelous ironic disruption of the cloacal gossip theories in the world.

Notes

1 Also cited in Gerald Vizenor, *Summer in the Spring*, 55, 152–153.
2 See reviews of *Navaho Witchcraft* by Julian H. Steward, *Social Forces* 21.4 (1944): 124–125 and Gladys A. Reichard, *Journal of American Folklore* 60.235 (1947): 90–92.
3 Also cited in Vizenor, *The People Named the Chippewa: Narrative Histories*, 8–9.
4 Also cited in Vizenor, *Fugitive Poses*, 24.
5 Also cited in Vizenor, "Trickster Discourse: Comic Holotropes and Language Games," 200.

Works Cited

Allen, Woody. *The Insanity Defense*. New York: Random House, 2007. Print.
Barnouw, Victor. *Wisconsin Chippewa Myths & Tales and Their Relation to Chippewa Life*. Madison: U of Wisconsin P, 1977. Print.
Brown, Leslie, "Irony," *The New Shorter Oxford English Dictionary*, Vol. 1. Oxford: Clarendon Press, 1993. Print.
Densmore, Frances. *Chippewa Music*. Bureau of American Ethnology. Washington, DC: GPO, 1910. Print.
Derrida, Jacques. "From *Différance*," *A Derrida Reader: Between the Blinds*. Ed. Peggy Kamuf. New York: Columbia UP, 1991. 59–79. Print.
———. *Marges de la philosophie*. Paris: Les Editions de Minuit, 1972. Print.

Dundes, Alan. "Earth-Diver: Creation of the Mythopoeic Male," *American Anthropologist* 64.5 (1962): 1032–1051. Rpt. in *Sacred Narrative: Readings in the Theory of the Myth*. Ed. Alan Dundes. Berkeley: U of California P, 1984. Print.

Geertz, Clifford. *The Interpretation of Cultures*. New York: Basic Books, 1973. Print.

Hooper, Ben. "National Poo Museum Exhibits Encourage Excitement for Excrement," *United Press International*, April 4, 2016, http://www.upi.com/Odd_News/2016 /04/04/National-Poo-Museum-exhibits-encourage-excitement-for-excrement /1131459795278/.

"Irony." *Urban Dictionary*, 2004. http://www.urbandictionary.com/define.php?term =Irony.

Lear, Jonathan. *A Case for Irony*. Cambridge: Harvard UP, 2011. Print.

Parsons, Talcott. Review of *Navaho Witchcraft*, by Clyde Kluckhohn. *American Journal of Sociology*, 51.6 (1946): 566–567. Print.

Rorty, Richard. *Contingency, Irony, and Solidarity*. New York: Cambridge UP, 1989. Print.

Sim, Stuart. *Derrida and the End of History*. New York: Totem Books, 1999. Print.

Tedlock, Dennis. *The Spoken Word and the Work of Interpretation*. Philadelphia: U of Pennsylvania P, 1983. Print.

Thorowgood, Thomas. *Jewes in America, or Probabilities, That the Americans Are Jewes*. London: Henry Brome at the Gun in Ivie-Lane, 1660. New York Public Library Digital Collection, http://digitalcollections.nypl.org/items/8c527043-06dc-15a6-e040 -e00a180659d7.

Vizenor, Gerald. *Fugitive Poses*. Lincoln: U of Nebraska P, 1998. Print.

———. *Literary Chance: Essays on Native American Survivance*. València, Spain: Universitat de València, Biblioteca Javier Coy d'estudis nord-americans, 2007. Print.

———. "Native Tease: Narratives of Irony and Survivance," in *Literary Chance: Essays on Native American Survivance*. València, Spain: Universitat de València, Biblioteca Javier Coy d'estudis nord-americans, 2007. 77–83. Print.

———. *The People Named the Chippewa: Narrative Histories*. Minneapolis: U of Minnesota P, 1984. Print.

———. *Summer in the Spring: Anishinaabe Lyric Poems and Stories*. Norman: U of Oklahoma P, 1993. Print.

———. "Trickster Discourse: Comic Holotropes and Language Games," in *Narrative Chance: Postmodern Discourse on Native American Indian Literatures*. Ed. Gerald Vizenor. Norman: U of Oklahoma P, 1989. 187–211. Print.

Part II
Sounding Race

• •

5

(Re)imagining Indigenous
Popular Culture
• •

MINTZI AUANDA MARTÍNEZ-RIVERA

High up in the P'urhépecha Sierra in the state of Michoacán, Radio Sapichu plays the latest banda song by La Arrolladora Banda El Limón, followed by a tune by Los Rayos del Sol, a *pirekua* group from the community of Angahuan. Other local radio stations throughout the sierra similarly alternate between regional Mexican music (cumbias, banda, norteñas, rancheras), pop, rock, and *pirekuas*. In addition, young people often organize rock and banda concerts followed, or preceded, by *pirekua* concerts. P'urhépecha youth are connected to the global popular culture/music trends, and their listening choices and interests are reflected in how they organize music concerts.

However, many people (and in some cases scholars) still imagine indigenous people as stuck in the past, removed from modernity and living "traditional lives." Influenced by the writings of Manuel Gamio, many scholars and the general public consider that indigenous persons cease to be indigenous if they partake of modernity (broadly construed). In this regard, popular culture, as a product of modernity, commodification, consumption, and mass media, is often considered antithetical to the experience of indigenous peoples. However, as some scholars and indigenous people have demonstrated, indigenous people not only partake of modernity but they are also active in the global community.

This chapter reframes popular culture as an integral feature of indigenous culture. By exploring the ways in which popular culture has been conceptualized, mainly the differences between U.S. scholarship and Latin American scholarship, and by contesting terms that scholars use to describe current indigenous cultural practices, such as "indigenous modernity" or "indigenous cosmopolitanism," I argue that we need to (re)imagine indigenous popular culture so that it more closely reflects current performances of indigenous culture and identity. To (re)imagine indigenous popular culture, I focus on two case studies. The first case study analyzes the indigenous rock movement in Mexico and in the United States. Indigenous rock groups have performed and recorded albums in Mexico since the mid-1990s. The two most recognized and popular groups are Hamac Caziim (Comcáac from Sonora) and Sak Tzevul (Tzotzil from Chiapas). In order to provide a hemispheric approach to the study of popular culture in Native American/indigenous communities, this section also engages with the works by David Walsh, Jeff Berglund, and Gail A. McKay that explore popular music in Native American communities in the United States. The second case study focuses on popular music in the P'urhépecha region of Michoacán, particularly in the community of Santo Santiago de Angahuan. While the *pirekua* is considered traditional music, in this chapter I argue that the *pirekua* is as much of an example of popular culture/music as indigenous rock. The principal goal of this chapter is to propose an alternative definition of indigenous popular culture, one that highlights the dynamism and plasticity of indigenous culture in order to contribute to the conversation on this important concept in the twenty-first century.

To begin our discussion on indigenous popular culture, and how/why indigenous people are considered "traditional" and thus unable to partake in modernity or popular culture, I briefly discuss indigenous identity politics in Mexico. Afterward, I compare how popular culture has been conceptualized in U.S. scholarship versus Mexican scholarship in order to understand how scholars have articulated indigenous popular culture, and propose a definition of indigenous popular culture. The last section of this chapter discusses in more detail the two case studies as well as the challenges of trying to (re)imagine indigenous popular culture.

Imagining Indigenous Identity for and in the Twenty-First Century

In previous works, I have discussed indigenous identity politics in Mexico and how most current conceptualizations, while highlighting changes in indigenous identity, are still influenced by Manuel Gamio's articulation of what is considered indigenous (Martínez-Rivera *Getting Married*). Since Gamio's canonical work *Forjando Patria*, Mexican conceptualizations of indigenous identities have developed in several waves. The first wave, the Revolutionary Wave, is heavily influenced by Gamio's work and argued that indigenous people had to be

(1) living in marginal zones such as mountains and deserts in the provinces; (2) living in extreme poverty; (3) dwelling in huts made from natural materials, far away from cities; (4) having a polytheistic and syncretic religion; (5) living according to their "traditional" customs; (6) speaking dialects and very little, if any, Spanish; (7) and "ignored" and "abandoned" by a national government that should have been "civilizing" them. (Alonso 478)

The main goal of the first wave was to educate and acculturate indigenous people into the national culture, to make them *mestizos*. Unfortunately, this list is still used today as a checklist to determine if someone, or something, is indigenous.

The second wave, which I call the anti-Indigenismo wave, is heavily influenced by the works of the five *magníficos*, a group composed of anthropologists Guillermo Bonfil Batalla, Arturo Warman, Margarita Nolasco Armas, Mercedes Olivera de Vazquez, and Enrique Valencia (*De eso que llaman*).[1] This wave focused on the hegemonic relationship between indigenous communities and the state and the effects of national policies to acculturate indigenous peoples. Bonfil Batalla, in particular, argues that indigenous communities are the roots of the Mexican nation, the *México Profundo* (1987). While highlighting the homogenizing and colonial limitations of the terms "indigenous" and "Indian," this group of scholars, as exemplified by Bonfil Batalla, highlighted the importance of culture and cultural practices (such as the cargo system) as ways to delimit who and what is indigenous.

The third wave, the multicultural turn, began with indigenous liberation movements (in the case of Mexico, the Zapatista Movement in 1994) and the emergence of indigenous scholars and activists. In this wave, the politics of indigenous identity were delimited by land, culture, and language.[2] In the late 1980s–early 1990s, throughout the continent, different indigenous groups began to fight for their autonomy and their civil rights using land claims, cultural practices, and language as markers of authenticity. Scholars discussed how indigenous political actors would embody (and challenge) the idea of what is indigenous as articulated by the government and nongovernmental organizations and used it for their advantage. And even though the multicultural turn was composed of indigenous scholars, leaders, and activists, Gamio's "list" was (and is still) used as a way to define indigenous identity.

The fourth, and currently ongoing wave, the Globalization wave, aims to move away from limiting representations of indigenous identity, while showcasing power dynamics that try to define what is indigenous. Scholars like Maximilian Forte (*Indigenous Cosmopolitanism*) and Mark Goodale ("Reclaiming Modernity") proposed the label "indigenous cosmopolitans" to move away from definitions of indigeneity that are rooted in place and stuck in an idea of tradition. In Marisol de la Cadena and Orin Starn's edited volume *Indigenous*

Experience Today, scholars explore what it means to be indigenous at the beginning of the twenty-first century. Claudia Briones, for example, examines the subculture of the *mapunkies* and *mapuheavy*, young Mapuches who like punk or heavy metal in Argentina. She argues that music serves to frame and empower young Mapuches in urban contexts. More recently, the volume *Modernidades Indígenas* (2007), edited by Orobitg and Pitarch, presents different case studies in which indigenous communities not only coexist with modernity but also produce their own understanding of modernity.

Current trends in indigenous identity conceptualizations, therefore, have moved from very narrow and limiting conceptualizations of what it means to be indigenous, to try to encompass and represent variability and cultural transformations. In my work, however, I move away from using qualifiers to describe indigenous identity, that is, using indigenous "cosmopolitanisms" or "modernities," and instead argue that *our conceptualizations of indigenous identity should already encompass cultural transformations*. Indigenous people use Facebook and cell phones and may go to McDonald's. That does not make them any less indigenous. This chapter is part of a larger project to reconceptualize ideas regarding indigenous identity, of which popular culture is an element.

Imagining Popular Culture

In his book *Cultural Theory and Popular Culture: An Introduction* (1994), John Storey argues that popular culture is influenced by how we define culture. According to Storey, popular culture may have four distinct meanings: as popularity (well-liked by many people); in relation to "high culture" (an inferior form of culture); as mass culture (work deliberately setting out to win favor with the people); and as peasant/working culture (culture made by the people for themselves). In his work, and by presenting the principal theoretical trends defining the term "popular culture," Storey argues for the interconnection of all the different definitions and uses of the term "popular culture." In his 2003 publication *Inventing Popular Culture*, however, Storey uses a more critical approach and presents an intellectual history of the concept. According to Storey, popular culture is a category defined by intellectuals to dismiss "the cultural practices of 'ordinary' people" (xii). In this regard, he is not seeking to analyze cultural texts as popular culture, but rather to "explore the changing intellectual ways of constructing texts as popular culture and how these intellectual discourses articulate questions of power and culture" (xi). Influenced by a Gramscian approach to culture and cultural studies, Storey highlights the power dynamics and hegemonic ideologies that influence the labeling of cultural texts as popular culture.

While Storey presents the different conceptualizations of popular culture and argues for an *interconnection* among the various definitions, most scholars choose one of the different conceptualizations. Nestor García Canclini argues that while Latin American, Italian, and even English scholars have conceptualized popular culture as a social group that defies capitalism and the nation, and that the study of subaltern groups could provide an alternative to capitalism, U.S. scholars have defined popular culture as cultural expressions that have mass marketability and mass appeal (24).[3] In this regard, U.S. scholars tend to conceptualize popular culture as a cultural text that is mediated by modernity, mass media, commodification, and technology, whereas in Mexico and in other parts of Latin America and Europe, theories of popular culture as a social group are strongly influenced by Gramsci's idea of hegemonic power.

In the Gramscian approach, popular culture is "a site of struggle between the 'resistance' of subordinate groups and the forces of 'incorporation' operating in the interests of dominant groups" (Storey 10). Nestor García Canclini, in his work *Las culturas populares en el capitalismo* (1982), analyzes folk art (*artesanías*) and folk celebrations to explore popular cultures in relation to modernity and the global market. In García Canclini's model, popular culture is defined as a social class.[4] Through his text, he aims to uncover how technology, commodification, and mass production of folk art transform and affect the production/authenticity of popular cultures.[5] What makes something popular, for García Canclini, is not the mode of production or markers of authenticity of a cultural artifact but the way that popular cultures use the objects (219). García Canclini's main argument is that the people, the artisans, should be protected, not the folk art. For García Canclini, the authenticity of folk art does not rely on the aesthetics or modes of production but on who made the object, why the object was made, and how it is used. In this framework, *popular* is conceptualized as a (social) position and an action (García Canclini 215). At the end of his text, García Canclini argues that indigenous people should join popular cultures (as a social group) because they share similar struggles as farmers, blue-collar workers, and the urban poor.[6] In García Canclini's framework, everything that is produced by (indigenous) artisans for their own use or the use of other (indigenous) people could be considered authentic popular culture. In this regard, indigenous communities are conceptualized as a type of popular culture in which individuals may have some agency and power over their own culture, but they may fall prey to the market, mass culture, and capitalist forces.

García Canclini argues that it is not easy to theorize a concept (popular culture) that is always in flight (25). Popular culture, as a form of cultural expression or as a social group, is constantly changing. Therefore, as soon as scholars agree on the term, the cultural expression or social group has transformed into something else. Moreover, popular culture, as a slippery concept, is always defined in relation to another phenomenon or social group, highlighting the inherent otherness of popular culture (both as a cultural expression and as a social group). In other words, we need to create a contrasting other to be able to talk about popular culture. Scholars, like Storey for example, have argued that we need to "fix" the meaning of popular culture so that the definition is not static and provides a more nuanced understanding of current cultural trends.

Based on how popular culture is defined (as a social group or as a cultural text) and how scholars relate it to indigenous communities, indigenous cultural practices are conceptualized differently. García Canclini argues that mass media or *popularidad* (basically the way that U.S. scholars define popular culture) serve as a way to homogenize cultural expressions and maintain the subjugation of popular cultures. Based on this argument, a logical conclusion is that popular cultures should be protected from mass media/*popularidad*. If indigenous communities are conceptualized as popular cultures, then indigenous cultures should also avoid mass media and cultural practices that are part of the *popularidad*. However, if we frame popular culture as a cultural text that engages with mass media, modernity, and commodification, and we unite it with an understanding of indigenous identity politics that are inclusive of all the different ways of being indigenous, then we can have a more nuanced and stronger representation of current indigenous cultural practices.

In this work, I am not using definitions of popular culture that focus on popular culture as a social/subaltern group: that conceptualization may serve as a way to further articulate indigenous people as removed from modernity or as passive actors in their own cultural production. While I recognize the theoretical possibilities of this conceptualization (popular culture as a social/subaltern group), in this work I want to focus on cultural practices and performances by indigenous people. Therefore, I define and use "indigenous popular culture" as cultural practices that are imagined as such both in and by indigenous communities, that are not used for rituals, and that have a ludic component. This ludic component is of crucial importance because this idea of play may reference mass media or something that is for pleasure. However, it does not negate the seriousness or social/political engagement of people participating in popular culture or the functionality of the cultural text.

Imagining Indigenous Popular Culture

As mentioned earlier, Native American and indigenous studies have moved away from static definitions of indigenous people as removed from modernity or as passive actors of modernity (most scholarship at least), to indigenous peoples as active participants in the global cultural scene. In relation to studies of popular culture, the way indigenous popular culture (as a practice and as a concept) is articulated also differs among U.S. scholars and Latin American scholars. In the case of Latin America, and because of how popular culture is conceptualized as a social group, indigenous groups fall under the umbrella of popular cultures. Moreover, and as I discussed in a previous work ("De El Constumbre al Rock"), if indigenous people engage with popular culture (as a cultural text) or mass culture, their authenticity as indigenous is questioned. To move beyond these limited and limiting portrayals of indigenous popular culture, I engage with Native American/indigenous studies to understand how indigenous popular culture has been conceptualized in the United States.

Among indigenous/Native American popular culture's scholars, I have found at least two trends. The first trend looks at the ways in which indigenous people have been represented by non-indigenous/Native American media. For instance, in his work *Tribal Television* (2014), Dustin Tahmahkera explores the stereotypical portrayal of Native Americans in television, mainly in sitcoms. He argues that this stereotypical portrayal follows a settler colonial mentality that serves to erase Native Americans and that the "culturally and socially multidimensional and fluid indigenous is practically neglected and absent" (3). Similar to Tahmahkera, the documentary *Reel Injun* (2009) explores Native American representations in film and the negative impact they have had on actual Native Americans. *Reel Injun* explores the history of the representation of Native Americans in film starting from silent films to the present. It discusses how most U.S. citizens have a stereotypical picture of Native Americans, a picture that has helped to marginalize living Native Americans. Television and films have contributed to the invisibilization of Native Americans by reducing them to one-dimensional caricatures. Moreover, both film and television have helped to further ideas and stereotypes of Native Americans as stuck in the nineteenth century (and a very problematic understanding of the nineteenth century at that). Both *Tribal Television* and *Reel Injun* conclude that we need a richer and more accurate representation of Native American people and their culture. *Reel Injun*, especially, ends on a hopeful note, discussing the rise of Native American filmmakers and projects by and for Native Americans.

Scholars have also explored how Native Americans/indigenous people have been and are active participants in the creation and shaping of popular culture. This second trend focuses on indigenous/Native American actors, both as consumers and as performers, in the creation or development of popular culture. In his canonical text, *Indians in Unexpected Places* (2004), Philip Deloria sheds light on different life stories of Native Americans who had a strong presence and influence in music, sports, technology, and film, all areas where indigenous people were not "expected" to be. Following in Deloria's footsteps, John Troutman further explores indigenous people in places where they are not supposed to be. In *Indian Blues: American Indians and the Politics of Music 1879–1934* (2009), Troutman unpacks the history of Native American (forced) participation in music programs organized by the Office of Indian Affairs (OIA). Those music programs had the goal of assimilating Native Americans and erasing their culture. Children who participated in those programs were taught Western classical music in the hopes of acculturating them into U.S. mainstream culture. However, what Troutman found was that "the practice of music, in a very real sense, provided a means by which American Indian people could strategically deploy their newfound U.S. citizenship—for example, to reinforce their tribal identities—in the face of OIA officials who sought to dismantle that core of their existence" (5). In his article "Indian Blues: The Indigenization of American Popular Music," Troutman further argues against the idea that musical fusions between Native American music and White-Anglo and African American music are new. Contrary to this, and as he highlights in his book, Native Americans have incorporated non-Native American music into their musical repertoire since the late nineteenth century. Music, in this regard, has served as a way to connect Native Americans to other communities while at the same time helping Native Americans preserve their culture (Troutman). Furthermore, Troutman argues, the articulation of outside music has helped new generations of Native American youth to connect with their own culture while helping them frame their identity in the current world.

In the volume *Indigenous Pop* (2016), editors Jeff Berglund, Jan Johnson, and Kimberli Lee compiled a series of articles that examine "the indigenous roots of American musical traditions, as well as the ways that popular (pop) contemporary and emerging (fresh) forms have led to innovative transformations and melding with tribal and Native traditions" (4). This volume moves away from stereotypes of Native American music to showcase the dynamism and richness of Native American music. The scholars in this volume clearly state that Native Americans do not lose their identity by using non-Native American music; contrary to this, Native Americans have "'indigenized' these entities, inventing new ways, Native ways, to employ music and song in many popular genres to convey Native thought and concerns" (7). Later in this chapter, I will discuss how this book explores the articulation of non-Native American music by Native Americans/indigenous musicians.[7]

Both types of scholarship, the one that highlights the uses of Native Americans/indigenous people, their language, and their culture, in popular culture, and the one that focuses on how Native Americans/indigenous people use and create popular culture, contribute to our understanding of Native American/indigenous experiences in the Americas. Native American/indigenous scholarship, then, provides a fruitful and productive path to explore indigenous popular cultural manifestations in Mexico.

(Re)imagining Indigenous Popular Culture: The Indigenous Rock Movement and the *Pirekua*

So far in this chapter, I have discussed how scholars have imagined indigenous identity, popular culture, and, more specifically, indigenous popular culture. My analysis has highlighted the challenges and, in some cases, the limitations of those three areas of study. Keeping in mind the limitations of portraying indigenous culture and identities, the case studies I discuss in the remainder of this chapter will allow us to reframe popular culture as cultural practices that are imagined as such in and by indigenous communities, as well as highlight the creativity and plasticity of indigenous cultures. My two case studies showcase two forms of indigenous popular culture: the indigenous rock movement—a form that articulates outside influences—and the *pirekua*—a musical form that is considered traditional P'urhépecha music.

The first form of indigenous popular culture (indigenous rock) is the one that most scholars have focused on, as exemplified by the edited volume *Indigenous Pop*, while the second form, a form that is considered traditional, has not been analyzed so far as popular culture, and I aim to flesh out some of the nuances of both forms of popular culture. As I will describe in a moment that for many indigenous communities, where musicians play punk, rock, reggae, hip-hop, and other musical genres, music is integral to their experience as indigenous people of the twenty-first century. A musical genre recognized as quintessentially P'urhépecha, *pirekua* is used for rituals, but it can also be performed for pleasure or ludic celebrations. Moreover, a new generation of musicians is creating new genres of P'urhépecha music that challenge the boundaries of *pirekua*. However, both forms of indigenous popular culture highlight the richness and plasticity of indigenous cultural practices and production.

The Indigenous Rock Movement

As mentioned earlier, Native Americans/Indigenous people are no strangers to the musical genres and cultural practices of non-Native American groups, and have participated in the creation of musical genres that are not considered Native American. And while some people are still surprised when they hear or learn about the indigenous rock movement, many of the principal or most famous groups and musicians, have been performing for over 20 years.[8] In a previous work analyzing the indigenous rock movement in Mexico, I discussed that the indigenous identity of musicians who play punk, progressive rock, rock, reggae, hip-hop, and other musical genres not considered indigenous, is constantly questioned by the media and even some scholars (Martínez-Rivera "'De El Costumbre al Rock'"). However, for the musicians and the members of the communities they belong to, they *are* indigenous, and rock, punk, reggae, or any other musical genre that they listen to or perform is also part of their experience as indigenous.

In *Indigenous Pop*, scholars explore the different ways in which Native American musicians articulate outside popular music within their culture. Jeff Berglund's analysis of Blackfire, a Diné punk band (Berglund, "Blackfire's Land Based Ethics), and Gail McKay's discussion of Cree rap/hip-hop performer Eekwool (McKay, "A Reading of Eekwool"), pay special attention to how musicians articulate popular music to their tradition, so that punk and rap/hip-hop are not transformations or adaptations, but examples of the "continuation of a long history of a vibrant and dynamic culture" (Walsh 175).

In his article "Babylon inna Hopiland," David S. Walsh uses James Clifford's concept of articulation to "demonstrate how Rasta Reggae discourse has been used to create a framework for understanding Indigenous plight and the social ills affecting indigenous peoples today" (155). Walsh analyzes the work of Casper Lomayesva, an award-winning reggae musician, in order to illustrate how Lomayesva articulates reggae with a Hopi worldview. I am further inspired by Walsh's use of articulation theory in relation to Hopi music and reggae to explain the "complex negotiation of tradition in modern contexts" (156). Articulation, as explained by Walsh, "recognizes human agency and ingenuity within living traditions, suggesting that tradition is not what existed from the past until today, rather what is articulated today about the past" (162). Therefore, for Walsh, reggae is not antithetical to Hopi tradition, but a continuation of that tradition.

Similar to the groups already mentioned, Hamac Caziim and Sak Tzevul also articulate "outside" music genres with their own traditional music.[9] Hamac Caziim is a punk group from Punta Chueca, Sonora, and they are Comcáac. They began playing in 1994 and performing publicly in 1996. Before they began performing they requested and received permission from their Council of Elders as most of their music consists of arrangements of Comcáac traditional music or oral narratives. Currently, they have performed in venues around Mexico, the United States, and Russia. They have two albums *Hamac Caziim* (2005) and *Ihamoc: Ano Caalam* (2014), and they have also been the focus of two documentaries. When they perform, they always dress in the traditional attire of their community and use their traditional face paint. While on stage, they address their audience only in Comcáac, notwithstanding the location of their performance. In 2010, I interviewed the members of Hamac Caziim as they participated in the Smithsonian Folklife Festival in Washington, DC.[10] For them playing punk and traditional/ceremonial music was not antithetical, rather, one served to reinforce the other. For example, as part of their participation in the Folklife Festival, they performed three times a day, twice with Hamac Caziim's repertoire, and once a day they performed Comcáac traditional/ceremonial music. Moreover, in our conversations they also mentioned how their music has helped young people in their community find pride in their language and culture.

Younger people have begun to form their own punk or rock groups in Punta Chueca, all with the help and support of the members of Hamac Caziim. Hamac Caziim's acceptance is not limited to the young generation; even the elders in the community attend their concerts and dance to their music. And although their fame has taken them to Russia and the United States, when at home they still work as fishermen. In the last three years, the members of Hamac Caziim have helped organize, as well as headlined, the Festival Xepe an Cöicoos celebrated in Comcáac communities. This festival invites and welcomes indigenous musical groups from other Mexican indigenous communities and has helped center Punta Chueca as a cultural enclave of Northern Mexico, not only for Comcáac culture but also for indigenous rock music.

Another famous indigenous rock group in Mexico is Sak Tzevul, a Tzotzil progressive rock group from Zinacantán, Chiapas. Sak Tzevul was formed in 1996, and although most of the initial members of the group have left, the group's main composer and lead singer, Damian Martínez, as well as his brother Enrique Martínez, the percussionist, continue pushing the group into new musical realms. The former members of Sak Tzevul have gone on to create their own jazz, reggae, or rock groups in Chiapas. Similarly to Hamac Caziim, Sak Tzevul has performed in many venues around Mexico as well as internationally. They have produced three albums *Antzetik* (2003), *Muk'ta Sot's* (2006), and *Xch'ulel Balamil* (2009). In contrast to Hamac Caziim's experience, the musical project espoused by the original members of Sak Tzevul was not originally accepted by the community at large. Damian and Enrique, children of traditional musicians, had to fight for the recognition of their music. By the mid-2000s, however, the group had been accepted by the community.

Their music features original compositions as well as arrangements of traditional music and oral narratives. They perform in Tzotzil, Tzetzal, and Tojolabal, and during their performances they wear the traditional dress of their community. Enrique, the percussionist, has also altered his drum kit to incorporate traditional drums. Through their attire, songs, and imagery during performances and music videos they form a continuous connection to their community and culture. Additionally, as part of their cultural, social, and political engagement with their community, they created a music school where children can learn their traditional music as well as other musical genres.

In 2009, they organized the first *Bats'i Fest: Festival de Rock Indígena*, where groups from Chiapas and Guatemala performed together for two days. Among the participants were Hamac Caziim, Santos Santiago (reggae in maya), and Lumaltok (rock tzotzil), groups that are still performing today. At present, the *Bats'i Fest* only lasts one day, and the last time it took place was in Ocozocoautla de Espinosa, Chiapas on September 30, 2016. While no longer headlining the *Bats'i Fest*, the impact of Sak Tzevul's contribution to the younger indigenous generation is invaluable, as many young people grew up listening to their music, or were even taught to play by them.

Although Hamac Caziim and Sak Tzevul originally received differing receptions in their communities, at present both groups are recognized for their contribution to the indigenous rock movement. As showcased by the *Festival Xepe an Cöicoos* and the *Bats'i Fest*, the rock movement has continued to expand and establish itself, and many indigenous communities throughout the country have their own form of musical articulation. For the younger generations that grew up listening to these groups, other musical genres, such as rock, reggae, punk, jazz, hip-hop, and rap, are not seen as foreign but rather as part of their everyday experience as indigenous youth.

The Transforming *Pirekua*

There are four different indigenous groups in the state of Michoacán. The eastern part of the state is home to Mazahua and Otomí, whereas Nahua settlements populate the coast. But the largest indigenous group is the P'urhépecha community, which occupies the area in the center of the state. The P'urhépecha had a vast and powerful empire prior to the Spanish Conquest, and they retain their status as the principal indigenous group in the area. Depending on how people are counted, currently there are between 125,000 and 200,000 P'urhépecha. At present, the P'urhépecha region is divided into four areas: Juatecharu isï (the Sierra or Meseta), Japondarhu (Zona Lacustre, the area surrounding the lake of Pátzcuaro), Sïrondarhu (la Ciénaga de Zacapu, the area near Zacapu), and Eraxamani (la Cañada de los Once Pueblos, the Ravine of the Eleven Towns).

P'urhépecha communities have a rich array of expressive cultural practices, such as different musical genres (e.g., brass bands, string music, orchestras), dances, rituals and festivals, food, material culture, traditional games, and oral narratives. Some P'urhépecha cultural practices have even gone global, such as the Danza de los Viejitos (Dance of the Old Men) or the way the Day of the Dead is celebrated in the region (Hellier-Tinoco). In 2010, the United Nations Educational, Scientific, and Cultural Organization (UNESCO) included P'urhépecha food and P'urhépecha music (specifically the *pirekua*) on their Intangible Cultural Heritage List (ICHL).

The *pirekua* is the traditional music of the P'urhépecha area. As defined in the ICHL, this type of music can be performed by men or women, young or old, and in many configurations (from a single musician to a whole chorus). In addition, the instrumentation also varies, from a string-only group (guitars, bass, and violin) to a full brass band. *Pirekua* performers, called *pirericha*, may also perform many musical genres, but *pirekuas* are mainly *sones* (3/8 time) or *abajeños* (6/8 time). *Pirekuas* can be performed as part of rituals, or for ludic purposes. As documented by Rocío Próspero Maldonado in the book *Pirekua: canto poco conocido*, members of P'urhépecha communities were not consulted or asked to participate in the nomination process. This definition of *pirekua* was articulated by government officials and not by practitioners of this cultural practice.

The inclusion of the *pirekua* into the ICHL sparked a huge and divisive debate among P'urhépecha musicians and activists, scholars, and government officials. In *Pirekua: canto poco conocido*, scholars, musicians, and activists aimed to redefine *pirekua* (versus the definition provided by ICHL) and trace its pre-Hispanic heritage, its musical and instrumental roots, its central component as part of P'urhépecha identity, and its current transformations (Márquez Joaquín). Moreover, and as a response to ICHL's definition, they provided their own definition of what *pirekua* is. In the introduction, Pedro Márquez Joaquín argues that the traditional definition of *pirekua* is "a song that expresses the thought, feelings and pride of the P'urhépecha people, where creators (composers) and the *pirericha* (performers) manifest all their talent, their creativity and their most profound feelings" (14).[11] Furthermore, *pirekua* music can be divided into three types: slow and melodious; *sones* and regional *sonecitos*; and fast-paced *abajeños* (Márquez Joaquín). This definition is more nuanced than the one provided by ICHL because it considers the P'urhépecha worldview. Recognizing how young singers and performers of *pirekua* are transforming the genre—as some groups are mixing in mariachi, banda, cumbia, bachata, and rap, and including electric instrumentation at times—Márquez Joaquín concludes that the best way of defining *pirekua* is that "*pirekua* is sung in P'urhépecha with diverse themes and rhythms, as well as different group compositions; it is the expressions of an artistic-literary-musical form that expresses the soul of life" (15).[12] The most important point, however, is that *pirekuas* have to be performed in P'urhépecha; if not, they are just regional songs (Márquez Joaquín).

Given the influence of immigration and an ever-growing access to world cultural trends, young P'urhépecha are, not surprisingly, experimenting with their traditional music. In his chapter "Kenda: *menkuisi, por siempre forever*. Analisis desde la mediación expresiva de la creación y la industria de la música p'urhépecha contemporánea," Edvar Dante Cerano Bautista analyzes the case of Grupo Kenda from the community of Cheranástico. For Cerano Bautista, Grupo Kenda is a prime example of P'urhépecha musical groups that create songs based on traditional *pirekua* (*sones* and *abajeños*) but perform them with electric instruments.[13] Grupo Kenda is known as performers of *música grupera*, and they have over ten musical records, most of them in P'urhépecha (only two are in Spanish). Grupo Kenda's music is known for its "modern" take on traditional *pirekua*, not only because they perform with electric instruments but because the lead singer's singing style is reminiscent of Spanish-language ballads or romantic songs. The themes addressed in their songs also move away from traditional *pirekuas* because they may address contemporary social issues.

I have conducted research in the community of Santo Santiago de Angahuan since 2006. Angahuan is home to one of the oldest and most respected *pirekua* groups, Los Rayos del Sol de Angahuan. And while most of the original members of the group have passed away, their nephews and grandchildren carry on their legacy. During my last research stay in the community, during the summer of 2016, I interviewed Tariacuri Soto, one of the members of Los Rayos del Sol.[14] During our conversation, Soto made a distinction between *pirekua antigua* and *pirekua moderna* (old *pirekua* and modern *pirekua*). Soto explained that while harmonies are important (old *pirekua* is supposed to be in minor tones), the determining characteristic of *pirekua antigua* is the lyrics. The lyrics have to be written in metaphors, and they have to transmit some form of teaching or knowledge. In other words, *pirekua antigua* transmits P'urhépecha culture's ancestral knowledge. Some groups, like Los Rayos del Sol de Angahuan, maintain the legacy of the *pirekua antigua*, while some of their members, such as Ta José Cortes Toral from Los Rayos del Sol de Angahuan, also compose new *pirekuas* following the style of *pirekua antigua*.

Soto mentioned that the *pirekua* started to change in the 1990s, with changes in instrumentation (the incorporation of electric instruments or instruments from other musical genres, like accordions), harmonies (songs in major tones), and lyrics (more aggressive lyrics, with sexual or violent content). And while modern *pirekuas* tend to narrate everyday events, similar to what old *pirekuas* do, the purpose of modern *pirekuas* is not to impart knowledge or a teaching, but to entertain. Moreover, musicians that perform the *pirekua moderna* incorporate elements of cumbia, bachata, rap, corridos, norteñas, and other musical genres. Some groups, according to Soto, simply borrow the music from popular songs and translate the lyrics into P'urhépecha. An example of this is a group that used the rhythm, melody, and harmonies from an Aventura song, a bachata group from New York City, but the song is performed in P'urhépecha with P'urhépecha themes. According to Soto, all musicians want their groups to do well and have a fan base, therefore some groups perform both types of *pirekuas*, *antiguas* and *modernas*, as a way to provide what audiences want. Groups that specialize in *pirekua moderna*, such as Grupo Kenda, Tanimu Pirericha and Checo Cacho y Angelitos, may also perform *pirekua antigua* on request, but the majority of their fan base is more interested in the *pirekua moderna*. According to Soto, these groups are more interested in having a fan base and making money than in preserving the *pirekua antigua*. And he does not blame them; they all need money to live and take care of their families. In fact, he has performed with *pirekua moderna* groups, although he prefers to perform and listen to *pirekua antigua*.

Soto made it clear that *pirericha* are not in agreement on how to define *pirekua*. Márquez Joaquín argues in his introduction to the book *Pirekua: canto poco conocido*, that a *pirekua* is any song performed in P'urhépecha. But Soto does not agree with this. He states that *pirekua* should refer to the music that follows the *pirekua antigua*, whereas the new transformations and modalities could be denominated *canciones en p'urhépecha* (songs in P'urhépecha). As a musician, Soto does not see anything wrong with transforming the *pirekua*, and he even likes the new genres and music performed in P'urhépecha. What he does not agree with is people calling that music *pirekua*. And even with the growing popularity of *canciones en p'urhepecha/pirekua moderna*, Soto is hopeful that *pirekua antigua* will continue to flourish and grow.

As mentioned earlier, because of its inclusion in UNESCO's ICHL, the study, analysis, and performance of *pirekua* are strongly contested. At this time, musicians, scholars, and government officials cannot agree on how to define *pirekua* and who has ownership of the music. In addition, and as Soto mentioned, new generations are changing the musical form to the point that some people say that certain groups are not performing *pirekua* but something else. But if people redefine *pirekua* as all music performed in P'urhépecha, as Joaquín Márquez concludes in his introduction, then rap and hip-hop performed in P'urhépecha would also be labeled *pirekua*. And, as Soto argues, that music (e.g., rap in P'urhépecha) is not *pirekua*, but *canción en P'urhépecha*.

The case of the *pirekua* serves as a clear example of the complexity of indigenous popular music and culture. From conversations with Soto, as well as with other P'urhépecha scholars, I learned that there are proposals for the creation of a new category for new musical creations and to delimit music considered P'urhépecha, even if it is performed in the language. The fact that the *pirekua* was added to UNESCO's ICHL greatly contributes to the tension in the debate because now the government also tries to influence and define musical production.[15]

Conclusion

This chapter has challenged us to (re)imagine indigenous popular culture; indigenous peoples have a variety of music forms, both for ritual and for ludic purposes. To do so, I first explored the different intellectual waves of indigenous identity politics in Mexico and the disparate ways in which the slippery concept of popular culture is conceptualized in both the United States and Mexico. These first puzzle pieces served to move us beyond limiting portrayals of indigenous people as removed from modernity, as well as restrictive conceptualizations of popular culture as a social group. In this regard, I defined popular culture as cultural practices of a ludic nature considered as such in and by indigenous communities.

An analysis of Native American/indigenous popular culture literature allowed us to see some of the intellectual patterns regarding the study of indigenous popular culture. The first trend discussed examined the ways in which Native American/indigenous people have been portrayed by non-Native American/indigenous media, whereas the second trend analyzed the different ways that Native Americans/indigenous people have contributed to popular culture. As part of the second trend, scholars have also explored the multiple ways in which Native American/indigenous people have engaged with and articulated popular culture.

The two case studies that I highlighted showcased the range of what can be classified as indigenous popular culture. As the case of Hamac Caziim demonstrates, the young men of the group combined punk with their traditional songs to create their own style of music that new generations of Comcáacs now see and embrace as part of their Comcáac identity. The second form of indigenous popular music, while focusing on the *pirekua*, seeks to move us away from stereotypes that all indigenous culture is inherently traditional. The case of the *pirekua* highlights the complexities of imagining indigenous music as only traditional (which is unfortunately reinforced by its inclusion in the ICHL), as this case supports the idea that indigenous communities have their own popular culture and music, and that they are constantly playing with and innovating on, their musical genres. In interviews, the members of Hamac Caziim have expressed how they use their traditional music as a foundation into which they mix punk. It can be said that groups like Grupo Kenda or Tanimu Pirericha use *pirekua* as a base and mix other musical genres into it. A significant difference, however, is that Grupo Kenda, Tanimu Pirericha, and others call their music *pirekua*, whereas Hamac Caziim, Sak Tzevul, and other groups will say that they perform Comcáac punk, Tzotzil rock, Mayan reggae, and other musical genres.

The (re)imagining that I propose in this work, that indigenous popular culture should be understood as cultural practices considered as such in and by indigenous communities and that are not used for rituals and that have a ludic component, highlights the fluidity, creativity, and plasticity of indigenous popular culture. In this regard, we need to move beyond static categories and further reframe what we scholars mean by "indigenous" and "indigenous culture" so that our conceptualizations better reflect and respect current indigenous cultural expressions and creativity. Moreover, indigenous musicians, artists, and scholars, as exemplified by Soto, are proposing their own terms, or categories, to describe their own cultural practices. Self-definition is key to helping us reimagine indigenous culture in and for the twenty-first century.

Notes

1 For an in depth analysis of the work and impact of the Five Magníficos, please refer to the work by Claudio Lomnitz *Deep Mexico, Silent Mexico* (2001).

2 Some scholars from this wave are Gunther Dietz, Laura Graham, Charles Hale, Suzanne Oakdale, Alcida Rita Ramos, and Terence Turner.

3 Peter Burke, in his work *Popular Culture in Early Modern Europe* (1978), conceptualized popular culture as the study of shopkeepers, factory workers, and lower classes in Medieval Europe and was one of the first scholars to articulate popular cultures as a subaltern groups.

4 He uses "popular culture" interchangeably with "subaltern groups." He also prefers to use "popular culture" instead of "traditional culture" or "oral culture" because "popular culture" allows for the study of the hegemonic relationship between groups and the resistance and struggles of subaltern groups.

5 García Canclini differentiates between popular culture (social group) and popularity (*popularidad*). For him, "popularity" refers to industrialized and mass cultural expressions.

6 This point was added in the 2002 revised edition; it was not in the original text. One can, therefore, infer that the Zapatista movement and other indigenous political movements influenced García Canclini's position on how to conceptualize indigenous peoples.

7 Scholars have also studied or mentioned how indigenous people, when excluded from the global/mainstream culture, create their own cultural spaces. Examples of Native American and indigenous groups creating their own spaces are the creation of the Native American Music Awards and the First World Indigenous Games celebrated in Brazil in 2015. Incorporated in 1998 to highlight the musical contributions and styles by Native American musicians in the United States and Canada, the Association of Native American Music Awards has more than 20,000 members, and the main offices in New York City hold the largest collection of Native American music. For more information, see http://www.nativeamerican musicawards.com/. The first indigenous games, the Jogos Mundiais dos Povos Indígenas, were held in Palmas, Brazil, from October 23 to November 1, 2015. The games were organized by Marcos Terena's Intertribal Council, the Brazilian Ministry of Sports, and the Municipality of Palmas. The games brought together over 2,000 athletes from thirty countries. Some people participated in competitive sports, while other groups showcased their traditional sports and games. The games also had a cultural and political component. For more information, see http://www.i-games2015.com/. More research is warranted on both of these cases.

8 I use "rock" as an umbrella term to refer to the indigenous popular music movement. I follow the use of "rock" as an umbrella term by the first compilation of rock music "De 'El Costumbre' al Rock" released in 2000 by the Comisión para el Desarrollo de los Pueblos Indígenas in Mexico.

9 I do not wish to repeat what I have written elsewhere ("De 'El Costumbre' al Rock"), but I want to highlight how Hamac Caziim and Sak Tzevul's musicians, specifically and forcefully, like to state that the inspiration for their music is their culture, that they use their traditional music and turn it into punk or progressive rock.

10 For more information on Hamac Caziim's participation in the Folklife Festival please refer to my article "De 'El Costumbre' al Rock."

11 "La pirekua es el canto que expresa el pensamiento, el sentimiento y el orgullo del
    pueblo p'urhépecha, donde los creadores (compositores) y los *pirericha* (intérpretes)
    manifiestan todo su talento, su creatividad y sus más profundos sentimientos." All
    translations are mine.

12 "La *pirekua* es cantada en P'urhépecha con temas, ritmos, y grupos de ejecutantes
    diversos, es la expression de un arte-literario-musical que expresa el sentir del alma
    y de la vida."

13 For Cerano Bautista, as well as all the collaborators of the book *Pirekua: un canto
    poco conocido*, the inclusion of electric instruments (electric guitar, electric bass,
    keyboards) is a clear sign of modernity.

14 Los Rayos del Sol de Angahuan is considered one of the premier cultural/musical
    institutions of P'urhépecha culture and music. One of the principal groups during
    the golden years of *pirekua* music (from the 1970s to the 1990s), the membership of
    Los Rayos del Sol has changed through the years, but the legacy of the group has
    passed from father to son. This new iteration of Los Rayos began some four years
    ago, but they follow the tradition of the original members. They mainly perform
    traditional *pirekuas*, although one of the members is starting to compose original
    pirekuas in the traditional style.

15 More research is needed to fully document the impact of the inclusion of *pirekua*
    in UNESCO's list.

Works Cited

Alonso, Ana María. "Conforming Disconformity: 'Mestizaje,' Hybridity, and the
    Aesthetics of Mexican Nationalism." *Cultural Anthropology* 19.4 (2004): 459–490.
    Print.

Berglund, Jeff. "Blackfire's Land Based Ethics." *Indigenous Pop: Native American Music
    from Jazz to Hip Hop*. Ed. Jeff Berglund, Jan Johnson, and Kimberli Lee. Tucson:
    University of Arizona Press, 2016. 155–178. Print.

Berglund, Jeff, Jan Johnson, and Kimberli Lee, eds. *Indigenous Pop: Native American Music
    from Jazz to Hip Hop*. Tucson: University of Arizona Press, 2016. Print.

Bonfil Batalla, Guillermo. *México Profundo: Una Civilización Negada*. 1987. Mexico City,
    Mexico: DeBolsillo, 2005. Print.

Briones, Claudia. "'Our Struggle Has Just Begun': Experiences of Belonging and Mapuche
    Formations of Self." *Indigenous Experience Today*. Ed. Marisol de la Cadena and Orin
    Starn. New York: Berg Publishers, 2007. 99–121. Print.

Cerano Bautista, Edvar Dante. "Kenda: *menkuisi*, por siempre, *forever*. Análisis desde la
    mediación expresiva de la creación y la industria de la música p'urhepecha contemporánea."
    Pirekua: canto poco conocido. Ed. Pedro Márquez Joaquín. Zamora, Mexico: El Colegio
    de Michoacán, Consejo para el Arte y la Cultura de la Región P'urhepecha, 2014.
    149–168. Print.

De la Cadena, Marisol, and Orin Starn. *Indigenous Experience Today*. New York: Berg
    Publishers, 2007. Print.

Deloria, Philip J. *Indians in Unexpected Places*. Lawrence: University Press of Kansas.
    2004. Print.

Forte, Maximilian C, ed. *Indigenous Cosmopolitans. Transnational and Transcultural
    Indigeneity in the Twenty-First Century*. New York: Peter Lang Publishing, 2010.
    Print.

Gamio, Manuel. *Forjando Patria*. 1916. Mexico City, México: Editorial Porrúa, 1982. Print.

García Canclini, Néstor. *Culturas populares en el capitalismo*. 1982. Mexico City, México: Editorial Grijalbo, 2002. Print.

Goodale, Mark. "Reclaiming Modernity: Indigenous Cosmopolitanism and the Coming of the Second Revolution in Bolivia." *American Ethnologist* 33.4 (2006): 634–649. Print.

Hellier-Tinoco, Ruth. *Embodying Mexico: Tourism, Nationalism & Performance*. Oxford: Oxford University Press, 2011. Print.

Lomnitz, Claudio. *Deep Mexico, Silent Mexico: An Anthropology of Nationalism*. Minneapolis: University of Minnesota Press, 2001. Print.

Márquez Joaquín, Pedro, ed. *Pirekua: canto poco conocido*. Zamora, Mexico: El Colegio de Michoacán, Consejo para el Arte y la Cultura de la Región P'urhepecha, 2014. Print.

Márquez Joaquín, Pedro. "Introducción." *Pirekua: canto poco conocido*. Ed. Pedro Márquez Joaquín. Zamora, Mexico: El Colegio de Michoacán, Consejo para el Arte y la Cultura de la Región P'urhepecha, 2014. 9–25. Print.

Martínez-Rivera, Mintzi. *Getting Married in Angahuan: The Tembuchakua and the Socio-Cultural Transformation of the P'urhépecha Culture*. Ph.D. Dissertation. Indiana University–Bloomington, 2014. Print.

———. "'De El Costumbre al Rock': Rock Indígena and Being Indigenous in 21st Century Mexico." *Journal of Latin American and Caribbean Ethnic Studies*. 9.3 (2014): 272–292. Print.

McKay, Gail A. "A Reading of Eekwool." *Indigenous Pop: Native American Music from Jazz to Hip Hop*. Ed. Jeff Berglund, Jan Johnson, and Kimberli Lee. Tucson: University of Arizona Press, 2016. 201–223. Print.

Pitarch, Pedro and Gemma Orobitg, eds. *Modernidades Indigenas*. Madrid and Frankfurt: Iberoamericana and Vervuert, 2012. Print.

Próspero Maldonado, Rocío. "Música p'urhepecha ¿valor cultural del pueblo p'urhepecha o patrimonio del mundo?" *Pirekua: canto poco conocido*. Ed. Pedro Márquez Joaquín. Zamora, Mexico: El Colegio de Michoacán, Consejo para el Arte y la Cultura de la Región P'urhepecha, 2014. 171–182. Print.

Reel Injun. Directed by Neil Diamond, Catherine Bainbridge, and Jeremiah Hayes. National Film Board of Canada, Rezolution Pictures, 2009. Film.

Storey, John. *Inventing Popular Culture*. London: Blackwell, 2003. Print.

———. *Cultural Theory and Popular Culture: An Introduction*. 1994. 5th Edition. London: Pearson Longman, 2008. Print.

Tahmahkera, Dustin. *Tribal Television: Viewing Native Peoples in Sitcoms*. Chapel Hill: University of North Carolina Press, 2014. Print.

Troutman, John W. *Indian Blues: American Indians and the Politics of Music 1879–1934*. Norman: University of Oklahoma Press, 2009. Print.

———. "Indian Blues: The Indigenization of American Popular Music." *World Literature Today*. 83.3 (2009): 41–46. Print.

Walsh, David. "Babylon Inna Hopiland." *Indigenous Pop: Native American Music from Jazz to Hip Hop*. Ed. Jeff Berglund, Jan Johnson, and Kimberli Lee. Tucson: University of Arizona Press, 2016. 155–178. Print.

Warman, Arturo, Guillermo Bonfil Batalla, Margarita Nolasco, Mercedes Olivera and Enrique Valencia. *De eso que llaman antropología Mexicana*. Mexico City, Mexico: Editorial Nuestro Tiempo, 1970. Print.

6

My Tongue Is Divided into Two

●●●●●●●●●●●●●●●●●●●●●●●

OLIVIA CADAVAL WITH

QUIQUE AVILÉS

Fordham University professor Clara Rodríguez observed that one of the lessons of the 2012 election was that "increasing numbers of Americans are moving toward a much more inclusive sense of what an American is." Rodríguez went on to say that the "earlier definition of an American, which was so prevalent in our media of the 1940s, '50s, '60s, and to a certain extent the '70s, has given way to a definition that reflects the great diversity of America today" (Levs 3). Salvadoran immigrant, poet, actor, theater director, ethnographer, and colleague Quique Avilés addresses this change at the beginning of the millennium:

> Like a snake, the United States of America begins to shed her skin and simultaneously grow a new one. Just the other day, the *New York Times* reported on this transformation. The people who trouble themselves pouring [*sic*] over data on population changes and trends estimate that by the year 2042 the country will have a new minority—White people. Ain't that something?

Quique continues,

> The new world order has brought with it globalization: A fast moving of information and ideas across the planet and the constant movement of people all over

the world having contacts and experiences like never before. The United States is no exception. For the first time in its history, Latinos or Hispanics are the biggest minority in the country. Diversity is not just something dictated by inclusionary laws, but a reality. America finds itself in an uncomfortable place. The airways are filled with nasty and ugly images of invading hordes of men at the border while on the ground, in our communities, people are falling in love with each other, getting married, and having babies. Part of America is resisting this with a sense of fear and rejection [accentuated by the 2016 Republican election debates]. Workplaces and institutions are still engaged in cultural sensitivity or diversity workshops. Others are skipping the workshops and going to hands-on experiences, feeling each other, sleeping with each other, and having babies. A multicultural United States now seems inevitable.

In this chapter, I engage Quique in a multisited cultural dialogue on issues of race, identity, diversity, and social advocacy. This dialogue has evolved over time through informal conversations, interviews, promotional materials, joint analyses, poetry, and performance, and, on his insistence, needs to "remain flexible, never a final version."[1] I bring to this mix cultural texts and references—Gloria Anzaldúa, W.E.B. Dubois, and Richard Bauman—that provide alternate contexts as well as analytic tools, while Quique brings his reflexive "tongue divided into two." I have recently written on this discursive approach that invites collaborative authority over cultural representation and challenges the curatorial hierarchy of voice and interpretation (Cadaval, "Imagining a Collaborative" 155–176; Cadaval, "Lesson in Presenting" 193–203; Baron 8–9). I was also inspired by Patrick Mullen's modeling a more dialogic research process that encourages "a more equitable association between researcher and subject" (119),[2] which George E. Marcus addresses in a recent *Cultural Anthropology* website discussion in terms of "internarrativity and epistemic partnerships and alignments" that result in a "collaborative analytic" ("Introduction: Collaborative Analytics"). In the case of this chapter, I strive to democratize the authorial analytic voice using various strategies informed by my curatorial experience. Writing in close collaboration with Quique, I engage him in conversations that chronicle his experience as a Latino immigrant in a Black city. I record, interpret, and return to him for commentary. This provides him with the authority to reflect on what he said, and at times, enhance or provide an alternate text on "the margins" of the draft, so to speak. Parallel to this conversational exchange, I listen to his other voice, his poetry, which raises our discourse to broader discussions on race, identity, diversity, and, to some degree, transnationalism. As I will later discuss, he renders his poetry as "verbal arts," transitioning from a literary poetic form to spoken popular culture.[3] I explore with him how he turns to ethnography, performance, and the spoken word to explore this "uncomfortable reality" created by the increasingly assertive Latino populations in this country and reimagines "a much more inclusive sense of what an American is." In the first section, "Differential Identity, Borderlands, and Double Consciousness," I propose to Quique some theoretical tropes or metaphors to frame our dialogue. Quique responds and frames his approach in "Verbal Arts as Spoken Resistance." This is followed by Quique's immigrant experience in Washington, D.C., touching on his flight from El Salvador and his encounter with the *barrio* and Chocolate City. We conclude with a discussion on a possible new American imaginary.

Differential Identity, Borderlands, and Double Consciousness

Through verbal arts, Quique imagines a cultural space generated by a diverse society where both alienation and new identities are generated (Bauman, "Differential Identity" 39). In our conversations and through his cultural production, we explore differential and deeply situated social identities in the crevices created by this "borderlands" space where first world meets third world, natives meet immigrants, immigrants meet themselves, Blacks meet Latinos, Latinos meet Blacks, Latinos meet other Latinos. Quique adds on the margin: "I would go as far that in a place like D.C. you can meet everybody and their mothers—the Turks, Afghans, Vietnamese, Koreans, and so on, and so on." These are the cultural borderlands first theorized by Chicana scholar and writer Gloria Anzaldúa: "The Borderlands are physically present wherever two or more cultures edge each other, where people from different races occupy the same territory, where under, lower, middle, and upper classes touch, where the space between two individuals shrinks with intimacy" (18). Anzaldúa describes viscerally this cultural space: "The U.S. Mexican border *es una herida abierta* (an open wound) where the Third World grates against the first and bleeds. And before a scab forms it hemorrhages again, the lifeblood of two worlds merging to form a third country—a border culture. . . . A borderland is a vague and undetermined place created by the emotional residue of an unnatural boundary. It is in a constant state of transition" (25). For Quique, it is the space in Washington where "people of different races, ethnic groups and identities are forced to co-exist in very cramped quarters." This is where he explores and encounters what W.E.B. DuBois describes as a "double consciousness." DuBois states, "It is a peculiar sensation, this double consciousness, this sense of always looking at one's self through the eyes of others, of measuring one's soul by the tape of a world that looks on in amused contempt and pity. One ever feels his two-ness—an American, a Negro, two souls, two thoughts, two unreconciled strivings, two warring ideas in one dark body, whose dogged strength alone keeps it from being torn asunder" (*The Souls* 2). Dubois foregrounds what scholars will later identify as differential identity, that is, identity emerging out of face-to-face social situations and interactions between people with different backgrounds, when he describes "this sense of always looking at one's self through the eyes of others." Dubois seeks to understand "the strange meaning of being black here in the dawning of the Twentieth Century," in the context of what he describes as "the problem of the color-line" (*Writings* 359), and he asks, "How does it feel to be a problem?" (*Souls* 1). In the twenty-first century, Quique's question is equally existential ("What does it feel like inside?"), as he explores an emergent and situated Latino identity in the context of the multiple societies of the nation's capital, fondly called by the majority African American population "Chocolate City, a term popularized by a song written by the funk band Parliament-Funkidelic."[4] At the heart of Quique's question is the emergence of a new American identity that he describes as "rooted in an East Coast experience and by a 'lower,' 'new' breed of Mezoamericans, *los salvatrucos*, Mexican tortilla cousins (not Mexicans, not Puerto Ricans, not Cubans)." In the 1980s, the composition of the Latino community in Washington, D.C, and in the East Coast generally, radically changes with the thousands upon thousands of Salvadorans fleeing from the war in their country. Quique, forever the chronicler, begins by trying to understand what it means to be a rural Salvadoran immigrant in urban Washington, D.C., usually building on stereotypes familiar to his audience. He continues to explore the larger Latino identity and asks: "What color is this latinhood? How does it do what it does?" (*Immigrant Museum* 8–9). And ultimately seeks to create a new imaginary, a new American society where the "tongue divided into two" leads to new dialogues and new possibilities: "My tongue is divided into two. . . . I like my tongue" (14–15). But by 2013, in the new millennium, Quique is blindsided by the experiences of a new multiethnic generation that he mentors, who are now born in the United States where they confront a new question. In the 1980s, they were asked, "where do you come from?" But today the question is, "where is your family from?" He calls them "*los híbridos*" the "children of Latinia." On the margins of a draft, he reminds me that this process of questioning and staking a place in the American imaginary is "informed and strengthened by the spaces created by the original civil rights movement, the Black Struggle."

Quique's Approach

Quique confronts this "Borderlands," its crevices, and its double consciousness through engaged performance, and more specifically through spoken word, or as later coined with his colleagues, spoken resistance. He examines, challenges, and dialogues with his colliding and converging social imaginaries of the urban Black and Latino D.C. worlds he lives in, often grounded in mass popular culture. He has not shirked his own personal monsters and rehab experiences as they reflect a major continuing crisis in this city. Like Ecuadoran immigrant performance artist José Torres Tama,[5] Quique experiments with a hybrid genre that taps experimental theater and performance art, visual arts, new media, poetry, spoken word, popular culture, politics, and social commentary. Like Tama, he explores the role of the artist as a social provocateur and one who chronicles a people's history. He searches language to express how immigrants understand their experience in this new world while helping to define this newness. How do they address the crisis that their very presence raises? He embodies the dilemma with stereotypical characters—among his favorites are the immigrant mother or the waiter—who interact with caricatures of the well-intentioned White local population, such as teachers and progressive-minded professionals working for social service agencies in the *barrio*. These scenes touch on a deeply embedded implicit racism disguised as somewhat patronizing tolerance toward new immigrants, people of color, founded on privilege—education, race, social and economic class—that does not escape Quique. While his Latino characters are somewhat endearing, he depicts liberal "White folk," who in fact constitute a large part of his audience, with merciless satire. Quique also invites them to put themselves in the shoes of the immigrant: "My work also confronts 'White people' as to how they know or understand their immigrant ancestry. I ask them "where were your folks from?"

Verbal Arts as Spoken Resistance

For Quique, language as verbal arts plays a central role in his journey, beginning with his earlier bewilderment and encounter with Black culture to witnessing and helping shape a new American identity. I use the term "verbal arts" as defined by Richard Bauman: "By the artistic use of spoken language, artistic verbal performance, is meant language usage which takes on special significance above and beyond its referential, informational dimension through the systematic elaboration of any component of verbal behavior in such a way that this component calls attention to itself and is perceived as uncommon or special in a particular context. It may validly be argued that all speech has an esthetic dimension, but it is the point at which awareness of the esthetic dimension is achieved, at which the esthetic is invoked and the speech is intended or recognized as special, which holds the key to artistic verbal performance and responses thereto" ("Differential Identity" 39). While Quique found this term "verbal arts" quite amusing, it also raised our conversation to the level of folkloristic discourse, without losing site of the poem, where he is most articulate and succinct. In line with Bauman's paradigm, Quique's verbal arts performances are shaped by, as well as create, a social context—by describing the world, he creates the world. For him, language is both challenging and transformative, both for himself and for his audience. After all performances, Quique insists in having a dialogue with his public. As Salvadoran scholar and colleague Nilda Villalta argues, his poems are "created to be spoken out loud . . . conceived and written with a live audience in mind" (Villalta, as quoted in *Immigrant Museum* 4). And Quique adds in the margins on a draft of an earlier version of this chapter "all these texts have remained flexible and have changed from performance to performance. There has never been a final version." In his poem "Barrio," he struggles with "trying to write about things that do not belong in poems" as he signifies immigrant realities, such as "real estate deals" that increase housing costs and push immigrants to cheaper areas. He struggles with "trying to balance civility and anger" but is driven by his belief in social advocacy through verbal arts performance, the essence of "spoken resistance." Initially he argues that "Trying to write things not saying what needs to be said . . . to put it down is very difficult," but he will advocate for the poets: "I say let the poets run the country/We'll be better off with books and pens/Instead of the misery of weapons" (18).

Both Quique and Anzaldúa are highly reflexive about language, further accentuated by their bilingualism, but unlike Anzaldúa, Quique only learned English when he came to Washington, D.C. While Anzaldúa engages the politics of language as she faces "how do you tame a wild tongue, train it to be quiet, how do you bridle and saddle it? How do you make it lie down?" (75). Quique finds in language the possibility of a space for imagining a new world, a new America. Interestingly, he is most comfortable writing in English throwing in expressions in vernacular Latino—an emergent barrio language that is a conglomerate of various Latino discourses, accents, vernaculars, reflecting a cultural diversity that distinguishes the D.C. Latino immigrant.

At different times in our conversations, Quique insists on the power of art for social change: "Through art we can say what needs to be said on our communities and in our times. The artist can speak for those who have no voice; have not found a place for their voice. Art allows for community to come together in a safe place where it can be put on the table; a safe place where one has license to be irreverent, offensive, put ideas out that may not be popular; raise ideas through characters." These characters are usually very accessible because they play off popular culture stereotypes.

Quique's Arrival from El Salvador

Quique leaves a war-torn El Salvador in 1980 at the age of fifteen and lands in the midst of an emerging Latino community right in the middle of Black D.C. Parodying statistical analysis he delivers a description of his homeland, "El Salvador at a Glance":

Area: the size of Massachusetts
Population: Not much left

Language: War, blood, broken English, Spanish
Customs: Survival, dances, birthday parties, funerals . . .

El Salvador
Little question mark
Midget with a gun in his hand
Belly button of the world. (*Immigrant Museum* 10)

The escalation of the civil war in El Salvador prompted an increase of Salvadoran immigration to the Washington Metropolitan area now estimated as
great as 200,000 people, primarily from the eastern part of the country. More
to the point, Quique adds, "Salvadorans change the city due to decisions made
on The Hill (U.S. Congress)." This growing population is part of what the Salvadoran press has called the "*Departamento 15*," playfully incorporating the area
as one more of El Salvador's fourteen political departments or provinces (Rodríguez 167–194). The Washington metropolitan area draws Salvadorans for
many reasons. Some come because the city is one of the sites for the sanctuary
movement, some have connections with transnational immigrant organizations,
and others have ties with family or friends from their hometown. They
encounter the Latino community and "*el barrio*," which offers some comfort,
some familiarity, a home away from home, as they confront that in-between
world, between countries, a "borderlands" that makes them the other, and labels
them "undocumented aliens."

Quique's Encounter with *El Barrio* and the Nation's Capital

Quique comes into a very recent and diverse Latino community also in the process of defining itself. Without a dominant ethnic group until the arrival of
the Salvadorans in the 1980s, the community has developed a distinct and inclusive sense of Latino.[6] It staked its space, *el barrio*, in the neighborhoods of Mt.
Pleasant, Adams Morgan, and Colombia Heights in the late '70s, with an annual
festival, with street murals, and with sporadic street theater performances organized by a small but active sector of the community addressing social protests
through the arts. A group of Latino leaders in *el barrio* organized the first Latino
festival to show the city how many Latinos live in D.C. so they could get more
resources from the city government. His brother Pedro Avilés was deeply engaged
in solidarity movements addressing political and social issues of El Salvador,
Nicaragua, Chile, Argentina, and South Africa. His sister Ana Elsa grew up
working in official D.C. as a staff member for councilwoman Hilda Mason, and
later as an organizer for SEIU (Service Employees International Union).

The *barrio* as a sense of place is a dominant presence in our conversations.
It emerges as the core of the Latino community and forms part of the cultural

landscape characterized by the city's diverse and historic neighborhoods, which are often invisible to the other D.C., the Federal City. In the 1960s, historian Constance McLaughlin Green labeled Black Washington the "Secret City": "Indeed at every period the before mid-twentieth century, except possibly for a brief span of time in the early 1870s, colored Washington was psychotically a secret city all but unknown to the white world round about" (vii). Ana Patricia Rodríguez (180) insightfully identifies this Federal City in Quique's poem "Barrio" as "this arrogant place" where he attempts to make sense of these "arrogant times," or as African American studies professor Acklyn Lynch calls, "these uncivilized times of war" (Spoken Word v). Without describing *el barrio*, Quique locates it and evokes the tenor of life here with its tensions and issues that confront its residents:

> Trying to write things
> Without naming names
> Not pointing the finger
> Not saying what the throat wants to say
> In these arrogant times
> In this arrogant place

To Quique *el barrio* is also a contested site:

> Trying to write about things that do
> Not belong in poems
> Real estate deals
> The increase and decline of property
> values. . . .
> Trying to write things about this place
> To say it right
> To put it down
> Is difficult
> Very difficult (*Let the Poets Run the Country* n.p.)

In this poem, the poet and activist come together to address issues and stimulate dialogue. Touching on common social nodes, testing out "socially appropriate ways," he creates and engages his audience, which usually consists of some of his colleagues from the Central American solidarity organizations and, as already mentioned, the more progressive-thinking, yet privileged, White social service or legal professionals that work in the *barrio* (Bauman, "Verbal Arts" 293). Upon rereading this poem, Quique observes that when he wrote it in 1992 gentrification was in its infancy, "*Barrios* are not *barrios* the way we defined them and understood them in those times. *Barrios* are now for wealthy, well-educated hipster white adoptive parents—very different and a lot more difficult," underscoring the increased urgency for the dialogue to persist.

Quique's Encounter with Chocolate City

Quique not only lands in a contested *barrio*, in a city of neighborhoods, in the Federal City, but in a predominantly African American city of migrants from Virginia and the Carolinas who formed part of the Great Migration from the South after the Civil War (Green 101–131). As described by Quique, "Here, a true encounter/bumping into each other happens: the complexities of 'official English' vs Black English and our own version of Spanglish." This city, divided by DuBois's "color line," had a binary Black–White consciousness and had no name for this recent immigrant Latino population. On the margin Quique adds: "This makes me think not of a duality but of triplicity—the outsiders squeezing themselves in the already established White vs. Black dynamic."[7] For Quique, it is a new and unknown territory. His experience of African Americans in El Salvador was limited to the music celebrities of the 1960s–'70s that he encountered in mainstream television programs broadcast in El Salvador—Stevie Wonder and Aretha Franklin; Black boxers—Muhammad Ali, Fraser, Foreman—and the famous fights. But now living in a Black neighborhood, he discovers that Blacks are mothers, children, and families like other ordinary people. He attends their schools, they become his friends and his assailants, and they model what "American" is. He learns their language. He describes his earliest experiences: "Nobody told us there were Black folks in the U.S. and a lot of Blacks did not know who or what Salvadoran was. Out there in the streets, there was a lot of ignorance, a lot of violence." Lilo González, Salvadoran immigrant musician and songwriter, and Quique's occasional collaborator, captures the tensions in this city where African American and Latino youths "live in neighborhoods divided by urbanization and gentrification projects, unemployment or underemployment, and urban crime, which often sets these populations against each other," (Rodríguez 192–193) in his song "La Mount Pleasant." Set to a reggae beat, he begins with these lines:

> Black killing Black / *Negro matando a negro*
> Black killing Latino / *Negro matando a latino*
> Latino killing Black / *Latino matando a negro*
> Latino killing Latino / *Latino matando a latino* (192)

However, Quique crosses the color line. He is admitted to the Duke Ellington School of the Arts, a high school dedicated to arts education and named for the American jazz bandleader and composer Edward Kennedy "Duke" Ellington, himself a native of Washington, D.C. This experience shaped Quique—he learned Black history; breathed in an environment of music, art, and jazz; read Black writers; and gained respect for the Black experience. Race was a new imaginary for him. In later years, this emerges in his very lyrical poem, "The Freckles of the Banana,"

Reminds me of me
Of my mother
Of my father
My skin . . . (Taylor)

And on the margins of a draft, Quique adds a cryptic note: "This poem also brings about the realization of the loneliness of the theater world—Ibsen, Albee, Miller, Shakespeare is them, not us." At another time he adds: "There are no parts for me in these plays." Academic racism takes a twist as he juxtaposes the "us" evoked by the freckles of the banana, "my skin," to them, the classic, mainstream writers that he read as a student in Duke Ellington.

He recalls how he first wrote angry political diatribes against Yankee imperialism and on the leftist struggles of the people of El Salvador and the rest of Latin America. He then gets into street theater thanks to his first summer job with the Afro-Latino Youth Theater working with young people to reduce racial conflict, funded by Mayor Marion Barry's Summer Youth Employment Program.[8] Later in 1985, he cofounds a theater group called LatiNegro, along with two Washington-born African American women, Michelle Banks and Valerie Peak, and another Salvadoran their age, Mario González. Quique, Michelle, and Valerie—all members of the Duke Ellington School of the Arts Class of 1984—met Mario hanging out in the neighborhood. Sitting on the building steps at the corner of 15th and Irving, they talked about why Blacks and Latinos were going after each other in such a violent way and decided to do something about it. Quique explains that back then "it was a time of crews and break dancing"—the first play the group produced was called "No Break Dancing Tonight." After that performance, the Latin American Youth Center proposed to adopt the group as one of their youth outreach programs. LatiNegro produced skits based on interviews with middle and high school students about issues in school, tensions with their peers, and issues with their families. LatiNegro would present unfinished skits back to the students, encourage a discussion on the characters and their situation, and involve the students in creating endings through examining different ways of dealing with the problems.

In 1992, Quique quits LatiNegro with the desire to do solo work—to write not for a group but for a single performer—and to establish himself as a poet in D.C.'s poetry scene. On the same steps where LatiNegro was born, Quique meets Joe Ray Sandoval, a poet-performer from Santa Fe who was part of the DCWritersCorps, an artists-in-service project founded by the National Endowment for the Arts and the AmeriCorps program. DCWritersCorps offered creative expression as an alternative to violence, alcohol, and drug abuse in underserved communities.

Joe Ray tells Quique about DCWritersCorps and introduces him to the director, Black poet Kenny Carroll. Aware of the growing Latino population, Kenny hires Quique. He sees that Quique is able to cross the color line. For Quique, this marks the beginning of an encounter with up-and-coming young writers and poets from different backgrounds, all happening with the emergence of the Spoken Word Movement.

Kenny is a member of the performance poetry ensemble Spoken Word, which according to African/American studies professor Acklyn Lynch is "committed to conscious raising. . . . In these uncivilized times of war . . . there is a need to return to the source . . . to the authentic self . . . even if saturated with contradictory images . . . through putting life to words as a means of setting the agenda for positive change. The Spoken Word claims its rightful place as a voice of concern and consciousness in the African American community" (Spoken Word v). With Kenny and the DCWritersCorps, Quique is exposed to the philosophy of Spoken Word, which resonates with his own experience in trying to make sense of his world. He is introduced to the growing tradition of poetry slams in the city—Quique participates reluctantly but the experience does expose him to a distinctive verbal arts aesthetic, as well as to a broad range of upcoming D.C. poets. According to Michelle Banks, Quique's longtime collaborator, colleague, and friend and a reviewer of this chapter, who grew up with him,[9] Kenny himself, a Black D.C. native urban poet and mentor, had at that time great influence on Quique. In his poetry, Kenny takes the pulse of his city with intimate, direct language that finds its mark in Quique's work:

> love becomes essential in a city
> where kisses are routinely
> interrupted by gunfire,
> where the law has replaced the lash
>
> it is imperative that we touch in a city
> where even the government is into drive-bys:
> they drive by the homeless,
> . . . the unemployed,
> . . . the elderly,
> they drive by people driving by

it is impossible to survive here

if there is no mirror for our souls . . . (Excerpts from "Poems from "My City" in
So What! for the white dude who said this ain't poetry 38–39).

As Michelle argues, Quique relates to Kenny because *"su trabajo es más moderno, más urbano, más "negro."* (His work is more modern, more urban, more "Black"). But she does clarify that the work with the Writers Corps was not totally new to Quique, "I feel like Kenny appeared after some groundwork we laid down with LatiNegro was already in place" (personal communication). In 2000, within this milieu of social consciousness and performance of urban expressive traditions, Quique together with Hilary Binder and Yael Flusberg forms Sol & Soul: a grassroots organization that "exists to use the power of art and creative process to transform lives, create community, and build a more just society" (*Immigrant Museum* 44). As part of Sol & Soul, an informal group including Quique organizes "Spoken Resistance" at the juncture of social justice and language to provide a forum and encourage young people to express themselves with poetry writing and performance.

From Salvadoran to Latino to New American

It is in this context of a diverse immigrant community in the midst of a predominantly Black city in the nation's capital, scarred by racism and discrimination, that Quique finds his new voice as an immigrant Salvadoran, as a Latino, and ultimately articulates the possibility of the voice of a new American. He begins by trying to understand what it means to be a rural Salvadoran immigrant in urban Washington, D.C. He first finds himself in the 1980s Third World imaginary, a cultural space created by the friction between the First and the Third World, and experiences that Norma Cantú describes as "the pain and joy of the borderlands—perhaps no greater or lesser than the emotions stirred by living anywhere contradictions abound, cultures clash and meld, and life is lived on an edge—come from a wound that will not heal and yet is forever healing" (29). I remember Quique participating in street theater, where the actors enacted the horrors of war and the interventionist policies of the United States in El Salvador and other Latin American countries. He is drawn by the work of the Black activist poet Ethelbert Miller with its sensuous rich imagery. He adds that he is "surrounded by a vibrant, local cultural fringe—leftist, liberal—with the poignant verse of Argentinian poet Alicia Partnoy, the songs of protest of Luci Murphy, the *nueva canción* songs of Rumisonko, and a pinch of punk hardcore music." But in his own work, Quique focuses on immigrant life in Washington, D.C. Like DuBois who outlines "the two worlds within and without the Veil" Quique delves inside the Salvadoran immigrant imaginary reminiscent of DuBois, stepping "within the Veil, raising it that you may view faintly its deeper recesses, the meaning of its religion, the passion of its human sorrow, and the struggle of its great souls" (*Writings* 359). And like DuBois, he looks at the ordinary people and their everyday experiences. He sketches out real-life situations of Salvadoran immigrants arriving from rural areas, who struggle to find themselves and survive in urban Washington. Quique explains: "My desire has been to dig deeper into the reality of Salvadoran peasant life and our stereotypes of people from the countryside—stereotypes I play with all the time." He taps the Salvadoran vernacular and its verbal arts aesthetic, mimicking regional posturing and accents. He creates characters signifying their specific realities—waiters serving young professionals who work in social agencies, new populations gentrifying their neighborhoods and forcing them to move to areas with cheaper housing, and mothers losing control over their children, who prefer speaking English—young people trying to fit in. He brings these characters to life with performances that merge poetry, monologues, music, visual images, and many languages, including English, Spanish, Black English, regional Salvadoran Spanish, and Spanglish. This is akin to Anzaldúa's sensitivity to the nuances of language in a social context. She explains that as "a complex heterogeneous people, we speak many languages. Some of the languages we speak are:

1 Standard English
2 Working class and slang English
3 Standard Mexican Spanish
4 North Mexican Spanish dialect
5 Chicano Spanish" (77)

But Quique counters: "These then become 'infected' by an energy in the D.C. Latino Spanglish experience that had no precedent." Quique sees the emergence of the new American, new identity, as language becomes more "polluted," more liberating, more creative.

In his Latino characters, Quique draws out these "great souls" with great sensitivity and humor, never as victims but as active agents in their new surroundings. As he presents these immigrant experiences, he not only entertains, but he touches on things familiar to all audiences encouraging dialogue, and maybe understanding and respect.

Latino as the Interstice between Immigrant and the New American

Through our conversations and throughout his cultural production, Quique's strength is his grounding in the local, but it is precisely this foundation that launches him into translocal, global discourses on race, hybridity, and the possibility of new identities. Quique's exploration takes him into "the wound," beyond the Veil, at the interstice between immigrant and the new American. He plays around with the image of the plumed serpent, the mythic Mesoamerican Quetzalcoatl in his unfinished first solo monologue "Crazy: Loco Culebra's Monologue," much like Anzaldúa evoking Aztlán, the imagined Chicano homeland and Coatlalopeuh, the snake, "descended from, or is an aspect of, earlier Mesoamerican fertility and earth goddesses" (49). *Loco culebra* muses:

> I remember the day I went crazy . . .
> And that's all I remember . . .
>
> And it's ok by me
> Not having a name
> A country
> An age
> . . .
> Because I can look at the world
> Through different eyes at any moment . . . (*Paper, Fabric* n.p.)[10]

Unlike Anzaldúa, who "has this fear that she has no names . . . that when she does reach herself . . . a lion's or witch's or serpent's head will turn around swallow her and grin" (65). Quique embraces this in-between space where he has no name, where he "can look at the world through different eyes at any moment" and ventures into the larger universe of Latino identity, torn by multiple consciousness, multiple identities. He adds from the margins of the page: "I chose to go with not just Salvadoran, but Colombian, Nicaraguan." He experiments with framing the question, "What color is this latinhood? How does it do what it does?" (op. cit. n.p.). Like DuBois, who "to the real question, "How does it feel to be a problem?" he responds, "I answer seldom a word" (*Writings* 363). Quique understands that the value is in the asking rather than the reply. He shifts from the question ("Where are you from?"), which linked him to a homeland, to a portrayal of Latinhood which bridges both realities— back home, increasingly more distant, and this new world he is helping to create and then on to a new American identity. As rightly suggested by Nilda Villalta, Quique is faced with that "cultural borderlands" or third space defined by Homi Bhabha, forcing the questions, "How are subjects formed 'in-between,' or in excess of the sum of the 'parts' of differences? How do strategies of representation of empowerment come to be formulated in the competing claims of communities where, despite shared histories of deprivation and discrimination, the exchange of values, meanings and priorities may not always be collaborative and dialogical, but maybe profoundly antagonistic, conflictual, and even incommensurable?" (2). Quique probes these "subjects formed 'in-between'" into the complexities of pluriculturalism, into the very core of this situated Latino consciousness:

> What does it feel inside?
> What color is this latinhood?
> How does it do what it does?
> . . .
> What language does it speak
> . . .
> What color is this latinhood of mine
> Is it black latin
> Brown latin
> White latin . . . .
> . . .
> Welfare recipient
> Registered voter
> Legal or illegal
> . . . (*Immigrant Museum* 8–9)

Ana Patricia Rodríguez ascertains that it is "exactly, in this line of questioning, Avilés gets to the heart of the matter that identity is performative, scripted, cited, and put to the test in daily exchanges within and between subjects . . ." (qtd. in Villalta 182). It is precisely through verbal arts performance grounded in the social context that he formulates the possibility of "representation of empowerment" in the context of "the competing claims of communities." As he reads a draft of this chapter, Quique observes that "in the last 15 years, it has become the issue of human dignity. How do my characters bring 'dignity' to the fray?" He presses on:

> Is it true what they are saying
> That this whole thing
> Is the simple ability
> To swallow the world at birth

Quique then forms part of this birthing process of an identity in the making, yet to become:

> Keeping it
> Learning to chew at it
> Letting it grow
> Letting it grow inside. (*Immigrant Museum* 9)

He captures the Latino experience, the immigrant experience of what historian Mai Ngai describes as "an 'impossible subject,' a person who cannot be and a problem that cannot be solved" (5); the subordinate class, an inassimilable class of racialized subjects, immigrants.[11] In his work an "oppositional consciousness" emerges, to use Tomás Ybarra Frausto's term; not to come to terms but to build another reality—a consciousness not fully colonized or mainstreamed—a consciousness of the inassimilable that ultimately seeks to create a new imaginary, a new American identity where the "tongue divided into two" leads to new dialogue and new possibilities. As Anzaldúa encrypts the body when she describes the borderlands, the "1,950 miles-long open wound . . . running down the length of my body" (24), Quique singles out his tongue as the central metaphor for this third space that allows for a new identity:

> My tongue is divided into two
> Not knowing which side should be speaking
> Which side translating
> . . .
> My tongue is divided into two
> A border patrol runs through the middle
> Frisking words
> Asking for proper identification
> Checking for pronunciation
> . . .
> I like my tongue
> It says what feels right . . . (*Immigrant Museum* 14–15)

He foreshadows his earlier struggle with language in his *loco culebra* monologue:

> I couldn't speak for a while
> my tongue did not understand life
> it was torn between languages
> when I first regained the ability to speak
> I was speaking quechua, for no reason,
> But it felt good
> then I remembered english and forgot spanish
> now I'm in between
> Trying to remember all
> And separate them . . . (*Paper, Fabric* n.p.)

Quique transcends what DuBois describes as "This waste of double aims, this seeking to satisfy two reconciled ideals . . . that has wrought sad havoc . . .

and at times has even seemed about to make them ashamed of themselves" (*Writings* 366). He chooses "pluralism," that is, "the engagement that creates a common from all that plurality" as defined by The Pluralism Project of Harvard University (1), and creates a new world to live in, even as he knows that he also happens to be in somebody else's world. He emphasizes that engagement is key: "My work aims to serve as catalyst for dialogue on social issues that are often full of tension, heated feelings, and emotions. I insist that performances are not one-sided—the audience must participate. All performances are followed by a post-performance discussion where audiences can comment, disagree, share their own experiences or simply give their opinion on the performance." For example, he states the following in talking about his audience and his characters:

> Yes, I know the reluctant anglo smile
> Shedding its skin and guilt
> Feeling western and professional
> The afro strut and anger
> Eating greens, walking jazz
> Shooting crap. Dying fast
> Yes, getting by, getting by (*Immigrant Museum* 1)

This new imaginary begins to take shape through the experiences of the young people he mentors. He discovers that these young people are different, they are now born here, and often only one parent is Latino—a Salvadoran mother married to a Mongolian dad; a Mexican father married to a Palestinian mother—greatly complicating their identity. What is their home language when their own parents don't speak each other's? Are they monolingual English speakers, or bilingual, or trilingual? In trying to understand differences to his experience, Quique observes, "When I first came, people asked: 'Where are you from?' Now people ask 'Where do your parents come from?'" Does the possibility of a new American emerge from this decoupling of American-born children from their immigrant parents? Quique describes an experience with some of these young people in a poetry-writing workshop in Arlandria, Virginia,[12] that puts to the test this question:

> So in the workshop, they developed stories and scenarios. They developed scenes that were mostly "ghetto" scenes. Drug dealers, prostitutes, people cheating on each other. They did this after having bitched and moaned about the stereotypes that other people had about them—"People say we migos, that we in gangs, that we have a lot of babies, that we illegal." And then I asked them, "Are you any of those things?" The resounding answer was "No." Then I asked, "Raise your hand if you were born in this country." The majority of the hands went up. And then

I said, "For those of you that were born here, do you feel like an American?" and again the resounding answer was "No." "Why not?" I asked and immediately, as if it was rehearsed, all of them said in unison, "Because of our parents."

Are their parents holding them back or is society rejecting them? What does it take to feel "American?" Do they feel it is desirable or undesirable to feel American, or both? Are they Mai Nagai's "inassimilable" or "impossible subject?" Is their response reacting to the engrained racism and discrimination in our society, or are they simply feeling out this new third space, imagining these new hybrid or multiple identities, or both?

Quique more fully explores these multilayered, multifaceted, and multidimensional voices and experiences of immigrants in *Caminata: A Walk through Immigrant America*. As he explains in the *Caminata* program:

> It brings to life the voices of an older Salvadoran woman who came to the U.S. almost twenty years ago to be with her children; a young Russian woman who is fluent in Spanish; an Iraqi refugee who came to the U.S. via Saudi Arabia after the Gulf War; and an immigrant from the Central African Republic who came to the U.S. as a youth and has been a youth worker for over 20 years. *Chaos Standing/El Caos de Pie* takes an honest look at the positive and negative aspects of multiculturalism, focusing on three of the most culturally diverse neighborhoods [Quique adds: culturally saturated hoods] in Washington, D.C. Through six human emotions—pain, joy, fear, hate, love, and anger—the performance's main character and narrator takes the audience on a non-apologetic journey of what happens when people of different races, ethnic groups and identities are forced to coexist in very cramped quarters.

Through verbal arts performance, spoken resistance, Quique takes this "non-apologetic journey" where we can glean the possibility of a new American. He invites us to join this journey in the unpublished poem, asking,

> Where would you birth your dreams
> What will you name them
> William, Inti, Jessica *sueño*, hope
> What would you teach your dreams
> Obedience,
> the long path of struggle and fight
> the power of our might
> Believing to do right . . .
>
> What will you teach your dream
> To pull the trigger or to sob

Would you teach poetry to it or beat it with a rod . . .
Where would you birth your dream . . .

Would you birth
A new American dream
Will you . . .

But Quique cannot leave this as the last word, recognizing that the birthing of a new American dream is a longer conversation, as he admonishes the new hybrid generations on the margins of the final draft: "For me, we are creating a new spine (backbone); making history, while most of this new generation keeps behaving as if they were immigrants, not Americans." Is it that he senses in them by "acting like immigrants" a feeling of disempowered not-belonging, or that "our 'Boxes' and language/conceptions to describe things haven't caught up with the reality of where we are."[13] Do we have the words for defining for ourselves this new third space?

Closing Reflections

In this chapter, we have traveled with Quique Avilés in a journey through the immigrant experience, through formulating a Latino identity, to imagining the new American. His stance is broad and inclusive. He explains, "I am interested in everyone who comes to the United States—we have in common this country that receives us." Quique first and foremost is a social activist whose medium is verbal art, "verbal art as performance, as a species of situated human communication, a way of speaking" (Bauman, "Verbal Arts" 291). He wields a direct poetic style, often using English and Spanish vernaculars, and reaches out to engage the other to see behind the Veil, examine a cultural borderland, to reach into the wound, "the wound that will not heal and yet is forever healing." He points without pointing, names without naming, frames the question and turns it every direction, and dares imagine a new society. His goal is to get the audience to name, question, and imagine, to enter the world of verbal arts. His philosophy has always been that we are all artists, and young people looking for a voice have always circled around him. These young people, the pluricultural children of immigrants, whom he has mentored, have prompted him to create the new American imaginary, a rewriting of the story of the United States, which in the words of writer Junot Díaz is "a new country emerging that has been in the making for a long time" ("Moyers" 2). Quique concludes: "The here is now, the now is here—and I'm sorry to tell you . . . but . . . it looks brown."

In this chapter, I have experimented with a dialogic collaborative approach, combining different modes of discourse—conversation, analyses, and verbal arts. Throughout this reflexive cultural conversation, Quique and I both play the role of chroniclers, framing a period of time in the Latino community in Washington, D.C., which contextualizes the thematic progress from immigrant to Latino to new American. I provide and control authority over the overall scholarly frame of the chapter; however, Quique's poetic expression/ interpretation develops the argument. It is an approach that sits uncomfortably with mainstream scholarship because it resists conventional interpretation of text. The analysis emerges out of the interaction between author and subject-author. It requires an effort to allow the poet to have equal voice, producing a different order of knowledge that combines the historical, experiential, poetic. This approach offers but a fragment of the larger story of immigration, race, and cultural identity in D.C. and in the United States; however, it provides an immediacy that exposes the frailties, the unanswerables, and the discontinuities of this narrative. We encounter palpable realities, uncertainties, and imaginings, yet the exchange between us provides no final word, no neat resolution. What persists is a "flexible changeable text" that invites the possibility of more dialogue and questioning the question. In today's social and political milieu, this may be a place to pick up the conversation with others.

Notes

1 I have written this chapter in collaboration with Quique Avilés. He has closely read and commented on an early draft and reviewed final copy. I also had an extensive interview with him. Other quotes come from program booklets and flyers. Quique and I go a long way back to when he first arrived in D.C. from rural Salvador. I was first his mentor; we worked together at the Centro de Arte and on oral history projects with the Latin American Youth Center. But when I was researching the Salvadoran community for a Smithsonian Folklife Festival program, I asked for his collaboration as a researcher and presenter. In time, our relationship developed into co-mentorship, and now, I have more to learn from him than he from me. As I come more and more to appreciate the centrality of cultural and social advocacy in my work with grassroots communities and cultural representation, I realize I have much to learn from his approach, from his explorations, and from the worlds he has portrayed, remade.

2 Patrick B. Mullen is editor of a special double issue of the *Journal of Folklore Research*, which presents collaborative research in the form of dialoguing essays between Pat and Jesse Truvillion on the case of Henry Truvillion and John Lomax. In addition, several authors, including myself, respond to this dialogue. Vol. 37, No. 2/3 (119–122 and 207–214).

3 I use the term "popular culture" as it is usually applied in Latin America to refer to folklore or expressive/spoken traditions. However, when I reference some of Quique's inspirations, I use the term as it is usually understood in the United States, as "mass culture."

4 In a personal email, Sam Smith shared a clip from *The DC Gazette*, October 11, 2007: "Things have changed since Washington was celebrated in a popular 1975 funk song as "Chocolate City." (Email. 11 January 2013).

5 This chapter was inspired by the panel "Chicano/a and Latino/a Performance Art: A Cultural Resource in Times of Crisis" featured at the American Folklore Society Meeting in New Orleans in 2013. Performance artist José Torres Tama formed part of this panel.

6 In *Creating a Latino Identity in the Nation's Capital: The Latino Festival,* chapter 2I address the makeup and history of the immigrant Latin American community of Washington, D.C., that contributed to shaping a distinctive, multiethnic Latino identity in the Nation's capital.

7 Novelist Viet Thanh Ngyuyen describes this rupture of binary politics in the case of Vietnamese immigrants: "The majority of the Americans regarded us with ambivalence if not outright distaste, we being living reminders of their stinging defeat. We threatened the sanctity and symmetry of a white and black America whose ying and yang racial politics left no room for any other color, particularly that of pathetic little yellow-skinned people pickpocketing the American purse" (117).

8 According to Quique, to this day it continues to be called the Marion Barry Summer Youth Employment Program.

9 In a recent panel, "Los Treinta: Thirty Years of Salvadorans in D.C. through Music and Poetry," featured in the On the Move: Migration across Generations program at the 2017 Smithsonian Folklife Festival, Michelle observed with affection that the only people she has known longer than Quique are her family, SFF2017_0701_OTM_Story_Circle_0004.wav.

10 Quique recalls: "This is when I get 'discovered' by Guillermo Gómez Peña at the Smithsonian; he was part of an exhibit."

11 See Ngai. She observes: "The legal racialization of these ethnic groups' national origin cast them as permanently foreign and unassimilable to the nation. I argue that these racial formations produced 'alien citizens'—Asian Americans and Mexican Americans born in the United States with formal U.S. citizenship but who remained alien in the eyes of the nation" (8).

12 A building complex in Arlandria, Virginia, was nicknamed "Chirilagua" because it housed an immigrant community from Chirilagua, El Salvador. Quique describes it as one of the many "transported versions of a displaced D.C. barrio that picked the suburbs to be their final destination."

13 From a conversation with linguist Amelia Tseng and an NPR interview with her; National Public Radio, *Code Switch*, A Prescription for "Racial Imposter Syndrome," June 07, 2017, http://www.npr.org/podcasts/510312/codeswitch.

Works Cited

Anzaldúa, Gloria. *Borderlands/La Frontera: The New Mestiza.* 4th ed. San Francisco: Aunt Lute Books, 2012. Print.

Avilés, Quique. "Caminata: A Walk Through Immigrant America." Dir. B. Stanley. Washington, DC Arts Center. 2002; 2003. Cadaval Personal Collection.

——. *The Immigrant Museum.* Mexico City: PinStudio and Raíces de Papel, 2003. Print.

——. *Let the Poets Run the Country.* Washington, DC: n.p., n.d. Chapbook.

——. *Paper, Fabric, String and Poetry: Poems/Poesía.* Washington, DC: n.p., n.d. Chapbook.

Banks, Michelle. Personal communication, November 6, 2012.

Baron, Robert. "Public Folklore Dialogism and Critical Heritage Studies." *International Journal of Heritage Studies* 22.8 (2016): 588–606. Print.

Bauman, Richard. "Differential Identity and the Social Base of Folklore." *The Journal of American Folklore* 84 (1971): 31–41. Print.

———. "Verbal Arts as Performance." *American Anthropologist* 77 (1975): 290–311. Print.

Bhabha, Homi. *The Location of Culture*. London & New York: Routledge, 1994. Print.

DuBois, W.E.B. *The Souls of Black Folk*. New York: Dover Publications, 1994. Print.

———. *Writings: The Souls of Black Folk*. New York: Literary Classics of the United States, 1986. Print.

Cadaval, Olivia. *Creating a Latino Identity in the Nation's Capital: The Latino Festival*. New York: Garland Publishing, 1998. Print.

———. "A Lesson in Presenting: The Smithsonian Folklife Festival Model," *Journal of American Folklore* 515.1 (Spring 2017): 193–203. Print.

———. "Imagining a Collaborative Curatorial Relationship: A reordering of authority over representation." In *Curatorial Conversations: Cultural Performance and the Smithsonian Folklife Festival*, co-editor with Sojin Kim and Diana N'Diaye. Jackson: UP of Mississippi, 2016. Print.

Cantú, Norma E. "Living on the Border: A Wound that Will Not Heal." *Festival of American Folklife*. Ed. Peter Seitel. Washington, DC: Smithsonian Institution, 1994: 26–29. Print.

Carroll, Kenneth. *So What! for the white dude who said this ain't poetry*. Washington, DC: The Bunny and Crocodile Press, 1997. Print.

Green, Constance McLaughlin. *The Secret City: A History of Race Relations in the Nation's Capital*. Princeton: Princeton UP, 1967. Print.

Levs, Josh. "The New America: What the Election Teaches Us about Ourselves." CNN .com. November 10, 2012. Web.

Lynch, Acklyn. "Spoken Word. Introduction." *Bad Beats Sacred Rhythms: Poetry*. Washington, DC: D.C. Community Humanities Council, 1993. v–viii. Print.

Marcus, George E. "Introduction: Collaborative Analytics." *Theorizing the Contemporary*. https://culanth.org/fieldsights/1170-introduction-collaborative-analytics Web. July 27, 2017.

"Moyers & Company." Junot Díaz in Rewriting the Story of America. Billmoyers.com. Web. December 28, 2012.

Mullen, Patrick B. "A Word of Introduction: Collaborative Research in Context." *Journal of Folklore Research* 37.2/3 (2000): 119–122). Print.

———. "Collaborative Research Reconsidered." *Journal of Folklore Research* 37.2/3 (2000): 207–214). Print.

Ngai, Mae M. *Impossible Subjects: Illegal Aliens and the Making of Modern America*. New Jersey: Princeton UP, 2004. Print.

Ngjuyen, Viet Thanh. *The Sympathizer*. New York: Grove Press, 2015. Print.

The Pluralism Project of Harvard University. "From Diversity to Pluralism." Web. February 17, 2016.

Rodríguez, Ana Patricia. *Dividing the Isthmus*. Austin: U of Texas P, 2009. Print.

Smith, Sam. Personal communication, January 11, 2013.

Taylor, Nate. Quique Avilés Poetry Recordings, "Banana Plant." Mediafire.com. 2012. Mp3.

Torres Tama, José. "Chicano/a and Latino/a Performance Art: A Cultural Resource in Times of Crisis." American Folklore Society Meeting. New Orleans 2013. Presentation.

Tseng, Amelia. National Public Radio. *Code Switch*. A Prescription for "Racial Imposter Syndrome." June 7, 2017. http://www.npr.org/podcasts/510312/codeswitch Web.

Villalta, Nilda C. "Despiadada(s) Ciudad(es): El imaginario salvadoreño más allá de la guerra civil, el testimonio y la inmigración." Dissertation, University of Maryland at College Park. 2004. Print.

7

Performing Nation Diva Style in Lila Downs and Astrid Hadad's *La Tequilera*

● ●

K. ANGELIQUE DWYER

Mexican-American pop singer Lila Downs and Mexican cabaret artist Astrid Hadad perform nation in their unique and respectively different interpretations of Lucha Reyes's iconic 1930s Mexican *ranchera* song *La tequilera*.[1] In what follows, I will analyze these two musical renditions through the lens of performance studies, a field that stems from anthropology, sociology, and theater. Because the body as medium of expression is the primary focus of this field, gender, sexuality, race, ethnicity, are all ripe for analysis. The interdisciplinary methodology applied here embraces a cultural studies approach that fosters intersectionality with the objective of moving beyond static constructions of identity. I use the term "performing nation" to analyze how Downs and Hadad embody and enact specific regional and national, ethnic and racial identities through costume choice, vocal inflection, song choice, and imagery. Though both Downs and Hadad reference Mexico in their performances of *La tequilera,* they do so by using a different context and tone. While Hadad's interpretation is grounded in Mexico and aided by the use of humor and irony, Downs's rendition is based in a transnational and contemporary pop setting.

A common cultural practice in popular culture is to assert one's sense of belonging through music in connection to land. Both artists chose to do so by remaking a classic Mexican song in manners that break the traditional framework on nationalism/regionalism and ethnicity. George Lipsitz argues that popular culture needs to be further explored "as a mechanism of communication and education, as a site for experimentation with cultural and social roles not yet possible in politics" (17). Though for some, remaking a song might be considered as a way to ridicule, Linda Hutcheon poses otherwise by stating that an ironic commentary is made through parody applied in the twentieth century, because instead of merely incorporating the referenced piece structurally, a critical distance is taken. This is why Hutcheon defines parody as "ironic imitation" (7). How can this be applied to the artists in question? In the case of Downs, this parodic imitation is found in her ability to mimic accents and tones, referencing a particular ethnic/racial group and socioeconomic status within Mexico. In her performance of *La tequilera* Downs is creating musical mimesis of working class immigrants who cross the U.S.–Mexico border to earn money for their family. For Hadad parody takes place through an opposition between costuming/props and the song's lyrics. In her rendition of *La tequilera* Hadad dresses as a *soldadera* from the Mexican Revolution (an icon that represents female agency and gender equality) when singing about a woman who is a victim both of her lover and of alcoholism. Parody as ironic imitation can also be applied to the racial performance of identity (as Judith Butler poses for gender performance) because there is an opposition between Hadad singing a traditional song in a genre used to strengthen displays of nationalism (*la ranchera*) and not being a mestiza woman, but rather of Arabic descent as the daughter of Lebanese immigrants. With this in mind, how, then, does each artist perform nation in *La tequilera*? How do they articulate their racial and ethnic identities in these two varying performances and to what end?

Hugh Seton-Watson argues that "a nation exists when a significant number of people in a community consider themselves to form a nation or behave as if they formed one" (5). Benedict Anderson finds that the community imagines itself as a nation. He argues that nation is "an imagined political community" (6). Anderson believes a nation is defined as a community because "regardless of the actual inequality and exploitation that may prevail in each, the nation is always conceived as a deep, horizontal comradeship" (7). Nationalism, in other words, is a construction, created or "imagined" by a community of people who consider themselves members. Their identification with this nation begins in an anthropological manner, with rituals, rites of passage, and ceremonies. To this effect, Mexican anthropologist Roger Bartra states that "lo mexicano" as such does not exist; it too is imagined and constructed by artists, musicians, intellectuals, and writers. These imaginations and constructions have been proudly adopted by Mexicans or admirers of "lo mexicano" situated within the nation-state or abroad, who shout the lyrics to José Alfredo Jiménez's "El rey"; whistle during *ballet folklórico* performances; purchase Frida Kahlo prints; visit Rivera's, Siqueiros's, or Orozco's murals; or read Juan Rulfo's "Pedro Páramo." "Lo mexicano," Bartra argues "existe principalmente en los libros y discursos que lo describen o exaltan, y allí es posible encontrar las huellas de su origen" (*La jaula de la melancholia* 14) / "Mexicanness exists mainly in books and speeches that describe it and exalt it. It is there that it is possible to find footprints of its origin." Bartra calls Mexican nationalism a myth that is put into practice every day within Mexico and within the cultural imaginings of Mexicans abroad. Bartra also differentiates between nation and nationalism. Though closely linked, they should not be confused: "operan en planos diferentes" ("they operate on different planes") he argues, "una cosa es la territorialización del poder político que se concreta en el Estado-nación, y otra cosa distinta es la forma ... en que se legitima la constitución de un espacio nacional" (*Oficio mexicano* 104) ("one thing is the territorialization of political power consolidated in the nation-state and something very different is the way ... in which national space is legitimately constituted"). In order to analyze Downs's and Hadad's performances of nation, both of Bartra's interpretations must be taken into account; that is, how Downs and Hadad enact, embody, entail, both a territorial reference (socially ascribed notions of identity), as well as the emotions related to the practice of nationalism (self-ascribed identity). As Bartra reveals, nation becomes a narration of myths and stories.

In "Remaking the Nation," Sarah Radcliffe and Sallie Westwood define nationalism as "a movement whereby symbols or belief attribute communality of experience to people in a regional or ethnic category" (15). They argue that national identity is "a wider and more multidimensional category than nationalism, as national identity can exist within subjects (collectively or individually) without there being a process of mobilization around a specific goal. National identities can mean different things to different people even within one nation" (16). Américo Paredes's coinage of the term "Greater Mexico" emphasizes this notion, which is true for the artists in question, whose identities are multiple, liminal.[2] When interviewed, Hadad argues that in addition to being Mexican of Lebanese heritage, other cultures that influence her identity are the Mayan philosophy found in the Southern Peninsula where she grew up, and the culture of the Caribbean, due to geographic proximity. Downs, on the other hand, is Mexican American with a Mixteca mother and a British father, raised between Oaxaca and Minnesota.

In "The Heterogeneous Isthmus," Thomas Sigler, K. A. Aliset, and I support the latter by arguing that ethnic boundaries can be thought of as fluid rather than fixed, and self-ascribed rather than inherited. Comparative studies of ethnicity by Wimmer (2008) and others describe empirical evidence that many individuals choose to occupy multiple ethnic categories simultaneously, implying that ethnic belonging is not determined by exclusive social group closure. (3)

Cultural displays of nationalism differ considerably in that they are staged within the nation or in a different geographic location, and according to Kate Ramsey these play "a big part in twentieth century nationalisms more generally" (346). Radcliffe and Westwood argue that "there can be a disjuncture between the national place and the national identity; the 'space of the nation' can be imagined by populations which have no 'place' in which to express and consolidate that identity" (20). They suggest that these "dislocated" populations re-create ties between people and place in the new land by generating a social or symbolic space dedicated to belonging and identification. This space, according to the authors, might be fueled by nostalgia: "memories, acts of remembering, within spatial/territorial boundaries are crucially productive of national identities and these productions are revisioned within popular cultures through festivals, television, songs and stories articulated with current politics to re-cast the political imaginary" (83). Just as Edward Soja claims "we live in times where 'postmodern geographies' are a commonality" (22). In other words, our common surroundings—streets, bridges, oceans—and our understanding of them, should be envisioned as malleable, rather than permanent. This should also be applied to our understanding of identity politics, as currently in the United States—and in many regions of the world—there is a beautiful disjunction between territory, language, and culture. Radcliffe and Westwood argue, "Identities are not static," and dislocated subjects living in a "dislocated sense of space" have "multiple subject positions" (24), which change and expand in time. The inclusive ethnic identification Downs and Hadad each (very differently) employ is what Radcliffe and Westwood refer to as "multiple subject positionality" (24). The artists in question position themselves in a liminal, Greater Mexican space, which is extended to the audience through song. To reference Josh Kun's *Audiotopia*, through music and lyrics listeners can visualize space and place "as a geography of belonging and identification" (188). The music of Downs and Hadad creates a liminal space of articulation identities with "multiple subject positionality" within a national (Hadad) and transnational (Downs) setting. How then does each artist narrate nation through performance?

Mariachi, *norteña*, and *trío* are subgenres of popular Mexican music, often referencing, or stemming from folk music. For the purpose of this chapter I will make reference to these genres by the names of the songs that correspond to them (i.e., *rancheras*, *corridos*, and *boleros*, respectively). The *ranchera* in particular is a type of song that reflects nation. It is socially accepted as representative of the nation, within and abroad. A common theme for *rancheras*, beyond love, beauty, and nature, is patriotism. Classic songs that are nostalgic of Mexican nationalism are Jorge Negrete *rancheras* like "México lindo y querido" (1950) and, regionally, "Ay, Jalisco no te rajes" (1950). These are *mariachi* songs charged with folk flavor that invoke patriotism and a sense of national community, read as racially and ethnically homogeneous to the Mexican cultural mainstream. There are classic *rancheras* such as these that remain over the years and are reproduced over and over again by other classic artists, such as Lola Beltrán or Pedro Infante, or more contemporary artists, such as Vicente Fernández, Luis Miguel, Alejandro Fernández, Lucero, Pedro Fernández, and Alicia Villareal. By singing a song like *La tequilera*, Downs and Hadad are—in their own way—referencing the past (a specific time period where national identity was forged and strengthened) and applying to it a contemporary critical framework (that expands conceptions of racial and ethnic homogeneity according to place of origin) in hopes that their listeners will look inward, reflect upon, and take forth expanding identity categories in the future.

¡El mariachi loco quiere bailar!: The Genre

The *ranchera* is accompanied by the rhythm and tone of a *mariachi* band. Though, recognized on a national scale, regionally, this music is native of the state of Jalisco. *Mariachi,* like other genres within Mexican popular music, is commonly male oriented, though female artists, such as Selena, Tish Hinojosa, and Lydia Mendoza in the United States, or Alicia Villareal, Ana Bárbara, and Lucero in Mexico, are widely popular in this genre (as well as Astrid Hadad and Lila Downs today). *Rancheras* are traditionally performed in full *charro/a* attire: boots, slacks (or long narrow skirt) with silver detail on the sides, white shirt, colorful bowtie, jacket, and sombrero. This masculine attire claims the seriousness of the genre as a representation of the nation. Donald Andrew Henríques explains that in the Mexican postrevolutionary era "as regional musical traditions became central elements in the project of cultural nationalism, mariachi emerged as a marker of national identity and symbol of *mexicanidad*" (viii). This *mexicanidad* was, and is arguably still, of course, patriarchal in nature. Mary-Lee Mulholland furthers the notion by arguing that

> mariachi does not exist *a priori* or *a posteriori* of *mexicanidad*, rather they are co-constitutive, constantly drawing on each other in an impulse to move forward and create a sense of past. It is this seemingly metonymic link between mariachi and perceived Mexican "essence" that allows mariachi to perform idealized and,

at times, hegemonic representations of Mexican identity. This essence is characterized as mestizo, macho and rural. (250–251)

Norteño (also referred to as *Tejano*) is another genre within popular music, specifically from the northern region of Mexico. Musically, *corrido* songs are accompanied by a *banda norteña* incorporating polka and accordion sounds. Its attire makes reference to the border in that it is no different from that of a U.S. cowboy: boots, slacks, jacket, button-down shirt, and cowboy hat. Like *country* music in the United States, it is known for its engaging storytelling. Similar to *rancheras*, María Herrera-Sobek finds that the *corrido* is generally authored by males. She elaborates: "These male authors have incorporated mostly masculine-oriented themes and a strongly patriarchal ideology. Nevertheless, there is nothing inherently male in the *corrido* or its structure, which can and does feature female protagonists" (xvii). She goes on to mention that the female protagonists that take part in this subgenre are typically represented from a patriarchal perspective.[3] Reyes being originally from Guadalajara, Jalisco, it is of course appropriate that she sing a *ranchera* about drinking *tequila*. As we will read in *La tequilera*'s lyrics, the author has chosen to discuss love, a common theme for *rancheras* in general. But he discusses love from the perspective of a woman who is betrayed by her lover. The chosen motif to discuss this is *tequila*, used to drown out sorrows and numb the heart. In this sense, not Alfredo D'Orsay as lyricist, but rather, Reyes as performer, is ascribing what is typically considered the male social code onto herself as a female singer.

Pídala cantando: The Song

The 1930s and '40s were decades of postrevolution, nostalgic for the sense of nationalism that Octavio Paz argues was born during the 1910 revolution (129). Continuing the trend of expressing and celebrating nationalism, Alfredo D'Orsay wrote *La tequilera* in 1937. It is a relatively well known *ranchera*, written specifically for Mexican actress Lucha Reyes who paved the road for women in this male-dominated genre. *La tequilera* has been subsequently sung by a legacy of Mexican female performers, such as Lucha Villa, Chavela Vargas, and Lola Beltrán, to name but a few.

Rhythmically, as the title suggests, the song seems to follow the demeanor of someone who is inebriated. As sung by Lucha Reyes in the late 1930s, the listener can hear drunken hiccups between verses. Within her performances of the song, Reyes appeared on stage with a bottle of *tequila* in hand, taking big swigs, approaching the audience and toasting with them, which to this day is a common practice for *rancheras* as performed in public venues (cockfights, *plazas*, and restaurants). The lyrics of the song speak of Mexican identity and at the same time bring forth gender specifications:

LA TEQUILERA/*THE TEQUILA DRINKER* (1937)[4]

Borrachita de tequila llevo siempre el alma mía	*My soul is always drunk on tequila*
para ver si se mejora de esta cruel melancolía	*With the hope that this cruel melancholy will get better*
Ay, por ese querer, ¿pues qué le he de hacer?	*Because of that love, what am I to do?*
Si el destino me lo dio para siempre padecer	*If destiny gave him to me to always suffer*
Aunque me haya traicionado no lo puedo aborrecer	*Even though he betrayed me I can't hate him*
Como buena mexicana sufriré el dolor tranquila	*Like a good Mexican woman I will suffer in silence*
Al fin y al cabo mañana tendré un trago de tequila.	*After all tomorrow I will have a shot of tequila.*
Me llaman la tequilera	*They call me tequilera*
Como si fuera de pila	*As if it were my first name*
Porque a mi me bautizaron	*Because I was baptized*
Con un trago de tequila	*With a shot of tequila*
Ya me voy mejor	*I better leave*
Pos', ¿qué hago yo aquí?	*What am I doing here?*
Disque por la borrachera	*Because of being drunk*
Dicen todo lo perdí.	*They say I lost it all.*

Within a traditional framework, the archetype of the Mexican woman reveals that she is meant to suffer in silence. A common expression in response to suffering is "carga tu cruz" ("carry your cross"), so as to reference the importance of Catholicism in the construction of gender roles. Though, interestingly, the way the singer deals with this pain is through drinking tequila, which typically is associated with male social behavior. Reyes was a proud *tequila* drinker, appearing frequently on stage with a drink or a bottle of *tequila* in hand.[5] When seen in this light D'Orsay's title and lyrics reflect the persona that Reyes was already performing: a strong, postrevolutionary, feminist woman.

A common element in Mexican epistemology is that of surviving current climates instead of thinking of how to change things, how to better them, or how to succeed. This settling and conforming attitude comes through in the lyric: "pues, ¿qué le he de hacer?" ("what am I to do?") common in Mexican speech. A feminist reading would argue that this adds to the passivity of the female role with regard to her pain and her condition. Low self-worth is also highlighted in the singer's inability to hate her lover in spite of his unfaithfulness. This is revealed in the lyric "aunque me haya traicionado no lo puedo aborrecer" ("even though he betrayed me, I can't hate him"). In all of these examples, with the exception of the drinking, the female voice that *La tequilera* represents is very much a traditional and patriarchal mention of the Mexican female archetype. *Tequila* (a male noun in Spanish, and something that is consumed in an act of asserting masculinity) provides the female singer with the strength to withstand her current pain and her ongoing suffering in life. The day-to-day drinking helps her forget her current situation and withstand the pain her partner brings her. Perhaps if *La tequilera* stopped drinking she would realize the severity of her lover's betrayal; she would confront him on his actions and move on with her life. But instead, she wallows in her pain and drowns it out. *Tequila* then, gives *La tequilera* both agency and passivity, simultaneously. As a motif for this song, *tequila* enables the portrayal of a strong *macha* woman, yet at the same time the image of the drunk female calls attention to the construction of the passivity of the female role with a traditional framework. Though we might read Reyes's behavior in this performance as forward—since women in this time period were not commonly seen drinking *tequila* from a shot glass, much less directly from the bottle, or publicly intoxicated—at the same time, this behavior is stagnant, in that it perpetuates her abuse. Due to being inebriated, *La tequilera* remains in a lethargic and nostalgic state enabling her to be blinded from reality, which would in turn propel action and change; she is active, however, in that she drinks in the way a man traditionally would. Put differently, within this context, *tequila* allows *La tequilera* to straddle both male and female gender roles.[6] A similar reading may be applied when considering class and race. Though Reyes is an affluent performer, her public consumption of *tequila* from the bottle aligns her racially and ethnically with the people, as a mestiza woman. A performer wanting to capitalize on her European heritage (and whiteness) might have chosen wine or champagne as the motif for her song, not to mention a different musical genre entirely.

Surely the long list of singers who have interpreted this piece over the years gladly took on this role not only as an opportunity to present themselves as leading females in the world of Mexican film but because of the liberating effect caused by embodying *La tequilera*. On the radio today we will find a different manner of female assertion, going so far as to view men as expendable, put in the words of Beyoncé in "Irreplaceable" (2006), "You must not know about me . . . I can get another man in a minute . . . I can find another you by tomorrow," or even to the extent of finding men as odious, as sung by Paquita la del Barrio in "Rata de dos patas" (2010), "Rata de dos patas . . . te odio y te desprecio ("Two legged rat . . . I hate and despise you."). As true to the era, D'Orsay does not go this far, his (somewhat) strong and independent female character is doomed to suffer forever: "el destino me lo dio para siempre padecer" ("destiny gave him to me to always suffer"). This lyric provides a dual reading, as the direct object pronoun "lo" can be understood as both her lost lover and/or as *el tequila*, which suggests that she will be a drunk for life. In both cases this notion of destiny is patriarchal in that it denies the woman the right to actively construct her own present life. The definite article "el" in "el tequila" also causes ambiguity in terms of Reyes referencing it as a drink that raises her up when all else in her life is suffering, or as the love that fails her. In this sense, the song becomes a lover's lament. As a farewell to her listeners, *La tequilera* admits that: "por la borrachera dicen todo lo perdí" ("because of being drunk they say I lost it all"). This final lyric suggests that the singer also feels responsible for the betrayal of her lover due to her drinking. At the end of the song, in the eyes of others (and it seems that in the eyes of the singer as well) she has lost it all: love, respect, and above all, dignity.

La reina de la canción ranchera: The Artist

Lucha Reyes was a young and attractive actress who began her musical and film career in the early 1920s in the United States, later returning to Mexico. She released her first LP while touring in Europe, introducing Europeans to Mexican music as a soprano singer. Upon her return to Mexico she recovered from a severe throat infection caught during her time abroad. She rested her soprano voice for one year, which resulted in the voice change that led her to become a *mariachi* singer. Interestingly, Reyes took *mariachi* music to Europe even before the talk of Global or World Music, as is studied in George Lipsitz's *Dangerous Crossroads*.[7] Within Mexico her presence shocked many, as Mexican society was not accustomed to seeing a female singer lead a *mariachi* band. Compensating for her petite figure was her strong voice and assertive attitude on stage, drinking and smoking as she sang along with the all-male *mariachi* band. Adding shock value, she spoke openly about drinking *tequila* regularly, and often did shots publicly, inviting the audience to join in. In the early 1930s she married film producer Félix Martín Cervantes (though later remarried twice) and her film career began in earnest. She died tragically at thirty-eight years of age due to alcohol and drug abuse.

During her performances Reyes dressed as a *soldadera*. This fact, along with her open and abundant drinking, references nostalgia for the Mexican Revolution. It also plays into the post-Revolution nation-shaping period. According to Alicia Arrizón, the *soldadera* figure "bears witness to the subject of feminism in the U.S./Mexico Borderlands" (70). Furthering this, Herrera-Sobek argues that "today, among women in both Mexico and the United States, *Adelita* is a symbol of action and inspiration, and her name is used to mean any woman who struggles and fights for her rights" (33). It must be noted that Reyes chooses to perform *La tequilera* dressed as a *soldadera*, and not in *charra* attire—as contemporary artists like Lucero and Alicia Villareal do— which would be the appropriate wardrobe to match the genre. In terms of class and race, *charro/a* attire is representative of national culture (high art), whereas the *soldadera* attire pertains to the clothing of a peasant (low art). This choice continues to align Reyes with the people, as a *campesina* from the agave fields of Jalisco, rather than an affluent mestiza woman who has studied opera and who has performed throughout Europe. It may be argued that by positioning herself in alignment to the marginalized (a *campesina*) with poor values (who drinks *tequila* in public) she finds the freedom to break traditional performance roles for women of her era. Additionally, this choice remits directly to what Herrera-Sobek notes earlier and furthers my analysis of Reyes as a performer who straddles both the male and female plain: she uses the *soldadera* attire (in addition to the open drinking) as a means of resistance, counterposing the passivity inscribed by the lyricist. Lucha Reyes sets the model as performer and originator for the female *ranchera* singer. How do subsequent performers who sing the same songs and address the same genre enter into dialogue with her performances and iconic image?

La nopalera: Astrid Hadad

Astrid Hadad is a Mexican cabaret artist of Lebanese descent who leads shows that incorporate song, stand-up comedy, audience participation and interaction, with multiple and elaborate costume changes.[8] As an artist, Hadad incorporates *ranchera* and *bolero* music into politically and socially committed satire in a 1930s cabaret style. Hadad seduces the spectator from the start of her performance, be it through her lyrics, her deep voice, her colorful costumes and makeup, her inversion of gender roles, her uncensored parodies, and her playfulness. Roselyn Constantino argues that Hadad critiques repressive systems of power by rejecting bureaucracy, elitism, and inflexibility. She rejects the government, religion, and family as institutions. She singles out the *vacas sagradas*: politicians, the president, the Pope, the conservative upper classes, and any other entity of hegemonic or social power (Constantino and Taylor 191). Hadad follows a line of assertive Mexican female writers and artists, such as Rosario Castellanos, Sabine Berman, Elena Garro, Elena Poniatowska, Jesusa Rodríguez, and Regina Orozco, to name a few. Gastón Alzate poetically and accurately describes her work:

> Sobre el cuerpo de Astrid se desarrolla no sólo la actividad de una orquesta de símbolos y voces, sino también un laberinto que exige que el espectador circule a lo largo de él para interpretar los diferentes elementos. Este laberinto es la ciudad

de México, la geografía, el escenario donde se confrontan las diferentes culturas que viven y hacen parte del territorio multicultural y multiétnico de la República Mexicana. (46)[9]

Hadad opens her interpretation of *La tequilera* by staggering onto stage center with a bottle of *tequila* in hand and takes her place before a rural landscape composed of a fake rock and a cactus.[10] Hadad's version of the song takes its artistic freedom in the performance aspect of the piece, which parodies and critiques Mexican gender roles and national culture. In Hadad's interpretation of *La tequilera* the song mimics Reyes's sweet voice inflection. She begins the song with a *mariachi* band coming on stage playing "El jarabe tapatío" (the Mexican Hat Dance) and then transitions to *La tequilera*. It is important to mention that "El jarabe tapatío" is a classic folk piece that within Mexico represents the state of Jalisco. Taken abroad, this song stands in for the nation. It is translated as "The Mexican Hat Dance" because the couple dances around the man's sombrero. The song concludes with the female dancer picking up the hat from the ground and placing it on her own head, arguably signifying she has obtained her partner's love and commitment. The instruments highlighted throughout *La tequilera* are violins, trumpets, and guitars, central to the *mariachi* sound. An artistic freedom that Hadad takes in the musical arrangement is that she adds a rock-infused chorus: "Tequilera, tequilera, rock, rock, rock" with a dissonant punk beat, adding irony to her performance of nation, as her interpretation of this song is anything but rock. By adding punk rock music, however, Hadad is referencing the contemporary and the marginalized. When this discrepancy between what is said and what is meant is applied to theater and to comedy, the discrepancy lies between the spectator(s) and the performer, incorporating certain elements like absurdity to this effect. Hadad inverts the meaning of the lyrics by her avant-garde gender-bending costuming.

Hadad's choice of costuming is a fusion of regional and pop culture elements. Dressed in an outfit resembling the typical costume of the state of Puebla "La China Poblana," Hadad wears a sparkling bustier and a red skirt made of a Virgen de Guadalupe print. From head to toe she becomes a symbol of the Mexican flag. By wearing the Virgen de Guadalupe on her skirt she is disempowering religion and deconstructing it as a symbol of Mexico. The red felt *charro* hat, the gun, and the holster, stand in for male (hyper) sexuality, whereas the makeup, long hair, and bangle earrings represent the feminine qualities of her persona. The result of this becomes the presence of a woman that is in control of her sexuality and sensuality; her bare arms and shoulders along with the bustier, add to this effect. In this particular costume Hadad references *la Adelita* or *soldadera* of the Mexican Revolution so as to embody this strength of character needed for her rendition of *La tequilera*, and to reference Reyes's original performance. In Semichon and Favre's documentary of the same title

La tequilera, Hadad speaks about her admiration toward Reyes, who she grew up listening to on the radio. Hadad states that in the 1940s Reyes was forbidden in some households: "sentían que era muy poco honrado oír a una mujer que cantara como los hombres" ("people felt that it was not honorable to listen to a woman sing like a man").

In *La tequilera*'s chorus, Hadad drags out the typical Mexican *grito*, or cry, of sorrow, to the point of becoming a child's whining cry, creating a response of laughter from the audience. Laura G. Gutiérrez notes Hadad's performances as "camp" because she uses excessive theatricality and same-sex masquerade to exaggerate the performance of women and critique gender roles in Mexico ("Reframing the *Retablo*" 73). Playing on this, and on the notion of irony as a tool aiding her performance of nation, Hadad takes a short whip and begins to whip herself as she sings: "Como buena mexicana sufriré el dolor tranquila" ("like a good Mexican woman I will suffer in silence"), again, received by her audience with laughter. With this, Hadad suggests that women put themselves in a position of becoming victimized. Her version of the song is altered through its performance, which adds a critical playfulness to it. This can only be interpreted as parodying the role of the woman D'Orsay creates; yet it also sheds light on Reyes's own characterization of herself. The body language Hadad uses in her interpretation of the piece is of a confident woman who plays with gender specifics. Her raspy voice comes off as masculinized, unlike that of Reyes, who sang with a strong, yet feminine, semisoprano voice. From a gender-bending standpoint, Hadad takes lyrics that are more consistent with the archetype of "la mujer abnegada," or the victimized woman, and sings them from the perspective of Freud's "phallic woman" (24). This idea of the phallic woman can be found in performers like Chavela Vargas, whose voice has been described as "la voz áspera de la ternura" ("the rough voice of tenderness") and who is known for her early cross-dressing, cigar smoking, drinking, and gun holstering. An open alcoholic and lesbian, Vargas continues to set the ground for subsequent female performers like Paquita la del Barrio, a rough mainstream Mexican *ranchera* singer. Commonly seen singing with a bottle of tequila in hand, Paquita la del Barrio screams her lyrics to "Rata de dos patas," and barks at the lost lover who betrayed her "Ojalá te mueras, perro desgraciado" ("I hope you die, disgraceful dog").

La tequilera is included in Hadad's 1995 album *¡Ay!*. The cover reveals a painted headshot of Hadad wearing a red felt *sombrero de charro* with silver accents. Her hair is braided, her earrings are big, and her makeup is dark and heavy, adding to the deep emotion within *ranchera* music. Physically, Hadad's head is raised, and she is singing what seems to be a *grito*, essential to the performance of this genre. On the cover, the words "y ha sido llorar y llorar" ("it's been nonstop crying") are placed by Hadad's mouth, representing the words she sings. Her body is submerged in water (or what could be imagined as tears) all the way up to her neck, read as the victimized position of suffering into which Mexican women allow themselves to be placed. In spite of the suffering and the complaining, the singing always continues: "carga tu cruz" ("carry your cross").

In Hadad's parodic performance, her intent is not to ridicule the tragedy and passion of Reyes's *ranchera* but rather to shock her audience by taking a classic fragment of national culture and altering it so as to make a commentary on gender constructions within the nation. Stephany Slaughter argues that cabaret artists such as Jesusa Rodríguez (Hadad's mentor) and Carmen Ramos "use revolutionary iconographies to imagine alternative present realities to traditional concepts of sex/gender/sexuality as they tease the spectator into considering gender in performance and gender as performance" (48). The genre of cabaret enables Hadad to critique the systems of power in a manner that is socially acceptable to her Mexican audiences, which is through comedy and irony. As the saying goes: "de broma en broma, la verdad se asoma" ("truth peeks out, joke by joke").

Entre copa y copa: Lila Downs

Lila Downs is a Mexican American singer born of a British father and a Mixtec mother. She grew up in Oaxaca and in Minnesota, incorporating her multicultural experiences into her songs, which she sings in English, Spanish, Mixteca, Zapoteca, and Maya. Though Downs released her first album entitled *La Sandunga* featuring Oaxacan folk songs, she is a trained opera singer with a background in jazz and anthropology. Downs's musical repertoire is vast and varied and includes several Grammy nominations and awards in the Contemporary World Music category, which is what led to the international marketing of her musical style. She incorporates a wide array of instruments, musical influences, and vocal inflections, and, in a constant manner, brings up the relations between music and language to culture and land. Brenda M. Romero states that Downs "creates stories within stories. She moves from one voice to another, from one sound icon to another. . . . she weaves a tapestry of sound, like a pattern on a Mixtec textile made audible" (259). *La tequilera* is included in Downs's 2006 album *La Cantina*. The songs in this album are all considered Mexican *cantina* classics. In other words, they are songs that speak of a certain Mexican cultural "authenticity." As Romero describes above, Downs takes these culturally authentic classic songs and weaves them with contemporary rhythms from different places, making them into something that modern-day audiences enjoy. Downs serves her listeners a sampler of World Music in a marketable pop package evidenced in the cover of the album, which features an Andy Warhol-like color effect on Downs's portrait where the artist is featured embracing her guitar, looking off to the horizon. The words "entre copa y copa" (between drinks) underline the image. In the center, the name of the artist appears in L.A. urban *cholo* calligraphy, followed by the name of the album, *La Cantina.*

Because of the musical diversity applied in Downs's work, critics were unable to categorize her music under only one label or genre; thus the terms "World Culture" and "World Music" were used and imposed by her critics. Due to her marketing by the Grammys as a "World Artist," and her international success, Downs's rendition of *La tequilera* takes artistic freedom to alter a classic authentic Mexican piece and turn it into a more widely consumed Latino-fused hit. Though, as we know, the song was not written as a *corrido* or ballad, Downs changes the rhythm of the song to a *norteña*, evident in the bouncy polka rhythm and the distinct sound of the accordion. Due to bands like Los Tigres del Norte, *norteño* music is often associated with migrant peoples who cross the U.S.–Mexico border in search of upward social mobility. As immigrants themselves they have spent their careers documenting through song the journeys and challenges that migrant people face.[11] This reveals and confirms that Downs's choice of altering the rhythm of the song to a *norteña* is not by chance, but rather a conscious choice as a transnational performer. Lipsitz's *Dangerous Crossroads* is based on the premise that the power of transnational capital means that all of us as listeners must become transnational too.[12] The book deals with the crossroads of contemporary culture, focusing on place and politics. Lipsitz examines a plurality of practices within popular/world music to understand how popular culture contains different meanings in different countries. Vocally, Downs applies a sense of musical mimesis (or ironic imitation, as was mentioned early on in the essay with regard to Linda Hutcheon's take on parody) by attempting to re-create particular voices commonly found in the local towns of northern Mexico. As Brenda Romero notes, "Lila is skillful at duplicating vocal timbres that resonate with ethnicities and she likes to explore the different dimensions of the voice and styles that predominate in particular areas of Mexico" (259). The vocal performance in *La tequilera* seems to invoke famous female voices of both *norteña* and *ranchera* music, still managing to keep her own style. Downs's rendition of the song also employs a 1990s techno beat. The fusion of both techno and *norteña*, seen formerly in Selena's 1994 "Techno Cumbia," takes on a modernizing effect, making the song more contemporary and adaptable to mainstream culture.

Unlike Hadad, Downs does not seem to question or critique the lyrics she sings. She sings them straightforwardly, suggesting that her agenda is not to discuss gender issues, but rather to provide her wide audiences with a bit of musical *mestizaje.* There *is* however an implicit presence of sexuality and gender, as well as race and class within her choice of genre. The notion of *norteño* music being male dominated has been changing within recent decades, typically due to the presence of sexy, attractive, young female singers in all male bands: Selena y *los Dinos* and Alicia Villaseñor with *Límite*, both big hits on either side of the border, and of course the female soloist, Jenni Rivera. Similarly, *norteño* music, as a genre that features the stories (*corridos*) of illegal immigration, drug trafficking, and other illicit activities, can be aligned to the marginalized. This is not to say that the consumption of this music is only limited to the working class, but rather that it celebrates those placed by society in the periphery.

What Downs does in *La tequilera* is true to her style as an artist: she takes fragments of classic/folk songs and fuses them to create something different and new. Though this musical intertextuality is a current trend, Downs's style is unique. She manages to erase land specificity, so inevitably present in folklore and folk music, enabling her to contribute to the creation of Greater Mexico cultural production. In other words, her music beyond the borderlands and into the U.S.–Mexican cultural imaginary. The objective is to reach a greater audience, making the final product available (and consumable) by all, regardless of ethnicity.

La última y nos vamos: Conclusion

Both Downs and Hadad's interpretations of Reyes' *La tequilera* place the song in an alternative field for different reasons: the former, due to musical arrangement, and the latter due to performance. Through their distinct versions of *La tequilera* both artists are performing nation and national identities as mobile and malleable, rather than fixed. Downs takes fragments of original folk culture (displaying an aura of cultural "authenticity") combined with contemporary rhythms, which result in a piece that contributes to the construction of new Mexicana/Latina culture. Her intention is to package her music in a "culture-ish" wrapping for an international market. Her priority as an artist is her music. Downs's performance alludes to a transnational, broader context of cultures that travel, traverse, and are transient within the musical genres she fuses. Her performance of national identities creates homage to plurality and diversity as both cultural and economic wealth. Her objective is to invite her audience not necessarily to reconstruct their (national and ethnic) identity but rather to inclusively overlook (geographic) borders. She opens a space of performance with the objective of reaching greater cultural (transnational) understanding. The identity Downs creates and enacts in *La tequilera* is that of a modern, commercial artist who has the ability to take iconic elements of culture and update them to create popular music that appeals to a wider market.

The identity Hadad creates and enacts in *La tequilera* is that of a cabaret artist who wants to create social critique and awareness, not through her musical talent and vocal range but through the performance of the songs she includes in her repertoire. Hadad is aware that her marketing as an artist is not due to her singing ability, but rather to the construction of cultural and social messages she produces through all of the elements she combines in her shows: costuming, performance, and critique. Hadad prioritizes her sociopolitical agenda over her music. What she does in *La tequilera* is also representative of her stylistically: Hadad takes original songs and provokes social consciousness by altering the performance and staging of each piece. She uses irony as a theatrical tool to aid her in inverting the meaning of what she is singing, and creating a space for negotiating questions of gender and politics. This irony, however, is not a direct attack on her audience; rather she filters it through other means, such as humor and parody, revealing how well she knows the Mexican public she addresses. Any other way of approaching social critique within Mexico (e.g., direct didacticism) would be disregarded by the public. The risk, however, is that the humor, costuming, and overall entertainment quality of her performance overpower the message. Hadad's performance of national identities suggests that Mexicans must become aware of the constructed nature of their society, from gender roles to politics, to religion. She demands (through irony, laughter, and shock value) that her audience reflect, question, and critique. She implies that men, but especially women, possess the ability to change, to reconstruct the roles that have been imposed on them by a patriarchal hegemonic society. She brings to mind that national and ethnic identities can question, change, negotiate, and move forward, as they rightly should.

In conclusion, Downs's objective is to perform a transnational nation for a world market. By using the *norteña* and fusing it with other beats she is performing a nation that is in movement, constantly changing, evolving, and transmuting. Hadad's objective is to look within the nation and its capital to create an ironic commentary on it. Hadad performs nation for the nation. She performs a straightforward nationalism that is altered in its staging, costuming, and presentation. Her message is to reflect, question, and deconstruct central Mexican cultural elements, only to reconstruct and recontextualize them, inviting her public into the process.

The contemporary panorama of Greater Mexico is as a space of articulation for liminal, plural, and mobile identities who need not mold into rigid categories of (racial, sexual, gender, ethnic, religious) identity. The artists in question perform nation(s) as interconnected. Like rivers in constant flow—often parting into brooks and streams, rising, and overflowing—Downs and Hadad's work models what the process of identification *should* look like because it is equitable and necessary for the society of today.

Notes

I wish to thank Claire Fox, who was instrumental in the conceptualization and early writing of this chapter. I am indebted to her guidance and mentoring. I am fortunate to have seen both Downs (May 2007 in Madison, Wisconsin, October 2012 in Iowa

City, Iowa, and October 2012 in St. Paul, Minnesota) and Hadad (May 2007 in Mexico City) perform live, which I highly recommend for anyone studying U.S./ Mexican intercultural studies. As someone who has personally dealt with identity negotiation, I thank these artists for continuing to inspire me.

1   Though Downs and Hadad are not performance artists per se their work can be described as *performative.* In this analysis I make use of Richard Schechner's broad and inclusive definition of performance, which reads that "performance must be construed as a 'broad spectrum' or 'continuum' of human actions ranging from ritual, play, sports, popular entertainments, performance arts, and everyday life performances to the enactment of social, professional, gender, race, and class roles, and on to healing and shamanism, the media, and the internet. . . . The underlying notion is that any action that is framed, presented, highlighted or displayed is a performance" (2). Schechner differentiates between what *is* a performance piece and what can be studied or seen *as* performance. My analysis stems from the latter.

2   Greater Mexico, a term coined by Américo Paredes in his 1958 study *With His Pistol in His Hand,* was initially used to describe the American Southwest or the U.S.–Mexico border, an area that Gloria Anzaldúa later named the Borderlands. The concept of Greater Mexico was further explored by José Limón, in *American Encounters,* who explains that the term "refer(s) to all Mexicans, beyond Laredo and from either side, with all their commonalities and differences" (3). Héctor Calderón calls it "América Mexicana" in his book *Narratives of Greater Mexico,* in which he studies the work of Chicano writers and their incorporation of the Borderlands in their work either as a location, as a subject, or as a framework. In "Expanding the Borderlands," Lynn Stephen suggests that due to current scholarship the term Greater Mexico may be used broadly to incorporate other cities within the United States that have large populations of Spanish speakers of Mexican heritage, like Chicago, New York, or Philadelphia

3   Jenni Rivera is an example of a female *corrido* singer who resisted the male-dominated perspective within the genre with songs like "Los ovarios" and "Jefa de Jefas." Rivera included a *corrido* rendition of *La tequilera* in her album *Mi vida loca.* The fact that she recorded the song as a *corrido* is not surprising for two reasons: (1) it is the genre for which she is most well known; (2) as an American singer with Mexican ancestry who asserts her identity from within the borderlands, this northern genre makes sense.

4   All translations are my own.

5   See *La tequilera* by Semichon and Favre.

6   Susana Vargas Cervantes' "Performing Mexicanidad: Criminality and Lucha Libre" highlights the limits of Mexican masculinity and femininity. It focuses on "redressing the raced, classed, gendered and sexualized limits of mexicanidad" (2). Though Vargas is analyzing lucha libre and criminality, they are similar to music and cinema in that gender performances become a spectacle for the nation.

7   For more on how mariachi traveled to Europe, see Henríques's full dissertation.

8   For more information on Lebanese immigrants in Mexico, see Liz Hamui-Halabe's "Christians from Lebanon and Jews from Syria in Mexico," *Immigrants & Minorities: Historical Studies in Ethnicity, Migration and Diaspora.* 16.1-2 (1997); and Theresa Alfaro Velcamp's *So far from Allah, So close to Mexico: Middle Eastern Immigrants in Modern Mexico.* Austin: U of Texas P, 2007.

9   Upon Astrid's body, not only is the activity of an orchestra of symbols and voices developed, but also a labrynth that demands the spectator to circle around it to

interpret its different elements. That labrynth is Mexico City, the geography: the stage where different cultures are confronted and become living part of the multicultural and multiethnic land that is the Mexican Republic.

10 Hadad performs *La tequilera* at a cabaret in Mexico City called La Bodega del Bataclán. The clip I analyze in this chapter is found in a documentary of the same name, made by French directors Semichon and Favre in 2000. Several different versions of *La tequilera* performed by Hadad can be found on YouTube in addition to Semichon and Favre's documentary: (1) on May 2010, a live version performed in the Historic Zocalo of Tlaxcala was uploaded. Using the same costume and attire, Hadad begins this performance reciting her anti-imperialistic version of "The Lord's Prayer" that reads like this: "al Tío Sam que estás en el país del norte: Santificado sea el nuevo orden. Vénganos tus dólares, Hágase tu voluntad, así en EE.UU. como en el mundo entero. Dános hoy nuestro McDonald's de cada día, perdóna a los cubanos y a los Yankees, como nosotros perdonamos a los de la DEA. No nos dejes caer en el nacionalismo. Y líbranos de los hombres de negocios chinos y japoneses. In God we trust. Shalom. Amen. Salúd." ("Uncle Sam who art in the northern country: hallowed be thy new order. Give us your dollars, Thy will be done in the United States as well as worldwide. Give us our daily McDonald's, forgive the Cubans and the Yankees [Americans] as we forgive the DEA. Lead us not into nationalism and deliver us from Chinese and Japanese businessmen. In God we Trust. Shalom. Amen. Cheers"). Immediately following, "La tequilera" begins and Hadad takes a big swig from her bottle of tequila and staggers across the stage; (2) On August 3, 2011, a live version was performed in San José del Cabo, Baja California Sur, in celebration of International Women's Day. The performance is the same as described in item 1; (3) On November 29, 2013, a live version performed in Obregón Plaza in Culiacán, Sinaloa, was uploaded. In this performance (with the exception of the red felt *charra* hat) Hadad's attire does not match her usual costume for this song, revealing that it might have been performed as an encore. Before reciting her version of "Tío Sam," she begins by educating the audience about the Mexican American War in 1848, and critiques Mexican's colonial graciousness even when being abused or taken advantage of. As the intro to *La tequilera* is being played, she recites a coquettish poem: "Cada vez que cae la tarde, me pongo a pensar y digo: 'pa' que me sirve la cama, si tú no duermes conmigo'. Salúd, Culiacán." ("Each afternoon I stop to think and I say: "what good is my bed when you don't sleep in it with me." Cheers, Cuilacán"). The audience roars in response; (4) On October 24, 2011, a live version of the song was uploaded featuring a performance at the Hollywood Forever Cemetery on October 22, 2011 in honor of the Day of the Dead. The song and corresponding choreography were unaltered, but because it was performed as an encore, she wore a costume that pertained to the previous song; (5) At Global Fest 2016 in New York, Hadad performs the same song and choreography in an all-black leather *quinceañera*-type dress, with a black *charra* hat. This non-corresponding costume, she indicates live, is due to "the Mexican economic recession." This is the first YouTube performance found where Hadad addresses her American audience in English. Before the song she recites her translation into English of "Tío Sam."

11 See "El santo de los mojados" (Pacto de Sangre. 2004); "Mis dos patrias" and "El mojado acaudalado" (Jefe de Jefes. 1997); "Tres veces mojado" and "La jaula de oro" (La banda del carro rojo. 2006).

12 Though the *rebozo* is a national symbol that goes beyond social classes, it is important to mention that it has been an iconic accessory associated with the peasant, the working class, and the indigenous woman. For these women, the *rebozo* has more of a practical use as it guards their face and neck from the hot sun, it warms their shoulders in the evening, it covers their head during the Catholic mass (a sign of respect performed by women), it carries their babies on their back while they work, and it provides privacy when they nurse their children. For the women who belong to upper and elite social classes, the *rebozo* is used during mass, while praying, or to accessorize an outfit. The main difference besides the utility versus accessory aspect I mention is the fabric. A traditional *rebozo* is made of an affordable and thin textile that is dyed and can then be embroidered. The fabrication of *rebozos* and other similar clothing is a common practice for peasant and indigenous women in their villages or in the big cities as a way to earn a living from tourists. These women typically use dark and wide *rebozos*, which allow for its multiple uses, and little embellishment. The *rebozos* used by women of upper social classes are typically embroidered, multicolored, and delicate, often not as wide. They are very similar to the *mantilla*, worn in Spain as they both have tassels on the end and are worn in similar cultural practices. The main difference between these is the shape: while *mantillas* are triangular, *rebozos* are rectangular. The comparison between *rebozos* used by upper-class women in Mexico as similar to a *mantilla* worn in Spain brings up the notion of class and race. In Mexico, traditionally the upper classes are socially constructed as being "more Spanish" (read: lighter skinned) than indigenous, and the working classes are socially constructed as being "more indigenous" (read: darker skinned). Middle class is traditionally accepted as a combination of both (read: mestizos), though one can be more predominant than the other based on skin color or surnames (e.g., Márquez de Prado is a surname of Spanish descent). Contrary to socioeconomics in the U.S., which easily allows for upward social mobility due to preapproved credit, Mexico's middle class is lower in number, making the gap greater between the working class and the upper/elite social status.

Works Cited

Alzate Cuervo, Gastón Adolfo. *Teatro de cabaret: imaginarios disidentes.* Irvine: Gestos, 2002. Print.

Anderson, Benedict. *Imagined Communities: Reflections on the Origin and Spread of Nationalism.* Revised Edition. London: Verso, 1983. Print.

Arrizón, Alicia. *Latina Performance: Traversing the Stage.* Bloomington: Indiana UP, 1999. Print.

Bartra, Roger. *La jaula de la melancolía: Identidad y metamorfosis del mexicano.* D.F.: Grijalbo, 1987. Print.

——. *Oficio mexicano.* D.F.: Grijalbo, 1988. Print.

Calderón, Héctor. *Narratives of Greater Mexico: Essays on Chicano Literary History, Genre, and Borders.* Austin: U of Texas P, 2004. Print.

Cervantes, Susana Vargas. "Performing Mexicanidad: Criminality and Lucha Libre." *Crime Media Culture* 6.2 (2010): 185–203. Print.

Constantino, Roselyn, and Diana Taylor, Eds. *Holy Terrors: Latin American Women Perform.* Durham: Duke UP, 2003. Print.

Downs, Lila. *La Cantina*, Narada World, 2006. LP.

Freud, Sigmund. *Introductions to Lectures on Psycho-Analysis*. New York and London: W. W. Norton & Company, 1989. Print.

Gutiérrez, Laura. *Performing Mexicanidad*. Austin: U of Texas P, 2010. Print.

——. "Reframing the *Retablo*: Mexican Feminist Critical Practice in Ximena Cuevas' *Corazón Sangrante*" *Feminist Media Studies*, 1.1 (2001): 73–90. Print.

Hadad, Astrid y Los tarzanes. *¡Ay!*, Rounder Records, 1990. LP.

Henríques, Donald Andew. "Performing Nationalism: Mariachi, Media and Transformation of a Tradition (1920–1942)." Dissertation. University of Texas at Austin, 2006. Print.

Herrera-Sobek, María. *The Mexican Corrido: A Feminist Analysis*. Bloomington: Indiana UP, 1990. Print.

Hutcheon, Linda. *A Theory of Parody: The Teachings of Twentieth Century Art Forms*. Urbana: U Illinois P, 2000. Print.

Kun, Josh. *Audiotopia: Music, Race and America*. Berkeley: U California P, 2005. Print.

Limón, José. *American Encounters: Greater Mexico, the United States, and the Erotics of Culture*. Boston: Beacon Press, 1998. Print.

Lipsitz, George. *Dangerous Crossroads: Popular Music, Postmodernism and the Poetics of Place*. London, New York: Verso, 1994. Print.

Mulholland, Mary-Lee. "Mariachi, Myths and Mestizaje: Popular Culture and Mexican National Identity." *National Identities* 9.3 (2007): 247–264. Print.

Paredes, Américo. *With His Pistol in His Hand*. Austin: U of Texas P. 1958. Print.

Paz, Octavio. *Laberinto de la soledad*. México: Fondo de Cultura Económica, 1959. Print.

Radcliffe, Sarah, and Sallie Westwood. *Remaking the Nation: Place, Identity and Politics in Latin America*. London: Routledge, 1996. Print.

Ramsey, Kate. "Vodou, Nationalism, and Performance: The Staging of Folklore in MidTwentieth-Century Haiti." *Meaning in Motion*. Ed. Jane Desmond. Durham: Duke UP, 1997. Print.

Reyes, Lucha. *15 Éxitos de Lucha Reyes*, BMG, 1997. LP.

Rivera, Jenni. *Mi vida loca*, Fonovisa Inc., 2007. LP.

Romero, Brenda M. "Lila Downs's Borderless Performance: Transculturation and Musical Communication." *Performing the US Latina and Latino Borderlands*. Ed. Arturo J. Aldama, Chela Sandoval, and Peter J. Garía. Bloomington: Indiana UP, 2012. 258–279. Print.

Schechner, Richard. *Performance Studies: An Introduction*. New York: Routledge, 2002. Print.

Semichon, Aurelie and Pierre Favre, dirs. *La tequilera*. MUZZIK, 2000. Film.

Seton-Watson, Hugh. *Nations and States: An Enquiry into the Origins of Nations and the Politics of Nationalism*. Boulder: Westview P, 1977. Print.

Sigler, Thomas, K. A. Aliset, and K. Angelique Dwyer. "The Heterogeneous Isthmus: Transnationalism and Cultural Differentiation in Panama." *Bulletin of Latin American Review*, 34.2 (2015): 229–244. Print.

Slaughter, Stephany. "Queering the Memory of the Mexican Revolution: Cabaret as a Space for Contesting National Memory." *Letras Femeninas*, 37.1 (2011): 47–70. Print.

Soja, Edward, W. *Postmodern Geographies: The Reassertion of Space in Critical Social Theory*. New York: Verso, 1989. Print.

Stephen, Lynn. "Expanding the Borderlands: Recent Studies on the U.S.-Mexican Border." *Latin American Research Review* 44.1 (2009): 266–277. Print.

Wimmer, Andreas. "The Making and Unmaking of Ethnic Boundaries: A Multilevel Process Theory." *American Journal of Sociology* 113.4 (2008): 970–1022. Print.

8

(Dis)identifying with Shakira's "Global Body"

•••••••••••••••••••••

A Path toward Rhythmic Affiliations beyond the Dichotomous Nation/Diaspora

DANIELA GUTIÉRREZ LÓPEZ

For five years now, since I became an international (nonimmigrant *alien*) Latina body in the United States, whenever I venture out to clubs and the lyrics "Let me see you move like you come from Colombia" play in the space, I am almost without exception asked to step into the middle of a circle and dance to the rhythms of the cumbia. While I usually do, my body excitedly following the sounds of "Hips Don't Lie" and others' apparent celebration of my identity, I also become intensely self-aware. Concern runs through me as I wonder whether my performance will adequately demonstrate my colombianidad, whether my hips will portray the sensual femininity they and I desire. I feel my body scoped for "authenticity" in the dance, an authenticity that I do not necessarily want to, nor should I, claim, since I racially do not belong to the communities of African descent this music genre calls home. And, still, I feel my hips in fact "lie." But what are they lying about?

International visibility has turned Shakira into a signifier for control. She and other Latin American bodies associated with her, mine in the preceding example, have become objects of the gaze and, therefore, of policing. Connection to (identification) or rejection of (counteridentification) these supposedly authentic signifiers—listening or not listening to Shakira's music, knowing or not knowing how to dance the cumbia, occupying or not occupying space in a nonfat (hourglass) body—almost automatically render personhoods like my own as worthy of belonging or as a target for exclusion from the nation I was born in, from Colombian diasporic settings, and from larger Latinx communities in the United States. However, *disidentifying* with Shakira's full performance functions as what Cuban-American scholar José Esteban Muñoz would call an alternate survival strategy (*Disidentifications* 4).[1]

In "Visualizing the Body: Western Theories and African Subjects," the introductory chapter to her book *The Invention of Women: Making an African Sense of Western Gender Discourses*, Nigerian scholar Oyèrónké Oyěwùmí argues that hegemonic Western centric, biologically determined epistemologies, "body-reasoning" (5) and "race-reasoning" (20), have universalized and naturalized gender difference through the prioritization of sight as *the* world organizing sense and principle. This has occurred even within social constructivist feminist critiques (3). Therefore, rather than fixating on and fixing the visuality of Shakira's body and audiovisual materials, which would replicate the imperial impulse Oyěwùmí describes, I propose a play with/in the ephemeral aspects of Shakira's music and persona to witness this process of disidentification.

As our own decolonial performance, in the following pages, I invite my readers on a journey in search of the potentialities of the "queer acts" (Muñoz "Ephemera" 5) I call *rhythmic affiliations*, bonds constituting and constituted by embodiments of race, ethnicity, gender, sexuality, class, (dis)ability, and their intersections. Instead of applying theory to popular culture texts, together we can add interpretive layers (Weheliye 9) to examples of life, sonic,[2] and migratory rhythms that make up Shakira's multimedia world. This way, through a methodology that African American studies and English scholar Alexander Weheliye terms "thinking sound/sound thinking" (8), we can build argumentative intensity (Agamben in Weheliye 16) toward the potential of disidentification. Ultimately, we will perceive how the traces and residues of the heard and felt (i.e., vibratory, emotional) rhythms that constitute at least a fragment of Shakira's beautiful lie,[3] can remix the limited, visual appearance of her "global body."

A refusal to answer the question of what the "lie" may be and, instead, an inhabitation of that "lie," a quotidian affective indetermination, is what animates many of us.[4] Through love for music, dance, and queer Latinidad, I tune in with others' lives, including those who died on June 12, 2016, at Pulse, a gay nightclub in Orlando, Florida, victims of a massacre that reflects countless homophobic hate crimes against queer communities. Therefore, I additionally propose the deployment of a pop-sense—inspired by Oyěwùmí's "world-sense" (3) in contrast to the Eurocentric "worldview"—as a disidentificatory technique to inhabit this indetermination. Rethinking the sonic, toward the transsensoriality of performance and the embodied experience of people of color and gender nonconforming individuals (Horton-Stallings 10), I offer the opportunities of the ebbs and flows of popular culture and the humanities at large to resist the racist, homophobic, and other bio-logic (Oyěwùmí 11) systems of oppression that allow and enable this violence to occur.

Tuning In . . .

Investigating Latin American and Latinx identities is a particularly rich practice given the region's complex history of ethnic blending, the processes of racialization of its population—often a consequence of the conquest and colonial sexual violence against women of color—and the ambiguity that ultimately renders many of us abject (Rodríguez 142). The characteristics of these pasts are habitually forgotten and perhaps intentionally erased in attempts to frame Latin American geopolitics as superior to that of other regions. This way, "we" imagine closeness to and perhaps even kinship with dominant white Euro-American society.

In her book *Sexual Futures, Queer Gestures, and Other Latina Longings* (2014), feminist scholar Juana María Rodríguez skillfully retells a story of Latinx racial identities:

> For many Latin@s these overlapping relationships to racialized colonial power live in intimate proximity; seen at the edges of family photos, whispered as ancestral lore. Where once we might have been seen as the criollo elite or the ascending mestizo middle class in our countries of origin, in the United States we become the racialized immigrant Other to Anglo-American whiteness; if once we had been mulato in relation to someone else's blackness, now Africa sticks to us like tar. Others might be invested in the refusal of European ancestry; however, that does little to diminish relationships to forms of colonial whiteness that are rarely encountered directly in decolonial discourses organized around "people of color." *And those who seek solace in direct uninterrupted Spanish lineage must at some point reconcile themselves to eight hundred years of Moorish occupation of the Iberian Peninsula.* Our hybridity as a product of colonial violence runs deep. (142; my emphasis)

These stories often appear or disappear through popular culture, creating and circulating racially sexualized stereotypes that, negatively marked, become the symbols of hegemonic History. Publics likewise receive these popular texts as confirmation of Latinx stereotypes, sometimes justifying the oppression of those who embody them (this may include rejection of one's own identity). Engaging with these histories through a pop-sense, a popular culture sensorial experience of the world, is an intentional act that reclaims Latinx empowerment from hegemony. This is especially significant for personhoods who not only embody these stereotypes but also derive pleasure from them. Shakira's celebrity persona, as well as the sounds and rhythms in her music, embody the aforementioned lost memories in an archive that brings forth the ephemeral gestures and movements of Latin culture and the material effects of her full performance. Given that for nonhegemonic communities, including "minority" or undesirable racialized communities in the United States "music has often been the mechanism for counterhistorical narratives, self-representation, and cultural empowerment" (Vargas x), soundscapes and audiotopias (including audiovisual materials) can function as primary sites for constructions of personhoods. The latter then have the power to bridge tensions at the borderlands between nations and their diasporas, and between these and other people who might participate in these contact-zones.[5]

In this sense, Shakira and her music function as an example of what Gloria Anzaldúa might call a borderland imaginary, "this space as the psychic, cultural, political site of collision, violence and promise [.... whose] musical representations demonstrate the negotiations of dual systems of power, knowledge, language, and culture that produce third ways of being" (Vargas xii). Just as exclusively following phenotype to make assumptions about identities and their histories re-creates ableist, gendered, and white supremacist violence, exclusively following Shakira's visual career and the logocentrism of lyrics would be a disservice, to say the least, to her performance. Therefore, I will first analyze the flux—creation and disruption—of Colombian/Latin American identities as they might be embodied in Shakira Isabel Mebarak Ripoll as a singer, a songwriter, a sexualized and racialized woman, a businesswoman, a UN ambassador, and recently, a mother.

"Shakira, Shakira!"

Shakira was born and raised in Barranquilla, a city on Colombia's Atlantic, that is, Caribbean, coast. Her father is a New York–born man of Lebanese descent and her mother is of Catalonian heritage (Cepeda 65). Having started her career in the early 1990s, Shakira released her second album, *Pies Descalzos*, in 1996. This project caught the eye of the international (primarily Spanish-speaking) market, including that of Miami-based Sony Discos (69). *Dónde están los ladrones?* (1998) followed as a great success. This last album was produced by Latin music star Gloria Estefan and her husband Emilio Estefan, after Shakira's relocation from Colombia to the United States (69), at a time when I remember Colombian migration of high-income classes to Miami had become routine. Entire families were fleeing the country, seeking to escape kidnapping threats or the terror of the possibility of those threats, made by the narco-trafficking guerrilla groups like the FARC and the ELN.

In 2001, having claimed certain creative independence from Estefan by insisting her album be composed of all new material (71), Shakira released her first bilingual album, *Laundry Service*. The album's first single, "Whenever, Wherever"—which incorporates worldbeat,[6] an integration of pop and rock with folk music, and Andean rhythms—became her best-selling song, topping both Britney Spears's and Madonna's releases in that same two-week period (71). The song peaked at number 6 in the United States, number 1 in the Billboard's "Hot Latin Tracks," and top-ten in Europe, especially the United Kingdom.

After more than fifty years of a civil war that has given Colombia the reputation of one of the most violent countries in the world, infested with drug lords (marijuana and cocaine) and "their" breast-enhanced female escorts,[7] many Colombians, local and diasporic, felt relieved to have Shakira represent us instead. It was perhaps the first time, since the famed Colombian soccer team participated in the French World Cup of 1998, that Colombia achieved the popularity granted by the international eye. This time, pride concentrated on one figure instead of two, René Higuita and Carlos "El Pipe" Valderrama, or eleven. Identification with Shakira's artistry, which managed a cross-over into the U.S. mainstream in a way that soccer never could, permitted Colombians within the naturalized nation and in the diasporas to release some of the shame that had followed us around (e.g., at airport security checks) for decades.

Nevertheless, Shakira's international recognition—grasp the exclusively mindful, that is, disembodied, connotations of Cartesian *cognition* (Oyěwùmí 3)—has not always been productive for personhoods continuously labeled subaltern. The creation of a "positive" Colombian identity necessitated the manipulation of Shakira's music, body, and politics. Shakira, who challenged the stereotype of Latina femininity, needed to be disciplined and possessed if she were to occupy the global spotlight. Shakira's international persona was seen as what Michel Foucault called a docile body, one "that may be subjected, used, transformed and improved" (Foucault 136).

Since 2001, when she released *Laundry Service*,[8] not only did the content of the rebellious costeña's rock songs change to describe more sexualized heteronormative encounters, but also her appearance underwent an explicit makeover. Thus I propose that Shakira's stardom, which scholars like María Elena Cepeda have attributed to her becoming a U.S. Latina/colombiana (69), has been based on the gendered racialization or attempted "whitening" of her persona. Her celebrity, especially in the United States, has relied on the reproduction of hierarchical power structures, including those of visual and audio media, and on the consumption and/or displacement of the people who then fall "below" her in scales of value: that is, black and queer communities within and outside Colombia, in Latin and non-Latin contexts.

Cepeda, author of *Musical ImagiNation: U.S.–Colombian Identity and the Latin Music Boom* (2010), argues that Shakira, as a public persona (64), served the media as an idealized transnational citizen (61). The author notes that her figure has shown a deterritorialization of transnational communities and their meanings (62), where she "may be interpreted as enacting the experience of multiple citizenships and multiple identities . . . Shakira therefore embodies the brand of 'strategic mitosis' or contextually bound identity shifts, that defines life in the United States for many Latin(o) Americans" (64). Ultimately, though, Cepeda describes what could be called disidentification with multiple identities and citizenship statuses, cultural and legal, "a shuffling back and forth between reception and production" (Muñoz 25), as a contradiction (Cepeda 63). This way, room for play in what Shakira's hybridity represents, in her indetermination or fragmentation (31), in her lies to hegemonic discourses across locales, is rapidly evacuated. Shakira's performance becomes colonized by origin stories,[9] by fixed (gender, genre, national, racial) borders, and by the naturalized identities on either side; that is, by what we superficially *see* in her, rather than what she fully performs and embodies.

In addition to being perceived as a docile body, just like "the global city is a strategic site for disempowered actors because it enables them to gain presence to emerge as subjects, even when they do not gain direct power" (Sassen in Gopinath 47), Shakira has functioned as a representation of a "global body." Even within academic writing, she has been reified and has been made available for the hegemonic gaze. While thanks to Shakira Colombian identities in multiple national contexts have gained presence, those who wish to identify exclusively with her new *image* and what it stands for seldom gain direct power. To be "recognized" as respectable Colombians, we are often expected to measure up to the standards that Shakira's privileged kinship to whiteness now demands.

In the following section, I illustrate the "whitening" process that has led Shakira to gain presence by becoming consumable "globally." As her transition comes to *light*, it is important to acknowledge that the definitions of this globality are in fact conditioned by privileged identities. Not everyone may access the global, and not just anyone can become palatable to those who represent the global.

Claiming the (Spot) Light

Launching Shakira's career as a singer of lyrics in English, in the Anglo and global markets, demanded visually lightening her appearance. Addressed in the February 2002 issue of *People in Español*, this transformation was termed an "evolution" (a naturalized advancement) in her image (Cepeda 77). In the earlier phases of her career, Shakira's rock ballads, fused with pop, dance music, reggae, and mariachi rhythms alike (65–66), required a standardized Latin American/Middle Eastern look: this included her "authentic" long, dark, wavy hair, and her "heavier" body.[10] Notice that this particular appearance permitted Shakira's mostly rock en español lyrics to speak not only of love but also about social issues such as abortion. In other words, her "woman of color" persona demanded she embody a political subject. For example, "Se quiere, se mata" (1996) has lyrics that center on abortion. Additionally, Shakira's consciousness of gender roles in "Pies descalzos" (1996), her love ballads, and her inclusion of "foreign," nonautochthonous genres in her music, are all political performances.

In 1998 the artist started playing with her hair color, dying it bright red as part of her rebellious rock and roll performance, as seen in the cover photo of her album *Dónde están los ladrones?* Then, Shakira became blonde—permanently. If her music videos showcase her with different-colored hair, we are looking at wigs, explicitly artificial, "unlike" her blonde hair. Through makeup (contouring) and lighting tricks that altered her skin tone, showcasing a paler hue, her features appeared slimmer. Shakira also lost weight over the years, further accommodating Euro-American standards of beauty, and literally occupying less space.

Most recently the Colombian artist has become an "ambassador" for Oral-B's Crest 3D White. Their slogan reads "Step into the spotlight with a Crest 3D White smile. Shakira believes that an amazing smile is how you connect to the world, and so do we. That's why we're teaming up to help everyone put their best and whitest smile forward" ("Crest 3D White"). The promotion of Crest 3D White reminds consumer publics that the road to superstardom, as demanded through the culture of care, is the individual's responsibility. Most importantly, it affirms that there is a direct link between hygiene/cleanliness, whiteness, and humanity (how you connect to the world). An updated neoliberal form of Shakira's *oral fixation*, this is again that bio-logic body- and race-reasoning Oyěwùmí delineates.

A political woman of color entering the realm of whiteness would be too much of a threat for the hegemony of whiteness. As such, Shakira also developed "apolitically." Now, in Colombia, a commercial for Crest 3D White still airs, with Shakira's *silent* presence—walking, hiding, smiling at the camera from within the walls of a colonial villa—narrated by an off-screen voice that says,

Todos buscamos la fórmula ideal para resaltar nuestra belleza y el poder de una sonrisa hace toda la diferencia. Por eso Shakira confía su sonrisa a la nueva pasta Oral B 3D White Perfection: remueve hasta 100% de manchas en tres días y ayuda a prevenirlas. Clínicamente comprobado. Cámbiate a la colección Oral B 3D White, perfecta para ti.[11] (June 2016)

We can perceive how, as a visually whiter version of herself, her *voice* (a singer's voice) started to wane. At perhaps her most *visible* moment, judging others' voices with a seat on the judges' panel of the TV singing competition *The Voice* for two nonconsecutive seasons (2013–2014), hers appeared inaudible. And still, if we actively *listened* to her, we could perceive that she's not just there to be *looked* at (Mulvey 837), as evidenced in an interview for *Entertainment News*, where she explains that she left *The Voice* to focus on her music and her children: "No, I wouldn't [go back], because it's so hard to be away from my family. Right now, [I'm] back into making music, and I'm gonna be going on tour pretty soon at the end of the year. I miss all that" (Drysdale).

It would be naive, or irresponsible, to assert that shifting racial and ethnic visual and thematic markers could be enough for anyone, in this case Shakira, to be read as white within dominant societies outside of Colombia. As Isabel Molina-Guzmán explains in her book *Dangerous Curves*, the light-skinned, blonde, thin Latin American artist will still not be recognizable as white in a global context (especially not a global north context). She can only position herself closer to dominant subjectivities inasmuch as she distances herself from her multiethnic roots (10–11).

Some might say, and I agree, that Shakira still performs her Lebanese heritage, mostly through the use of belly dancing as an essential component in her shows and videos. "Ojos Así"[12] (*Dónde están los ladrones?* 1998), one of the greatest hits in Colombia and internationally, was an unapologetically outspoken song that embraced Shakira's radical hybridity, rhythmically, linguistically, physically, and through the movements of the "original" rendition and the force of hips that don't lie. However, the multiethnic background that once provided her with the ambiguous positionality that created space for her "global" body now increasingly highlights her affiliation to whiteness as well.

For example, Shakira's song "I'm a Gypsy" (*She Wolf*, 2009) relates her bonds to the Catalan culture, which is heavily influenced by the Moorish inhabitation in Spain. Yet, by sharing the screen with Spanish tennis star Rafael Nadal in that video, the media text connotes dominant European-ness far more that it does the Catalan culture that seeks differentiation from the nationalist state. Shakira's skin additionally glistens in their sensual scenes, her body a lighter hue than the "talk, dark, and handsome" olive skin of the athlete. Therefore, Shakira's current flight from the status as a woman of color, of the aforementioned histories she embodies, her use of Arab instruments and sounds in songs like "I'm a Gypsy" sometimes merely mirror violent processes of Orientalism and cultural appropriations.

In 2005, four years after her debut in English, when she had dyed her hair blonde and had begun losing weight, Shakira released the album *Oral Fixation Vol. 2*. This album featured the most-played song on the radio in U.S. history (Cepeda 75): "Hips Don't Lie." Framed by the jungle flora on screen, Shakira's "exotic" Latinidad, the sensuality of her racialized body, enjoyed by the gaze of the camera's close-ups on her back, waist, and, of course, hips, facilitated the artist's first steps toward engaging in conversation with her global audiences. A Colombian flag painted on and fully covering one of the walls in the video additionally claimed the nation's spotlight on the global stage. And still, one of the most circulated questions in the media at the time wondered if Shakira had sold out (75).

In this "Hips Don't Lie," however, the cumbia, an Afro-Colombian genre that has traveled north and south through Latin America, from Perú to Chile, and from México to the United States—and in the video, its traditional dress and dance—still played an essential role in constructing Shakira's global body. This stage in Shakira's career shows how her celebrity status functioned through her remaining visually and audibly marked, possessing an "authenticity" explicitly available for consumption by "everybody" else. I use the word "possess" here, because the distinction between ownership and affiliation is crucial, as it may require the claiming of an identity or positionality, versus the performance of disidentification with different notions of race and ethnicity as presented in popular culture.

Casting a Shadow

Scholar Ruth Frankenberg states, "whiteness makes itself invisible precisely by asserting its normalcy, its transparency, in contrast with the marking of others on which its transparency depends" (Frankenberg in Carroll 7). Following this account, I propose that in order to become supposedly more visible and privileged, from 2005 forward, Shakira struggled to unmark herself, make her histories as invisible as possible. She did so by more explicitly marking others in the "global south" as racially Other. In other words, she visually proved not only that she was available for consumption but also that she had the ability to consume others. Over the past six years, Shakira literally took the stage traveling from one side of the globe to the other (i.e., her *The Sun Comes Out Tour*, with performances in countries in South and North America, Europe, Asia, and Africa), and she also projected herself as a "global voice" in the official songs for the soccer World Cups of 2010 and 2014. In the latter, she performed as an advocate for one of the world's ("apolitical") passions, assuming a position of privilege.[13]

The artist's interpretation of "Waka Waka (Esto es África/This Time for Africa" (*Sale el Sol*, 2010) for the South African 2010 FIFA World Cup became one of the best-selling singles of all time. This furthered Shakira's rise in fame. The music and lyrics of Shakira's song used a riff from the 1986 hit song "Zamina mina (Zangaléwa)," by Cameroon's makossa (genre) group Golden Sounds, which later changed its name to Zangaléwa (the original song paid tribute to

African cavalry soldiers who fought during World War II). The riff probably echoed in Shakira's musical repertoire, since the Cameroonian song became popular in Colombia thanks to West African DJs in the Atlantic coast's city of Cartagena. This city, where an ample part of the (segregated) country's Afro-Colombian population resides, still embodies colonial histories of the slave trade, as it was the primary port of entry of enslaved people to the South American continent. Barranquilla, Shakira's birth city, was likewise a "primary physical and cultural port" pioneer in the shaping of Colombia's musical scape (Cepeda 68).[14]

However, when Shakira performed "Waka Waka" in 2010, it produced disappointment within South Africa for not having a local interpret the official World Cup song. If the light-skinned Latina's appropriation of these rhythms was already problematic, she was additionally complicit in the homogenization of the African continent and its heterogeneous populations. Shakira visibly capitalized on Africa for celebrity status in a way similar to previous imperial agendas. While some might argue that these sounds are part of her identity, having grown up where she did, no matter how true this may be, it is essential to understand both Shakira's white privilege within Colombia and her mirroring of hegemonic whiteness outside in order to understand her complicity in oppressive processes.

Four years later, Shakira debuted her second FIFA World Cup song, "La La La," from the album *Shakira*, this time in Brazil in 2014.[15] Less anchored to a particular history, Shakira held the spotlight again. She did not explicitly play the role of the colonizer but instead claimed a "global" positionality akin to whiteness—transparent and invisible. This song, which has versions in both English and Spanish, resorts to a "universal" "la la la" vocal that audibly brings the "whole" world together. Many might say that because this one "la" sound does not belong to anyone, then everybody can sing along. However, this so-called universality is exclusionary. First, there are numerous language groups around the world who could not pronounce the "la" sound,[16] and second, assuming that everybody can say "la" is additionally an ableist claim. That is not to say that affiliations are not possible, hegemonic and queer alike. I will return to this in the next section.

Focusing on the visuality of the "La La La" video is compelling on two levels: (1) it reproduces racial and gender hierarchies through popular music, displaying the presence Shakira has gained through her "whitening" process; (2) the video is an example of the potential disempowerment her movement entails for other(ed) people. I engage with this song more than with "Waka Waka," because it was released the same year as Shakira and Rihanna's collaboration "Can't Remember to Forget You." The simultaneity of their release further speaks to the politics of racialized heteronormative femininity and to Shakira's positionality on the spectrum.

To begin, notice that Activia sponsored the "La La La" music video, directed by Spanish national Jaume de Laiguana. Their slogan, a play on the English lyrics, reads: "Dare to feel good." The yogurt campaign manifests in the video through the constant drawing of a smiling mouth at the bottom of the performers' stomachs. The imagery then alludes to a happy and, of course, "healthy" universalism, embodied in the protagonist's, Shakira's, global body and voice. Much like her participation in the Oral-B ad campaigns, this music video references a notion that the universal body can buy comfort and fit into dominant beauty standards through mass-produced commodities. A guise for this kind of exploitation, Shakira and Activia's campaign supported the World Food Programme, the food assistance branch of the United Nations; ironically, it is possible that this program would not need to exist if the capitalist system the artist and the company rely on were to be dismantled.

Furthermore, the video splits the scene among racial lines, and it demarcates the boundaries of presumably cisgender masculine and feminine spaces. "La La La" starts with the image of two black children holding a soccer ball. Immediately, the video cuts to the visual of drums and the sounds of Afro-Brazilian rhythms. Carlinho Brown's voice functions as an epilogue to the rest of the song's lyrics, as he sings in Portuguese. Black presumably cis men's bodies take the stage, muscular backs uncovered, banging on giant drums once again. Then, Shakira appears in the frame, her blonde hair and light skin a contrast to the men who are now in the background. She seems to lead a musical army. Cut after cut, as in flashes, the audience encounters the busts of some of the most famous soccer players in the world. Their skin colors, unlike those of the background musicians, are mostly light hues. Of the ten, there are two exceptions to this rule: Brazilian Neymar da Silva Santos Júnior, and French Éric Sylvain Abidal. Overall, the fixation on players' heads creates a gendered and racialized image. Their cameos are juxtaposed with scenes in which traditional Brazilian *garotas*—carnival dancers—appear behind Shakira, their full and almost naked bodies on display.[17] When close-ups of women are included, they feature only women's eyes or lips, makeup representing team flags, objectified fetishes.

As it is in fact a song for the FIFA World Cup, the appearance of national flags becomes a provocation (along with the lyrics, "I dare you"). The goal is to prove which nationality, which races, and ultimately which people are the best. What could be a celebration of "all" national identities, which I do not mean to say is not itself dangerous, is overshadowed by the "global" omniscient voice that narrates them, daring each nation to be superior. Shakira's embodiment of universality—she does not really have any specifically cultural garments attached to her body in the video, unlike a lot of the other bodies, who, for example, carry headdresses or turbans—rests on her opposition to the other women in the video, as the lightest-skinned person on camera. The singer's ability to shine casts a shadow on the rest when she refuses the stereotypical

Latinidad all other women in the video are forced to play. This is not to say that she has to perform as the hot Latina she is expected to play. What is unclear, and serves the violence of whiteness, is that she is portrayed as "naturally" exceptional.

Moreover, although in one shot she carries the Colombian flag—a symbol she can own—across the screen, it is her affiliation with her Spanish partner, Catalan soccer player Gerard Piqué, with whom she lives in Barcelona, Spain, which is exalted. Their music–soccer union is confirmed most compellingly by the presence of her one-year-old son Milan (born in 2013) in the music video. Shakira therefore becomes the only woman in the video who is not hypersexualized through her race, and she is also marked as a mother.[18] In *Impossible Desires*, Gayatri Gopinath explains that the status of the diaspora with regard to the nation fully depends on the heterosexual female abroad (101). Shakira's performance of a mother figure in the "La La La" video serves as an example of this process, as it symbolically represents the artist giving birth to a whiter generation in the diaspora.

Implementing our popular culture world-sense, where it becomes essential to traverse media genres, I encourage my readers to consider a supporting example of the cis-heterosexual woman ensuring the status of the diaspora vis-à-vis the home nation: Shakira and Piqué's "World Baby Shower." Carried out through UNICEF, this project is oriented toward earning money for children in need—perhaps the children in the global South against whom Shakira's children are now positioned. While the project might be productive in terms of essentially needed capital, the pictures on the baby shower's website reproduce ideas of a model, white family set out to fulfill their manifest destiny: saving "thousands of lives and [giving] babies a healthy start in life" ("World Baby Shower, Home").

Now the World Baby Shower has had its second edition with the birth of Sasha Piqué Mebarak in January 2016. This time, the heteronormative family extended their call, asking people to host their own baby shower. This interpellation, "You don't have to be a celebrity to make a difference . . . your child can be a blessing" ("World Baby Shower, About the Shower"), reproduces the nuclear family's modus operandi, making it seem both normal and exceptional simultaneously. Acknowledging that social change indeed needs everybody's cooperation, the sale of gifts in the "World Baby Shower" lets the onus fall on individuals (especially the expectant mother) to "fix" inequalities that need the restructuring of systems of power. And I must say, there is an eerie similarity between the sale of gifts for the baby shower and the sale of Crest 3D White and Activia.

It is arguable that regardless of her performance for the baby shower campaign, Shakira actually does not fit the white cis-heteronormative mold. First, the artist has expressed she does not intend to get married, a compulsory practice in heterosexual normativity; and, second, Piqué (born in 1987) is younger than she is (born in 1977), interrupting normalized narratives where women are expected to be younger than the men with whom they are involved romantically/sexually. While I agree with these arguments, it is also key to consider that although Shakira may not perform a sublime heteronormativity, in proving her heterosexual femininity she does contribute to the invisibilization of other nonnormative or queer modes of being in the world (Gopinath 123). So, while identifying with Shakira might give presence to some of her "disempowered" fans, groups of queer followers cannot gain much power through this identification. Some of us are empowered mostly through disidentification, or through what I have called rhythmic affiliations, ties made queer by the displacement of the power of the visual, and toward the reception of ephemeral gestures and the queer audiotopias Gopinath describes to conceptualize a queer diasporic framework (58).

The music video of "Can't Remember to Forget You" serves as an example of a missed opportunity for Shakira to actively empower her queer audiences. In this dual work with Barbadian singer Rihanna, another artist who has gained visibility in dominant U.S. society,[19] the video displays homoerotic discourses through the women's body language. Although some might argue for Rihanna's "queer" identity, and thus the visibility of queer communities, the lyrics they sing and the imagery they draw from deny this queerness altogether. Most of the video is an assembly of shots cutting from Shakira to Rihanna in individual frames. The scenes they perform together, though charged with same-gender desire, in fact attend to "the ultimate male fantasy" (105).

Several components evince the importance of a man's (un)presence in this video. On the one hand, the lyrics of the song leave no ambiguity regarding the gender of the characters' intended lover. In the song, Shakira's lyrics read: "The way he makes me feel, yeah. . . . He a part of me now." Then, after the chorus, Rihanna continues: "I go back again / fall off the train / land in his bed / repeat yesterday's mistakes." These phrases explicitly state that the lover uses the masculine pronoun "he." Perhaps the only aspect that remains unclear is whether or not they are both singing about and to the same man. On the other hand, they show the amount of power this man holds over them. He not only makes them struggle with and fail at their own determinations (falling off the train), but, if they act, they do it for him: they follow. In unison, they confess they would rob and kill for him. Finally, as the video presents, they would roll around in bed with another woman, as long as it were for him. When they share the screen they do not actually express desire for each other. In fact, they seem to feel more desire for the walls against which they dance during their individual takes, or even for the objects that surround them: the femme stiletto heels they wear and play with on the bed. Same-gender desire is thus but a foil that works instrumentally to please the omnipresent male gaze, further represented through the almost clichéd phallic imagery of the two women smoking cigars (Gopinath 123).

The inclusion of Rihanna's body in the video seems as instrumental as the queer-baiting trope of woman–woman desire. Rihanna's presence on screen in the English version of the song prevents Shakira from being fully read as the stereotypical sexualized Latina and allows her to continue to build her image as a "global body." The Colombian artist becomes the bridge that communicates Spanish-speaking Latin America and the English-speaking Caribbean to Europe and the United States. This is accomplished through the contrast of her own light skin (whiteness) with Rihanna's blackness.[20] As if to confirm this racialized discourse, the bed they lie on mirrors their bodies in a black and white striped pattern. In this case, the livability of the black Latinx community becomes threatened. A group that has already been relegated to the margins in Latin America, the United States, and other white supremacist contexts, becomes even more invisible, illegitimate, and impossible.[21]

The material consequences of these scenes for women who *do* identify as lesbian, bisexual, queer, or other, and especially for those who might be looking for representation and recognition in this music, could be devastating. Queer desire "translates" into the world as something only legitimate, and even mandatory, if performed for heterosexual male audiences. Our right to exist becomes conditional. What is more, these kinds of media representations obligate some of us to "choose" among the different axes that our personhoods comprise: if, for example, I wish to identify with Shakira on the basis of our feminine Latinidad, I am almost coaxed to deny my queerness; if I wish to embrace my queerness, I am compelled to reject Shakira's representations of heteronormativity. In other words, in order for my subjectivity to be recognized by others, I need to prioritize between my nationality and ethnicity and my sexual orientation, disregarding that my personhood is in fact the result of intersecting identities that should not and cannot be disarticulated (Cohen 440–441).

Still, recoding Shakira's performance by "acknowledging what is disturbing about [her] familiar [mostly visual and lyrical] practices" (Muñoz 70) enables disidentificatory pleasures to emerge. This recoding is possible when we *center* Rihanna's presence onscreen. The Barbadian singer invites a "queer" reading of the text: "Queerness in this case references an alternative hermeneutic, the particular interpretive strategies that are available to those deemed "impossible" within hegemonic nationalist and diasporic discourses" (Gopinath 22). Perverse spectators (95) who disidentify with Shakira's visual progress narrative and her historical forgetfulness (89) can complicate a critique of these popular culture products.

The tacit knowledges (Rodríguez 99–100) of audiences of color responding to these two particular artists might displace, recode, the meaning of the cigars:

"recognizing the archival moments available in the quotidian ... [veers] us into the space beyond official documentation, into the warm dark abyss of remembrance and potentiality" (102). The cigars are a product of the Caribbean that, given economic and political relationships to the United States might become fetishized or be found unacceptable. Yet, in the video they can give perceptibility to the marginalized bodies and labor associated with them. In the words of Weheliye, this constitutes "afro-diasporic studio tricknology" (8). These feminine figures consuming the cigars and luring hegemonic audiences to desire them might also "trick" audiences into becoming complicit with politics they may not otherwise support. This way, we can attend to the polysemy of multimedia products such as those of popular music, ultimately allowing for multiple forms of affective interactions among people across borders of nations and diasporas. These practices of recoding, disidentifying with explicit meanings, ultimately create what Gopinath terms "affective geographies" and "affective loyalties." I accompany this scholar by offering rhythmic affiliations, affective loyalties that center bodily, sonic, audiovisual (heart) beats, through the activation of a pop-sense that decenters whiteness.

Rhythmic Affiliations: Playing Queer Vibes

Affective ties can function to generate space for people, even within abjection, but they likewise carry the risk of reproducing discrimination (Rodríguez 32–33). Shakira, for example, has become both physically and audibly recognizable internationally. Nevertheless, as I continuously sense in everyday conversations with Colombians and read in current magazine articles,[22] she also represents a figure of "betrayal" to her home and to the people who long to identify with her but who can no longer reach her newly constructed values. On the one hand, many Latin Americans can literally no longer understand the words she sings and the messages she conveys and embodies due to the language barrier. On the other hand, her constructed kinship to whiteness initially depended on her limited embrace of Latin American popular music, so engagements with reggaetón and merengue in songs like "She Wolf/Loba" (*She Wolf*, 2009), "Rabiosa" or "Loca" (*Sale el Sol*, 2010) are perceived as potentially artificial and demeaning to those in the culture on which she now capitalizes.[23]

So, it is arguable that Shakira's career has centered a visual transformation. However, as audiences, we should engage additionally with her rhythms, with her use of lyrics in Spanish, English, and French (even if we don't understand them), and with her most recent emphasis on collaborations with artists like Carlos Vives, Nicky Jam, Prince Royce, MAGIC!, and Black M (*El Dorado*, 2017). We should experience her performance as a whole. Then queer, antiracist, and nonableist potentialities emerge, some more vibrant than others, as Shakira uses her spotlight to make others perceptible internationally.

So refusing the compulsion to merely identify or counteridentify with Shakira's nationality or her look, what could it mean to inhabit the perpetually-in-motion, ephemeral space that her music creates? In the following pages, I explore three tracks of rhythmic affiliations by surfacing the sonic traces of Shakira's performance. Following these threads excavates the intensities (Weheliye 74) of Shakira's popular culture performance and hopefully prevents racialized subjectivities' from "falling out of history" (75).

I do not mean to say that listening or dancing to music is in any way devoid of social violences and processes of oppression[24]—as safe spaces like nightclubs can easily become locales for hatred. However, I appreciate that decentering visuality and creating spaces for transsensory media might bring forth possibilities for queer kinships, built on aural affective loyalties that move beyond the "black and white" dichotomy of nation and diaspora. Disidentifying with "global" bodies and connecting to archives of "queer audibility" (Gopinath 58) might be an empowering gesture for people whose personhoods function as transnationally as musical histories, audiotopias, and the back and forth vibrations that sound waves permit.

First, I will take a moment to make an unlikely connection that extends the meanings of the "la la la." Accompanying these sounds, we can specifically speculate about additional populations toward which Shakira's 2014 World Cup song can gesture and with whom her audiences may affiliate. In this first example I propose that "La La La" (*Shakira*, 2014) resonates with a popular song by Naughty Boy[25] featuring Sam Smith, also titled "La La La" (*Hotel Cabana*, 2013).

The video for the 2013 song follows a young child, presumably a young boy. We see him move from the living room of what seems to be his home, to the streets of La Paz, Bolivia, and down to the depths of a mine. From the beginning, the audience attends the child as he, with his Chow Chow puppy, runs away from the abusive yelling of an older man, perhaps his father. The child then walks into an exercise studio, from where he is run out, again by screams, but this time from a woman the spectator has just seen working out, leading a group of other women, whose mascaras drip down their faces (from crying?). This time, he leaves the studio with an older man. Face covered in dirt or ash, this man had been *playing music* out of the boom box at the fitness studio.[26] The three characters, boy, dog, and man stop on the street to purchase a bleeding heart for the boy. The older man stuffs the heart in the left inner pocket of the child's jacket. Next, we encounter a *dancer*. The dancer[27] performs at a traffic light (for money?), in a carnavalesque costume that covers the dancer's body from head to toe. Finally, the now four main characters walk away from the city, into the mountains (near Potosí, Bolivia).[28] All but the dog continue down a dark tunnel. At the bottom, they encounter a statue of a devil. The older characters hug the boy goodbye, comforting him as he cries. Then they walk away. The child is left behind with his two index fingers covering his ears, as he sings "la la, la la la la la, la la na na na," blocking the threat of the devil away, just as he had blocked the abuse of the man at the beginning of the video, and the yelling by the woman at the studio.

The video's imagery does not directly correspond to the song's lyrics. Through a textual analysis, it is arguable that this is a love song that represents a relationship coming to an end. However, I want to focus on the metaphor that runs through both the video and its lyrics, especially in the chorus: "I'm covering my ears *like a kid* / when your words mean nothing, I go la la la / I'm turning up the volume when you speak, / cause if my heart can't stop it, / I'll find a way to block it" (Naughty Boy; my emphasis). The "la la la" in the song and the geographical setting of the video—located through the clothing the boy wears (hat and socks)—signal a racialized and childish, perhaps even spoiled, population. While it is problematic that this representation could easily replicate discourses that once validated the conquest of the Americas (South America in this case), where indigenous populations were deemed defenseless, childlike indigenous savages that needed rescue (Wynter 283–302), I wish to emphasize that this video *features* a rebellious child (accompanied by marginalized characters) who escapes the violence of those who are supposed to hold power over him.

Following Naughty Boy's video, I propose that Shakira's affiliation with that child, and the sounds he uses to protect himself, could recode her 2014 World Cup performance. These questions then emerge: is Shakira refusing to listen to the people her videos racialized, sexualized, and treated as childish? Or is she the infantilized and racialized woman who refuses not to listen to hegemonic discourses? Could she be compelling her audiences to cover their ears and sing "la la, la la la la la, la la na na na" with her, protecting themselves from cisheteropatriarchal white supremacy? In that case, Shakira would represent the marginalized, yet more privileged, characters that accompany the boy throughout the video and urge him to block the unintelligible words of power.

I do not intend to give answers to these questions. Like autoethnography, this journey in search of rhythmic affiliations "is not interested in searching for some lost and essential experience, because it understands the relationship that subjects have with their own pasts as complicated yet necessary fictions" (*Disidentifications* 83). Instead, I offer their indeterminacy to the readers, as a gesture and as a practice of survival. In other words, I provide an example of the ways playing with Shakira's performance constitutes a decolonial process in which my—and hopefully others'—existence is made possible, even within regimes of power.

Second, I feel Shakira's performance resonating with the Dominican bachata genre in two modalities. On the one hand, as previously mentioned, the guitar in the bachata and the genre's vocal woes echo the guitar and vocals of the flamenco genre. While it is primarily the Romani communities in Spain who move, dance, and sing to the rhythms of their Arab, Middle Eastern, and South Asian traditions, Shakira's signature "yodel-like shadings"—sounds that have been attributed to her Lebanese heritage (Cepeda 66)—reverberate throughout her discography. The Colombian artist and the Dominican genre meet, as they acknowledge their shared histories. On the other hand, Mario Baro explicitly recorded a bachata version of Naughty Boy's "La La La" song (still in English). This is one among multiple other remixes of the song.

Why pay attention to the bachata version? One, two, three, four. While the bachata is particularly popular among some Latinx communities in the United States, as well as among non-Latinx groups who take "Latin rhythms" classes in different institutions, this genre has been significantly vilified within classist (and racist) groups in Colombia. One, two, three, four. Similarly, though bachata was born in the Dominican Republic, the genre now occupies a vilified status in its "home" nation. Deemed the product of "lower" over(t)ly-sexual, socio-economic classes (closer to Haitian Blackness), bachata is held in contrast to merengue, a relatively desexualized dance with a military-like tempo is governmentally endorsed as the national music genre (the genre of a dominant class that strives to prove its imperial blood). One, two, three, four. Finally, bachata in particular—and the people affiliated with the genre—continues to be ostracized not only because it interrupts the Christian-centric, antierotic, disembodied experience of "whiteness" in Latin American countries, but because, I propose, it does so through the sensuality of dance and the drama of voice that responds to calls by/for the beloved, not unlike the Muslim calls to prayer. One, two, three, four. The fourth beat punctuates the dance by an instant of the hip movement for which Shakira and belly dancing in general are so well known.

If we let Shakira's "La La La" rhythmically and affectively turn us toward Baro, then it is possible for us as her audience to simultaneously turn our attention toward marginalized Latin American and Other communities. By animating our pop-sense and following this track of rhythmic affiliations, we can center those who enjoy the bachata genre regardless of its classed, sexualized, and racialized connotations within hegemonic white supremacist society. Once more, rhythms reanimate sonic migrations that have traveled across Latin America, Europe, the Middle East, and South Asia.[29]

Finally, as a third track I offer the rhythmic affiliations—genres, instruments, beats—of the cumbia, the genre with which I began this chapter, as it is remixed into "Hips Don't Lie." The Colombian cumbia carries with it the beat of African drums and the chants and sorrows of slavery. Two of the most famous contemporary cumbia artists are Totó la Momposina and Petrona

Martínez. Both of these women were born in the department of Bolívar, in the Caribbean coast of Colombia, which is the same region through which the rhythms of the "Waka Waka" entered the country.

Furthermore, through this sonic archeology, we can attend to how, on the one hand, the rhythms of the Afro-Colombian cumbia have traveled south, transformed into Chilean cumbias. While the latter no longer explicitly echo Black voices, they harmonize the voices of working-class issues in the southernmost regions of South America. On the other hand, trekking north, the cumbia has affiliated, perhaps not explicitly but rather queerly, Shakira's musical performance, and those of us who disidentify with her, to artists like Mexican-American Selena Quintanilla.

Selena herself, though born in Lake Jackson, Texas, built off of the Afro-Colombian music genre in songs like "Baile esta cumbia," "Techno cumbia," and, less explicitly, "Como una flor." The artist and her music

> resonated with those who desired to claim their racialized sexuality within structural systems that aim to fix their bodies to a disempowered status.... Selena utilized the stage as a dance floor in ways the queens, disenfranchised racialized women, fags, and Latina/o youth had "worked it" during the days of disco and freestyle. (Vargas 192)

In connecting us with Selena, Shakira's music additionally moves us toward those disenfranchised by U.S. hegemony, audibly countering the "whiteness" her image seems to represent. What is more, through the rhythmic affiliation between these two women, the histories of racialized women, fags, and youth are not only recovered, our existence acknowledged and legitimated, but a bond is also created between indigenous and black people and histories, who have been pitted against one another in efforts to prove our humanity to whiteness (Wynter 293).

Queer (sound) waves and world-making resulting from disidentification with audible archives continue to resonate and emerge in San Antonio, Texas, over twenty years after Selena's murder, as the cumbia touches groups like Girl in a Coma (active since 2006). The all-female Indie-rock band jams and dances to the rhythms of the now Tejanx rendition of the cumbia genre: their performances have (re)covered songs by '90s Latina diva Selena, including "Si una vez." Nina Diaz performs the vocals and plays the guitar, Phanie Diaz rocks the drums, and Jenn Alva owns the bass. This way, the three queer Chicana women not only honor their ethnic identity they also invoke Anglo bands, like the English rock band The Smiths, interpreters of the song that inspired the group's name. These invocations recall Shakira's early career, when she found her rockera personality, setting her aside from other Colombian artists, by listening to American bands and artists like Nirvana, Aerosmith, and Tom Petty

("Shakira"). She remixed their rhythms into pop music that also gestured toward reggae and mariachi genres, among others. Much like Selena borrowed from Shakira's national music, Shakira also honored Selena's heritage.

Ultimately, through these examples of rhythmic affiliations, we can witness how Shakira revives artists, genres, and histories. She does so through her musical play in a way that might resonate for some with the way W.E.B. DuBois remixes spirituals in his *Souls of Black Folk* as he creates sonic–textual interactions that transverse black song and European poetry: "DuBois uses rhythm as a figure to delineate the grounds of empirical knowability" (Weheliye 105).[30] In other words, sonically and in the mainstream arena of pop culture, Shakira provides her fans with the tools to recover the lives and experiences of racial groups that hegemonic history relegates to minor stories.

Notes

1 Through my citation of Muñoz's work, I want to intentionally invoke Black radical, Chicana, and women of color feminist traditions that engage with ideas of double, oppositional, differential consciousness as developed by scholars like W.E.B DuBois, Audre Lorde, Franz Fanon, Cherríe Moraga, and Chela Sandoval, among others.

2 I choose to center the sonic, rather than the audible, for the sonic encompasses the vibratory component that allows many hard of hearing people to experience music. Recommended view: "'Sin palabras', el primer café para sordos en Colombia" (08.09.2017).

3 Recall "Beautiful Liar," a 2007 single by Beyoncé, featuring Shakira.

4 See Trinh Minh-ha's (1989) deliberation on stories, lies, fiction, and Truth.

5 Contact-zones are "social spaces where cultures meet, clash, and grapple with each other, often in contexts of highly asymmetrical relations of power, such as colonialism, slavery, or their aftermaths as they are lived out in many parts of the world today" (Pratt in Boast 57).

6 This hegemonic denomination of music genre centers whiteness, rendering the lives it represents unmarked.

7 See the relationship between beauty, plastic surgery, and violence, in Taussig (2012).

8 What perceptions could the title of this album create in the public, when much of the diasporic Latin American population works in the service sector in the United States?

9 See Andrea Smith's engagement of Judith Butler's concept of origin stories in "Queer Theory and Native Studies: The Heteronormativity of Settler Colonialism" (2010).

10 Released in 2010, the song "Gordita," featuring Latin American rap/reggaetón artist Calle 13, describes Shakira's early-career body. Translated into English, the title of the song means "fatty," a term of endearment in large parts of Latin America, however, also racialized and classed.

11 My translation: We all look for the ideal formula in order to highlight our beauty and the power of a smile makes all the difference. That is why Shakira trusts her smile to the new toothpaste Oral B 3D White Perfection: it removes up to 100% of

the stains in three days and helps prevent them. Clinically proven. Switch to the Oral B 3D White collection, perfect for you.

12 "Ojos Así" was released in an English version in Shakira's following album, *Laundry Service*.

13 In Colombia, soccer has been deeply political, linked through funding and fandom to the armed conflict: many (even internationally) remember July 1994 as the month when Colombian soccer player Andrés Escobar was shot dead by drug cartel orders. He was killed in retaliation for having scored an own goal perceived to have caused Colombia's elimination from the FIFA World Cup that year.

14 Alexander Weheliye's analysis of W.E.B DuBois's *Souls of Black Folk* as a remix that functions much like contemporary DJing practices provides a compelling example of how enslaved people's onto-epistemologies were articulated through popular song, and of how modernity and today's hegemony of whiteness depend on a racial rift that others these articulations (82–87).

15 The 2014 FIFA World Cup theme song was Jennifer López and Pitbull's "We Are One (Ole Ola)."

16 For example, East Asian languages like Mandarin and Korean.

17 See histories of people of color, especially black women, on display in Coco Fusco's "The Other History of Intercultural Performance" (1994).

18 Years earlier, she had presented herself as *the* Mother on the cover of her sixth studio album *Fijación Oral Vol. 1* (2005), as she appropriated the popular image of Madonna with child.

19 From the English-speaking Caribbean, Nicki Minaj, raised in Queens, New York, is the only other artist with a similar level of success as Rihanna in the United States. Still, neither is comparable to Shakira in the reach they have had: Nicki has only toured the United States and Europe; Rihanna's "Anti World Tour" included North America, Europe, and only one stop in Asia; whereas, until her "El Dorado World Tour" which will only stop in the Americas and Europe, Shakira's previous three worldwide tours ("Anfibio," "Mongoose," and "Oral Fixation") included performances in North and South America, Europe, Africa, and Asia. This does not necessarily speak to the talent of these three artists, but it does resonate to their politically racialized affiliations.

20 It is worth acknowledging that Rihanna's skin is of a lighter hue than many black Americans or others of African descent, and this constitutes a privilege within the United States, if not also in her country of origin.

21 Artists like Jennifer López, whose heritage from Puerto Rico could gesture to Afro-Caribbean lives and histories, have mostly capitalized on the Latina image that negates Blackness, even while capitalizing on the hip-hop culture so prevalent in NYC.

22 See Colombian magazine *Shock*'s article titled "¿Qué pasó Shakira? Antes eras chévere" (*Redacción Shock*, 2017).

23 In 2016, she lent her voice to a sensual gazelle in Disney's *Zootopia*. While she reached a new level of success with her participation in this movie, this also represents a reproduction of a Latinx racialized and animalized sexuality.

24 Two examples: (1) bachata often oozes themes of misogyny in its lyrics, which are simultaneously experienced on dance floors as harassment; (2) Maluma, a Colombian artist with whom Shakira collaborated in her 2017 album, has been accused of perpetuating rape culture through his reggaetón lyrics (Cantor-Navas, 2017).

25 Shahid Khan, whose stage name is Naughty Boy, is an English artist of Pakistani descent.

26 Ian Pons Jewell, who directed Naughty Boy's video, wanted to showcase the wrestling community of La Paz.

27 I do not want to assign a gender to a character who is not performing one, even though some may say the dancer's frame *looks* like that of a man. Histories of gender violence have relied on assumptions about how people look.

28 Some might be reminded of *The Wiz* (1978) or of *The Wizard of Oz* (1939).

29 I do not want to suggest that these sonic migrations have not been the product of violent processes, and I do not want to homogenize very different cultures, but it is important to acknowledge the connections that exist regardless. Also, I use the word "across," because I do not want to ascribe directionality to these migratory patterns, directionalities that have often been used to teleologically mark geographies of progress, from ancient periods, to (Western) modern civilization.

30 Colombian music group Bomba Estereo is known for its mixes of "psychedelic cumbia." The lead singers voice is intentionally recognizable as following this musical tradition. Nevertheless, the reason I do not engage with them in this chapter is because, this far, and regardless of their last album's ("Amanecer") international success, they do not have a global reach comparable to Shakira's.

Works Cited

Boast, Robin. "Neocolonial Collaboration: Museum as Contact Zone Revisited." *Museum Anthropology* 34.1 (2011): 56–70. Print.

Cantor-Navas, Judy. "Citing Sexist Lyrics, Public Funds Withdrawn from Maluma Concert in Canary Islands" *billboard*. August 15, 2017. http://www.billboard.com /articles/columns/latin/7904969/maluma-sexist-lyrics-concert-spain-canary-islands -funds-pulled. Web.

Carroll, Hamilton. *Affirmative Reaction: New Formations of White Masculinity*. Durham: Duke UP, 2011. Print.

Cepeda, María Elena. *Musical ImagiNation: U.S.–Colombian Identity and the Latin Music Boom*. New York: New York UP, 2010. Print.

Cohen, Cathy. "Punks, Bulldaggers, and Welfare Queens." *GLQ: A Journal of Lesbian and Gay Studies* 3 (1997): 437–465. Print.

"Crest 3D White." *Oral-B*. 2016. http://www.3dwhite.com/en-ca/. Web.

Drysdale, Jennifer. "EXCLUSIVE: Shakira Opens Up about Why She Wouldn't Return to the 'Voice' Again." *Entertainment Tonight*. 7 May 2017. https://www.msn.com/en-us /music/news/exclusive-shakira-opens-up-about-why-she-wouldnt-return-to-the-voice -again/ar-BBBz7p7. Web. 14 Jul. 2018.

Foucault, Michel. *Discipline and Punish: The Birth of the Prison*. New York: Random House, Inc., 1995. Print.

Fusco, Coco. "The Other History of the Intercultural Performance." *TDR* 38.1 (1994): 143–167.

Gopinath, Gayatri. *Impossible Desires: Queer Diasporas and South Asian Public Cultures*. Durham: Duke UP, 2005. Print.

Horton-Stallings, LaMonda. *Funk the Erotic: Transaesthetics and Black Sexual Cultures*. Chicago: U of Illinois P, 2015. Print.

Minh-ha, Trinh. "Grandma's Story." *Woman, Native, Other: Writing Post-Coloniality and Feminism*. Bloomington: Indiana UP, 1989: 119–152 Print.

Molina-Guzmán, Isabel. *Dangerous Curves: Latina Bodies in the Media*. New York: New York UP, 2010. Print.

Mulvey, Laura. "Visual Pleasure and Narrative Cinema." *Film Theory and Criticism: Introductory Readings*. Eds. Leo Braudy and Marshall Cohen. New York: Oxford UP, 1999: 833–844. Print.

Muñoz, José Esteban. *Disidentifications: Queers of Color and the Performance of Politics*. Minneapolis: Minnesota UP, 1999. Print.

———. "Ephemera as Evidence: Introductory Notes to Queer Acts." *Women & Performance: A Journal of Feminist Theory* 8.2 (1996): 5–16. Print.

Naughty Boy feat. Sam Smith. "La La La." *Hotel Cabana*, Naughty Boy Recordings, 2013.

"Naughty Boy 'La La La' (feat. Sam Smith) by Ian Pons Jewell." *Promo News*. May 3, 2013. http://www.promonews.tv/videos/2013/05/03/naughty-boy-%E2%80%98la-la-la%E2%80%99-ft-sam-smith-ian-pons-jewell. Web. 3 May 2013.

Oyěwùmí, Oyèrónkẹ́. "Visualizing the Body: Western Theories and African Subjects." *The Invention of Women: Making an African Sense of Western Gender Discourses*. Minneapolis: Minnesota UP, 1997: 1–30. Print.

"¿Qué pasó Shakira? Antes eras chévere" *Redacción Shock*. 2 Feb. 2017. https://www.shock.co/cultura/articulos/shakira-antes-eras-mas-chevere-79119. Web. 14 Jul. 2018.

Rodríguez, Juana María. *Sexual Futures, Queer Gestures, and Other Latina Longings*. New York: New York UP, 2014. Print.

Shakira. *Pies descalzos*, Sony Discos, 1996.

———. *¿Dónde están los ladrones?*, Sony Discos, 1998.

———. *Laundry Service*, Epic Records, 2001.

———. *Fijación Oral, Vol. 1*, Epic Records, 2005.

———. *Oral Fixation, Vol. 2*, Epic Records, 2005.

———. *She Wolf*, Sony Music Entertainment, 2009.

———. *Sale el sol*, Epic Records, 2010.

———. *Shakira*, RCA/Sony Latin, 2014.

———. *El Dorado*, Sony Music Latin, 2017.

"'Sin palabras', el primer café para sordos en Colombia" *El Espectador*. 9 Aug. 2017. http://www.elespectador.com/noticias/actualidad/sin-palabras-el-primer-cafe-para-sordos-en-colombia-video-707164. Web. 14 Jul. 2018.

Smith, Andrea. "Queer Theory and Native Studies: The Heteronormativity of Settler Colonialism." *GLQ: A Journal of Lesbian and Gay Studies* 16.1-2 (2010): 42–68. Print.

Taussig, Michael. *Beauty and the Beast*. Chicago: Chicago UP, 2012. Print.

Vargas, Deborah R. *Dissonant Divas in Chicana Music: The Limits of La Onda*. Minneapolis: U of Minnesota P, 2012. Print.

Weheliye, Alexander. *Phonographies: Grooves in Sonic Afro-Modernity*. Durham: Duke UP, 2005. Print.

"World Baby Shower." *UNICEF*. 2016. http://www.worldbabyshower.org/. Web.

Wynter, Sylvia. "Unsettling the Coloniality of Being/Power/Truth/Freedom: Towards the Human, After Man, Its Overrepresentation—An Argument" *CR: The New Centennial Review* 3.3 (2003): 257–337. Print.

9

Voicing the Occult in Chicana/o Culture and Hybridity

• •

Prayers and the Cholo-Goth Aesthetic

JOSÉ G. ANGUIANO

> Everything that I do from the music to
> my art work, they're like sigils or
> amulets. I create these paintings and
> I make this music to protect me from
> those that wish me harm.
> —Rafael Reyes

The boundaries and genres of popular culture or subcultures often parallel racial and ethnic divisions of the broader culture. While overt forms of pop culture segregation like the "race records" of the 1920s seem relics of the past, invisible color lines nonetheless persist. Discursively, many music genres still represent or are linked with racial categories. Historically, in the United States musical genres like rhythm and blues served as a catch-all category for black music and served to distinguish "white" categories, such as country, roots, or folk music. Like racial categories themselves these genre associations have shifted over time as Latinos and other groups position themselves within genres and as technology alters the reach and capabilities of creativity. The globalization of media technologies and the dissemination of popular culture around the world facilitates an unprecedented access to popular culture that establishes affective resonances between listeners/viewers even as hierarchies of race, class, gender, and sexuality linger. The linkages also produce unexpected hybridities that may challenge racial assumptions, binaries, and divisions.

Chicano/Latino cultural production has a long-celebrated history of hybridity, of linguistic and cultural duality, and of navigating the "third space" between the American black–white racial paradigm. The recently formed band Prayers exemplifies Chicano modes of cultural hybridity that coalesce disparate and often contradictory elements to forge new visions of popular culture and race. Prayers is also representative of a shift in popular culture and subculture demographics where young people of color are venturing into scenes formerly deemed off limits and transforming them from the inside. In Southern California and many parts of the U.S. Southwest many underground rock subcultures like rockabilly, punk, and metal have become primarily Latina/o scenes.

Prayers brings together two subcultures (cholo and goth) previously deemed aesthetically and racially incompatible. The band's music and aesthetic construct a dark new vision of race and popular culture by presenting and smashing a series of binaries: cholo/goth, Chicano/white, straight/gay, male/female, violence/passivity, and sacred/occult. The band's aesthetic finds its full expression in the multiple music videos that showcase a menacing hybridity of occult references, Chicano gang culture, postpunk synthesizer music, and a *llorona*-wail vocal delivery. The band visually and sonically references occult imagery of both goth and Mexican culture to build a common affective language. This hybridized cholo-gothic realm that encompasses multiple iconographies comes together in the setting, music, clothes, and bodies to form a mystical barrio aesthetic.

Exploring the occult in Chicana/o hybridity and identity in this chapter also concerns analyzing a secondary meaning of occult as hidden or mysterious and how it speaks to secret pleasures and connections, and unpredictable ways that popular culture and music establish and destabilize identities. In this case, Prayers represents a wider and darker Chicana/o experience of growing up between (music) cultures: where R&B oldies and hip-hop fade into Pet Shop Boys and Christian Death, where Catholicism fuses with indigenous folk healing, where Vicente Fernandez's hypermasculinity bumps into Morrissey's morbid introspection, where rigid heteronormativity and gender-queer icons share the same headphones, and where we declare blood-claims to neighborhoods and feelings of statelessness. The personal, sometimes secretive, and ephemeral nature of listening to music makes it a critical site to excavate these hidden links and tensions.

The following sections of this chapter explore the origins of the band Prayers and the cholo-goth aesthetic as rooted in the wider musical context of Chicana/o interest in darkwave sounds and the experience growing up around gang culture. I argue that an interest in "dark" sounds and the "gothic" context of growing up Chicana/o in Southern California shape the hybrid cholo-goth musical and visual expressions I analyze in the music videos for "Black Leather" and "West End Girls."

Prayers and the Origin of Cholo-Goth

Formed in 2013, Prayers, is an electronic-goth music duo from San Diego, California, comprising vocalist Rafael Reyes and DJ Dave Parley. Initially calling their visual and musical aesthetic "kill wave," the band's recognition increased since it embraced the "cholo-goth" label. "Cholo-goth" is part branding/marketing ploy, part attempt to reconcile and define singer Rafael Reyes's performed cholo aesthetic paired with dark wave electronic music created by Dave Parley. Indeed, Rafael claims membership in one of San Diego's oldest Chicano gangs and presents himself on stage as a prison tatted gang member with a taste for the occult and shoe-gaze goth music. Rafael, who goes by the stage name Leafar Seyer, performs with a shaved head that reveals a tattoo-covered scalp, a black leather jacket, form-fitting black jeans, and black boots. Dave is the tall stoic beat maker, with frizzy hair and dressed in all black, creating a dark sonic canvas. The pair met in the independent music scene that spans the San Diego/Tijuana borderlands.

While Rafael's Prayers persona attempts to establish a mythos of a hardened Chicano gang member that one day stumbled into electronic goth music, his history as a member of other dark wave bands, visual art shows, and self-published memoir reveal sustained efforts to craft and express an artistic vision he labels "occultwave" under different guises and mediums. Before starting Prayers, Reyes played with a few goth-inspired bands in the San Diego area, including Baptism of Thieves and Vampire, along with a solo project named Nite Ritual (Holslin). In 2011, he published *Living Dangerously*, largely based on his life experience in San Diego graffiti crews where he went by the moniker "Lotus Day" (Hartman). He has also exhibited visual art in both Los Angeles and San Diego under the name "Baby Boy" (Lecaro; Lamb; Thompson). Reyes's interest in visual design and fashion make him the primary force behind the band's emblems, fashion, and art direction of music videos.

Chicana/o Darkwave Legacies/La Onda Obscura

Cholo-goth music may seem unexpected or bizarre, but that sentiment stems in part from the marginalized or forgotten Chicano/Latino presence in rock music history and the racialization of music genres. For despite seminal and transformative Chicano/Latino contributions to rock and roll—from Ritchie Valens to Question Mark and the Mysterians through Carlos Santana, Los Lobos, and Ozomatli, to name a few—Chicanas/os, and Latinas/os in general, have never been acknowledged as central to rock music scenes (Reyes and Waldman; Loza; Avant-Mier). If musical impact is seldom acknowledged, the Chicano/Latino audience is even less so. Disregard of U.S. Latinas/os as consumers and listeners of rock music operates on many levels and through various discourses that legitimize the invisibility of the Latina/o rock fan. Prevalent among them, and informing many others, are (1) rock's long-standing black/white dichotomy, (2) the music industry's erroneous belief that there is no Latino "market" for rock or at least not one for English-language music, and (3) "sonic stereotypes" that narrowly define what type of music Latinas/os listen to and consume. Despite an acknowledgment of black and Latina/o contributions to the development and popularization of rock music, rock is nonetheless read (heard) as "white" music primarily consumed by a white audience (Mahon 5–10). The academic literature on Latinas/os in the rock music scenes is growing and uncovering Latino presence and contributions as performers and listeners/supporters of music scenes across time periods and subgenres. This section briefly reviews Chicano/Latino participation in punk and postpunk genres as a direct influence on the music produced by Prayers and historical context for the band and their audience.

This history represents an "occult" or hidden history of rock at the intersections of race and aesthetics. Evident in the synth pop sounds and directly expressed in interviews, Prayers proclaims inspiration and admiration for postpunk British dark wave music, such as the Pet Shop Boys, along with American punk and gothic bands, such as Christian Death. Reviewing recent Chicana/o/Latina/o identifications with punk aesthetics and punk bands like the Sex Pistols, and the postpunk sounds of the Smiths (Morrissey) and Siouxsie and the Banshees supports the argument that cholo-goth must be contextualized as part of a larger Latino interest in alternative rock genres and particularly an investment in British dark wave music.

To be sure Chicanos, like many other American youth, followed the music trends of British "invasion" imports since the Beatles and the rock music that followed. Chicano R&B group Cannibal and the Headhunters even got to open for the Beatles in the summer of 1965 in support of their second American tour (Reyes and Waldman 73). Besides sharing the same bill Chicano affinity for British rockers is well documented in literary and ethnographic writing.

In the novel *The Autobiography of a Brown Buffalo* (1972) acclaimed Chicano novelist Oscar Zeta Acosta is haunted and fixated on the song "A Whiter Shade of Pale" by British group Procul Harum. Unable to explain what the song meant to him other than to say "the song moved me deeply. It reminds me of Luther's 'A Mighty Fortress Is Our God'" (35). The song's somber tone and psychedelic imagery reflect the narrator's state of mind. But, more importantly, for many Chicanos that grew up listening to 1967's "A Whiter Shade of Pale" the song's deep organ riffs, R&B feel, and slow-dance rhythm felt familiar and organic to the way Eastside bands like Thee Midnighters were mixing rock and roll, doo wop, and Latin rhythms in that same era. The sound belonged to the barrio even if the group did not. In the 1970s El Chicano would incorporate Latin jazz into this soulful rock sound and call it "the brown sound." The interaction between British and Chicano sounds continued with the emergence of punk and postpunk rock at the forefront of youth culture in the late 1970s and into the 1980s.

When bands like the Sex Pistols, the Ramones, Patti Smith, and others introduced the world to the antiauthoritarian aesthetic of punk many Chicanas and Chicanos quickly joined the subculture as an audience and performers. It is worth noting too that some rock historians have made the case for Ritchie Valens and other Chicano groups, such as Question Mark and the Mysterians of the 1960s, as proto-punk rockers that paved the way for later iconic punk acts (Reyes and Waldman 135; Taylor 16). This suggests punk is not simply a style that was adopted but one indebted to Chicano/Latino contributions. Regardless, Chicano/Latino youth were attracted to the avant-garde fashion trends, the political edge of the music, and a culture that embraced "misfits."

Michelle Habell-Pallán's work on *punkeras* from the greater eastside of Los Angeles documents that rock and roll music has long been an outlet for disaffected Chicana/o youth seeking alternative aesthetic and political realities. Habell-Pallán argues that punk music was attractive to Chicanas and Chicanos because "it was a site where identities outside of ethnic stereotypes could be embodied" (153). Moreover, Chicanas from East L.A., such as Teresa Covarrubias (of the Brat) and Alicia Armendariz Velasquez (of the Bags), found an aesthetic to voice a fierce feminist critique of both Latino and American culture. Explaining the popularity of the Sex Pistols among Chicanos, Habell-Pallán argues that the fetishization of British rockers is about exoticizing an Other, a Great Britain of oppositional styles that can be used to resist U.S. racism and Chicano patriarchy. This transnational connection is what George Lipsitz names "families of resemblance," similar aesthetic and political interests that connect diverse individuals across time and space (162).

As the punk aesthetic transformed in other directions the Latino community followed along as an audience for bands like Siouxsie and the Banshees. Recent papers on the Latino audience of Siouxsie and the Banshees argue that women of color and queer listeners built unique spaces of listening and socializing through the music. Iván A. Ramos argues that "Siouxsie Sioux, gives queer and female listeners a relational space rooted in a feminist goth aesthetic consonant with their sense of double difference." And Richard T. Rodríguez notes that Siouxsie Sioux's various attempts to resist categorization or disidentify with punk scene origins ultimately dislocate the band from a largely white and male aesthetic. These disidentifications parallel Chicana punks disidentifying with traditional American and Mexican culture and suggest listeners felt connected with the political and aesthetic modes of punk and postpunk bands.

Another Latino-British postpunk connection that has garnered much media attention is Latino fandom of the Smiths and their singer Steven Morrissey (aka Moz or Morrissey). While many Latino fans followed the Smiths and Morrissey in their heyday in the mid-1980s, Southern California in the mid-1990s saw a vibrant revival of the band's music and aesthetic among many second-generation Latino youth. Despite the band being disbanded and Morrissey's career all but finished, Latino youth built an ardent fan culture that included social crews, club nights, an annual convention, and a tribute band (Sweet and Tender Hooligans) led by the self-proclaimed Mexican Morrissey, José Maldonado; Los Angeles was transformed into Moz Angeles after their idol (Anguiano 89; Devereux and Hidalgo 197).

Inexplicably and unintentionally, the Smiths and Morrissey's passionate lyrics of disappointment, rejection, isolation, and contradiction reached a young Latino audience coming of age in a racialized, marginalized, and impoverished environ of Los Angeles. British "dark wave" music—which included bands like the Smiths, the Cure, and Depeche Mode—featured industrial-sounding beats and drums, often coupled with brooding lyrics, found a home in Southern California at a time of changing demographics and devastating neoliberal economic policies. The destitute sounds of Thatcher-era Manchester, England, resonated with Chicano/Latino youth in the barrios and the suburbs of Los Angeles. The majority of Morrissey's Latino fans came from the working-class neighborhoods of South L.A., Orange County, and the vast eastern corridor that runs from East Los Angeles into the Inland Empire. Depictions of Southern California as Hollywood glamour and affluent Beverly Hills suburbs mask these communities; Sandra Tsing-Loh playfully calls this other L.A. "lesser Los Angeles."

Gustavo Arellano of the *Orange County Weekly* argued that media coverage of Latino Smiths and Morrissey fans is "universally condescending, if not outright racist" (3). Nor is the first time that Chicanos have been attacked on the basis of their fandom. For example, Howard Stern ridiculed fans of Tejana icon Selena after her tragic death and much of the media's coverage expressed bewilderment at the outpouring of grief in the Latino community (Paredez 71). Devoted Latino Morrissey fans and Selena fans are examples of what José Esteban Muñoz calls an "affective excess" that marks Latinos as nonnormative and therefore un-American, in this case, for caring too much, for the wrong stars (70). Historically, fandom itself has been viewed suspiciously as a potential pathological disorder, a font of irrational violence, or at the very least a negative side effect of modern culture (Jensen), but race and ethnicity add a further layer of stigma and marginality. Cholo-goth enters the fray as the latest dark wave trend from the Chicano/Latino community that challenges boundaries and expectations.

Mi Vida Gothica: Gangs and Social Death, as Roots of Cholo-Goth

Musical cultures are as much about affective impulses as aesthetic principles. For example, anger was one of punk's main emotional registers. However, punk's rage and Latinidad were not always viewed as compatible or connected. In other words, some believed Latinas/os had nothing to be angry about. In this same way Chicano/Latino interest in gothic culture is confounding to some that believe they have nothing to be melancholy or miserable about. This section explores some of the "dark" realities facing many Chicano/Latino youth growing up in Southern California and the aesthetic strategy of Prayers to channel histories of violence, loss, and vulnerability into a musical outlet that elevates pain and suffering to the sublime. In a YouTube interview for the website desmadre.com Rafael explains the origins of the song "Gothic Summer":

> The summer where I grew up, in the Chicano neighborhood I grew up in, there was fucking gang shootings: who's going into jail; who's coming out of jail. Summer was fucking gothic. It was Dark as fuck. "Gothic Summer" for me is an homage to my cousin Wicked from Sherman and to 1994. That year, 1994, is the year all this shit went down everywhere, all over California. If you were born or were around that time you know those times were savage as fuck. That's what "Gothic Summer" is about: being a Chicano growing up in the neighborhood and summers there you're dodging everything—hate, bullets.

Rafael's quote highlights cycles of violence, incarceration, and despair that characterized his youth—and by extension youth of his generation. Rafael uses "gothic" here to refer not to the subculture but instead the feelings of misery and dejection in the face of street violence and institutional violence. Cornel West has written eloquently about how youth caught in these vicious cycles develop a culture of nihilism built on "the lived experience of coping with a life of horrifying meaninglessness, hopelessness, and (most important) lovelessness" (14). A lack of "love" can also be understood as a lack of opportunity, support, or fairness that can be missing from personal and institutional relationships. Sociologist Victor Ríos argues that institutions like the police, schools, media, community centers, and even families have turned toward focusing solely on punitive practices for youth deemed delinquent, in what he labels the "youth control complex" (xiv). Given this context, many youths turn toward gangs for protection, brotherhood, and a sense of belonging (love) not found in other spaces. Rafael Reyes himself expressed in interviews that he joined a gang to protect his family from street violence that targeted anyone not part of a gang. From real and fictionalized narratives of hardship Reyes constructs a soundtrack of Chicano gothic experience that relishes and finds meaning in "dark" affective sensibilities.

Prayers mines these feelings of hopelessness and contempt, pairs it with a postpunk darkwave aesthetic, and offers it back to the audience as art and amulet. One of these aesthetic manifestations is frequent reference to Satan as the only refuge for the broken and wicked: "I sin in his name because nothing else remains," wails Reyes on the track "Drugs" that details his addiction to the "wicked ways." Much like abused and neglected youth turning toward gangs as "familial support" the devil in Prayers's anthems understands and accepts without judgment even if it comes at a cost. Indeed, gang life may be metaphorically described as a deal with Lucifer that offers certain appeal but may ultimately cost you your life or soul. In other songs the devil is channeled as masculine aggression and power that lashes out at enemies that lurk everywhere. On "Pentagram Medallion" Reyes warns "come at me sideways and I'll show you I'm about it." Psychologically, we should read/listen to these aesthetic manifestations of the "fallen angel" not just as a common theme of gothic subcultures but also as suggestive of an attempt to deal with trauma and crisis.

Of all the gothic summers Rafael endured 1994 stands out as especially dark. His statement "you're dodging everything—hate, bullets" references not only gang warfare but also the wider sociopolitical context of Southern California in the mid-1990s. Most significantly, 1994 is the year that California voters approved Proposition 187. The controversial state proposition sought to deny all social services, including nonemergency medical services, to undocumented immigrants, and required state employees, such as teachers and healthcare workers, to monitor the residency status of the people they served (Santa Ana 67). The Latino community largely viewed the bill as a nativist and racist attack on Latinos of all legal statuses. While the proposition was eventually ruled unconstitutional it marked the rise of a conservative backlash to roll back progressive legislation intended to assist people of color or immigrants. Subsequently, voters in California approved Proposition 209 to end affirmative action at the University of California and Proposition 227 to ban bilingual education in K–12 schools in 1996 and 1998, respectively (Santa Ana 239). When Rafael claims the era was "savage as fuck" he is also describing the institutional violence and social death perpetuated by the state on bodies deemed undesirable and dangerous.

For social scientists the concept of social death implies both abstract and material results of legal, cultural, political, and discursive mechanisms that render certain bodies "living nonbeings" (Cacho 6) or as Sharon Patricia Holland argues people "dead to others" (18). The marginalized, criminalized, and racialized are not only rendered insignificant to society but also disproportionately placed at risk for actual death. The politics of social death can take many forms, such as Ruth Wilson Gilmore's definition of racism as "a death-dealing displacement of difference into hierarchies that organize relations within and between the planet's sovereign political territories" (16). Chicano urban studies scholar Raúl Homero Villa notes that the motif of social death is among the most persistent in Chicano literature and cultural production (156). The barrios of Southern California serve as containment zones for people of color; the barriers to many notable barrios are marked by physical proximity to railroad tracks, freeways, and toxic industrial zones, and reinforced by social barriers, such as discriminatory housing covenants. In the literature analyzed by Villa "The barrio is a social and physical 'dead end,'" a dark and gothic place where residents use their resiliency and creativity to survive against the odds (160). Moving past death by attrition, Rosa Linda Fregoso has examined how various national and transnational forces have coalesced into what she labels a "necropolitical order" that precipitated horrific femicide in Ciudad Juárez and other parts of Latin America: "The necropolitical order, as 'contemporary forms of subjugation of life to the power of death' thus results from these overlapping forces, a heterogeneous network of deployers of violence: the confluence of state armies, paramilitary groups, private armies, private security firms and armies of drug lords and ruling elite" (114). For Prayers, then, the theme of death is not simply an aesthetic curiosity of the Anglo gothic tradition but rooted in the many faces of death that haunt the barrios of the world. Prayers offers a musical channel to lament, to be vulnerable, and to channel powerful dark forces. Under this regime of death, death can feel like the only end to suffering: "Only death can set me free from my sorrows . . . from tomorrow" laments Reyes on the track "Only Death Can Set Me Free."

"Gothic Gang Throw It Up": The Homeboy Aesthetic Goes Gothic

As an entry point into a world of the macabre and mystical Prayers aestheticizes and shrouds gang culture in a mystical world of demons, dark rituals, and existential tragedy. Chicano street or gang culture is a central theme in Prayers's lyrics and visual aesthetic. Gang culture references, symbols, and the use of youth who embody the "cholo" in music videos stamp their visual work with a defiant authenticity and allow Reyes to interpolate the cholo's sinister presence into a gothic aesthetic—they become monsters and demons of a different order.

The band's videos feature countless menacing Latino men, often shirtless, tattooed, shaved from the head, with dark sunglasses, and in hard stances. Rodríguez notes that "The homeboy aesthetic is at once the subject of admiration and fear. It is embraced and resisted as a mode of working-class sensibility and a marker of cultural difference. For those who adopt it, the aesthetic is conscientiously contoured by repetition, but its tenor is decidedly implacable and cocksure" ("Queering the Homeboy" 128). Reyes invokes the sense of fear and admiration by using the cholo aesthetic to assert a hypermasculine defense of his music but also project what he sees as a resilient family structure. Prayers builds from the homeboy aesthetic a new gothic vision that links cholo culture and goth culture through the tropes of marginality, death, and the occult.

The band's aesthetic is fully realized in the multiple music videos that showcase a menacing hybridity of satanic references, Chicano gang iconography, postpunk synthesizer music, and a *llorona*-wail vocal delivery. Prayers creates stunning contrasts in music videos that visually exploit various dark personal and societal tensions. The band's music and aesthetic challenges listeners and unwanted onlookers alike on multiple fronts by presenting and smashing a series of binaries: cholo/goth, Chicano/white, straight/gay, male/female, violence/passivity, life/death, and sacred/occult. Prayers mines the occult imagery of both goth culture, with unsubtle references to Lucifer and mysticism, and Mexican culture, with allusions to *La Santa Muerte* and Mexican spiritualism practices.

As is standard in many gothic or film noir approaches all of Prayers's music videos are shot in black and white. Other gothic conventions include using cemeteries as the natural site of their lamentations. For Rafael the cemetery takes on a particularly mournful quality as he visits his father's actual grave in the video for "Gothic Summer," and the same grave appears in videos for songs "West End Girls" and "Black Leather." Added to this classic gothic trope, however, are other "sinister" spaces of the barrio that include graffiti-filled alleyways, railroad tracks, abandoned city lots, empty churches, dark street corners, and heavily fenced backyards. These are liminal spaces of the barrio where shady figures lurk of the human and the supernatural variety.

The move to bring the cholo aesthetic and goth subculture together is embodied in Rafael Reyes himself, who performs as a self-identified gang member whose body is covered in gang-related tattoos—including those revealed on his shaved head—while wearing black leather jackets and black clothing more associated with gothic or punk subcultures. Prayers's gang affiliation is voyeuristically documented by music outpost Noisey in its short 2016 profile of the band. The short documentary prominently features Reyes's Sherman "homeboys" as they pose, kneel, flex, and look menacingly into the camera. In a central and repeating shot the Sherman gang, with Reyes in the center, pose shirtless as the camera zooms into their torsos crammed with gang related tattoos. An exploitative gaze is produced with slow-motion shots that gawk at cholos throwing up gang signs, lifting weights, and posing next to barrio murals. The voyeuristic gaze is also confirmed by Reyes offering to "decode" for Noisey the various gang letters and numbers used in tattoos, jerseys, and graffiti.

Many of these men are also used in Prayers's music videos to create the cholo-goth aesthetic or to add a sense of authenticity to the hard-life lyrics of the music. In the music video for "Young Gods" Prayers recruits the Sherman gang to stage a full-scale gang melee in an alley. The extent to which the band pursues social realism is evident in behind-the-scenes footage that shows a director unable to control real skirmishes from breaking out on set.

The music videos are filmed in and around the Grant Hill area of San Diego, California. This neighborhood is directly to the north of historic Chicano Park and Barrio Logan in the southern section of San Diego. This part of town is historically Mexican and a site of important Chicano political and cultural activism, most notably the community mobilization around creating Chicano Park (Cockcroft; Villa 172). Unlike typical depictions of San Diego as a tourist mecca filled with beaches, Spanish missions, and year-round sunshine, Prayers strips the city's sunny veneer to reveal a gritty community in the shadows of metropolitan wealth. In the aforementioned video "Young Gods" an aerial shot of the barrio begins in an alley where the staged gang fight has just occurred and floats up to capture San Diego Bay in the background along with glossy downtown skyscrapers. The shot contextualizes the Grant Hill neighborhood and the Sherman Grant Hill gang used in the video as a fight to not just survive neighborhood violence but also institutional violence meted out by municipal politics. "Young Gods" portrays gang-life hardships following a common gang film trope of violence, incarceration, and the potential for redemption; however, in the music videos for the songs "Black Leather" and "West End Girls" the Sherman homeboys and their cholo aesthetic are deployed to create a uniquely shadowy cholo-goth universe.

"Black Leather Possess My Soul"

The song (and accompanying music video) "Black Leather" was released as a single in early 2016. The single and music video feature a collaboration with Kat Von D, a tattooist turned reality TV star best known for the show *LA Ink*. Von D is a celebrated Latina (born in Mexico, of Argentine descent) in the alternative rock scene. Von D's black-clad clothing style, dark hair, and tattoos aligns with the Prayers aesthetic, making her an easy choice to star in the video for "Black Leather." Von D is the central protagonist in the video, with Reyes and his cholo-goth crew lurking in the shadows of various shoot locations. The video's aesthetic and affective mood turn up the goth side of the cholo-goth equation full tilt with backlit stone crosses, cemetery scenes, serpents, witchy women, spectral cholos, and a fog machine working overtime. Lyrically, the song is a gloomy and introspective reflection on trauma ("my body resembles a broken home") and transformation ("I'm shedding my skin, I'm letting go") from a tortured soul. This music video is emblematic of how Prayers constructs their aesthetic using coherent themes of darkness in the mood, music, clothes, and bodies depicted.

The title "Black Leather" is somewhat ambiguous but may refer to the custom of wearing black leather motorcycle jackets in gothic and other underground rock cultures. Various persons don the black leather jacket in the video and Reyes wears a three-quarter-length black jacket (it's unclear if it's leather) throughout the scenes. The black leather jacket has a long association in popular culture with rebelliousness, cool, and youth cultures going back to Marlon Brando in *The Wild Ones*. Symbolically, "black leather," suggests a bleak emotional shroud that envelops our protagonist but fits well like a stylish leather jacket. The lyrics match Parley's dark electro mood beat that seems inspired by black-and-white werewolf and vampire cult classics. With the focus on melancholic feelings and atmospheres the video focuses on creating a corresponding affective resonance through its imagery instead of a coherent narrative.

The camera moves between prowling behind Von D as she traverses the esoteric cholo-goth landscape to watching Reyes and company as supernatural lurkers. The chiaroscuro lighting techniques, occult symbols, and foreboding figures build a fantastical hybridized gothic realm. The first half of the music video features cutaways from Von D to an eerie cemetery scene where Reyes delivers the lyrics amid phantasmagorical figures and symbols. A shirtless homeboy with dark sunglasses stands ominously behind a cemetery cross as the opening shot of the video. From here the camera jumps between other supernatural sequences. One visual features a nude homeboy kneeling before a grave stone with his back turned toward us as a large boa constrictor slithers across his full-back skull tattoo. The skull and serpent visual is common gothic iconography that symbolizes the persistence of knowledge even in death. The nudity also invokes Salvador Dalí's famous skull optical illusion "In Voluptus Mors." Another key visualization is a shot of three cholos standing guard atop a mausoleum. Shirtless and holding lighted votive candles they stand watch as surreal gargoyles. The votive candles are a subtle reference to Mexican spiritualist rituals of lighting votive candles in prayers seeking everything from love to protection from witchcraft—often the prayers are made to unsanctioned folk saints, such as La Santa Muerte or Jesús Malverde. More importantly, the gargoyle as symbol of the grotesque is equated with the grotesque figure of the cholo in our society. Reyes understands the fascination and terror they inspire and recontextualizes their presence in a paranormal context. As the action of the video moves to a more conventional club setting the grotesque or monstrous nature of the cholo remains intact.

As Kat Von D—the object of our desire and perhaps witching—makes her way to the club, Reyes and crew are already waiting. Reyes sits in a leathered booth surrounded by his tatted homeboys as he calculates his approach. In the club scenes the homeboys are fully dressed but their swagger and tattoos still mark them as different and dangerous. One close-up features a homeboy with various tattoos scrawled across his full face. The general shape and dark color of the tattoos across his face and bald head register as skull-like or ghoulish. Perhaps frightened by the collection of "monsters" inside Von D exits the club into a dark alley only to be finally confronted by the ghostly apparition of Reyes. The camera fades to black as the two protagonists finally face off but not before a final close-up of Von D eerily singing the back half of the song's chorus: [black leather] "possess my soul." A literal reading suggests that Reyes's persona possesses Von D in a patriarchal sense of the word as a man who pursues and finally secures his prize. However, we may also read Reyes as a representation of sinister energies, feelings, and preferences that cannot be denied or suppressed. The concluding shot links back to Prayers's somber themes of clashing forces. In this case it takes the shape of monstrous bodies and desires. Where cholo and gothic bodies are juxtaposed and masculine desire is pitted against female sexuality and agency.

"In a West End Town, a Dead End World"

"West End Girls" by Prayers is a cover of the original 1984 song by the Pet Shop Boys. The original song is a 1980s British synthpop classic that features lead singer Neil Tennant melodically flowing through a tale of social class pressures exemplified in the divide between west and east London. In the Prayers version the soft melodic chorus and flow are hijacked-at-gunpoint by a faster, industrial-sounding melody backed by a hard-hitting drumbeat provided by Travis Barker of Blink 182 fame; the song's lyrics are screamed and howled by Reyes. Visually, the Prayers video transports us from London streets in the original video to noir scenes in the barrios of San Diego (The West End Town of Prayers's vision). The black and white video opens on a shot of a train speeding past a cemetery on either side and fades into a shot of gothic women and "cholo" men walking along the same train track. The train symbolizes a dark unstoppable force that sweeps through the barrio and is embodied in the cholo-goth congregation. This group is the reimagined "East End boys and West End girls" of the original song. Here the East End boys are depicted as apparent gang members and the West End girls an assortment of women in gothic attire. The original song's commentary on social class in England is reformulated as a visual clashing of race, gender, and subcultures. While the most obvious juxtaposition in the video is of gothic and cholo culture, layered into this contrast are intersecting social hierarchies of race, gender, and sexuality.

Gothic culture as a white aesthetic is reinforced by the brown bodies of the Chicano men in the video that visually contrast with the pale makeup of the gothic women. The distinction serves to suggest gothic culture comes from outside the barrio; perhaps it sweeps through unexpectedly like the train that opens the video. Although not all of the women in the video present as white the gothic subculture has always been understood as signifying whiteness. The raced and gendered division of brown men and "white" women also imbues gothic culture with so-called feminine qualities, such as pacifism, mystery, and vanity, which stand in contrast to cholo culture depicted as masculine, aggressive, and intimidating. In one illustrative camera shot the camera zooms into a gun tucked in the back waistband of a cholo as he holds hands with a gothic woman. Most of the women featured wear black feminine dresses of different styles, some resembling punk looks, others 1920s flapper style. The clothing of the women further conveys the clash of subcultures in contrast to the white T-shirts, sports jerseys, and backward baseball caps of the homeboys.

The normative heterosexuality Rodríguez finds underpins the homeboy aesthetic appears in the video as well as in shots that feature heterosexual couplings between the cholo men and gothic women. However, two brief shots feature a sapphic kiss, but the images must be read as "framed" by the male gaze of the homeboys in the music video and in the audience. The queer kiss is quickly eclipsed by longer shots of homeboys engrossed in a handshake and followed by a slow close-up kiss between a heterosexual pairing. The heterosexual *carnalismo* or brotherhood of the cholos—and the video's aesthetic gaze—quickly shores up any sexual ambiguity, including an earlier sequence of a cholo getting his nails painted black. Romantic and aesthetic pairing is also used to resolve the apparent subcultural incompatibility.

This remix of the "East End boys and West End girls" conflict is resolved by finding literal and figurative common ground. Linked by a familiarity with death and social marginality, goths and cholos come together in the music video at a cemetery, with death as a literal and aesthetic meeting ground of the two subcultures. Michel Foucault famously described the Western cemetery as a prime example of his concept of heterotopic spaces—real and imagined spaces of layered meanings and otherness. Not only is the cemetery a common thematic of gothic culture but also a liminal space of the city where they are free to explore dark interests and even forbidden romance. The cholo-goth mass gather among gravestones as the camera pans in to tarot cards with pentagrams and medieval devils played atop a blanket with Aztec iconography—its own type of pagan idolatry. The cemetery is understood to be a haunted place, in this case, by people "dead to others." Alone together they drink, smoke, read tarot cards over gravestones, and pair off. In the end the contrasting categories of white/brown, male/female, straight/queer are resolved by the video's final sequence in which a cholo-goth couple linger in a kiss, only to be interrupted by the gothic woman reaching for the cholo's handgun and firing it at the camera/audience. This final gesture breaks the established passivity or pacifism of the gothic subculture and adds a level femininity to male gang culture, and thus presents a symbolic embrace of duality.

Dark Rituals of Gender and Sexuality

Chicano studies scholars have established popular music as a space where gender and sexuality identities play out and where norms are tested and transgressed, however fleeting, and new identities are explored (Espinoza; Bragg and McFarland; Vargas; Pérez). Prayers's cholo-goth aesthetic is no exception as we see a variety of critical and uncritical gender and sex politics play out in their music, videos, and interviews. Reyes's gender performance and the representations of masculinity and femininity in the band's videos showcase both liberating impulses and masculinist pitfalls. The cholo and gothic influences of Prayers's gender and sex politics appear a duality of conflicting modes of being, the former conservative and aggressive and the latter ostensibly more open and transgressive. However, as analyzed later in the chapter the gothic subculture's supposed egalitarian social norms often mask heteronormative and patriarchal impulses as well.

Coming from a hypermasculine Chicano and gang culture background Reyes seems quite aware that his interest in gothic music and gothic body adornment throws his masculinity and sexuality into question for anyone holding strict patriarchal views on Chicano masculinity. Prayers's videos display scenes in which Reyes wears black lipstick, uses eyeliner and other makeup marks, and paints his nails black. Prayers also routinely acknowledges its many aesthetic influences including various queer-identified British artists, such as Pet Shop Boys, and Reyes posted a picture with Boy George on the band's Instagram account. Another notable picture on the social media account featured Reyes posed nude, reclining on a velvet couch. The homoeroticism of the image led to a barrage of homophobic comments and alleged death threats. Asked about why some men and women resist duality or a spectrum of gender expression Reyes explained:

> It's not their fault. Society and religion has [sic] poisoned their minds. They are afraid of real freedom. They are slaves who live in fear of self-liberation. Only through vulnerability can we empower them. Someone has to be the sacrificial lamb ... to experience a fulfilling life both genders must embrace it's [sic] counterpart. Repressing what nature has given us is ignorant and shameful. (Ruin)

Reyes implies he is a gender martyr (using the language of ritual) as he pushes against narrow definitions of Chicano masculinity by making himself vulnerable through his art. Indeed, Reyes and his bandmate Dave Parley's contrasting personalities and traits represent a form of duality. Parley is the yin to Reyes's yang as he rarely speaks on camera and is less physically intimidating, and his calm nature appears to be a grounding force to the volatile energy inside Reyes. In the interview by Noisey Reyes remarked on the opposing energies of each: "I'm filled with hate but he [Parley] gives me love and shows me that I am loved." Their unguarded affection toward each other also serves as a model for young men to express affection for and between other men.

In a different tone and style, Reyes's commentary on masculinity also echoes recent scholarly and creative work that seeks to subvert rigid notions of Latino masculinity. The anthology *Muy Macho: Latino Men Confront Their Manhood* (1996) showcases personal reflections from writers and scholars as they come to terms with how machismo has shaped their sense of self. Similarly, research by Gabriel S. Estrada and Alfredo Mirandé interrogates the patriarchal binds and mythology of Latino masculinity and suggests new understandings of masculinity are needed, whether they come from pre-Hispanic traditions as Estrada suggests or a grounded praxis of Latino experience as advocated by Mirandé. Using popular culture, subcultural identifications, and esoteric interests Reyes builds and disseminates to his audience his own compelling and flawed conception of masculinity.

Although the rhetoric of masculine vulnerability, duality, and openness are laudatory ideas to champion, a closer examination of the band's gender and sexual politics reveals various contradictions most apparent in the underlying hypermasculinity of their espoused masculine vulnerability and an uncritical use of female bodies in their videos.

Despite seeking to upend gender stereotypes and the notion that "queer" interests lead to queer sexuality, Reyes, defends his gender fluidity and vulnerability by relying on violent hypermasculinity—asserted by him and his homeboys—to protect his gender "transgressions." In other words, he relies on the same patriarchal force that established those parameters in the first place. In the face of backlash Reyes validates his heterosexual masculinity through his credentials as a gang member and displays of heterosexual prowess. In one illustrative example Reyes posted a picture of a scantily clad woman propped on top of him painting his nails black. Thus, even as he attempts to disrupt gender norms there is often a simultaneous move to shore up and protect his heterosexual masculinity, sometimes at the expense of women. Reyes also often refers to women in his circle as "lovers," a word that connotes romance and relationships outside of patriarchal monogamy. However, Reyes's many "lovers"—which he never gives name too—also reinforce his male virility and heterosexuality. Indeed, many of the women in Prayers's music videos function as little more than sexualized props.

As analyzed earlier, an exploitative male gaze that depicts women as sexual objects structures the music videos for "West End Girls" and "Black Leather." Even Kat Von D's fierce, independent television persona is reduced to being sexy gothic prey for Prayers's "sinister" male desires. The video for "Ready to Bleed" also features a representative scene in which nude women suggestively lick blood off of Reyes's body. The image is a subversion of Catholic transubstantiation rituals but comes at the expense of women's bodies. The gothic aesthetic may lend a different tone or tint to the representations, but many are nevertheless rooted in patriarchal tropes that are familiar depictions of women in music videos for other music genres.

Nor are goth subcultures free of different forms of gender inequality, despite its celebrated sexual and gender egalitarianism. While goth subcultures are characterized as allowing both men and women to challenge normative gender roles and explore taboo sexual fetishes (Brill 9), gothic scenes remain connected to a wider patriarchal structure and ideology. Research on gothic subcultures suggests a greater sense of agency for women as they actively resist normative scripts of female sexual agency by exploring nonmonogamous and queer relationships (Wilkins 332). Moreover, many women (and men) in the goth scene assert an oppositional stance toward traditional standards of feminine beauty. Indeed, the use of fishnet and PVC clothing, white makeup, dark hair, and accessories such as dog collars stand in direct contrast to many "mainstream" markers of female beauty and strike a purposely "ugly" juxtaposition. While androgyny is a defining trait of gothic subcultures many aspects are tilted toward femininity and feminine traits.

However, ethnographers have also noted the various limitations and contradictions of gothic representations of the "feminine." Joshua Gunn reads goth fetishization of "death chic," the skinny, pale, and delicate body as originating from misogyny of the wider culture (41). Similarly, Spooner, argues that men in the goth scene actually value patriarchal notions of femininity, such as dressing up and expressing melodramatic emotions. And Wilkins argues that unequal gender relations in the goth scene prevail in "the compulsion to dress sexily and to be sexually available, the continued objectification of women as recipients of predatory and critical male and female gazes, and the maintenance of gendered double standards in individual sexual relationships" (329).

This subcultural context suggests that the contradictions and limitations of Prayers's gender and sex politics are not just products of Latino or gang machismo but of larger systems of patriarchy, including gothic subcultures. Epitomizing the Prayers aesthetic of clashing forces, gestures toward sexual and gender empowerment smash into deeply ingrained masculinist and sexist belief systems. The result is a spectacular musical aesthetic that is dramatic, defiant, and tragically flawed—in other words gothic.

Conclusion: "Occult" Histories of Chicano Identity

Prayers's cholo-goth aesthetic is a unique vision that is rooted in the history of overlapping subcultures in Southern California and other Chicano barrios. It represents the latest development in the long history of Chicano communities innovating style and popular culture trends through a playful and resourceful cultural hybridity that pushes against real and imagined boundaries—even as it struggles and stumbles with its own contradictions. Prayers uses the term "occult" to speak to their interest in gothic subcultures and mystical ritual, yet, it is also important to consider the secondary meaning of "occult" as hidden or mysterious and how it links to secret pleasures and connections, and the unpredictable ways that popular culture and music establish and destabilize identities. In this case, Prayers represents a wider Chicana/o experience of listening to music or following trends that defy racial or cultural expectations, of race rebels and misfits that use popular culture as their weapon of choice. Through a critical hybridity of ostensibly incompatible music genres or subcultures Chicano musicians and listeners remix their lives and tastes into the soundtracks of rock subcultures and popular culture innovations and trends.

Prayers must also be read as part of a longer "occult" history of Chicanos in the alternative scene, where music is central but also connected to other forms of popular culture. For example, the *Love and Rockets* comic book series by the Hernandez brothers has been a fixture of the alternative comic scene since 1982. The comic book series, widely read by Latinos and non-Latinos, createed a vast cast of multicultural misfits influenced by the sociopolitical milieu of life in Southern California (Aldama 89). Also, in an article titled "David Bowie in Aztlán" playwright Gregg Barrios recently detailed his work in the 1970s putting together a Chicano sci-fi opera based on David Bowie's *Space Oddity* with high school students in Crystal City, Texas. Bowie's outsider persona and alien themes resonated with Chicano students that felt alienated and literally treated like Martians.

Each generation of Chicanos/Latinos struggling to fit established racial and cultural norms finds in alternative pop culture a place to locate their own identity and voice despite internal and external barriers. In an interview question about growing up being into gothic culture in a tough Chicano neighborhood, Rafael Reyes exclaimed, "It was very difficult yet I found purpose in it. My forbidden fruit, my secret lover. It was worth every ass kicking that I endured" (Ruin). It is not uncommon to hear Chicano/Latino pioneers in alternative culture say they felt ostracized or physically threatened for being different, yet it is often that difference and struggle that propels new visions and sounds that change everything, even if for just one "dark" cholo-goth moment.

Works Cited

Aldama, Frederick Luis. *Your Brain on Latino Comics: From Gus Arriola to Los Bros Hernandez*. Austin: U of Texas P, 2012. Print.

Anguiano, José G. "No It's Not Like Any Other Love: Latino Morrissey Fans, Masculinity, and Class." *Masculinities: A Journal of Culture and Identity* 2 (2014): 80–107. Print.

Arellano, Gustavo. "Their Charming Man: Dispatches from the Latino Morrissey Love-in." *OC Weekly*. September 12, 2002. Web. February 2009.

Avant-Mier, Roberto. *Rock the Nation: Latin/o Identities and the Latin Rock Diaspora*. London: Continuum, 2010. Print.

Bragg, Beauty, and Pancho McFarland. "The Erotic and Pornographic in Chicana Rap: JV vs. Ms. Sancha." *Meridians* 7 (2007): 1–21. Print.

Brill, Dunja. *Goth Culture: Gender, Sexuality and Style*. Oxford: Berg Publishers, 2008. Print.

Cacho, Lisa Marie. *Social Death: Racialized Rightlessness and the Criminalization of the Unprotected*. New York: NYU P, 2012. Print.

Cockcroft, Eva. "The Story of Chicano Park." *Aztlán: A Journal of Chicano Studies* 15.1 (1984): 79–103. Print.

Devereux, Eoin, and Melissa Hidalgo. "You're Gonna Need Someone on Your Side: Morrissey's Latino/a and Chicano/a Fans." *Participations: Journal of Audience and Reception Studies* 12 (2015): 1–21. Print.

Espinoza, Dionne. "'Tanto Tiempo Disfrutamos . . .': Revisiting the Gender and Sexual Politics of Chicana/o Youth Culture in East Los Angeles in the 1960s." *Velvet Barrios: Popular Culture and Chicana/o Sexualities*. Ed. Alicia Gaspar de Alba. New York: Palgrave, 2003. 89–106. Print.

Estrada, Gabriel S. "The 'Macho' Body as Social Malinche." *Velvet Barrios: Popular Culture and Chicana/o Sexualities*. Ed. Alicia Gaspar de Alba. New York: Palgrave, 2003. 41–60. Print.

Foucault, Michel. Trans. Jay Miskowiec. "Of Other Spaces." *Diacritics* 16.1 (1986): 22–27. Print.

Fregoso, Rosa Linda. "'We Want Them Alive!': The Politics and Culture of Human Rights." *Social Identities* 12.2 (2006): 109–138. Print.

Gilmore, Ruth Wilson. "Fatal Couplings of Power and Difference: Notes on Racism and Geography." *The Professional Geographer* 54.1 (2002): 15–24. Print.

González, Ray, ed. *Muy Macho: Latino Men Confront Their Manhood*. New York: Anchor Books, 1996. Print.

Gunn, Joshua. "Dark Admissions: Gothic Subculture and the Ambivalence of Misogyny and Resistance." *Goth: Undead Subculture*. Eds. Lauren M. E. Goodlad and Michael Bibby. Durham: Duke UP, 2007. 41–64. Print.

Habell-Pallán, Michelle. *Loca Motion: The Travels of Chicana and Latina Popular Culture*. New York: NYU P, 2005. Print.

Hartman, Kendra. "San Diego's Underworld Finds Light in New Book." *SD News*. San Diego Community Newspaper Group. 2011. Web. May 2016.

Holland, Sharon Patricia. *Raising the Dead: Readings of Death and (Black) Subjectivity*. Durham: Duke UP, 2000. Print.

Holslin, Peter. "New 'Occult-wave' Band in Town." *San Diego City Beat*. San Diego City Beat. 2012. Web. June 2016.

Jensen, Joli. "Fandom as Pathology: The Consequences of Characterization." *The Adoring Audience: Fan Culture and Popular Media*. Ed. Lisa A. Lewis. New York: Routledge, 1992. 9–29. Print.

Lamb, Mariko. "Urban Gallery Shakes Up Art Scene." *SD News*. San Diego Community Newspaper Group. September 2011. Web. March 2016.

Lecaro, Lina. "Lina in L.A.: Two Whore and a John." *LA Weekly* January 15, 2014. Web. February 2016.

Lipsitz, George. "Cruising the Historical Bloc: Postmodernism and Popular Music in East Los Angeles," *Cultural Critique* 5 (1986): 157–177. Print.

Loza, Steven Joseph. *Barrio Rhythm: Mexican American Music in Los Angeles*. Champaign: U of Illinois P, 1993. Print.

Mahon, Maureen. *Right to Rock: The Black Rock Coalition and the Cultural Politics of Race*. Durham: Duke UP, 2004. Print.

Mirandé, Alfredo. *Hombres y Machos: Masculinity and Latino Culture*. Boulder: Westview P, 1997. Print.

Muñoz, José Esteban. "Feeling Brown." *Theatre Journal* 52 (2000): 67–79. Print.

Paredez, Deborah. "Remembering Selena, Re-membering *Latinidad*." *Theatre Journal* 54 (2002): 63–84. Print.

Pérez, Leonor Xóchitl. "Transgressing the Taboo: A Chicana's Voice in the Mariachi World." *Chicana Traditions: Continuity and Change*. Eds. Norma E. Cantú and Olga Nájera-Ramírez. Urbana: U of Illinois P, 2002. 143–163. Print.

Ramos, Iván A. "Nicotine Stains: On Siouxsie Sioux's Racial Publics." Experience Music Project Pop Conference. Seattle, WA. April 14, 2016. Conference Presentation.

Reyes, David, and Tom Waldman. *Land of a Thousand Dances: Chicano Rock n Roll from Southern California*. Albuquerque: U of New Mexico P, 1998. Print.

Ríos, Victor M. *Punished: Policing the Lives of Black and Latino boys*. New York: NYU P, 2011. Print.

Rodríguez, Richard T. "Queering the Homeboy Aesthetic." *Aztlán: A Journal of Chicano Studies* 31.2 (2006): 127–137. Print.

———. "'Red Over White': Siouxsie's Disidentifications." Experience Music Project Pop Conference. Seattle, WA. April 14, 2016. Conference Presentation.

Ruin, Renee. "Destiny, Magick and Musick: An interview with Leafar Reyes of PRAYERS." Blog post. *Renee Ruin*. October 14, 2015. Web. March 2016.

Santa Ana, Otto. *Brown Tide Rising: Metaphors of Latinos in Contemporary American Public Discourse*. Austin: U of Texas P, 2002. Print.

Spooner, Catherine. *Contemporary Gothic*. Islington, UK: Reaktion Books, 2006. Print.

Taylor, Steven. *False Prophet: Field Notes from the Punk Underground*. Middletown, CT: Wesleyan University Press, 2003. Print.

Thompson, Elise. "Lisa Derrick and Rafael Reyes with his sculpture, Magdalene's Temple." Web blog photo post. *L.A. Beat*. January 13, 2014. Web. May 2016.

Tsing-Loh, Sandra. *Depth Takes a Holiday: Essays from Lesser Los Angeles*. New York: Riverhead Books, 1996. Print.

Vargas, Deborah R. "Rita's Pants: The Charro Traje and Trans-Sensuality." *Women and Performance* 20 (2010): 3–14. Print.

Villa, Raúl Homero. *Barrio-Logos: Space and Place in Urban Chicano Literature and Culture*. Austin: U of Texas P, 2000. Print.

West, Cornel. *Race Matters*. New York: Vintage, 1993. Print.

Wilkins, Amy C. "So Full of Myself as a Chick:" Goth Women, Sexual Independence, and Gender Egalitarianism." *Gender & Society* 18.3 (2004): 328–349. Print.

Zeta Acosta, Oscar. *The Autobiography of a Brown Buffalo*. New York: Vintage, 1989. Print.

Part III

Racialization in Place

•••••••••••••••••••••••

10

Ugly Brown Bodies

• • • • • • • • • • • • • • • • • • • •

Queering Desire in *Machete*

NICOLE M. GUIDOTTI-HERNÁNDEZ

The ugly exists, we often assume, both parallel to and in conflict with the beautiful. In fact, we could argue that beauty is thought of as technique while ugliness is an innate and unchanging form of irregularity that can even be linked to disfigurement and by extension, disability. But when we take ugliness and its "irregularity" seriously we can learn that those qualities, usually thought of as transparent and unchanging, are actually highly mobile as well, a technique of self-presentation just like beauty. So even though aesthetes would say ugliness cannot be mirrored in beauty, I argue that the two affective stances share a context-specific hailing (prediscursive interpellation and identification of being something) and a technique of presentation and representation. Thus this chapter has three aims: (1) to think through and theorize ugliness as generative, using queer studies as a frame; (2) to contribute to a growing body of scholarship that makes available objects of study that are not marketed or studied as queer; and (3) to think about how a queer aesthetic of the ugly, and understanding the ideological work that the ugly performs, and in particular how it might help us think differently about the place of Latino/as and their overdetermined brown bodies in the Americas. A queer aesthetic of the ugly illuminates some of the key components of racialized, sexualized, and gendered subjects, namely, the question of nation, the militarization of the border, and the attendant violence visited upon ugly brown gendered bodies.

The ugly-queer connection is fraught with problems. Turning to ugliness as a signifier of queerness and aesthetics has the potential to pathologize difference. However, theorizing the ugly as a queer aesthetic practice also has tremendous potential, for it provides a generative alternative to heteronormative forms of racialized masculinity. To call something ugly is to express negative affect and a negative subject position. And even when scholars attempt to engage the idea of ugliness in a sustained manner, we end up talking about beauty; it is as if we cannot help ourselves. As a result it is hard to see the ugly as anything less than the flip side of the beautiful; or to put it differently, as anything more than just an unfortunate lack, an absence, an irregularity. Though ugliness can be a way to mark difference, and to distinguish ourselves from what does not look like us, or from what makes us uncomfortable, ugliness also contains great power, a bold—if often unappreciated—means of articulating identity. In our race-soaked world, beauty has long been allied with white skin. Within the simple binaries that so often define our perceptions, dark skin (heretofore referred to as "brown") is ugly. The damage caused by this binary, across the gamut from institutional racism and to the daily insecurities of brown boys and girls around the world, is incalculable. Negative affect and the damage are manifest in the reproductive labor performed by people of color who are seen as always already nonnormative. And yet there is also great power within this awful concept.

We do not have a robustly developed language of aesthetics and negative affect centralized in the ugly as a category, except for queer studies discussions of monstrosity, loneliness, isolation, and marginalization. Because of this, the idea that "brown is ugly," can also become an antinationalist articulation of ethnicity and embodiment. Toward that end, this chapter reads Robert Rodriguez's 2010 film *Machete* as evidence of the ugly as a queer aesthetic practice.[1] While not marketed as a "queer text" and often disavowing a queer fan base, the film nonetheless cultivates nonnormative senses of desire. With its generic conventions and its presentation of ugly brown bodies as monstrous, *Machete* is rife with queer interpretive possibility both in its aesthetic engagement with ugliness and brownness and in its revelation that gender performances of masculinity are not tied to biology.

The characters that populate *Machete* are bodies viewed as undesirable, bodies that are deficient or partially incapacitated, or bodies that cannot move freely in spaces, which all evoke the scholarly and critical hallmarks of queer studies, disability studies (particularly research on freaks and the suffering associated with capitalist domination [Fritsch]), and fat studies. A brief review of the literature suggests that the bodies foregrounded in *Machete* centralize nonnormative forms of desire, what Sianne Ngai has called the "morally degraded and seemingly unjustifiable status of these feelings, [which] tends to produce an unpleasurable feeling *about* the feeling" produce negative affect, shame, and an opportunity for reinterpretation of the states of being (10). With the visual text created in film "saturat[ion] with socially stigmatizing meanings and values; and syntactically negative," images "are organized by trajectories of repulsion rather than attraction," ground the affectively ugly world that produces the racialization of difference (Ngai 11). Further, Hames-García and Martínez, in *Gay Latino Studies: A Critical Reader*, argue, "narrating stories from nonqueer perspectives not only transfers some of the burden of queer representation, but also interrupts heteronormative logics that refuse marginalized subjects their place in the intermeshed cultural fabric and history of their communities" (6). Thus, following Hames-García and Martinez's lead, the burden of representation in this chapter is not about finding homosexual subjects in theorizing the ugly. Rather, the focus is to keep the category of queer as open or unfixed and to think through why the dominant heteronormative worldview deems brown masculine bodies failed and excessive, and thus, nonetheless, reinforce the idea that whiteness generated from an ongoing sexual colonialism is the mechanism by which all brown bodies are queer in the first place, irrelevant of sexual orientation or self-presentation.[2]

Curtis Márez has articulated Mexican masculinities as "a scatological vocabulary that marks [brownness] as out of place" (102). The sense of feeling brown, or of affectively being out of place, codifies the ugly as aesthetic and produces visual pleasure for the audience. Negative affective responses, along with racialized gender and sexual destabilizations, are marked as ugly. By theorizing the queer potentiality embedded in the "ugly" I use evidence from Rodriguez's film *Machete* (2010), set in Austin, Texas, to account for racialized masculinities. To do so, Rodriguez traffics in a range of film genres—from horror to pornography, from B movies to Blaxploitation films, Hong Kong cinema to "narco" films—all linked by their low social status and sharing in excess. Indeed, just as queerness can destabilize class notions of beauty, Rodriguez's genres of choice destabilize classic notions of cinema. Rodriguez's cinema, in general, deploys "incongruent emotions" and representations that are at once repulsive and attractive while also beautiful and ugly (Aldama 57). Thus genre pastiche, alongside a film with representations that antagonize those who militarize the U.S.–Mexico border and attempt to physically remove or harm the brown, ugly, underclasses, exposes the psychobiography of heteronormative scripts. Excessive representations of brown bodies under surveillance and evil white men open up possibilities for being masculine beyond orthodox conceptions. Thus this chapter uses a queer analytic lens to account for unintended and unforeseen cultural phenomena in *Machete* that transgress conventional understandings of gender, sexuality, and race by making ambiguous the boundaries between normative and nonnormative bodies. In terms of its placement in larger Latina/o and Chicano/a and American cinematic studies, the film represents a camping sensibility and performance of exaggeration (Ybarra-Frausto 5)[3] of what Rosa Linda Fregoso has called the impulse "to overly emphasize the view of [Chicano] films as reflections of 'the real world'" (2).

Providing an alternative to the Chicana/o and Latina/o realism imperative, camp is a performance of bad taste and ironic value, which disrupts notions of high art and aesthetics, in queer and feminized parody. Sontag's definition of camp ostentatious, exaggerated, affected, theatrical frivolity that critiques middle-class pretentiousness maps nicely through Rodriguez's filmmaking practices. As a filmmaker, Rodriguez always deploys explicit parody of stock types or cinematic stereotyping of Mexicans and Latina/os, which is representative of "a social conversation that reveals the mainstream's attitudes about Others" (Ramírez Berg 4). Camp provides the intensification of emotion not through femininity but by overcompensating for what is perceived as racialized forms of masculinized failure. Rerouting gender, sexuality, and desire to brown improper subjects exaggerates what the dominant society projects onto ugly bodies or that they are seen as having little use-value beyond their labor. Overall, this film is a queered up, camped up expression of the parodic aspects of gender, sexuality, and violence. Together, they articulate the institutional failings and successes of brown affect, abjection, and corporeality.

The Ugly

The context in which the word "ugly" is uttered to describe an object, for example, reflects the normativity of our social order and our aesthetic choices and says less about the object itself and more about our values and value more broadly. Meg Wesling has called this "queer value" through her reading of sexuality. "[T]he psychic realm of desire and the material realm of accumulation and exchange," she argues, is the result of affective labor (107). In this way, accrual of aesthetic value is materially derived from the ways in which bodies labor. In the context of ugliness, the production of negative affect is the reproductive labor performed by people of color who are, when viewed via the dominant lens of colonialism, seen as always already nonnormative.

But what about the ugly as not just a point of view, or negative subject position, but as a performative utterance, or a performance more broadly? To date, there is no comprehensive theory of "the ugly," only two treatises—Umberto Eco's *On Ugliness* (2000) and Sianne Ngai's *Ugly Feelings* (2009)—which both describe the affective and historic registers of ugliness. Far more pages, needless to say, have been written about what constitutes beauty; in those moments when ugliness is discussed, it is typically evoked just as a shadow underbelly to prove what is indeed beautiful. Hence, aesthetic judgments and value judgments are often inseparable from difference in categories of race and gender. When negative affect expressed in hailing the ugly surfaces, it is a failure of performance without a context for invention or intervention, a failure of meaning, if you will.

The position of lack in performative utterances of negative affect ultimately give us little from which to theorize, or rather become *the* thing to theorize. My focus is on how such ideas become moral matrices for exclusion of nonconforming bodies by hailing them as ugly, the site of negative affect and semantic or linguistic failure. In staking the claim that ugliness produces something of value other than beauty, I want to suggest that here lies the potential of the ugly: as a nonnormative, nonconforming, and ambiguous destabilization of aesthetic meaning, which produces a markedly powerful form of desire and desirability that localizes in the material body. We usually associate ugliness, needless to say, with a *lack* of desirability; but, if we follow a Freudian line of thought about the feelings of love and hate as ambivalence, then both sets of feeling come from a similar expression of libidinal pleasures and frustrations through disidentification. Predetermined scripts of naming the ugly are normalized acts of aggression that create dysphoria for the subject who is deemed ugly while the individual performing the speech act disidentifies with the ugly subject. In other words, violence in the speech act is about demarcating belonging and desirability or the inverse, exclusion. Language codifies vitriol toward the body, and the materiality of the body forms the basis for creating ideas of race, sex, and gender differences as essentially tied to negative aesthetic value embodied in ugliness.

While we know that racialized, sexualized, and gendered notions of difference are not essential or innate properties, by departing from a normative idea of phenotype and physical beauty, and staking desire in the ugly, we can fracture universal truths about ugliness. Queer potentiality means seeing the ugly as something other than a failure of aesthetic normativities. We can "use this experience of failure to confront the gross inequalities of everyday life in the United States" (Halberstam 4). Considering the excessive nature of negative affect, then the speech act and visuality overdetermine what is ugly, what Williams has called "gross," which is predicated on "designat[ing] excesses that we wish to exclude," and "often displace" (159–160). If we take the repulsive quality of unseemly emotion and repellent visuality as a visceral, bodily expression of sensation, it has a logic of displacement at its core. Such displacement attempts to cordon off a fixed register of desire, visual pleasure, and gendered sexual constructions of the sexual fantasies that regulate psychosocial imaginaries. When ugliness is cordoned off, and relegated to the margins, normative aesthetic and sexual identifications are reproduced, identifications that garner force in the visual realm by displacing sexual violence through discursive violence. Yoking ugliness to sexual desire makes clear how proximity is determined by what we see and how we interpret what we see.

One of the most pertinent ways in which desire, aesthetic value judgment, and the idea of the ugly function as failure is in the visual field. Visuality, or "the gaze," or "the male gaze" figures erotic pleasure in film (Mulvey 835). While this dominant view represents the ways that patriarchal power has functioned to subordinate women as sexual objects on screen, it says nothing of the ways operating with a queer sensibility exposes subordination and asymmetry, an instability and exclusion that produces marginal sexualities and desires (Sedgwick 10). Mutual exclusion applies to the ugly–beauty paradigm and does not resolve the problem of brown embodiment or affect, that is further intensified with rejection and exclusion. The scatological feeling that permeates our social and sexual lives in a heightened antiterrorist, anti-immigrant climate is exemplified in *Machete*'s formalism: visual techniques add lines, distortions, and grain to the text, literally making the film brown so that it has a 1970s Mexploitation feel. That brown feeling, coupled with the ugly immigrant landscape that Luz/Shé/Ché and Machete inhabit, mobilizes desire around the social world's ultimate undesirables. For the viewer's cinematic pleasure is garnered, not through the bodies of stereotypical, hyper(hetero)sexualized women but instead through gender-bending practices. Here, cinematic pleasure occurs through the homoerotics of fanboy and fangirl attachments to ugly affect and bodies.

Ugly Origins

We cannot understand the film *Machete* without accounting for the contemporary context of narco-trafficking as state power in Mexico and the daily existence of day laborers amidst a climate of hostile vigilantism, increased Immigration and Customs Enforcement (ICE) policing post-9/11, and the dire need for more humane treatment of migrants and immigrants. The film opens with Machete fleeing Mexico as a political refugee on the heels of witnessing his wife be decapitated by Torrez, the head of a Mexican drug cartel. The film's plot is fueled by Machete avenging his symbolic castration when he becomes a hired assassin to kill Senator McLaughlin, only to learn that he has been set up to take the fall in order to get the senator reelected. As Machete hides from law enforcement, he links up with Luz, the mythical leader of "the network." In these opening scenes, Machete looks larger than life: pockmarked face, aged, sculpted muscles, leather clad, tattooed, long brown hair and battle tested, despite the fact that he is 5'6". Luz's long brown hair, brown skin, cutoff jeans, tank top, and Doc Martens contribute to the working-class aesthetic she is meant to represent. Luz had a doppelgänger or secret identity later revealed as "Shé," a former Central American guerrillera who runs an underground immigrant support network. Their relationship in the film is determined by a love of justice, being falsely criminalized for being and/or caring for immigrants, and stopping the corrupt senator and his henchmen from profiting off the labor and incarceration of undocumented immigrants. In this process of stopping McLaughlin and Booth, his political spin doctor, Machete learns they work with Torrez, profiting from drug smuggling together. Machete and Luz then unite the immigrant network to triumph over McLaughlin and all of the border vigilantes. In Rodriguez's cinematic fashion, a delicious form of destruction ensues for the film's ninety-minute arc.

Throughout the violence and vengeance that unfolds, Rodriguez establishes three basic groups of people. Luz's "network" consists of dishwashers, day laborers, and cholos (gang members), and in depicting this ramshackle group, the film references various sanctuary movements: Harriet Tubman's Underground Railroad that helped over 100,000 enslaved Africans escape from bondage in the United States to Canada between 1810 and 1850, and the sanctuary movement in Mexico and in the southwestern United States that housed Central American refugees in the 1970s and 1980s who were fleeing the U.S.-backed civil wars that tore their countries apart.[4] Showing that narcotrafficking and border violence are fueled by a burgeoning U.S.-based upper class consumer market for drugs and cheap manual labor, Booth (played by Jeff Fahey), who has a crew of under-the-table gardeners employed in his home, and his crack-addicted daughter, April (played by Lindsay Lohan), represent dual markets for informal workers in the shadows of NAFTA (North American Free Trade Agreement). The film also shows the rise of the Latina/o middle class, who climb the social ladder by joining the U.S. border patrol and ICE (U.S. Immigration and Customs Enforcement) and police their own people, as exemplified by Agent Sartana (played by Jessica Alba). Mimicking brown invasions of immigrants crossing the border without being caught to the literally browned and gritty film stock that takes us mimetically back to the 1970s, in its representational strategies, the film conjoins the ugly–beautiful for a unified aesthetic feel.[5] It ends with a mass of Mexican farmers, gardeners, nurses, doctors, bikers, dishwashers, and urban youth, a ragtag army armed with everything from sketchbooks to machetes, rebelling against the corrupt political system McLaughlin represents and its not-so-strange bedfellow the Torrez Cartel of Mexico—a return of the repressed and abject.

The first instantiation of what constitutes ugly brown sexualized affect in the film is located on the body of Danny Trejo, the actor who plays Machete. Trejo is covered in tattoos and acne scarred, lacking any hint of stylized and artificial beauty, which reads as the fashioning of the Machete character in Rodriguez's grotesque tradition (Aldama 61). These direct signifiers of racial and social status like acne-scarred skin suggest a lack of access to cosmetic medical treatments at peak hormonal periods in puberty; the abundance of age, tattoos, and the thematic context of multiple tattoos speak to familial and national memorializations on the one hand, and past IV drug use on the other (Ocaña Perez). Trejo's body, as visual text, represents a racial and social monstrosity in its clearly marked Mexicanidad (the tattoo on his chest harkens to revolutionary Mexico—a woman in a sombrero like on a calendar and cholo[6] visual repertoires of stylized calligraphy, female family members, and prison time served) at the same time that it represents a queered bodily history of incarceration, policing, and colonialism that made being brown racially, sexually, and affectively different.

Trejo's overly signifying ugly body (the tattoos and his skin) codifies "feeling brown," where José Esteban Muñoz describes the affect of Latinos and Latinas as "often off," making "the affective performance of normative whiteness minimalist to the point of emotional impoverishment" (*Cruising Utopia* 206–207). As a result, there are two disparate forms of brown affect generated by Machete's body in the filmic text: (1) Machete's own personal excessively contained and flat affect coupled with an excessive corporeal presence and (2) a transfer of that excess as an amplified intensification of these feelings to the point that they become campy and humorous, and ultimately undo normative masculinities (Ngai 52). These registers of disparate affect can be seen as an aestheticized vision of the ugly. While Rodriguez claims that *Machete* is designed as "a very fun movie and there's nothing to change because it's not a political movie," it is no coincidence Rodriguez chose Trejo to be Machete (Roberts). Though Rodriguez typically resists any deeper interpretations of this work, *Machete* is an outright performative negotiation of conventional stereotypes of ugly Mexican and Latino/a masculinities because of Trejo's body. The "fun" or pleasure comes from using extreme and campy violence for comic effect and making ugliness an aesthetic project that reverses historical racial and gendered orders of normativity (Roberts).[7] Rodriguez went so far as to say that when Trejo "walks onto the set, he is Machete, and it was without us really ever rehearsing it. By osmosis, I guess we had rehearsed it over the past 14 years because he just knows how to play that character and plays it really well" (Radish). That Trejo "naturally or essentially" performs expected stereotypes and his affect reflects "feeling brown" (Muñoz). The "osmosis" also signals what Solórzano-Thompson and Butler argue: Trejo's body has become a pinto (Chicano prisoners and their art) textual reference to his roles in over 200 feature films, roles that are nearly all the same or roles that are all variations on a very specific type, and have made him "known worldwide for playing the dangerous Mexicano in . . . exploitation films" (Solórzano-Thompson and Butler). Trejo's presence can also be read as a kind of brown virtuosity. That is, Trejo has mastered ugliness from all angles, its technical, sonic, affective, corporeal effects: he embodies the conventions of nonnormative ugliness so much so that his performance of technique is seamless. This mastery was no doubt learned through repetition and mimesis of what the audience potentially wanted to see of him, and from his own life history told through the color of his skin and its tattoos and scars. This is not a docile body as Foucault might describe, one that is disciplined in the image of the state. Rather, if we take it seriously as a historical text, Trejo's body—and thus Machete's—carries with it a history of cultural, social, racial, and gendered overdetermination. And to write off Trejo's seamless assimilation of the formalistic conventions of being an ugly brown criminal would be a big mistake. His repeated performance of a similar character also signals an exceeding professionalism, and the kind of racialized labor brown bodies are expected to perform in the entertainment industries like film, reproducing authenticity (Paredez 6). The performance also demonstrates how Trejo has cultivated and practiced the queered, ugly, brown persona to the point that the director cannot even disassociate his performance repertoire from it.

To further Rodriguez's point about osmosis or what has been labeled brown virtuosity, when Trejo speaks to mainstream media outlets like *Latina Magazine*, they cannot help but comment on his ugliness: "With a face that would make Osama Bin Laden flee his cave, Trejo most often gets offered bad-guy roles. His only request when he signs on? 'They can do anything they want, but have to die at the end,' he says" (Ocaña Perez). But then, backpedaling on their wholesale acceptance of Trejo's ugliness, the magazine tells readers that "[h]e lives a few doors down from his mom. 'The only problem is that when my friends coma round [*sic*], the neighbors all want to call the police. 'They don't exactly look like regular citizens!'" Showing the ideology of ugliness at work, the piece jokes that Trejo's face is ugly and frightening enough to scare even the world's most feared terrorist, and then at the same time disavows the fact that this means he is undesirable. Instead, the argument doubles back to Trejo and his friends' negative subject position—they are, he acknowledges, not "regular citizens." That is, they, like he, are brown, tatted up, and not seen as a part of the national body. Evoking his mother and the fact that he likes to grow roses called *labios de mujer* (women's lips, which could also be a double entendre for vaginal lips), become the normalizing factors that push back against his nonnormative *cara dura* (hard face) and that of his friends, which makes people want to call the police because masculine Mexicanidad is ugly and criminal. The story deploys the ugly only to use mothers and roses to reheteronormativize desire, and Trejo more broadly as a good man. And that reheteronormativization is critical to Trejo's discussion of his craft, and his request that these ugly characters die at the end of his films.

Trejo as lead also exemplifies a political form of reverse casting, where "color specific . . . nontraditional ways . . . [mock] ethnic lines" (Sun 87). Reverse casting stakes difference in Machete's nonnormative body as a stand-in for the brown, ugly, abject masses, while all of the white male bodies in the film are represented as bereft and corrupt, another gleeful nod to the Blaxploitation film (Ongiri). Trejo overperforms his mockery of what constitutes both a traditional hero and the stereotyped Mexican criminal. He embodies the "three fs" that are a cornerstone of Mexican cinema and are often used to depict the Mexican criminals—fuerte (strong), feo (ugly), and formal—in his gritty face, and his formal and restrained speech (e.g., the tonally deadpan proclamation "Machete don't text"). The result is that the viewer's gaze is unsettled, rather than alighting on a traditionally beautiful female body, as is so often the case, we cannot avoid Trejo's intensive physical presence, and thus we gaze throughout the film on his male body. Machete is figured as excessively manly, as if to compensate for his brown queerness, because his subject position is outside the symmetry of white heteronormative masculinity. His excessive corporality hits the spectator over the head with the idea that we desperately need to view him as a man.

And while Trejo has cultivated this persona, there is a way in which the script seems to force a hypermasculine drive onto Machete. That hypermasculinity unsettles gender normativities, as if Rodriguez poses indestructability as the overcompensative response to brown men's bodies being vulnerable to practices like deportation, incarceration, and violence.[8] This is a body that has mastered itself, all within the context of multiple historic traumas, both psychic and physical. When working in tandem, the virtuosity in performing the ugly alongside Mexican conventional notions of masculinity shows how one brown body can be subjected to violence, over and over again, and can absorb it, and in the process generate affective difference for racialized, sexualized, and gendered subjects.

Machete's brown masculinity also pushes back against the ways in which he is read as queer, a kind of fear and anxiety the script reenacts ad nauseam. For example, even though he is dressed in black jeans, combat boots, a sleeveless white T-shirt, and a leather jacket, Machete poses as the new gardener, armed with an axe and weed whacker to enter Booth's house. The eastern European bodyguards question him, and then let him pass into the home, stating, "Did you ever think about why we let Mexicans into our homes just because they have garden tools? No questions asked, you just let 'em right in." With a dramatic pause for effect so that the viewer ponders the irony of a gardener who does not look like a gardener, and to set up what one journalist called the best movie attack scene of "weed whacker abuse," Trejo's excessive corporality is the exact opposite of the unintruding nature of a normative Mexican gardener's body, which is invisibilized in the process of his labor (Alexander). We only see the normative gardener's labor, not the Mexican gardener himself. The social landscape renders the garden tools visible as signifier, like the bodyguard states above. The push back against perceived labor and racial normativity ("Mexican" becomes a racial category of invisible labor) is ridiculous by overstating it. Such structures of feeling make way for an emotively flat Machete to gain his power by wielding garden tools—fetishized objects of loss, labor, and economic abjection—to defeat xenophobic individuals who benefit from immigrant labor. While the bodyguard's initial reaction is dismissive, revenge with the weed whacker uncloaks the queer terrorist potential in fear of the immigrant body itself.

Ugliness makes the immigrant body and its labor invisible through the works performed with the grotesque in this film. Machete and Luz's bodies map and catalogue an accumulation of violence (Aldama 61). Jack Halberstam has argued that ugliness is a key point of identification. In "link[ing] [the] struggle of the rejected individual to larger struggles of dispossessed," Halberstam makes clear how difference and outsiderness express the potential embodied in nonnormativity (120). In this sense, and aesthetically speaking, ugliness is generative because rejection is the base of individual and communal subject formation and allows a certain kind of mobility. Being hailed as ugly provides a different way of being in the world and can make a person a bit more mobile, because the world desires that person less and thus focuses on him or her less, just like immigrant labor. Thus Machete's constant hailing through ugliness, and Luz/Shé's butch presentation as a taco truck operator and a Central American whose past is intimately tied to struggles for liberation,[9] makes them both ideal leaders for an immigrant revolution. Their being yoked through the rhetoric of ugliness and brownness affords them tremendous mobility as society's outcasts and undesirables—they are invisible until disruptive. The ugly offers dysphoria as a viable operating strategy for queer world making, because it is a site of displeasure and grotesqueness. Ugliness initially draws attention to itself only to be dismissed.

Luz, who doubles as Shé, on the other hand, is the archetype of masculine normativity but mapped onto a female, brown body: she is calm, reserved, stoic, and in control of her emotions, making her blend in as a laborer in the informal economy. And even though she presents as butch because of the ungendering nature of the labor she performs, she nonetheless signals marginal racialized femininity in a heteronormative context. At the same time, she also represents the ways in which the femininity of women of color is always already in question: she is viewed as nonnormative, and somehow less than the white or light-skinned women who are made into sexual objects in the film. Shé/Luz's queerness comes from the butch inscription of the actress Michelle Rodriguez independent of this role (her bisexuality beyond the frame) and is further amplified by the ways in which the director tries to objectify her body as femme but nonetheless registers masculine affect and presentation, a kind of "irregular" or differential femininity. Further, the uncontrollable nature of her body, not as the site of reproduction but as a guerrilla revolutionary warrior, queers her even more so. In turn, Luz/Shé's conventional masculine gender performance queers Machete's position as the ugly antihero as well. And Machete's masculinity as an overperformance, juxtaposed with that of Luz/Shé, makes her inhabit the space of female masculinity. They are foils to one another.

Thus masculinity is not tied to biology or essentialized maleness; rather, it is a social construction. If we take *Machete* as a response to the heteronormativity that makes Machete and Shé/Luz queer, then "the ugly" is the film's best way to articulate a kind of "grotesque realism [that] degrade[s], bring[s] down to earth, turn[s] their subject into flesh" (Bakhtin 20). Here, the grotesque conflates brown bodies with innate disfigurement and genetic inferiority, invoking revulsion as response. While the grotesque gets conflated with ugliness, the two concepts need to be separated out for us to appreciate what is happening here: for when this film and the larger anti-immigrant, anti-Mexican political climate reproduce the notion that "Brown is indeed ugly," the film makes fun of this sentiment and essentially celebrates the fact that ugliness, to some degree, is a means of refuting and disavowing not only the ethnonationalism of the 1970s, but the violence of antibrown, anti-Latino politics. While Machete and Shé/Luz's flesh as brown and ugly is amplified because of their precarious position in the economy as laborers in the informal economy, their corporeality, alongside that of the other Mexican underclasses in the text, ultimately rounds out the film's queered notions of ugly masculinities.

Ugliness also intimately links the market position to day laborers and street vendors like Luz and Machete: Since the 2008 economic crash, American laborers have been crowding out Latinos for day labor positions because there are fewer jobs in every sector.[10] Machete's rejection as a day laborer in the film's opening scene where he tries to get work as a gardener, and Luz's position as a mobile street vendor who sells to day laborers, are both linked to the increased joblessness rate since the economic crash in 2008, and how people are more selective and willing to pay less and less for temporary labor, making it difficult for people to make the wages of 2008. But it also suggests that proper affect, proper dress, and the proper performance of normativity within the world of informal economies are more important than ever because people want to pay less, have less to spend, and do not want to hire someone menacing. Machete's rejection as a day laborer and Luz's service to male immigrants are linked to potential criminal and nonnormative appearance. Luz demonstrates the normalized physical characteristics of nondescript Latina immigrants selling tacos who are able to blend in to the literal landscapes that they are caring for, creating, and constructing. Machete, however, sticks out, and is somewhat intelligible, highly mobile, and threatening because of the way he is dressed.

"Oye feo, ¿quieres pelear?"

Machete's racial castration as a rejected day laborer, and Luz's double castration as a butch female street vendor, echo the monstrosity of Jasbir Puar and Amir Rai's theory of the "monster, terrorist, fag." In pushing back against earlier scholarship on queer monstrosity, they argue, "the construct of the terrorist relies on a knowledge of sexual perversity (failed heterosexuality, Western notions of the psyche, and a certain queer monstrosity) [and] normalization

[which] invites an aggressive heterosexual patriotism that we can see, for example, in dominant media representations" (107). It is the symbolism of the Mexican gardener as weed whacking potential terrorist, and mobile street vendor
cum displaced Central American revolutionary, that play with the ideas of
queer monstrosity. At the same time, even as the film uses these tropes, the secondary read of the text overcompensates with campy and excessive heteronormativity for Machete and Luz to the point that it seems forced. Both are a
perversion of the symbolically castrated Mexican gardener and street vendor,
which are nonnormative because of their brown affect and faces. They are not
humble and grateful but read as aggressive, which contrasts greatly with the
heterosexual patriotism of the border vigilantes in the film, like Senator
McLaughlin, who shoots pregnant immigrants at the border in the name of
protecting American families and security. Instead, it is the loaded symbolism
of both figures being read as slashers and not gardeners or harmless taco truck
vendors performing reproductive labor that makes them queer monstrosities—
they are threats to the nation. Further, Luz's butch machete-toting past
ruptures narrative masculinist histories of Central American liberation movements; she is a potentially emasculating butch figure. The film's embodiment
of the immigrant as terrorist is announced in the sentiments of the senator
who gleefully and campily states "red rover, red rover, let the terrorists come
over." Because Machete and Luz are the extreme cases of the terrorist immigrant, a kind of indestructible garden tool–wielding, taco-slinging, gun-
toting anti-patriots, Rodriguez reverses the castration complex enforced upon
Machete and Luz more locally and allegorically on the bodies of Mexican day
laborers, gardeners, and street vendors by literally making them into the monstrous, a relentless "figure of the individual to be corrected [which] is first and
foremost the racialized and deviant psyche" (Puar and Rai 124). Their deviant
and racialized psyches cannot be "fixed" because out-of-place masculinity
defies the concepts of nation (United States and Mexico) and lacks a context.
Further, Luz and Machete stand as sexual and social terrorists, individuals
who mobilize homosocial desire in the name of terrorizing the United States
with their nonnormativity. Internalized homophobia structures the discourse of the patriot in the United States, and Mexican culture permeates
everyday life to make Luz and Machete sexual and national outsiders. The senator and his hired thugs' inability to control Machete and Luz's kinetic anti-
state activity makes this nonnormative sexualized threat against the United
States that much more palpable.

After overcorrecting for what can be perceived as the "monster, terrorist,
fag," Rodriguez takes us further into informal economies: in a pivotal scene
halfway through the movie, Machete learns of a con where a mark is provoked
into fighting another guy with the promise of winning half the bets if he wins
the street fight. The con's success relies on one's sense of inflated masculinity

(a sense of being *chingón*)[11] to think he can beat the other fighter who physically trains to be unbeatable. This scene stages a human version of the banned Mexican cockfight, another phallically charged sport, where people bet on roosters that fight each other with razor blades attached to their legs.[12] The scene's interdeterminacy visually references the cockfight because of the secrecy of the location, the marginalized Mexicano day laborers who encircle the fighters, and the man who takes the bets, who is counting on the participants to make the wrong bet. These visual cues suggest that the new configuration of the cockfight is not with roosters but with male bodies. In fact, Jerry García has argued that the cockfight "can be interpreted as a homoerotic dance between the cocks themselves, between the two human handlers, and between cock and man" (116). By removing the rooster-cock from the scene and replacing it with brown, ugly, bestial bodies, levels of mediation between man and rooster are cut to produce a site of homoerotic performance, leaving us with the men as stand-ins for the cocks. On the heels of being rejected for work, Machete is goaded into fighting the con man and does so while eating a breakfast taco. In fact, he is goaded by the con man through the utterance, "Oye Feo, ¿quieres pelear?/ Hey ugly, do you want fight?" This hailing of the queered, racialized, and abjected subject instantiates Machete as highly visible and self-aware of his position as ugly *because* he responds by entering himself in the fight. Interpellation of the subject shows ugliness's ideological work at play in the moment of recognition, but what Machete does with the hailing unravels the predetermined con script where he is supposed to lose the fight. The con comes undone through Machete's disinterested and almost bothered affect: he eats his breakfast taco, anticipating the punches of his opponent in the style of Hong Kong cinema, and patiently waits for the con man to defeat himself. A calm Machete waits for the man to slash his arm off on a sharp, exposed beam, and is declared the victor.

In addition, the breakfast taco centralizes a number of pleasures. Many Tejanos will come to verbal blows about the origin of the breakfast taco, another one of Rodriguez's campy love letters to places and things he, and by extension, the film, holds dear. Most importantly, winning a fight while eating food is absurd. That Machete unseats the con man and his trained cockfighter all while eating a breakfast taco locates us undeniably in a Tejano landscape to camp up the violence, staging a parody of masculinity. Reworking the stereotypes of the cockfight with the disinterested eating leads to debates about the extent to which an artist's ironic reinterpretation of an established paradigm can be discerned by the audience, inadvertently recapitulating the scenarios they seek to subvert (Guitiérrez 86). Rodriguez thus counts on the audience to know four things in order for the camp to work. First, violence and humor are intimately linked in restaging what may be the quintessential site of performing homoerotic Mexicano masculine excess, the cockfight. Second, he counts on the audience to know that eating a breakfast taco during a fight scene is absurd. Thirdly, instead of making Machete hypermacho and enraged in this scene, he seems disinterested and more focused on eating his taco that is not linked to homosocial bonding but bodily satiation. Fourth, the minimal nature of the speech and the economy of his gestures, as Freud would describe it, make it funny (Freud 33). So while one might interpret this symbolic cockfighting scene as solely a reproduction of transnational Mexicano masculine excess, we get a campy and critical rendition of it because the centrality of a breakfast taco foregrounds distinctly Texas Mexican foodways.

While the symbolic cockfighting scene has the potential for representing Machete's raw carnality, Rodriguez directs our gaze onto Machete's displeasure in the fight by putting the focus on his consumption, and hence digestion, of the breakfast taco. His aphonic mouth and silent, disinterested eating mark the queerness of this scene, because desire is directed toward food, an inanimate object that provides pleasure, and not on the physical fight, which would stereotypically indicate Mexican masculinity. This becomes one of the many sites by which we attach ourselves in the humoristic pleasure of the scene's campy absurdity. Machete's apathy toward the fight suggests there is more pleasure in the consumption of the breakfast taco than in the fight itself, taking us to another kind of eroticism in food, because the object of desire is the taco, not the other male-cock. All of these loaded cock homoerotics queerly cultivate and simultaneously thwart the affective category of macho as always already seeking out physical conflict as part of subject formation; instead, food is a more primary object of desire. In other words, the human cockfight's stripped-down baseness and conservation of bodily force and emotion positions Machete not as a slasher (a horror film character who relentlessly attacks with a knife or razor), but as a calculated thinker who manages his affect and focuses on his eating. Desire is generated in the consumption of the food and the rejection of bodily contact or physicality, an asexual queer gesture that finds physical pleasure in eating rather than the homoerotics of cockfighting.

In another scene that stages queer brown sexual contact, Machete breaks into Booth's house, the white drug lord, and takes advantage of the two things he holds dear: his wife and daughter. Here Rodriguez uses two other hyperbolic genres—the Mexican telenovela (a melodramatic television form often dealing with taboo themes, such as relationships between people of different races and social classes) and the porno flick—to show how and justify why women develop a sexual interest in Machete: because his difference and ugliness are marketable and can provide success in the market of Internet-for-profit porn. This is one of the few places in the film where the text camps up the interweaving of erotic pleasure with white women (Mulvey 835). Rodriguez stages heteronormative fantasy by making the white women of the house desire the forbidden body of the Mexican gardener, suggesting other racialized sexual possibilities. In an utterly implausible scene except for in the Robert Rodriguez film world, after Machete takes control of Booth's house, Booth's wife and daughter April take advantage of a bad situation and decide that they should make a porn film with Machete and sell it on the Internet. April begins to shoot the film, repulsed by what her mother sees in Machete. But upon second look, she realizes that her disgust and his ugliness are precisely the queer things that will make her homemade porno sell. The sexual fantasy of a pockmarked, tatted up Mexican gardener having sex with an upper class white woman and her mother shows that these upper class white women are agents in sex work/marketing their bodies, an aspect of global economies and web commerce. Second, April's desire to draw attention to herself with this mom and daughter pornography collaboration suggests the desire to capture not only a niche market but also, the "(post) feminist ethos emphasizing . . . independence and agency through a neoliberal discourse of freedom of choice" (Nikunen and Paasonen 36). Taking this neoliberal discourse of choice as its backbone, the women in this particular scene are subjects of their own making, engaging in nonnormative incestuous sexual acts. Machete's queer brown body authorizes, and is the conduit for, incest. Third, the scene relies on Blaxploitation as its textual interlocutor because it posits "masculinity that is empowered by a sexuality that, in terms of [a] film's visual display, it barely enacts" (Ongiri 174). Like in the other sex scene with She/Ché in the first thirty minutes of the film, there is a "rigid display of emotive and physical inaction," quite the opposite of the stereotyped brown body and its supposed capacity for hyper or optimal sexual performance. Thus, even though the script wants us to believe that Machete's sexual prowess is active and macho, it demonstrates how use of the penis is "remarkably ideologically, visually, and physically static and stationary" and visually absent (175).

Here, the gardener fucks the white man by seeming to fuck his wife and daughter (we do not know if Machete actually has sex them) in their porn film. While we could read this scene as Machete fucking his way to liberation, he is relatively stationary in the scene, and the corny soundtrack that chants his name softly, "Machete, Machete, Machete," accompanied by the shaking of maracas, only makes that projection of sexual prowess all the more campy. Still, the body of the passing day laborer/Mexican gardener, labeled a threat to economic security and at the same time the site of economic profit, is even found to be terrorist for a white male heteropatriotic national imaginary because it represents neither the nonnormative nor idealized sexual partner in the case of the homemade porn film. It is also a kind of hypermasculinized heteronormative revisioning of the sexual/gender politics of racial castration. For fear of Machete being confused with the monstrous nonheteronormativity, where "queerness as sexual deviancy is tied to the monstrous figure of the terrorist as a way to otherize and quarantine subjects classified as 'terrorists,' but also to normalize and discipline a population through these very monstrous figures," Rodriguez uses this porn scene to make sure that this sexual terrorist is not a fag in any way, shape, or form (Puar and Rai 125). In other words, public heteronormative desire for Machete's queered body, which originally is an object of disgust for almost all of the women in the film, attempts to break the notion of the ugly other who is quarantined, and sexually and racially disciplined. But that desire also facilitates other nonnormative sexual practices like incest. Further, the reinstantiation of brown heteronormativity is a response to the connection made between terrorism and contemporary discourses about the sexually deviant homosexual brown body. Celebrating Machete's indefatigable physicality, but not necessarily sexual drive, the camp comes when the monstrous becomes less so with the hybrid Mexploitation-porn citation as comedic excess and impossibility.

After the porn is shot and the women pass out, Machete delivers the two naked women to church in a hearse where his brother, Padre Benicio del Toro, receives them, pushing the campy absurdity further. Even though this intertextual reference to Blaxploitation mentioned earlier might position these women as sexually exploited by Machete, the fact that he is the gateway for their incestuous sex scene indicates the contrary. Instead of exploitation, the incest and porn flick indicate knowing and consenting subjects performing sexuality in a global economy for profit. That Machete delivers them to a church, at some level, positions Machete having some sense of morality and redeems the social death of incest symbolized in the hearse so that they can become "good people," as Padre Benicio del Toro nervously and campily states—the moral corrective to the pornographic scene.

Overall, these grotesque combinations of ugliness and desire, either posited in the eros of eating a breakfast taco while participating in a human cockfight or a quirky ploy to sell web porn, demonstrate *Machete*'s cultivated representation of seeking out pleasure in the encounter with excess (Aldama 59). Excessive drives for food and market access via racialized ugly immigrant male bodies are sexual disruptions that verge on the implausible, queering these staged interactions in the film. Overcompensating for the ways the dominant culture queers Mexican immigrant male sexuality, the foregoing scenes represent a kind of horror for the white male patriarchies that they dismantle (Booth's home, his wife, his daughter, etc.). Shortly thereafter, Senator McLaughlin kills Booth. The fear and fascination embodied in the ugly immigrant also establish masculinities that are not always attached to male bodies. Thus one could argue that the body being read as out of place contributes to why he is considered "ugly."

Blaxploitation, Aural Pornographies, and Butch Masculinities

In the several scenes of contact between Machete and Luz/Shé, she offers a particularly striking performance of masculinity. She is detached, affectively flat, gritty, aggressive, and politically conscious, a mode of existence that destabilizes normative Latina standards of femininity. In contrast to the racial history of brown women being seen as overly sexualized, Luz/Shé is viewed as less feminine compared with April (Lohan's character) but still sexualized because of the way camera angles linger on her legs, breasts, and eventually her leather clad ripped toroso. Rodriguez's performance as Luz/Shé riffs on the stoic ways people interpret the masculine affect of Ché Guevara (her male tocayo) and a previous filmography that has cast her in butch professions like boxer, surfer, cop, and combat pilot, among others. The composite affective archive of Michelle Rodriguez's performance mark her as a leather-clad butch, even though she has insisted that she wants to be femme, feminine, or "sexy" in her roles. Michelle Rodriguez stated, in a 2010 interview,

> You know what was amazing to me? Finally not having a frickin' cop outfit. I'm so tired of these butchy polyester outfits. It seems every time I do something I'm wearing some government outfit—it's so annoying. With the exception of *Fast and the Furious*, I'm always in uniform. I'm always like, "Can I just get rid of this butch outfit and be hot for once?" (Minaya)

Such animated agitation and annoyance about being read as butch follows Sianne Ngai's argument that problematic feelings demonstrate an exaggerated responsiveness to the language of others, a kind of deflecting away from the excess of her body being read within the signs of masculine gender performance (32). Lauding the hope to find men who are manlier than she, Rodriguez articulates her frustration in being typecast butch herself and overall gender expectations ("Michelle Rodriguez Discusses Love Life").

When we first lay eyes on Luz/Shé in the opening credits, she brandishes a leather eye patch and a huge assault rifle that dwarfs her body. The rifle covers what will later be her "leather daddy" clothing of bondage, discipline, dominance, and submission, but with a bikini top, washboard abs, and combat boots, a negotiation of hard femme performance. Multidirectional erotics are mobilized via sexually ambiguous masculine gender performance because her character is not marked as a lesbian but is nonetheless notably butch. The toughness in commanding the assault rifle only adds to the BDSM (bondage, dominance, submission, and masochism) Latin American Revolutionary sexual fantasy that it evokes for the audience. This is in extreme contrast with the quotidian Luz who wears cutoff shorts, combat boots, and a tank top while serving tacos to day laborers.

It is the quotidian Luz that intercepts Machete in her taco truck after his paid assassination gig goes sour. She yells, "You're all over the TV cabrón, come on, get inside!" This salutation of brotherhood names the stupidity of his actions, the gravity of his situation (he is fucked), and the masculinized affective bonds they have generated through shared political interests in immigration. She takes him to her run-down shack in east Austin. From the outside, the structure tells a story of poverty and subsistence. Inside, however, the home exhibits a kind of *rasquache* (resourceful repurposing of materials in a Chicana/o aesthetic) domesticity: the kitchen is the primary point of entry, bearing a surplus of canned foods, pots and pans, and kitschy Mexican curios like plastic chiles and ajo hanging from the vent. The bedroom also bears these same rasquache touches, including a beaded wood curtain, a fringed lamp, a velvet painting of a Mexican bandido, and an East Indian textile bedspread and pillow shams. Machete and the viewer pan to newspaper clippings pegged to a wall. We see a photo of Luz picking cotton as a child, under the headline, "Mujeres rebeldes llevan la revolución," "Shé Sobrevivirá?" ["Rebel Women Lead the Revolution" and "Did Shé Survive?"]. This archive of feeling, to use Ann Cvetkovich's words, shows both the ordinary and extraordinary nature of trauma in the lives of queer and displaced subjects. Cognitive dissonance is also staged in this scene in the contrast between how Luz/Shé actually lives her daily life and the mythologized repertoire of images of Shé that adorn her dresser. One in particular stands out, which imitates, both in color scheme and form, the iconography of Ché Guevara.

In a beret, svelte, feminine body with curves and stylized hair and machine gun, this is a femmed up, glammed up icon of a female revolutionary and a contrast with the butch-presenting Luz. Nonetheless, both figures are sexually self-possessed in their gender presentations. When Machete asks if she is indeed Shé, she responds, "Shé's a myth," and begins to pass an egg on his forehead. A ritual *limpia*, or cleaning, meant to take away "pollution" in the form of curses or bad luck, this is a further queering of Luz as a *bruja* or white witch in that she is a butch harnessing what is thought to be feminine power. When read in the context of white magic or *bruja blanca* that is used for good in Mexican and Chicano folk traditions, the flatly stated phrase, "try not to bleed on the bed," takes on a new valance. If Machete bleeds on her bed, his wounds will not ruin the sovereignty of her sleep-space as sexual space, but rather, she too will have the same *maldición*, or affliction, that he is afflicted with, by touching his blood. As the *limpia* proceeds, Machete forcefully grabs her hand in a sexually suggestive manner, beginning a long stare between the two. She lays him forcefully on the bed, and in the process cracks the egg beneath his body. He touches her leg and she slaps him, stating "Cuidado, don't start what you can't finish . . . Machete." She is a fighter rather than a lover. Luz's knowledge of Machete is in the legend, and he coyly argues, "Maybe the legend is better."

With this utterance, 1970's Blaxploitation-pornographic music begins to play and Luz hurls herself on top of Machete. We do not see anything, but the proximity of her body to his, and the pornographic track suggests that they are about to have sex.

The stock pornographic music that is equated with the sex act masks or conceals the queerness of the scene: sonic signification through soul music that doubles as a porn track. Here that sonic text performs a gendered and racial sleight of hand. Not only does the music mark an intertextual moment of homage to a 1970s Blaxploitation genre, it also destabilizes presumed homonormativity between the two masculinized revolutionary comrades to reinstate a gender order where Luz/Shé can only be read as female and Machete as male. The director thus makes gender and sex temporarily bound to biology. Because Luz initiates their presumed sexual contact, and she is the aggressor, the music nonetheless marks the exchange as queer, forced, and formulaic, both in his ugly desirability coupled with her butch gender presentation. Yetta Howard has described filmic moments where "aversion to the way [one] looks and sexually identifies" mark "ugly sex, [through] desire-as-aversion, [which] becomes a crucial mode of alienation . . . that manifests in relation to the figure of the lesbian" (50). Two things are relevant to this scene marking "ugly sex": first, from the white heteropatriarchal view, nothing could be more repulsive than two immigrants coded as masculine having sex. Second, while the text does not completely code Luz/Shé as lesbian (even if the actress who plays her is bisexual), the desire-as-aversion mode operates as ugly sex.

When Machete awakens, he finds a fried egg that under the bed which triply signifies the following: (1) He is cured of his ailments from the *limpia*, (2) the egg picked up so many impurities from him that it was completely fried, and (3) from a queer perspective, their sexual encounter sizzled because it was so ugly that it was hot. Again mobilizing the Freudian notion that love and hate are similar kinds of emotional responses, the Mexploitation interpretation is campy, and the folkloric reading is rendered queer in the face of colonial regimes of sex, sexuality, and remedy healings. Here filial brotherhood transforms the extremely bad ojo through the feminized practice of folk healing performed by Luz at the same time it banks on the masculinized homosocial bonds they share as revolutionaries to facilitate the sexual encounter.

What is most interesting about Luz is not her role in the network but the ways in which she most concretely represents a kind of normative masculinity in her gender performance throughout the film. In the sex scene with Luz and Machete, Rodriguez sutures genre conventions of pornography and horror, creating a systematic logic of excess. As Linda Williams argues, "Porno is the lowest in cultural esteem, gross out horror is the next lowest" (161). Nonnormative sexual encounters between butch Shé/Ché and Machete and April and Machete in the porno flick are all nonreproductive behaviors. The nonstable gender and/or racial categorization of the encounters is oversignaled by the odd placement of porno music to indicate that sex is about to happen. The music signals a reorganization of desire around ugliness and affinity and marks the queerness of such events.

In the moment when Machete realizes that Luz is indeed Shé much of the plot has progressed. Despite Luz's denial throughout the film, there is also a sublime aesthetic component to this recognition. They each identify themselves in the other person, brown revolutionary outcasts against the world, which results in a kind of utopian moment of seeing the self in the other—a mutual recognition of ugliness. It is not a sentiment-laden moment of intense, feminized emotion; rather, the moment of recognition is fleeting, utilitarian, and transitory. Here, the utilitarian nature of the sexual interaction shows that desire is situational and, at times, politically necessary as a point of identification.

Ugly affect reemerges in the final scenes in the form of disability. When Shé appears from the back of an ambulance, entirely clad in leather and sporting an eye patch to cover the gaping hole where her eye used to be, exclusion in physical disfigurement becomes a source of vengeance. The missing eye is the result of an attack by a vigilante sheriff, played by Don Johnson, and marks her as a freak. Rodriguez transforms the female monstrosity of disfigurement into a stylized femme leather butch that mimetically references Machete's intense corporality in this very same scene. Looking pissed off about her missing eye, the affect is in stark contrast with the bikini top, which is somewhat modest, as her breasts are contained but visible. When the physician asks, "How's the eye," she grumpily scoffs, "What eye?" to suggest it was not necessary in her ability to see the world clearly. If we were to see what was under the patch, it would disrupt the aestheticized beauty of violence that Rodriguez creates in this leather disability scene, and readily instantiate her as ugly, as a freak. Further, to look under the patch would be to engage affinity between queer and ability studies, something that gets negated by covering disability. It would require the viewer to make connections between backbreaking injuries immigrants suffer as an incurred cost of their manual labor. Instead, Shé's butch retort, despite her femme costuming, conjoins brown disfigured immigrant bodies (bodies that are overworked and mangled throughout the film) in the final shootout scene.

Staying consistent with the generic tropes of Hong Kong Cinema, made most famous in America by John Wu, Shé/Luz functions as potential sources of both violence and beauty. Luz/Shé is driven to perform violence in order to protect the precarious subject positions of undocumented immigrants, and that violence is aestheticized to both expose the simultaneous ugliness of the gore and the beauty of the cinematic montages. Such choreographed violence, with her position as a butch and at other times as a non-gender-conforming individual, marks the balletic staging of queerness. But she does not exhibit the butch sensitivities or excessive emotion that much of the literature on butch women outlines. Instead she is deadpan, angry, and ornery, with a death wish to take down those who terrorize immigrants. Luz/Shé is symbolically castrated first because her body is female and second because her eye is missing. In some ways, that gendered form of loss in disability is remedied in her activities in a guerrilla war against border vigilantes. Similarly, Machete's weapon of choice, which gave him his namesake, plays on several other scenes where the objects of abjection (the machete and garden tools) are transformed as a result of his symbolic racial castration. Tropes of this Mexican gardener or field-workers like the photo of Luz as a child picking cotton, present the immigrant as benign and docile, obedient, and asexual. This in turn amplifies their non-white bodies that labor and are symbolically castrated, signaling another kind of ugliness, that of undercompensated labor. In fact, David Eng has argued that racial castration is the simultaneous management of racial and sexual difference (5). According to Eng, castration anxiety universally applies to men, but he reminds readers that sexuality and thus the castration complex are not disparate or independently articulated domains. Instead, "the sexual effects of the fetish are also racial effects" (5). Thus an intersectional approach to race, sexuality, and gender, equal forces in subject formation, makes castration anxiety always already racialized and sex as an impossibility. Dysphoria, in the face of symbolic castration (degradation and dehumanization), is a strategy for navigating the world that labels you castrated, disabled, and ugly.

Queer Utopia: Ché Guevara Strikes Again

The dysphoria of queer world-making becomes a utopia of sorts in the film's final scenes: a revolution of shovel-wielding gardeners, dish washers armed with pots and pans, ex-Central American Revolutionaries toting machine guns, cholos with sketch books, homegirls, informal laborers with paleta carts, nurses in short skirts and platform shoes, agricultural workers armed with pitchforks and long-handled hoes, and low riders mounted with machine guns. These are the parting images Rodriguez leaves us with. Machete has traded up for this final battle against the border vigilantes, driving a motorcycle armed with two huge rotating machine guns that spit 100 rounds in 30 seconds. He leads the rag-tag army that surges around him, bearing their crude tools-turned-weapons, these downtrodden men and women bent on avenging the castration complex that immigrants bear in their daily degradation and dehumanization.

In this scene, we see that it is not just the drug cartels that symbolically castrate Machete by murdering his wife or border vigilantes that symbolically castrate Luz/Shé in mutilating her eye; they are stand-ins for the many others like them. Neoliberal economies, Mexican complicity in NAFTA, and U.S. imperialism all contribute to the localized symbolic castration of immigrants more broadly. Their freakishly overworked bodies and lack of citizenship evokes the broader transnational symbolism of abject Mexican service providers on both sides of the border. In this utopian revolutionary scene, Machete is joined by Luz, who has "come out" and acknowledged that she is indeed the famous Shé. As a Latina guerrilla, Luz/Shé dons an eye patch and a leather bikini top and pants along with a loaded AK-47, sexualizing the revolution and Michelle Rodriguez's body as if to extinguish her female masculine acting persona. In addition, the web-porn-making, incest-engaging, ex-drug-addict April reemerges in the final scene of the film as the figure of the penitent whore who dons a nun's habit, after finding herself naked in Padre Benicio del Toro's church, to avenge her father's death. By taking out numerous vigilantes, April and Shé/Luz's political losses become parallel when they fight the same vigilantes for different reasons. Both women further inhabit the hypermasculinized space of the direct combat of border warfare. There is something hyperbolic and yet uncanny about this form of racialized (female) masculinities that Rodriguez develops in this film. As mentioned earlier, by the end, Machete and Luz are not out of place, but become part of histories of revolution—their queerness is avowed and disavowed in this scene. In this new articulation, "histories of revolution" and nonnormative masculinity, in particular Machete's ugliness and Luz's "female masculinity" become the new social order. Immediately following the victory over the vigilantes, the camera lingers on his stony expression; no words are uttered. All he does is silently raise his machete to signal the remedying of the original loss through castration. Mexicano farmers with pitchforks, cholos with sketch books, and gardeners with long-handled hoes stand beside him. They remedy their symbolic and social castration through the battle scene. But this is not all.

Rodriguez's film is rife with queer possibility for the future, or what Muñoz describes as "the rejection of a here and now and insistence on the potentiality or concrete possibility for another world" (*Cruising Utopia* 2). *Machete* is a film defined by its odd affective registers: the sexually nonnormative abject Mexicano service providers that populate the film's landscape, Machete's consistently commented upon ugliness alongside Luz's highly mobile, street-vending butch instantiation, and the persistently flat affect symptomatic of both the action genre and the film's inescapable brown corporeality. Racism and sexism do not operate as separate discourses but instead contribute to the ridiculous affect of the film, a kind of queer possibility. Ultimately, normativity is temporarily unseated, in various places throughout the film, if we apply a critical read of such masculinities. Further, those opening scenes hailing the ugly seem overdetermined by the time we get to the end of the film, creating a kind of complicity with Chicano nationalist scripts on the one hand, but at the same time hinting at dissonant and potentially queer masculine formations that vie for the viewer's attention on the other. The unintended consequences of *Machete*'s queer potentiality for radical productions of ugly new worlds are temporary and ephemeral in the face of Rodriguez's imposition of steroidal heteronormativity and racialized brown masculinities (what often are called machismo or the chingón) in both Luz and Machete. Even though the flat affect mimics white action hero requisites of performance, Machete and Luz's brown bodies show that we cannot escape the conditions of exploitation or feeling brown. Nonetheless, Machete and Luz cannot permanently inhabit the queer future of potential because the movie script will not let them. Rodriguez's love letter to the exploitation genre (a fanboy act of desire in and of itself) put straight women and queer women into scenes as to leave no doubt about Machete's heteronormative masculinity. These queer traces (fanboy love and fragile nonnormative racialized masculinity) show the affectively limited nature of permanently imagining another form of utopian eros of nation, of gender, of sexuality, and race as the ugly.

Even in the final scene, when I hoped Machete would ride off alone into the dark, Agent Sartana, played by Jessica Alba (often read as another *Malinche*—sexual betrayer of the imagined Chicano nation—for denying her Mexican American ancestry early in her career), reinserts herself (dressed as a sexy cop) into his future after the fight to deliver him a Green card. Agent Sartana is the potential for a heteronormative coupling of the Mexican antihero and a newly politically conscious former ICE agent, what Mark Rifkin has called "the attendant presumption of heterocouplehood as the atom of social life that helps position other logics of identification, affiliation, and self representation" (36). While the permanent residency Sartana provides hints at a heteronormative future, and maybe even ugly babies, reading the scene another way yields a queer possible futurity for Machete, by seeing them as a queer family, conjoining the ugly and undesirable Machete with a highly desirable and positive affect–evoking Jessica Alba. If Whitney Davis's call for "an alternative to, the social relations of juridical kin or real biological family" (310) holds sway in this final scene, and, given that Machete's reproductive legacy is short-circuited with the decapitation of his wife and child in the opening scenes, this coupling might be a nonjuridical family in the sense that they are mixed status (Sartana is an ICE agent and U.S. citizen; Machete is an undocumented outlaw).

But we might also see this ending as reflective of what Muñoz further calls "virtuosity and failure . . . [as] queerness's way" (*Cruising Utopia* 17). The utopian futurist ending of *Machete* and the violence by which Machete and Luz reclaim the self and thus win the race war. In the ugly registers of Mexploitation, it is somehow more pleasurable and utopian that homicidal violence is enacted by people of color, queers in leather, and penitent drug-addicted whores. The final scene is futurist utopia with an imposition of steroidal masculinity. The feo, fuerte, y formal in campy, seemingly forced performances of both Luz and Machete's masculinities provide a future alternative that is outside of straight expectations for beauty, providing ugliness (both literally and figuratively) as the celebrated alternative. Such ugly brown aesthetics are made flesh in Machete and Luz's (crip) bodies, providing dysphoria as a strategy for social change. Ugly brown masculinities are the failure of ethnonationalism (brown is ugly), which is what gives the film a kind of queer potentiality. The display of affiliations, gestures, and communal imaginings of excess at the film's end deploy the eros of violence as a resolution to the mistreatment of ugly queer brown bodies, as a remedy to Machete and Luz's primal loss of family and autonomy, and symbolic castration. The film's failure, in other words, shows the unintended queer ruptures, the possibility of a fleeting and ephemeral utopia alongside a normative, violent, macho world, the possibility of which the film disavows with every avowal.

Notes

1   I use the notion that brown is ugly as the antinationalistic and affective foil to the 1970s black and brown power movements that claimed each subject position as beautiful.

2   In the introduction to *Radical History Review* Special Issue 123 (2015), Cowan, Guidotti-Hernández, and Ruiz argue that we cannot imagine the history of sexuality without a discussion of empire. Given that the subjects who populate the *Machete* text are Latina/o (native born and immigrant), their proximity to long-term U.S. intervention in the sending nations and contemporary minority communities makes this reading of sexuality also about a history of empire and displacement.

3   While the notion of performative excess harkens to Tomas Ybarra Frausto's theory of rasquachismo, it is discussed in the longer, book-length version of this article.

4   See María Cristina García's *Seeking Refuge: Central American Migration to Mexico, the United States, and Canada* (Berkeley: U of California P, 2006) for a fuller account of the sanctuary movement.

5   Fredrick Aldama argues that all of Rodriguez's films conjoin the ugly and beautiful in a grotesque aesthetic accumulation of violence. *The Cinema of Robert Rodriguez* (Austin: U of Texas P, 2014), 61.

6   "Cholo" loosely refers to Mexican American gang members and an aesthetic style of self-representation in clothing (khaki Dickies pants, a white T-shirt layered with a flannel shirt with the top button open).

7   Ben Walters further argues that Tarantino's films use extreme violence for comic effect, where "homicidal vengeance is heroism" (21). Rodriguez's *Machete* shares the ethic in formalistic practice and Tarantino friendship. "Debating *Inglourious Basterds.*" *Film Quarterly.*63.2. (Winter 2009): 7.

8   Amy Ongiri (2010) more explicitly touches on this trope.

9   See Lorena Muñoz, "Tamales . . . Elotes . . . Champurrado: The Production of Latino Vending Street-Scapes in Los Angeles," which examines the gendered and sexual complexities of street vending and informal economies in Los Angeles. The intimate relationship between normative gender performance and the success of women's bodies in vendingscapes mirrors the ways in which Luz's nurturing butch persona is executed in the film.

10 Jordan, Miram. "Hispanic Employment Down, Immigrants Returning Home."
    http://www.workingimmigrants.com/2008/12/. Retrieved 5/11/11. In the third
    quarter of 2008, 71.3% of Latino immigrant workers were either employed or
    actively seeking work, compared with 72.4% in the same quarter a year earlier,
    according to a new study by the Pew Hispanic Center, a nonpartisan research
    organization. The 1.1-percentage-point drop "marks a substantial decrease in the
    labor-market participation of Latino immigrants," says Rakesh Kochhar, the Pew
    economist who prepared the report. Vela, Rafael. "Blue Collar Competition
    Drives Out Some Migrant Workers." December 16, 2008. http://thehispanic
    institute.net/node/1141. Retrieved June 10, 2011. In a 2006 study, Theodore,
    Valenzuela and Mélendez found that the median hourly wage for day labor was
    $10.00 an hour, with 4% of the total survey sample earning less than the federally
    mandated minimum wage of $5.15 per hour. E. Meléndez, N. Theodore, and
    A. Valenzuela. "Day Laborers in New York's Informal Economy," in E. Marcelli,
    C. Williams, and P. Joussart-Marcelli, eds., *Informal Work in Developed Nations*.
    London: Routledge, 2010. 414–415.
11 *Chingón* signifies the ultimate in Mexican culturally specific normative expres-
    sions of aggression. It also translates to "badass" in slang.
12 While some might argue that the scene mimics boxing, my reading centers on
    Machete's conservation of bodily movements in Hong Kong cinema style as a
    mediatory force of the body like the rooster in the cockfight.

Works Cited

Aldama, Frederick Luis. *The Cinema of Robert Rodriguez*. Austin: U of Texas P, 2014.
    Print.

Alexander, Bryan. "Best Attack Scene in 'Machete; Is Danny Trejo's Weed Whacker
    Abuse." NBCUniversal Media *NBCWashington .com*. 26 Aug. 2010. Web. 8 Dec.
    2015.

Bakhtin, Mikhail. *Rabelais and His World*. Bloomington: Indiana UP, 1984. Print.

Cowan, Benjamin A., Nicole M. Guidotti-Hernández, and Jason Ruiz. "Sexing Empire:
    Editors' Introduction." *Radical History Review* 123 (2015): 1–8. Print.

Cvetkovich, Ann. *An Archive of Feeling: Trauma, Sexuality, and Lesbian Public Cultures*.
    Durham: Duke UP, 2003. Print.

Davis, Whitney. "Queer Family Romance in Collecting Visual Culture." *GLQ: A Journal
    of Lesbian and Gay Studies*. 17.2–3 (2011): 309–329. Print.

Eco, Humberto. *On Ugliness*. New York: Rizzoli, 2001. Print.

Eng, David. *Racial Castration: Managing Masculinity in Asian America*. Durham: Duke
    UP, 2001. Print.

Fregoso, Rosa Linda. *The Bronze Screen: Chicana and Chicano Film Culture*. Minneapolis:
    U of Minnesota P, 1993. Print.

Freud, Sigmund. *The Joke and Its Relation to the Unconscious*. New York: Penguin, 1983. Print.

Fritsch, Kelly. "On the Negative Possibility of Suffering: Adorno, Feminist Philosophy,
    and the Transfigured Crip to Come." *Disability Studies Quarterly* 33.4 (2013): n.p. Web.

García, Jerry. "The Measure of a Cock: Mexican Cockfighting, Culture, and Masculinity."
    I Am Aztlán: The Personal Essay in Chicano Studies. Los Angeles: UCLA Chicano
    Studies Research Center P, 2004. 109–138. Print.

García, María Cristina. *Seeking Refuge: Central American Migration to Mexico, the United
    States, and Canada*. Berkeley: U of California P, 2006. Print.

Guitiérrez, Laura. *Performing Mexicanidad: Vedidas and Cabereteras on the Transnational Stage*. Austin: U of Texas P, 2010. Print.

Halberstam, Jack. *The Queer Art of Failure*. Durham: Duke UP, 2011. Print.

Hames-Garcia, Michael Roy, and Ernesto Javier Martínez, eds. *Gay Latino Studies: A Critical Reader*. Durham: Duke UP, 2011. Print.

Howard, Yetta. "Alien/ating Lesbianism: Ugly Sex and Postpunk Feminist Dystopia in *Liquid Sky*." *Women & Performance: A Journal of Feminist Theory* 21.1 (2011): 41–61. Print.

Jordan, Miram. "Hispanic Employment Down, Immigrants Returning Home." Workingimmigrants.com. *Working Immigrants* 30 Dec. 2008. Web. May 11, 2011.

Kant, Immanuel. *Critique of the Power of Judgement*. Ed. Paul Guyer. Cambridge: Cambridge UP, 2001. Print.

Márez, Curtis. "Brown: The Politics of Working Class Chicano Style." *Social Text* 48 (1996): 109–132. Print.

Meléndez, E., N. Theodore, and A. Valenzuela. "Day Laborers in New York's Informal Economy." *Informal Work in Developed Nations*. Ed. E. Marcelli, C. Williams, and P. Joussart-Marcelli. London: Routledge, 2010. 135–153. Print.

"Michelle Rodriguez Discusses Love Life, Admits She's Gone 'Both Ways.'" *Fox News Entertainment*. Fox News Network, October 1, 2013. Web.

Minaya, Marcell. "Michelle Rodriguez 'Tired of Butch Roles.'" *Digital Spy*. Hearst Magazines UK, August 21, 2010. Web. January 15, 2013.

Mulvey, Laura. "Visual Pleasure in Narrative Cinema." *Film Theory and Criticism*. Eds. Leo Braudy and Marshall Cohen. 5th ed. New York: Oxford UP, 1999. Print.

Muñoz, José Esteban. *Cruising Utopia: The Then and There of Queer Futurity*. New York: NYU P, 2009. Print.

——. "Feeling Brown: Ethnicity and Affect in Ricardo Bracho's *The Sweetest Hangover (and Other STDs)*." *Theatre Journal* 52.1 (2000): 67–79. Print.

Muñoz, Lorena. "'Tamales . . . Elotes . . . Champurrado . . .' The Production of Latino Vending Street-Scapes in Los Angeles." Diss. U of Southern California: Los Angeles, 2008. Print.

Ngai, Sianne. *Ugly Feelings*. Cambridge: Harvard UP, 2007. Print.

Nikunen, Karrina, and Susanna Paasonen. "Porn Star as Brand: Pornification and the Intermedia Career of Rakel Liekki." *The Velvet Light Trap* 59. (Spring 2007): 30–41. Print.

Ocaña Perez, Damarys. "5 Shocking Things You Never Knew about Danny Trejo." *Latina*. Latina Media Ventures, LLC, 2 September 2010. Web. January 15, 2013.

Ongiri, Amy. *Spectacular Blackness: The Cultural Politics of the Black Power Movement and the Search for a Black Aesthetic*. Charlottesville: U of Virginia P, 2010. Print.

Paredez, Deborah. "*Day In, Day Out*: Lena Horne's Diva Citizenship." Unpublished manuscript. 2012. MS.

Puar, Jasbir, and Amit Rai. "Monster, Terrorist, Fag: The War on Terrorism and the Production of Docile Patriots." *Social Text* 20.3/72 (2002): 117–148. Print.

Radish, Christina. "Robert Rodriguez and Danny Trejo Interview *Machete*." *Collider*. Complex Media Inc., August 29, 2010. Web. July 1, 2011.

Ramírez Berg, Charles. *Latino Images in Film*. Austin: U of Texas P, 2004. Print.

Rifkin, Mark. *When Did Indians Become Straight?* London: Oxford UP, 2011. Print.

Roberts, Sheila. "Interview with Robert Rodriguez. Danny Trejo and Michelle Rodriguez." *MoviesOnline*. MoviesOnline. Web. July 4, 2011. http://www.moviesonline.ca/movienews_18320.html.

Sedgwick, Eve Kosofsky. *Epistemology of the Closet*. Berkeley: U of California P, 1990. Print.

Solórzano-Thompson, Nohemy, and Tia K. Butler. "Danny Trejo's Body: Immigrant Males, the Border, and Citizenship in the American Imagination." *Bad Subjects* 81 (2011): n.p. Web. July 30, 2011.

Sontag, Susan. "Notes on 'Camp.'" *The Partisan Review* 31.4. (1964): 515–530. Print.

Sun, William H. "Power and Problems of Performance across Ethnic Lines: An Alternative Approach to Nontraditional Casting." *The Drama Review*. 44.4 (2000): 86–95. Print.

Vela, Rafael. "Blue Collar Competition Drives Out Some Migrant Workers." TheHispanic Institute.net. The Hispanic Institute, December 16, 2008. Web. June 10, 2011.

Walters, Ben. "Debating *Inglourious Basterds*." *Film Quarterly*. 63.2. (2009–10): 19–22. Print.

Wesling, Meg. "Queer Value." *GLQ: A Journal of Lesbian and Gay Studies* 18.1 (2012): 107–125. Print.

Williams, Linda, "Film Bodies: Gender, Genre, and Excess." *The Film Studies Genre Reader IV*. Ed. Barry Grant. Austin: U of Texas P, 2012. Print.

Ybarra-Frausto, Tomás. "Rasquachismo: A Chicano Sensibility." *Chicano Aesthetics: Rasquachismo*. Phoenix: MARS, Movimiento Artiscico del Rio Salado, 1989.

11

"Bitch, how'd you make it this far?"

• • • • • • • • • • • • • • • • • • • •

Strategic Enactments of White Femininity in *The Walking Dead*

JAIME GUZMÁN AND RAISA ALVARADO UCHIMA

Set in modern-day United States, *The Walking Dead* is a horror spectacle that explores the extent to which humans are willing to go to survive a postapocalyptic universe. Since its initial airing in 2010, the graphic novel–inspired series has amassed a considerable viewership, tripling its ratings in less than four years and consistently holding the number one spot in the eighteen to forty-nine demographic. At the time of its sixth season finale, 18.4 million viewers tuned in to watch the series, prompting the network to renew the show for an eighth season before the premiere of season seven. *The Walking Dead* is nothing short of a cultural phenomenon that further boasts numerous successful ventures, such a thriving graphic novel series, podcasts, video games, horror-themed attractions (Universal Studios), and a widely successful talk show, *The Talking Dead*, a show dedicated to discussing the exploits of the previously aired program. A popular culture powerhouse, *The Walking Dead* is a representative horror fixture that carries with it great ideological weight. Far from solely representing the survival tactics of a group of people, the television show offers poignant commentary respective to race and racialized performances in a twenty-first century, U.S. landscape. Specifically, we look toward the ways whiteness is performed when the common enemy is the undead.

The Walking Dead has amassed considerable scholarly inquiry, from analysis of masculine representations (Ho; Sugg), inquiries of family relationships in an apocalyptic world (Ambrosius and Valenzano), to articles exploring the evolution of the zombie trope (Bishop). Yet scholarship has not explored race as an additional variable that characters must negotiate in a postapocalyptic context. *The Walking Dead*, not unlike the horror genre, is notorious for "killing off" its limited people of color characters, and, while the series has also been known for killing off white, secondary characters, at the time of its seventh season premiere there remain four white characters that have survived the entirety of the series—Rick, Carl, Daryl, and Carol. There is much to be said about the limited and at times transgressive portrayal of people of color within the show; however, in an effort to pinpoint the invisible racialized center we turn our attention to whiteness as it exists within the series. More specifically, we focus on white femininity as enacted by character Carol Peletier (played by Melissa McBride). Carol is an interesting character in relation to whiteness because she is a person who is acutely aware of the racialized performances that were necessary for survival preapocalypse and further is a person who exploits these racialized performances to survive the postapocalyptic world. Further, in relation to other white women throughout the series (Beth, Lori, and Andrea), Carol is the only character who has successfully transitioned from a secondary, passive survivor to a successful and well-respected leader. This chapter focuses on the trajectory of Carol as a white female character, marking and playing with the ways white femininity is treated within popular culture. In order to explicate this analysis on white femininity this chapter will present the following four sections: first, we briefly set the context of the program; second, we flesh out whiteness and white femininity; third, we analyze Carol's mastery of white femininity throughout the series; finally, we look toward the ways racialized representations in the media shape everyday interactions and beliefs.

The Zombie and the Apocalyptic World

The origins of the zombie can be traced to the Haitian religion, voodoo; however, its existence in U.S. American popular culture is considerable as the zombie, much like other monsters, is a representative figure depending on the context (Cohen 4). The zombie stands apart from other monstrous figures (e.g., vampires, werewolves, ghosts) in that it "manage[s] what no other monster had ever been able to do: it destroy[s] the world" (Poole 200). Through a complete obliteration of life as we know it, the zombie forces both survivors and viewers alike to reimagine a world where the dead roam the world and humans live as prey. Further, the disarray resulting from the zombie apocalypse is not confined to structural manifestations of human civilization (i.e., the destruction of metropolitan cities and government); instead social relationships are transformed. This is further complicated when one considers the zombie itself as a monstrous creature.

A zombie is unique to other monsters because of its likeness to human beings well into its later stages of decomposition. Decaying flesh, missing limbs, and an insatiable appetite for flesh—the zombie ultimately maintains its human form, roaming the Earth with artifacts (clothes and jewelry, for example) from its past life. This "confusing resemblance . . . never goes away" as survivors are literally faced with what they will become if they die (Paffenroth 9). For the remaining humans, surviving this world and avoiding the zombie transformation means they must engage in a redefinition of society itself. Past vocational training, if not relevant to killing, or healing, humans, is disregarded, as survivors must become proficient in foraging, building alliances, and killing. In this regard, viewers of the zombie apocalypse become invested in the transformation survivors must undergo to continue to stay alive. Each week we see humans in situations where previous or expected social norms are questioned and on several occasions deemed obsolete. Further, while the illusion of a post-race universe remains a prominent feature of most postapocalyptic scenarios, in *The Walking Dead* survivors are forced to both resist and create new ways of raced and gendered *being*. This is especially true as we consider white femininity and the strategic qualities that shape its existence in a postapocalyptic world.

Whiteness and White Femininity

Whiteness can be best understood as the unnamed racial hierarchical system that has shaped most of the world. As Charles W. Mills argues, "Whiteness is a system of domination and exclusion," an ideological construct that systemically, socially, and culturally privileges white people and white performances (i.e., western notions of civility and etiquette), while simultaneously policing and disciplining behaviors that are not aligned (451). A notable raced and ethnic marker, whiteness has been so normalized that it is perceived as invisible—an "unmarked norm against which other identities are marked and racialized, the seemingly un-raced center of a racialized world" (Rasmussen et al. 10). This invisibility is of great relevance when theorizing race as it "present[s] a constellation of challenges for rhetorical scholars" who seek to delineate the ideological pervasiveness of whiteness (Crenshaw 254). How do we mark something deemed so "normal" and therefore nonexistent? Still scholars have analyzed whiteness in its numerous manifestations; from studies that focus on whiteness as a strategic rhetoric (Moon "'Be/coming' White"; Nakayama and Krizek) to the evasive strategies used to avoid discussions of white supremacy (Dace; DiAngelo) scholars note everyday performances that represent larger systems of structural domination. For the purposes of this chapter, however, we focus on the intersection of gender and race, specifically white femininity.

White feminine performances are notable in their relationship to white patriarchy functioning as both "subordinate" and "complementary" to "European men of the same class/ethnicity" (Deliovsky 121). White women are *expected* to fulfill their role as literal and symbolic "bearers of the white race," while remaining passive and obedient to societal and patriarchal expectations (Deliovsky 121). This conditioning begins early as Moon describes the discursive choices used to enculturate "good" white girls to simultaneously embrace and deny whiteness through discursive choices (Moon "White Enculturation" 179). More specifically, through the perpetuation of whitespeak, euphemism, and hyperpoliteness, Moon argues that white girls are taught to avoid engagements with white supremacy and instead act in a way that bolsters white heteropatriarchy. These strategies are not confined to white girls as white women also gain empowerment through their alignment to "white hegemony and supremacy" and often "willingly deploy" performances for the purpose of both benefiting and surviving white heteropatriarchy ("White Enculturation" 182). Yet, while white femininity "constitutes the locus through which borders of race, gender, sexuality, and nationality are guarded and secure," white women's subordinate role within white patriarchy also poses a threat to white patriarchy, nationhood, and white supremacy since their complicit performances are needed for the perpetuation of these systems of domination that have stratified and structured society (Shome 323).

Yet, even though white femininity is literally and symbolically necessary for the continuation of white patriarchy, these dominant systems do not protect white women completely. Their protection is guaranteed insofar as their performances help maintain the status quo. If white women stray from the enculturation process and act in ways that deviate from what constitutes a "'good' white girl," girls and women alike are disciplined and policed into not transgressing further. Deliovsky writes, "the activities of self-surveillance, self-improvement and self-correction are the psychic expressions of normative 'white' femininity rooted in 'white' culture" (121). In this way, white femininity, like whiteness, can be seen as a "reiterative performance—an identity that is maintained and naturalized through our everyday communication" (Warren 8). Similar to the narrative of consistently checking one's body for any signs of zombie infections, white women must be hyperaware of their performance and how closely they conform to societal expectations. White women play a pivotal role in the maintenance of white patriarchy; however, they are also essential players in the potential destruction of white supremacy. Thus we explore white femininity as it plays out in popular culture, for often televised depictions offer a mirror to better understand race and cultural practice in our daily lives.

It is through this theoretical paradigm that we critically interrogate Carol Peletier's strategic performances of white femininity in AMC's *The Walking Dead*. Crenshaw urges scholars to locate unspoken constructions of race where "the power of whiteness is invoked but its explicit terminology is not, and investigate how these racialized constructions intersect with gender and class" (254). Carol's performances are an ideal site to consider identity construction because her character offers an opportunity to analyze white femininity as both expected norm and a site to challenge white patriarchy. Of the eighty-three episodes of *The Walking Dead* available to date, we focused on the fifty-seven episodes that featured Carol. We then coded these episodes and marked scenes in which Carol was the focus of the narrative and hyperaware of her embodied performances. Following this overview we organized the exemplars into three thematic categories. The first theme, "complicit white femininity," marks Carol's *complicit* servitude to white patriarchy, as represented through her initial, submissive, secondary character status. Carol is most submissive in relation to three different representations of white patriarchy: her abusive husband, the male leaders of the group, and her religious beliefs. The second theme, "embodied white femininity," considers the ways Carol *embodies* both her own ideal notions of white femininity while simultaneously reinventing herself outside of these patriarchal confines. This is most prevalent as she negotiates being a mother and group leader, two roles that cannot coexist within the show. The third theme, "strategic white femininity," looks at Carol's masterful manipulation of whiteness. Free from past ties to heteropatriarchy she becomes an actualized fighter, skilled in combat and survival by manipulating societal perceptions of race and gender.

Complicit White Femininity

"I got beat up, life went on, and I just kept praying for something to happen. But I didn't do anything. Not a damn thing." ("Consumed")

The first two seasons of *The Walking Dead* follow survivors as they negotiate the new world. Zombies outnumber humans, and people have learned that survival is predicated on alliances and staying clear of large metropolitan areas. Audiences first meet Carol, her husband Ed, and their daughter Sophia as they join Rick Grimes's (series protagonist) group. Carol's initial character representation is focused on her relationship with Ed and the physical and emotional abuse he inflicts on her. Passive in her mannerisms and speech and careful to avoid eye contact, Carol is depicted as a victim of her environment long before the undead walked the earth. As a survivor of domestic violence, Carol's white femininity is rooted in domestic survival as she must appease an abusive partner that controls all aspects of her life. This is initially evident in episode three, "Tell It to the Frogs," where Carol, along with the other women in the group, is recurrently shown fulfilling domestic responsibilities (laundering, cooking, and cleaning). Through the gendered designation of labor, audiences are confronted with patriarchy's presence amid the zombie invasion via the women's participation but more acutely through Carol's full complicity. In the scene, the women are visibly frustrated with the labor they are assigned and start complaining about the domestic responsibilities. In reaction, Carol looks toward her husband's menacing stare, and softly murmurs, "It's just the way it is" ("Tell It to the Frogs"). Her compliance is further seen in the episode when the women start to vocalize their anger toward Ed, reprimanding him for his controlling treatment of Carol. In response Ed slaps Carol in front of the women, which leads to the women collaboratively fighting Ed. Noticing the physical scuffle, Shane (fellow group member) rushes Ed and assaults him violently until Ed is comatose. In the aftermath, Carol runs to Ed's side repeating, "Ed, I'm sorry . . . I'm sorry, Ed, I'm sorry . . ." ("Tell It to the Frogs"). Carol's actions and responses to this scene are highly raced and gendered as she is firmly aligned with the patriarchal authority and survival of her white husband. While her responses are largely informed by repeated physical and emotional abuse, her compliance with labor and submission to her white male abuser are representative of the performative behaviors needed to survive her preapocalyptic world. Carol knows that survival is predicated on remaining submissive, quiet, and obedient to a patriarchal figure, whether it is her abusive husband, the group's white male leaders, or her deity.

As the show progresses, her performances of white femininity persist well after her abusive husband Ed is killed. Specifically, her motivation as a character and identity performance shift to mothering her daughter Sophia and keeping her safe. This is accentuated in season two when Carol's daughter Sophia is lost during a zombie raid and Carol becomes consumed with finding her. Notably, Carol receives little attention in the series at this time, even though the majority of the second season is devoted to finding her daughter. The only time Carol is present is as a background fixture; appearing only to fulfill domestic responsibilities, while the white male leaders of the group (predominantly Rick and Daryl) traverse the surrounding areas making the sole physical effort to find Sophia. Throughout this part of the journey, Carol continues to put her faith in white patriarchy for protection as she confines herself to her living quarters. Her grief and frustration are centered in the first episode of the second season entitled, "What Lies Ahead." In the episode, Carol seeks solace from her grief via Christianity, delivering the following monologue:

> Father forgive me, I don't deserve your mercy. I prayed for safe passage from Atlanta and you provided. Prayed for Ed to be punished for laying his hand on

me and for looking at his own daughter, whatever sickness was growing in his soul. I prayed you put a stop to it. Give me a chance to raise her right, help her not make my mistakes. She's so fearful. She's so young in her way. She hasn't had a chance . . . please don't let this be my punishment, let her be safe, alive and safe . . . punish me however you want but show mercy on her. ("What Lies Ahead")

The monologue is notable as it depicts Carol's performative commitment to white heteropatriarchy via religious practice. Specifically, Carol chooses to pray to the "Father" aloud, placing her role as wife and mother at the forefront of her prayers. Carol remains stripped of any agency related to raising and protecting her daughter, from Ed or zombies, and instead repeatedly asks the Father for "protection" in an expression of raced and gendered religious devotion. In the monologue she is kneeling before a cross, silently weeping, and clasping her hands obediently. In the context of a postapocalyptic world, survival remains reliant on how obedient, selfless, and small she can be. Further, though the majority of the second season is devoted to finding Sophia, Carol is never actively leading search groups to find her own daughter; rather, her faith remains firmly placed in patriarchy and the decisions and commands of the *white* men in her life. Despite the existence of a new world, Carol remains deeply committed to those qualities and strategies that have kept her alive.

In the first stage of her performative negotiations, Carol is portrayed as a docile and helpless secondary character that privileges her wifely, religious, and motherly identities. Yet these performances do not last. Season two marks a major point of departure for her character. Once the group discovered that Sophia had "turned" into a zombie, Carol underwent a dramatic transformation. With her husband and daughter dead Carol loses faith and begins to redefine herself.

Embodied White Femininity

"At the prison I got to be who I always thought I should be, thought I should've been." ("Consumed")

Stripped of her immediate ties to white heteropatriarchy, Carol undergoes a performative transformation. She no longer asks for forgiveness, punishment, or jobs from the Father or male leaders of the group and instead begins an autonomous journey of survival and self-discovery. Yet this second stage of her character transformation is not linear as Carol finds herself in a battle between societally imposed expectations and who she needs to become to survive the zombie apocalypse. In the second thematic cluster spectators observe the liminal space from which Carol operates, embodying leadership not connected to normative white femininity and defying expectations of white motherhood ascribed to her body.

The first representation of this liminal negotiation is present in the episode entitled, "I Ain't a Judas." In the episode Andrea, a former group member, visits Carol's group in an effort to mediate peace between the two factions. Tensions are high, and in an effort to avoid an impending and violent confrontation, Carol privately speaks to Andrea, seeking to find a peaceful resolution with as little bloodshed as possible. During their conversation Carol says to Andrea, "you need to do something . . . you need to sleep with him. Give him the greatest night of his life. You get him to drop his guard. Then when he's sleeping, you can end this" ("I Ain't a Judas"). Carol explicitly talks not only of deceiving and killing another human but also about the strategic use of sex for white women. This scene highlights Carol's awareness of raced and gendered performances; as Andrea is in a romantic relationship with the leader of the antagonizing group, Carol's suggestion harkens to her earlier performances of submission. When Ed would become violent she would succumb to his every whim even though other women in the group would find his erratic behavior problematic. It is only at this stage in her character evolution that Carol begins to vocalize her acute awareness of white femininity. Audiences are privy to her internal struggle and her budding desire to subvert expected norms. This is further seen in her caregiver role for all the children in the survivor group.

Motherhood, for Carol, continues to be a central motivation in the third season as Carol takes on the maternal role within the group. She ensures survivors are being fed ("Seed") by cooking and making meals with the limited provisions at their disposal, and takes on the caregiving responsibilities when survivors are ill, cooling their foreheads with wet cloths and changing bandages when necessary ("Sick"). For Carol, this role is so all encompassing that in a third season episode, she assumes child delivery responsibilities, practicing C-sections on female zombies in preparation for Lori's delivery. Yet past societal expectations of white femininity are not crystallized until she is introduced to Judith (Lori and Rick's daughter). Lori dies from childbirth, leaving Judith in the care of her husband Rick and their first-born Carl ("When the Dead Come Knocking"). However, after Lori's death, Carol becomes the primary caretaker of Judith. She is seen carrying Judith in most scenes and is also depicted feeding and rocking Judith to sleep more than any other member of the group. At this point in the series, the only major role Rick and Carl have in Judith's life is deciding what her name should be. The imposition of maternity on white females, in this case Carol, is also highlighted when Michonne (lead black female character) interacts with Judith.

In the fourth season, Beth asks Michonne to hold Judith for a few minutes; Michonne awkwardly takes Judith in a nonverbal display of discomfort and unfamiliarity. It is apparent that Michonne's association with motherhood is far different from Carol's attached and nurturing style: she is more comfortable wielding a katana than holding a newborn ("Infected"). Michonne is portrayed from her initial introduction as a strong, independent, and knowledgeable fighter with no familial ties. Michonne's raced and gendered expectations are interesting in that they draw attention to the oppositional representation of Carol, the central white woman of the group. Where Carol is assumed to be loving, soft, and nurturing, Michonne is entrusted with weapons, invited to raids that may result in her death, and looked upon for council when major decisions are made. Far from the white, female impositions on Carol, Michonne is treated as a masculine, hard, and authoritative presence. This point in Carol's character development represents the budding tensions she feels with past performances of white femininity and whom she wants to see herself become. As her previous conversation with Andrea highlights, Carol is privy to the power of raced and gendered performances, especially when they are placed on white women's bodies. It is at this time that viewers witness Carol's early departure from what is expected of her as a white woman as she begins to negotiate the roles she is expected to fulfill for the group.

In the first episode of season four titled, "30 Days Without an Accident," Carol is shown reading fictional stories to the children in the group in a makeshift library within an abandoned prison compound. Yet, as soon as she is left alone with the children, she discards the teacher pretense, puts away the children's books, and opens a chest filled with knives. As a white woman, caring and reading to children, she poses no threat. The group has placed her in this role because they view Carol as a loving and caring surrogate mother, and while others are tending to crops, or "manning" the borders, they rest assured that their children are being well taken care of. Carol negotiates the role of surrogate mother to begin covertly teaching children self-defense, something that was highly contested within the group. Thus motherhood for Carol has transformed from caregiving and nurturing into teaching children to be self-reliant and not seek protection from parents or other adults. In essence, she is actively rejecting the core ideals of white motherhood since there is no place in this new world for normative white motherhood (i.e., Sophia met her fate specifically because as a child she relied solely on her mother for protection).

Interestingly within the episode two white girls (Lizzie and Mica) lose their father and Carol promises their dying father that she will look after them. However, when she took up this burden she focused predominantly on making sure both Lizzie and Mica would become independent and self-reliant to ensure that she would not be burdened with "looking after them" as she had promised their dying father. In one instance, rather than consoling Mica after Mica survives a zombie attack, she tells her, "Honey you are weak, you lost your nerve. You have to trust your gut and you have to act fast every time" ("Infected"). Later in the season, Lizzie accidentally calls her "mom," and even though Lizzie quickly apologizes for the slip-up Carol responds, "don't call me mom" ("Indifferent"). To a child, Carol is quick to correct their false characterization of her (something she later does to a boy in the Alexandria community when he finds out she has been sneaking guns from the armory). However, with other adults, Carol takes note of the power of invisibility within the continued performative act others have ascribed to her body.

As she rejects the identity of mother she reinterprets "caregiving" into eliminating any possible threat that might hurt other members of the group. This is exemplified when people from the group develop a sickness that can only be cured by medicine they do not have. Rather than rely on selflessness and faith, traits that have contributed to her survival preapocalypse, Carol takes it upon herself to kill the sickly in order to prevent the sickness from spreading. This is a radical transformation since earlier in the same season Carol was one of the caretakers of the sick and wounded. While the need to survive propels her to kill sickly humans, her "good" white feminine performances also makes her invisible to others as a possible suspect in the murder; to the point that Tyreese (the boyfriend of one of the people Carol murdered) asks Carol to look after his sick sister, Sasha, while he goes on a scouting mission for medicine ("Isolation"). This moment in Carol's trajectory is significant as it is the first time Carol is willing to take action not approved firsthand by white patriarchal leaders. At the end of this second thematic cluster, Carol completely disassociates herself with the group's imposed role of caregiver and white motherhood.

This is the last time viewers see her in the background of the group dynamics. In the third and most recent transformation, after her return to the group from a brief hiatus, Carol places herself as a rightful leader of this group alongside Rick and Daryl by masterfully using the facade of white femininity as a strategic ploy to ensure her and her friend's survivability.

Strategic White Femininity

"Everything now just . . . consumes you." ("Consumed")

After considerable turmoil and loss, a new world order exists. Morality and societal expectations are now largely frivolous subjective constructs, and while the characters in the show have learned to navigate the new world in recent seasons of the series, it is apparent that gendered and racialized expectations remain. It is because of these remaining expectations that Carol strategically employs white femininity as a survival strategy. The difference between this phase of Carol's performances and the previous is that she becomes more publicly pronounced and purposeful. There are three particular instances that spotlight this transition: Carol helping save Beth, being introduced to a new community (Alexandria), and Carol's strategic rescuing of Maggie.

In the fifth season, Daryl and Carol go out on a rescue mission to save Beth, who has been taken hostage by another group set up in a hospital. In an episode entitled, "Consumed," Carol, Daryl, and Noah (a new member of the group) are about to be captured by the group stationed at an abandoned hospital. Before they are cornered, Carol frantically runs out of the building aimlessly and into an oncoming car. In the context of a postapocalyptic world, Carol running into an oncoming car in this manner frames her as a woman that has relied on the protection of others to survive rather than as a cunning and skilled survivor herself. Thus here she strategically performs the "damsel in distress"—a dominant normative white feminine role that consistently reifies the role of white men as protectors. The opposing group, not suspecting that a white woman would purposefully throw herself onto oncoming traffic, takes her body away on a stretcher thereby ensuring the safety of Daryl and Noah.

Another instance that highlights Carol's strategic manipulation of white femininity is evident in her group's survival in the community of Alexandria. After much scavenging and fighting, the group seeks refuge at Alexandria, a self-sufficient oasis for survivors. In the episode titled, "Remember," the group must do two things in order to gain access to Alexandria: relinquish their weapons and be interviewed and recorded by Alexandria's leader Deanna. One by one the group members walk over to a cart and place all their weapons in a pile that will be transported to the community's armory. The last person to disarm is Carol. In a very tactful and strategic manner, Carol proceeds to clumsily remove the semiautomatic rifle strapped to her back. As she places the weapon on the pile, Carol looks over at the white woman overseeing this transaction and gives her a faint smile. The woman, whose job in the Alexandria community is to record all the weaponry, gives Carol an understanding grin. The moment is a knowing and coded one as the two white women acknowledge how out-of-character having a gun is for their suburban, white, middle-class aesthetic. Their role preapocalypse was certainly not reliant on semiautomatic weapons, and so the clumsy maneuvering of guns is expected. While Carol in no way embodies this weakness, her smile, or alignment with white feminine expectations, is necessary so that she can move through Alexandria freely and without suspicion.

Later in the same episode, viewers witness Carol's private taped interview with Deanna. Apart from learning about the incoming survivors, the interview process is used to assess job placement within the compound as Deanna wants to ensure community members are given jobs that complement their past vocations. In the taped interview Deanna asks Carol what she did before the apocalypse, Carol replies, "I did laundry, gardened, um . . . always had dinner on the table for Ed when he came home. Um . . . I miss that stupid wonderful man every day. You know, I really didn't have much to offer this group, so I think I just became their den mother. And they've been nice enough to protect me" ("Remember"). Carol is very purposeful in framing Ed as a wonderful husband, playing into the representation of an ideal, white heteropatriarchal family: the man works, while the wife has dinner on the table every night. She wants Deanna, and by extension the new community, to perceive her as a defenseless widow that correctly performs gendered and raced expectations. Further, she does not acknowledge her daughter Sophia at all throughout the interview, choosing instead to represent herself as a woman that never got the *privilege* of having children and thus will gladly become a proxy mother for the community. She knows that she needs to cultivate the assumption that she is weak, obedient, and nurturing so that she can remain unsuspected. Here white femininity offers a convincing veil behind which Carol can hide. At the end of the interview, Deanna asks Carol where she sees herself most useful at Alexandria, and she replies, "Oh, um, hmm. Well, I'd like to be involved in the community. Do you have anything like Junior League? I'm a real people person" ("Remember"). Carol masterfully convinces the new community that she adheres to normative expectations and thus should be labeled "safe" and nonthreatening.

Carol is ultimately assigned a domestic role in the community and chooses to further perpetuate "good" white femininity via outfit choices, choosing to wear baby blue cardigans and pastel colored blouses in subsequent episodes. Through her strategic wardrobe ensemble Carol uses her appearance as a transgressive space. For instance, Carol is able to unsuspectingly join conversations with other white women in Alexandria in order to gather vital information on the community (i.e., the location and shift schedule of the armory). Carol takes full advantage of the suburban makeup of their geographic context, masterfully fulfilling the expected role in order to secure information for her group.

The perception of Carol as a passive and weak white woman goes beyond the walls of the Alexandria community as she takes advantage of the expectations others impose on her body. This is evident in season seven when an opposing group, led by Negan (the newest villain of the series), takes Carol and Maggie hostage. In the episode titled, "The Same Boat," Carol and Maggie are seen in a room within the opposing group's compound with their hands and feet bound by duct tape. Unable to escape or use weapons, Carol chooses to strategically enact weak and submissive white femininity as a line of defense. She wiggles within her confines and is eventually able to grasp a rosary within her pocket, stroking it, and forcing herself to hyperventilate. Maggie looks at her from across the room, assesses that it is a performance, and "joins in" by trying to calm Carol. When the women of the antagonizing group return to the room, they are greeted by a screaming Maggie and a hyperventilating and crying Carol. One of the women looks toward Carol and says, "She's a nervous little bird, ain't she," while the other asks Carol, "Bitch, how did you make it this far?!" As they remove the gag from her mouth, they see Carol clutching a rosary. "Oh, you're one of those," a captor states as another continues, "What are you so afraid of, are you actually afraid to die?" Two things happen in this exchange: first, Carol once again presents herself as a nonthreatening individual so the assailants drop their guard; second, Carol extends her performance of "good" white femininity by bringing attention to Maggie's real pregnancy. This performance is embellished even more when the religious iconography of the rosary is put into context. Representing a "good" white Christian woman, Carol strategically manipulates her captors to believe she has survived this far by mere luck. In contrast to the first season, she no longer seeks divine intervention through a patriarchal figure; instead she uses religious artifacts as performative flair. In essence, Carol maneuvers the rosary with precision just like a rifle in order to ensure the safety of both herself and Maggie.

It is only through Carol's final transformation that she employs the advice she presented to Andrea back in season three. Carol knows she must use the presumptions people have about her to manipulate her environment and secure the survival of her and her group. Carol no longer employs white femininity because of her connection and investments in white patriarchy; instead she uses these "good" white feminine performances as tools to gain valuable information and to appear unassuming, and nonthreatening.

Conclusion

Over the course of the series, Carol's transformation is staggering. She begins as a battered and defenseless woman submitting to her domestic hell for daily survival. As zombies multiplied and in-group alliances became more important, her identity performance began to change to account for these new circumstances. In the second stage of her trajectory Carol begins to depart from societal expectations, understanding that surviving a postapocalyptic world is predicated on the necessity of self-transformation. Being perceived as a docile, innocent, white mother, Carol starts to alter expected performances. In the third stage of her transformation, Carol uses white femininity as a disguise to garner vital information and invisibility and to ensure that others will not look toward her as a threat. Carol continues to survive via her manipulation of gendered and raced expectations. While most characters in the series have shown a radical transformation, Carol's evolution is unique in that it represents a sophisticated and multilayered survival strategy. Not only has she become an acute killer, forager, and leader (often saving the entire group from violent exchanges), she has equally mastered raced and gendered expectations, which has helped her manipulate the people around her for her and her group's survival.

Throughout the series, *The Walking Dead* has been able to present a white body that is cognitively aware of her whiteness. This self-awareness has simultaneously helped Carol understand the necessity of strategically employing performances of white femininity in order to persevere. It is within the context of a zombie apocalypse that Carol understands that these performances can indeed be altered—as Moon indicates, "since identities are not preconstituted nor static, [a critical understanding of white enculturation] can enable us to find points of dis/rupture of hegemonic identification practices" ("White Enculturation" 299). In the fifth season of the show, following the group's stay in the Alexandria community, Carol tells Rick, "You know what is so great about this place? I get to be invisible again" ("Forget"). As Carol enters Alexandria, a community that is a visual representation of the quintessential imaginary of U.S. American suburbia, she blends into her surroundings like a chameleon able to effectively manipulate expected gendered and raced performances to her advantage. Invisibility is not a characteristic of whiteness, rather a privilege imposed on white and white-appearing bodies, and rather than follow dominant expectations Carol is able to strategically manipulate others through "good" white feminine performances.

Throughout Carol Peletier's survival narrative, a couple of questions resonate with us: In what ways do popular culture texts challenge expected normative "good" white girl performances? What is the potentiality of white femininity when identity is perceived as performative rather than essential and static? Finally, if whiteness can indeed be pinned down in popular culture texts, how can embodied performative acts help to connect the lived experience of white privilege to the systemic domination of white supremacy? Whiteness is not invisible, and continuing to perpetuate this misconception will only deter the progress of transgressive racialized and gendered performances. It is precisely this transgressive potentiality that makes Carol so fascinating. Despite there being numerous white survivors throughout the series she is the only character that uses her whiteness as a survival strategy. Conversely, her fellow white survivors continue to operate from an assumption that whiteness is the invisible center from which *other* bodies are raced. Continuing to ignore the existence of whiteness in popular culture characterizations, and society at large, will be as inane as framing Carol, this banal unassuming white woman clutching a rosary, as some poor defenseless nervous little bird.

Works Cited

"30 Days Without an Accident." *The Walking Dead*. Writ. Frank Darabont, Robert Kirkman, Tony Moore, Charlie Adlard, and Scott M. Gimple. Dir. Greg Nicotero. AMC, 2013. Television.

Ambrosius, Joshua D., and Joseph M. Valenzano III. "'People in Hell Want Slurpees': The Redefinition of the Zombie Genre through the Salvific Portrayal of Family on AMC's *The Walking Dead*. *Communication Monographs* 83.1 (2016): 69–93.

Bishop, Kyle William. *American Zombie Gothic: The Rise and Fall (and Rise) of The Walking Dead in Popular Culture.* Jefferson: McFarland & Co, 2010. Print.

Cohen, Jeffrey Jerome. *Monster Theory: Reading Culture.* Minneapolis: U of Minnesota P, 1996. Print.

"Consumed." *The Walking Dead.* Writ. Frank Darabont, Robert Kirkman, Tony Moore, Charlie Adlard, Matthew Negrete, and Corey Reed. Dir. Seith Mann. AMC, 2014. Television.

Crenshaw, Carrie. "Resisting Whiteness' Rhetorical Silence." *Western Journal of Communication* 61.3 (1997): 253–278. Print.

Dace, Karen L. "What Do I Do with All of Your Tears?" *Unlikely Allies in the Academy: Women of Color and White Women in Conversation.* Ed. Karen L. Dace. New York: Routledge, 2012. 76–88. Print.

Deliovsky, Katerina. *White Femininity: Race, Gender & Power.* Halifax & Winnipeg: Fernwood Publishing, 2010. Print.

DiAngelo, Robin. "White Fragility." *The International Journal of Critical Pedagogy* 3 (2011): 54–70. Print.

"Forget." *The Walking Dead.* Writ. Frank Darabont, Robert Kirkman, Tony Moore, Charlie Adlard, and Corey Reed. Dir. Daniel Boyd. AMC, 2015. Television.

Ho, Helen K. "The Model Minority in the Zombie Apocalypse: Asian-American Manhood on AMC's *The Walking Dead.*" *The Journal of Popular Culture* 49.1 (2016): 57–76.

"I Ain't a Judas." *The Walking Dead.* Writ. Frank Darabont, Robert Kirkman, Tony Moore, Charlie Adlard, and Angela Kang. Dir. Greg Nicotero. AMC, 2013. Television.

"Indifference." *The Walking Dead.* Writ. Frank Darabont, Robert Kirkman, Tony Moore, Charlie Adlard, and Matthew Negrete. Dir. Tricia Brock. AMC, 2013. Television.

"Infected." *The Walking Dead.* Writ. Frank Darabont, Robert Kirkman, Tony Moore, Charlie Adlard, and Angela Kang. Dir. Guy Ferland. AMC, 2013. Television.

"Isolation." *The Walking Dead.* Writ. Frank Darabont, Robert Kirkman, Tony Moore, and Charlie Adlard. Dir. Daniel Sackheim. AMC, 2013. Television.

Mills, Charles W. "Race and the Social Contract Tradition." *Social Identities* 6.4 (2000): 441–462. Print.

Moon, Dreama. "'Be/coming' White and the Myth of White Ignorance: Identity Projects in White Communities." *Western Journal of Communication* 80.3 (2016): 282–303. Print.

———. "White Enculturation and Bourgeois Ideology: The Discursive Production of 'Good (White) Girls.'" *Whiteness: The Communication of Social Identity.* Eds. Thomas K. Nakayama and Judith N. Martin. Thousand Oaks: SAGE Publications, 1999. 177–197. Print.

Nakayama, Thomas K., and Robert L. Krizek. "Whiteness: A Strategic Rhetoric." *Quarterly Journal of Speech* 81 (1995): 291–309. Print.

Paffenroth, Kim. *Gospel of the Living Dead: George Romero's Visions of Hell on Earth.* Waco: Baylor UP, 2006. Print.

Poole, W. Scott. *Monsters in America: Our Historical Obsession with the Hideous and the Haunting.* Waco: Baylor UP, 2011. Print.

Rassmussen, Brigit Brander, Eric Klinenberg, Irene J. Nexica, and Matt Wray. "Introduction." *The Making and Unmaking of Whiteness.* Eds. Brigit B. Rasmussen, Eric Klineberg, Irene J. Nexica, and Matt Wray. Durham: Duke UP, 2001. 1–24.

"Remember." *The Walking Dead.* Writ. Frank Darabont, Robert Kirkman, Tony Moore, Charlie Adlard, and Channing Powell. Dir. Greg Nicotero. AMC, 2014. Television.

"Seed." *The Walking Dead*. Writ. Frank Darabont, Robert Kirkman, Tony Moore, Charlie Adlard, and Glenn Mazzara. Dir. Ernest R. Dickerson. AMC, 2012. Television.

Shome, Raka. "White Femininity and the Discourse of the Nation: Re/membering Princess Diana." *Feminist Media Studies* 1.3 (2001): 323–342. Print.

"Sick." *The Walking Dead*. Writ. Frank Darabont, Robert Kirkman, Tony Moore, Charlie Adlard, and Nichole Beattie. Dir. Billy Gierhard. AMC, 2012. Television.

Sugg, Katherine. "*The Walking Dead:* Late Liberalism and Masculine Subjection in Apocalypse Fictions." *Journal of American Studies* 49.4 (2015): 793–811.

"Tell It to the Frogs." *The Walking Dead*. Writ. Frank Darabont, Robert Kirkman, Tony Moore, Charlie Adlard, Charles H. Eglee, Jack LoGuidice, and Gwyneth Horder-Payton. Dir. Gwyneth Horder-Payton. AMC, 2010. Television.

"The Same Boat." *The Walking Dead*. Writ. Frank Darabont, Robert Kirkman, Tony Moore, Charlie Adlard, and Angela Kang. Dir. Billy Gierhart. AMC, 2016. Television.

Warren, John T. *Performing Purity: Whiteness, Pedagogy, and the Reconstruction of Power.* New York: Peter Lang Publishing, 2003. Print.

"What Lies Ahead." *The Walking Dead*. Writ. Frank Darabont, Robert Kirkman, Tony Moore, and Charlie Adlard. Dir. Ernest R. Dickerson, and Gwyneth Horder-Payton. AMC, 2011. Television.

"When the Dead Come Knocking." *The Walking Dead*. Writ. Frank Darabont, Robert Kirkman, Tony Moore, Charlie Adlard, and Frank Renzulli. Dir. Daniel Sackheim. AMC, 2012. Television.

12

Bridge and Tunnel

• • • • • • • • • • • • • • • • • • • •

Transcultural Border Crossings
in *The Bridge* and *Sicario*

MARCEL BROUSSEAU*

Arguments about what the U.S.–Mexico border is, or should be, reached fever pitch in the United States in 2016, as the U.S. presidential elections staged a broadcast referendum on nativism and immigrant rights, and nationalism and so-called globalism, among other conceptual political dichotomies. Within this rhetorical conflict, the basic image of the U.S.–Mexico border, the operative abilities of the border to open or to close to human traffic, and the border's role as a medium between the cultures of the United States and Mexico, were all sublimated into infrastructural metaphors. Most strident was the prospect of "the wall," a foreboding chimera promised by the Republican presidential candidate (Gonyea). Against this image, the Democratic presidential candidate mobilized the slogan "build bridges, not walls" ("Hillary"). In either case, the border was imagined as a site where national cultures expressed themselves and communicated through forms of infrastructural media. Indeed, although valenced as political prolepses, the imaginary border infrastructures of the 2016 campaign have well-worn analogues in the lived U.S.–Mexico borderlands,

*The author would like to thank Domino Perez and Rachel González-Martin; he also wishes to thank Katherine Kelp-Stebbins for her inspiration regarding this piece.

where some 650 miles of fences and walls, and numerous railroad, automobile, and pedestrian bridges already mediate the borderline. These objects, distributed along the border, linking and dividing cities and towns such as El Paso and Juárez, San Diego and Tijuana, and Ambos Nogales, have, in the words of political theorist Peter Andreas, "escalat[ed] . . . state control" over "old and diverse" transcultural practices in the borderlands, including trade, economic migration, smuggling, coyotaje, and everyday border crossing (8, 29). At the same time, infrastructural technologies serve as powerful "images and symbols" determining "public perception" of the borderlands, informing a "border enforcement" system that is as "audience-directed" or "expressive" as it is "instrumental" (9–11).

The expressive, or symbolic, border infrastructure rhetoricized by the candidates of 2016 also has analogues in contemporary popular cultural representations of the U.S.–Mexico borderlands. The "escalation of border policing" over the last two decades or so, as analyzed by Andreas, among others, is reflected in the shifting settings of filmic narratives about the borderlands (3). Over a half-century of American film, representations of border crossing as a cultural practice have ranged imaginatively from the casual, albeit portentous stroll through the checkpoint at the beginning of Orson Welles's *Touch of Evil* (1958), to the quick and illicit chain-link-fence jumping in Robert Young's *Alambrista!* (1977), to the harrowing crawl through a transborder sewer tunnel in Gregory Nava's *El Norte* (1983), to the congested auto-crossing of Steven Soderbergh's *Traffic* (2000). In this brief catalog of the imagined border, a changing architecture of connectivity and restriction is made visible, comprising checkpoints, surveillance technologies, interrogation sites, fences, roadways, and civic infrastructure. Regardless of the apparent evolution of border settings and their set-pieces, these movies make clear that border crossing is a practice correlated to infrastructural objects, and that these objects introduce distinct cultural and technical effects upon the act of crossing, by requiring specific knowledges and abilities, among them language skills, legal documentation, legal and extralegal affiliations, physical endurance, and awareness of land and materials. In this way, the expressive borders shown on film imply and even diagram the instrumental borders of lived cultural practice, not unlike the border symbols wielded by politicians as "representation[s] of state authority" (Andreas 8).

This chapter examines the representation of border infrastructure, and its role in mediating cultural practices of border crossing, in two recent productions, the FX television show *The Bridge* (2013–14), and the feature film *Sicario* (2015). I argue that these filmic expressions of the U.S.–Mexico borderlands complicate prevailing "stereotypes that shape a mediated border spectacle" by framing the border as a series of technical spaces that separately and differently mediate distinctions of race, nationality, gender, and sexuality (Sowards and

Pineda 73). By framing the U.S.–Mexico border as distributed among infrastructure such as bridges and tunnels, and by narrativizing these objects as instruments of cultural practice and as cultural symbols, both *The Bridge* and *Sicario* emphasize the processual nature of the border, and its "collaborative," binational construction (Hernández 127–130). As symbols and as settings, the border infrastructure on display in these visual fictions expresses border crossing as a practice whereby "human actor[s are] decentered onto the technical object[s]" that mediate their crossing—bridge, car, checkpoint, identificatory documents—and interpellated as subjects through this mediation process (Siegert, "Doors" 8). Border culture emerges, in this framework, as a network of relations between infrastructural objects and knowledge practices that produces nationalized, racialized, legalized subjects. However, as *The Bridge* and *Sicario* show, the "humanoid–technoid" relations of border culture also produce antinational, invisible, nonlegalized subjects (Siegert, "Doors" 7). This internal distinction in border culture, whereby the border simultaneously articulates cultures of visibility and invisibility, legality and illegality, affirms Gloria Anzaldúa's definition of a borderlands as an "unstable, unpredictable, precarious, always-in-transition space lacking clear boundaries" (243). As seen in *The Bridge* and *Sicario*, although infrastructures of control in the borderlands symbolize the regulation of cultural and territorial difference, they also lay the groundwork for new cultural practices and territorial formations.

Geographically, *The Bridge* and *Sicario* represent a centralized section of the U.S.–Mexico border. *Sicario* begins and ends in the Arizona–Sonora borderlands, particularly in Ambos Nogales; a middle portion of the narrative also takes the characters to El Paso–Juárez, where *The Bridge* itself is set. These border cities are significant as historic sites of binational coordination regarding border enforcement. As historian Kelly Lytle Hernández relates, El Paso and Nogales were agreed upon in 1945 as the primary cities where the U.S. Border Patrol would deport undocumented Mexicans into the control of the Mexican government. These arrangements represented a shift in border policy whereby the two nations cooperated to control the deportation process, as opposed to the U.S. acting unilaterally (127). The predicate of transnational cooperation is intrinsic to the narratives depicted in *The Bridge* and *Sicario*, since the protagonists of each production are law enforcement agents operating in collaboration on both sides of the border. In each production, the bridge functions as the infrastructural symbol and setting for collaborative, binational, legalized border crossing, much as it did in the twentieth-century border histories cited by Hernández, wherein, for instance, the U.S. Border Patrol would meet Mexican officers in the "'middle of the bridge' that connected Presidio, Texas, to Ojinaga, [Chihuahua]," in order to transfer Mexicans for deportation (128). The bridge, as explored in both productions, is a legitimized channel for transcultural crossing practices mediated by binationally proscribed techniques for territorializing space and codifying identities. However, both *The Bridge* and *Sicario* propose the tunnel as an alternative infrastructural symbol and setting for border communication. Within the narrative of each production, the tunnel emerges as an illegitimate channel that, by mediating a border-crossing culture predicated upon deterritorializing space and concealing identities, undermines the nationalized distinctions enforced on the bridge

In relation to infrastructural forms such as bridges or tunnels, border cross-ings may be considered as media operations, or as what media theorist Bern-hard Siegert, among others, calls *cultural techniques*. In this framework, culture "does not exist independently" of its technological constitution (Siegert, *Cultural* 9); rather, "culture begins with the introduction of distinctions" (14). In the geohistorical borderlands referenced by *The Bridge* and *Sicario*, border culture emerges with the introduction of national and racial distinc-tions correlated to techniques of war and border enforcement—including legal and cartographic media—techniques which, in the words of Hernández, enforced the "racialized marginalization of Mexicans in the borderlands" (148). Although the 1848 Treaty of Guadalupe Hidalgo, which codified the new U.S.–Mexico border, conferred legal U.S. citizenship on roughly 120,000 U.S. citizens, it did so through the identity of racial whiteness, a status that "the great majority of Mexican [Americans] did not enjoy . . . social[ly] and legal[ly]" (Bowen 32, citing Amaya 16). This attainment by Mexicans of "American citi-zenship" without the agency of "American identity" is correlated to the "loss of property rights . . . political [rights] and linguistic rights" that occurred when Mexicans were displaced into the United States, and into separate states, by the legal and cartographic production of the border (Carbado 637; Bowen 32, citing Amaya 16). As Hernández shows, the technical maintenance of the border as a stable cartographic and legal object during the twentieth century continued "deeply rooted racial divides arising from conquest and capitalist economic development," ultimately instituting a culture of coop-eration between the United States and Mexico based on a racially—and there-fore biopolitically—informed "legal/illegal divide" (222). Within this rubric, legitimized border crossings between the United States and Mexico operate as constructions of identity, moments during which subjects are categorically processed by infrastructural media against an archive of cultural distinctions in order to attain the status of legality.

The fictional narratives *The Bridge* and *Sicario* dramatically process the oscillating distinctions of the borderlands: U.S.–Mexico, El Paso–Juárez, Spanish–English, evil–good, female–male, legal–illegal, friend–foe, criminal–police, federal–state, local–global, brown–white, clean–corrupt, alive–dead, the list goes on. Technologies like IDs and badges, guns and cars, language and gesture, bridges and tunnels, clothing and food, maps and newspapers medi-ate and communicate these distinctions. Culture is produced and communities are networked through the communicative practices of using these technologies. Narrative tension occurs as characters negotiate communities, switch sides, deviate from stable identities, and build new connections. Both *The Bridge* and *Sicario* are thus dramas of *nepantla*, "the Nahuatl word for an in-between state, that uncertain terrain one crosses when moving from one place to another, when changing from one class, race, or sexual position to another, when traveling from the present identity into a new identity" (Anzaldúa 180). In Anzaldúa's framework, "the border is in a constant nepantla state," as "a bewildering transitional space" symbolized by "borderline[s]" but also by bridges, by structures that "span liminal (threshold) spaces between worlds" (180–181, 243). Indeed, one of Anzaldúa's diagrams of nepantla is an abstract rendering of an infrastructural tunnel, road, or bridge between "waystations" (220). Another of Anzaldúa's diagrams represents nepantla as a "dismember[ed]" female body, which, although a reference to the Aztec goddess Coyolxauhqui, is the symbol around which the first season of *The Bridge* revolves, and implicitly, the mourning symbol haunting the backstory of *Sicario* (226).

Anzaldúa defines nepantla as a cause for "bouts of dissociation of identity, identity breakdowns and buildups" (181). In this formulation, she concurs with Siegert's assertion that "identity is nothing which humans own by nature but is a cultural construction of media" (Siegert, "Fictitious" 30). Framed by the theory of Anzaldúa and Siegert, and by the historicization of Hernández, the U.S.–Mexico borderlands can be seen as a site in which identity and subjectivity are formed in relation infrastructural media and their role in processing cultural distinctions. To further this line of critique, the act of viewing *The Bridge* and *Sicario* must likewise be seen as an encounter with border culture wherein the viewer becomes interpellated as a border subject, an "audience," in Andreas's terms, given the power to act upon the "images and symbols" determining "public perception" of the borderlands (9–11). This is to say that, as expressions of the U.S.–Mexico border, *The Bridge* and *Sicario* function as instruments that allow viewers to cross into border discourse. In what follows, I further examine the cultural technique of border crossing as it is separately practiced and processed by bridges and tunnels in *The Bridge* and *Sicario*. While contextualizing these expressions of border infrastructure and cultural practice in medial and historical analysis, I also seek to ascertain their effect on the larger discourse surrounding the U.S.–Mexico border as it occurs in popular culture.

Bridge

Every episode of *The Bridge* begins with a cold open, followed by a title sequence featuring scenery from the El Paso–Juárez borderlands. The production company that designed the sequence, yU+co, describes it as "an impressionistic montage exploring the divide between the two countries [that] fluidly moves between the two sides of the border . . . [evoking] the gritty mood of the show [and] ending with the titular bridge that links the two cities and their inhabitants together" ("The Bridge"). This description focalizes the bridge as the icon of *The Bridge*; its image provides what the philosopher Georg Simmel calls an "aesthetic value" for the show, in that it "gives to the eye the same support for connecting the sides of the landscape as it does to the body for practical reality" (6). The bridge that ends every title sequence provides the viewer with a visual object that "mak[es] directly visible" the division between the United States and Mexico that the title sequence has fluidly dissembled (6). However, as the bridge makes the divided landscape apparent, it also proposes itself as the connective medium reconciling the discontinuity between the United States and Mexico. By overlaying an image of the bridge with the title, *The Bridge*, yU+co creates a semiotic chain that aligns the bridge as an icon with the bridge as a symbol. These signs perform indexically as well: the image of the bridge indicates a specific place in El Paso–Juárez, and the title, *The Bridge*, references television rhetorics through its font and formatting. The title card provides the viewer, in Simmel's terms, with a "single timelessly stable visualization which reality never displays and never can display" (6). This visualization ultimately establishes the television show itself as the bridge between the viewer and the reality of the border, but in its imagery it promises a difficult crossing for the viewer, as indicated by the reddish swarm of brake lights and the noise of jammed traffic.

What neither the title sequence nor yU+co's description of it indicate is that the montage does not end with one bridge but rather two. The last image shown before the title card depicts the toll plaza of the Bridge of the Americas at night, facing north. This scene cuts away to an aerial shot of the Santa Fe Bridge—four miles upriver—also facing north. Glaring brake lights in both images provide iconic continuity. Therefore, the title sequence does not culminate with "the titular bridge," but rather with two bridges conflated in a narrative of heavy transborder traffic. Furthermore, the title card does not necessarily depict the Santa Fe Bridge, but rather, a flipped image of the Santa Fe bridge, in which the normally west-to-east curving structure angles from east to west, bracketing the show's title on the left side of the screen. This disorientation of the bridge underscores the fictionality of the show, but it also detaches the Santa Fe Bridge from its specific material history, from its particular identity as an architectural structure. By conflating two border bridges, and by deforming the image of one of those bridges—and indeed, of the entire borderscape— *The Bridge* subtly begins every episode by destabilizing the identity of El Paso– Juárez. The system of bridges and borders that mediate cultural distinctions is deconstructed and reconstructed through the techniques of television in order to fit the aesthetic parameters of the medium. This process, by which

The Bridge breaks down the bridge(s), draws attention to the ways in which media technologies produce culture symbolically, through medial constraints. As media theorist Kate Marshall argues, when infrastructure is put to work in narrative fiction, it functions in multiple ways, "form[ing] at once the physical and figurative connective tissue between persons, or operat[ing] as material symbols that produce the social and describe it." Furthermore, Marshall declares, the multivalence of infrastructure, its "movement through registers of meaning," allows infrastructure to identify "its status as media object . . . through which [narrative media] identify their own operations as media" (82). Therefore, when the television show channels the "empirical historical objects" of the Bridge of the Americas and the Santa Fe Bridge into images and lines to be conflated and redrawn, it raises questions about those bridges as channels themselves, or as media that process cultural distinctions (Siegert, *Cultural* 9).

The Bridge's conflation of the bridges of El Paso–Juárez into a singular narrative symbol fulfills, in Marshall's terms, a cliché of infrastructural modernity. This cliché contains two major aspects: "The first is that, when invoked, the reference to infrastructure always refers to physical structures and to the collectivities conjoined by them, that there is always 'something metaphoric' about infrastructure. The second is that these structures tend to remain invisible until blocked, broken, or struck by catastrophe" (Marshall 81–82). In its narrative use of the bridge(s) of El Paso–Juárez, *The Bridge* agrees with this cliché in various ways. The bridge is utilized less as a symbol and setting of communication than of miscommunication. There are implicit, routine bridge crossings made between the United States and Mexico by numerous characters on the show, but these crossings are not made visible as material practices. Only through narrative development does the viewer learn that a certain character, like *El Paso Times* journalist Adriana Mendez (Emily Rios), lives in Juárez, and must commute across the bridge daily for work. Although full-frame transition shots of the bridge occasionally function, quite literally, to bridge the narrative as it shifts to Mexico or the United States, visual and auditory cues like buildings and music are used more often to signal to the viewer that characters, and the story itself, have successfully crossed from Juárez or El Paso, or vice versa.

The Bridge uses the bridge more consistently as a site and sign of conflict and blockage. In the first two episodes of the show, full-frame transition shots of traffic on the bridge give way to narratives set within that traffic: as Juárez detective Marco Ruiz (Demian Bichir) drives toward the border checkpoint in the first episode of *The Bridge*, he is stuck in traffic, and he takes the time to buy pan dulce from a vendor, while talking to El Paso detective Sonya Cross (Diane Kruger) over the phone ("Pilot"). Traveling with Sonya into Juárez in the second episode, Marco again drives in traffic, talks with his wife over the phone, and then engages Sonya in a conversation ("Calaca"). In these scenes, the blockage of the bridge as a communicative device compels the use of other

media, like the phone—which transmits more seamlessly across the border—
and fosters more immediate, local communication, like face-to-face conversation. The bridge is reframed not as a single channel connecting two points but
as a node in a network of communication through which, in Anzaldúa's terms,
one may "chang[e] from one class, race, or sexual position to another" (180). As
he negotiates traffic, Marco also negotiates his cultural positions as Mexican,
as middle class, as detective, as male, and as husband, through his subjective
acts of crossing the border, buying pan dulce, and talking on the phone with
his investigative partner and with his wife. These identificatory acts undertaken
in bridge traffic are themselves metonymic of the "bureaucratic effort [that pro-
duces] legal mobility," which is actually causing all the traffic. As he crosses
the bridge, Marco's dissociated identities will be subsumed into the customs
process as it attempts to distinguish between "citizen/subjects and possible
interlopers" (Siegert, "Fictitious" 20).

In *The Bridge*, the bridge is a tool for processing border subjects that enacts
"identity breakdowns and buildups" that enforce cultural distinctions of class,
race, sexuality, gender, and nationality (Anzaldúa 181). In crossing the bridge,
border subjects are "decentered onto the technical object[s]" that mediate their
crossing—bridge, car, identificatory documents—and interpellated as subjects
through this mediation process (Siegert, "Doors" 8). These media, and the cultural distinctions they articulate, draw upon a "technical a priori," or an archive
of practices with specific cultural implications in El Paso–Juárez (Siegert, "The
map" 14). Historian David Dorado Romo assigns a date for the local use of
bridges as technologies for articulating distinctions in race, nationality, gender, or sexuality, recounting that "Until January 1917 El Paso and Juárez citizens could freely cross back and forth between the two countries without need
of a passport." Romo quotes an oral history in which El Paso resident Mike
Romo recalls the following: "Coming from Juárez across the Stanton Bridge
they never asked you for any identification. They didn't ask you for anything. . . .
You could go and come back and nobody ever bothered you. You could bring in
whatever you wanted." Another voice, belonging to Cleofas Calleros, recounts,
"Everyone was happy, coming and going without any customs restrictions, any
immigration restrictions, any health department restrictions" (228). The idyllic sense of connectivity expressed by these local voices contrasts with the
more violent and disruptive border environment that emerged after U.S. entry
in World War I and the passage of the Immigration Act of 1917. While the war
created a climate of interdiction on the border, whereby smuggling and espio-
nage were guarded against, the Immigration Act created biopolitical protocols
for controlling the bodies and mobility of border crossers (228). The bureaucratic processes established during this historical period include the institution of passport controls at "'regular immigration ports of entry.'" These "paper

barriers" revised the bridges of El Paso–Juárez as sites for identity construction along bureaucratic lines (Torpey 118–119).

As Romo asserts, in El Paso–Juárez, the effect of the new border controls of 1917 was that "El Paso and Juárez became separate communities" (229). In this new arrangement, the bridge, which had previously served as a geographic link, became a barrier that instead communicated as what Hernández calls a "corridor of migration control" (125). At the end of this corridor, Mexican border crossers had to endure more than a paper barrier, as U.S. officials subjected them to procedures that processed their physical and cognitive faculties in terms of pseudoscientific medical and social criteria, including imbecility, idiocy, homosexuality, physical defectiveness, contagious disease, and illiteracy, among others. These controls, along with local hysteria about the possibility of Mexican border crossers spreading typhus in El Paso, transformed the international bridge in El Paso–Juárez into an inspection and disinfection site at which every immigrant from the interior of Mexico and all "second class" citizens of Juárez had to submit to an inspection of their naked body, be sterilized with insecticides like gasoline, and have their clothes fumigated before being allowed to leave the bridge. These biopolitical measures, whereby U.S. officials quarantined and violently deconstructed Mexican bodies, continued until the mid-twentieth century (Romo 233–237). In these historic scenes the bridge's ability, in Simmel's phrasing, to "support" Mexican bodies as they communicate between "the sides of the landscape," clashes with U.S. policies that reject Mexicans upon arrival (6). Bureaucratic bottlenecks on the bridge begin here, as race and identity are conflated in the control and categorization of Mexican bodies.

Beginning with the international bridge blocked by the interlinked, dismembered corpses of a poor woman from Mexico and a comparatively wealthy woman from the United States, *The Bridge* is ostensibly confronting this legacy of asymmetric violence and biopolitical control. Indeed, the first season of *The Bridge* anchors its plot with a series of questions addressing structural inequality and its effect on borderland bodies: "There are five murders a year in El Paso. In Juárez, thousands. Why? Why is one dead white woman more important than so many dead just across the bridge? How long can El Paso look away?" ("Pilot"). Despite the cogent premise of these questions, and their invocation of the bridge as a symbol of connection and failed communication between the United States and Mexico, the plot of the first season is displaced into a serial-killer whodunit, in which the antagonist, David Tate (Eric Lange) seeks vengeance for a car accident that killed his wife and son on the Bridge of the Americas. Rather than Mexicans experiencing the bridge as a site of traffic, identity reconstruction, and bodily harm, it is white U.S. citizens like Tate, who are most transformed by the act of crossing. Tate's subsequent violence against Mexicans, including his murders of the wealthy scion of Mexican elites who caused the accident, and of Marco's son (as retribution for Marco's affair with Tate's wife, which inadvertently led to the accident), are framed as a tragic vendetta that does not actually reconcile the structural inequality between the two nations. Histories of cultural prejudice and physical discipline enacted by the United States against Mexican citizens are repressed in the reddish glow of traffic, in the aesthetic value of the bridge, which is inverted, not only in the show's title card but also in its narrative, to reflect the generic priorities of television as a medium.

The communicative power of the bridge is further qualified in *Sicario*, in which aesthetics are more specifically linked to practices of binational cooperation and law enforcement. A frantic set-piece early in the movie follows a U.S. special operations force on a mission to capture a high-ranking member of the Sonora cartel from Juárez for transfer to the United States. As the force crosses the border, its convoy of sport utility vehicles streaks at high-speed, in miniature detail, across aerial shots of the Bridge of the Americas and the surrounding borderlands. An earlier mission briefing scene has already revealed that Mexican Federal Police are meeting the convoy at the border and escorting them through Juárez to the courthouse where the prisoner will be given into the custody of U.S. marshals. The depiction of the bridge-crossing into Mexico, valenced ominously through a series of aerial shots of the borderline, overlaid with the rhythm of helicopter blades and droning cellos, asserts the efficiency of binational control over the sprawl and noise of the borderlands. The speed and precision of the special-ops convoy, particularly in contrast to the traffic jam in the northbound lanes of the bridge, seems to indicate the ability of the two nations to construct a clear channel for communication, albeit to deliver U.S. law enforcement personnel to destinations in Mexico.

This communicative potential of the bridge is belied by the convoy's return crossing, with its prisoner, Guillermo Diaz (Edgar Arreola) in tow. As the convoy approaches the bridge, closed-circuit dialogue assures the drivers that "agents at the border are waving traffic through to get [the special-ops team over] as quickly as they can." This promise is quickly revised as a "fuck-up": an aerial shot simulating helicopter surveillance reveals that a car has broken down farther ahead, and that no additional lanes on the bridge can be cleared. The convoy will be stuck in traffic. As helicopters circle overhead, the special-ops team, including the film's protagonist, FBI agent Kate Macer (Emily Blunt), and the mysterious Department of Defense consultant Alejandro (Benicio del Toro) scan the surrounding cars for potential cartel gunmen. Indeed, as forewarned during the mission briefing, two cars are flanking the convoy, with armed men inside preparing for an ambush. With traffic on the verge of clearing, the gunmen make their move, but they are slaughtered by the powerfully armed members of the special-ops force in a brief engagement. As traffic begins to move, the convoy starts up again. The camera scans across the remaining car-nage, capturing the faces of dazed but impassive drivers, before cutting away from the bridge.

The depiction of bridge-crossing in *Sicario* is designed to narrativize the skill and command of government institutions, particularly the ability of U.S. agen-cies like the CIA, FBI, armed forces, federal marshals, and Customs and Bor-der Protection, to interlink and manage the border, in further collaboration with Mexican government agencies, such as the Policía Federal. In this way, *Sicario* echoes the cultural politics of *The Bridge* by depicting binational law enforcement as a set of shared cultural practices and prerogatives mediated by shared transborder infrastructure. However, the plotting of *Sicario*, like that of *The Bridge*, also emphasizes that despite the ability of these agencies to com-mand and control transborder infrastructure, the traffic and noise produced by policing the border always threaten communication, even among privileged subjects. The law enforcement personnel guiding the mission routinely assert the problematics of this traffic. Despite the film's connotation of Juárez as a "Beast," both Alejandro and the U.S. marshal supervising the mission argue that "the border" will be the site of any potential conflict, not the city itself, presumably because of the potential for disorganization and blockage on the bridge.

The bridge in *Sicario* ultimately functions to articulate a Manichean set of distinctions that supersede cultures of law enforcement or even nationality. With the U.S. marshal's admonition at the mission briefing that, "anyone not in this room is a potential shooter," border culture is reduced to a division between friend and foe, in which the briefing room, and by extension, the mil-itary convoy, comprises its own cultural order. The disorientation of this arrange-ment is particularly felt by Kate, who shouts to herself, "What the fuck are we doing?" as the members of the special-ops team gun down the groups of armed young men in bridge traffic. Back in the United States, she vents her frustration about the border crossing, and the unclear rules by which the convoy acted, in an outburst to CIA operative Matt Graver (Josh Brolin): "That was fucking illegal! You want to start a war? . . . You just spray bullets . . . and . . . there's just fucking civilians everywhere." By taking recourse in the terminology of law, Kate attempts to assert a more nuanced distinction into the friend-and-foe divide followed by the special-ops squad, a distinction that Matt dis-misses. "This is the future, Kate," he states, "Juárez is what happens when they dig in."

With his casual use of the signifier "they," Matt asserts the distinction of friend and foe—or us and them—as the proleptic culture of the borderlands, a culture of sustained war that Kate's recourse to the term "civilian" qualifies but does not dispute. This is the thesis of *Sicario*: Border culture has become subsumed into the culture of war—particularly the so-called War on

Drugs—and all other cultural distinctions may be re-marked in relation to the cultural distinctions necessary to warfare. In this context, the bridge becomes a site where visual identificatory markers, such as race and class, are further qualified in terms of the friend/foe distinction regardless of legal documentation or other bureaucratic media. As the special-ops team scans the bridge in the thick of traffic, two specific potential adversaries emerge: a red Chevrolet Impala, and a green Honda Civic with mismatched bodywork, each car containing four young brown-skinned men with casual clothes, some bearing visible tattoos. These vehicles and their passengers are profiled in resonance with what Hernández calls the "dimensions of gender, class, and complexion" that historically informed "the Border Patrol's targeted enforcement of U.S. immigration restrictions" (10). As the scene unfolds, the transformation of the stereotype of the illegal migrant into the enemy combatant is made complete when weapons are observed in the young men's' hands. From this moment in the narrative, battle seems inevitable; all that remains for the special-ops force is a radio clarification of "the rules" of engagement, an indication that the force is operating as a military unit, and not in the capacity of law enforcement (*Sicario*).

By turning the Bridge of the Americas into a battlefield, *Sicario* asserts that the U.S.–Mexico borderlands is less a transnational, transcultural space marked by a "visible boundary" than it is a "*zone*' . . . structured by clamp points and strong points" (Vismann 55). As media theorist Cornelia Vismann states, military discourse such as the "zone" finds cultural expression in the term "no man's land": a site where "aesthetical perception . . . habitual order, and . . . 'men' . . . disappear" (54). This violent replacement of the bridge as a connective symbol, with a "terrain of indeterminacy," would seem to gesture toward Anzaldúa's definition of nepantla, except that it does not foster identity breakdowns and buildups, but rather the "negation of identity [and] all kinds of orders linked with identity" (Vismann 56–57). While *Sicario* stages this cultural collapse only as "an arrangement of perception in the moment of death threat," it does so in the context of open binational cooperation, at the most conspicuous site of transborder cultural exchange, as vendors hawk trinkets, and citizens physically negotiate the borderline with their cars and their bodies (Vismann 54). In four minutes, *Sicario* asserts, the bridge, as both a symbol and an instrument of crossing and transcultural exchange, as a site of racial discipline and identity construction, can be reduced to a no-man's land, a zone where both crossing and culture become suddenly implausible.

Tunnel

"Estoy hasta la madre de vivir como una rata [I'm tired of living like a rat]," cartel leader Fausto Galvan (Ramón Franco) complains to his assistant, Obregon

(Daniel Edward Mora), halfway through the second season of *The Bridge*. Increased scrutiny by the new presidential administration in Mexico, and covert U.S. action beyond his knowledge, has pushed Fausto further underground, so to speak. He laments that he is not able to exploit the wealth he has attained. Some days he sits behind the wheel of a large speedboat, dry-docked in his warehouse. He dreams of traveling to Norway to see the fjords because "they look relaxing" ("Lamia"). By the end of the following episode, Fausto is fleeing a raid by the Mexican Marines through a series of underground tunnels. As he runs, he kills two of his henchman in order to limit his risk. "I'm surrounded by leeches," he explains to Obregon ("Goliath").

A rat surrounded by leeches: Fausto is overdetermined by the symbolism of the parasite. His presence in *The Bridge* allows for a rethinking of the structure diagrammed above, in which the bridge articulates, or makes visible, distinctions in race, nationality, gender, and sexuality, and enforces these distinctions through paper barriers and the physical discipline of bodies. Fausto does not communicate as himself through the formal media comprising law and order; he conceals himself at the center of underground networks and uses the bodies of henchmen and corrupted officials on both sides of the border to connect himself to the state. Although law enforcement officials on *The Bridge* frame Fausto and his cartel as a sign of an "[un]clean house," or as a cancer of the system needing to be "take[n] out," it is clear, from the enforcement histories recounted above that the figure of the parasite is a construction used to determine systems of law and order ("Yankee"). As Siegert argues, citing Michel Serres, the disorder represented by Fausto does not emerge after the construction of order, but rather produces it: "We do not start out with some kind of relation that is subsequently disturbed or interrupted; rather ... The origin lies with the pirate rather than the merchant, with the highwayman rather than the highway" (Siegert, *Cultural* 21). Categorizing and excluding Fausto as illegitimate pirate, as narco boss, is the means by which the state establishes its symbolic control over political and commercial relations. It is not for nothing that Obregon attempts to pacify Fausto by reminding him why he is underground: "You know how it is boss. New president, new administration. They're trying to show how tough they are by going after you. They want to look like they've got big balls" ("Lamia"). Fausto the outlaw provides the symbolic conditions of possibility for law, but in this he is not unique. There were narco bosses before Fausto, and there will be narco bosses after him. He is a rat, surrounded by leeches that could take his place as a parasite of the state.

Seemingly beneath the system and yet within its bowels, unseen, Fausto moves through tunnels, both to conduct his business and to evade his capture. In scripting this particular form of infrastructure, *The Bridge* deviates from *Broen/Bron,* its Swedish–Danish source material. While *Broen/Bron* mobilized the symbol of the bridge in ways akin to those mentioned earlier, it did not provide a figurative counterpoint in the form of the tunnel. In *The Bridge* there are at least four tunnel systems mediating underground communication around El Paso–Juárez. One system includes the caves through which Fausto flees—identified by the Mexican Marines as "sewers" ("Goliath"). The other three tunnel systems span the border. Two of them, belonging to Fausto, have been compromised: as he recounts, one tunnel caved in and the Border Patrol sealed the other ("Maria"). The other cross-border tunnel provides a setting for a criminal subplot in *The Bridge*'s first season. Ostensibly used to sneak migrants across the border, it instead becomes a conduit for ransom money, guns, and corpses.

While the bridge connects the landscape of El Paso–Juárez and serves to mediate between cultural distinctions of race, gender, nationality, and sexuality, the tunnel undermines the clarity of those distinctions. Tunnels mediate a different kind of subjectivity than bridges, one that does not necessarily negotiate control over the landscape and the bodies that connect it, but rather invokes the power of the unseen and the unknowable. In the context of the U.S.–Mexico border, tunnels do not mediate formal systems of laws or protocols that condition movement. They function informally, as open secrets, invisible channels that must be maintained to be useful and concealed to be maintained. Tunnel networks on the border become visible as symbols of underground power only when they are brought to light and made visible, and yet this visibility transfers the power of the tunnel to the realm of law and order. According to Cynthia Sorrensen, discovering and displaying knowledge of border tunnels is both a material and a symbolic act of control that allows the state to "assure the public that each discovered tunnel has been shut down, that safety has been brought to bear on the situation, and that control of the subterranean is extending into new border spaces" (342). Just as Fausto serves the state as a symptom/symbol to control, at the same time that he hollows beneath it, so too do the tunnels he uses.

The presence of tunnels in the fictional geography of *The Bridge* also indicates a symbolic agenda on the part of the show, because transborder tunnels are not considered common to El Paso–Juárez during the modern enforcement era beginning in 1917. Among the 180 tunnels discovered by the Border Patrol since 1990, only one tunnel was located in El Paso–Juárez, under the Rio Grande (San Diego Union-Tribune). Storm drains running into the river have functioned as smuggling tunnels; a well-known one crossed the river near the campus of University of Texas–El Paso (Campbell 261). However, lacking evidence of tunnels does not necessarily indicate a lack of tunnels in El Paso–Juárez. It could mean a lack of operational control by state power. At the same time, because they are tunnels, the tunnels in *The Bridge* lack any visual cues indexing them to the real landscape of El Paso–Juárez. Rather than reflecting local infrastructure, they might be considered symbols of the border at large.

The tunnel enters the show as a symbol of clandestine migration, as a means for migrant bodies to escape the discipline of official channels like the bridge. However, the show reveals tunnels to be precarious and destabilizing environments, sites of nepantla and risk. When Charlotte Millwright (Annabeth Gish) and her employee Cesar (Alejandro Patiño) explore the crumbling migration tunnel that opens into her ranch property, they encounter an altar and a skeleton, which compel Charlotte to flee from the structure. "Board it up," she commands César, turning her back on the scene. Immediately, the show cuts to a cattle truck; as the camera moves inside the trailer, the viewer notices a group of migrants steadying themselves among the cattle ("Calaca"). With this interconnected sequence, equating the bare life of the tunnel to that of the cattle car, *The Bridge* makes a layered critique of clandestine migration. The hazards of disappearance and death in the underground tunnel are weighed against those of an aboveground tunnel—a repurposed trailer—in which migrants are animalized and placed at risk of dehydration and hyperthermia. This complementary system of tunnels—a stationary one, literally underground, and a mobile one, concealing migrants under the guise of commerce—indicates that tunnels are also technologies that discipline bodies. However, tunnels do not discipline bodies by identifying them—or "decenter[ing]" them "onto . . . technical object[s]" like bridges and passports—but rather by disappearing them, or decentering them *into* technical objects to avoid identification (Siegert, "Doors" 8). The stakes for migrant bodies in this context are not merely exclusion, but invisibility: either to be marked in terms of nationality, race, class, and gender, or to be unmarked by the state, bare life.

Although tunnels are not common to the modern era of border enforcement in El Paso–Juárez, they do index an older period of exclusion and invisibility: the Chinese Exclusion Act of 1882, which outlawed Chinese immigrants and inaugurated an ongoing era of human smuggling on the U.S.–Mexico border. Before border distinctions between U.S. and Mexican citizens were institutionalized, the Chinese Exclusion Act produced what historian Nancy Farrar calls, "an 'underground railroad' [in Juárez that could] take [Chinese migrants] to New York, Chicago, or San Francisco" by means of "smuggling firms" using an "organized system" of houses, hideouts, and tunnels (19). Both El Paso and Juárez apparently contained an underworld of "secret tunnels and passages" that linked "Chinese buildings [and] made it possible for Chinese to enter one house and exit through another house several doors or blocks away." Farrar also cites "some immigration authorities" who "alleged that the tunnels . . . actually extended under the Rio Grande" (20). While *The Bridge* invokes this history of subaltern survival with its meditation on tunnels and clandestine migration, it ultimately identifies tunnels more with the smuggling firms than with the migrants. As the show's first season progresses Charlotte and Cesar become smugglers themselves, participants in the criminal underworld networked through their tunnel. The migrant subplot of the show gives way to a drama about drug running, and the tunnel is thematized less as a means of concealing subaltern communities than as a metaphor for concealing criminal conspiracy.

As the plot of the second season of *The Bridge* unfolds, it becomes clear that the infrastructural symbol the show uses to identify itself—the bridge—is ironic, if not anachronistic. The connectivity between the United States and Mexico—as sketched by the frantic violence and double-crossings of the show's script—does not reduce to the bridge, as a regular port of entry, with its official identificatory techniques and exclusionary traffic. The tunnel, with its ability to blur boundaries, to encase the parasites of the state, and to mobilize unseen power, is the symbol of season two, and yet the tunnel is itself too structural to fully represent the transborder systems of *The Bridge* as it attempts to limn the government–corporate–criminal relationships of its imagined El Paso–Juárez. The final infrastructural symbol put forward by *The Bridge*, as it pits government agencies against one another on both sides of the border, is the network itself, a series of abstract, fluctuating connections that represent how, in Sorrensen's words, "sovereignty practices extend beyond territorial boundaries [and] intersect with illegal activities" (330). Tunnels and bridges are both interlinked within this symbolic framework, as are the phones and Internet services characters use to communicate, the radios to which they listen, and the televisions that they watch, and on which they are watched. Yet, even as components of shared networks, tunnels and bridges demarcate "divergent" cultural forms and practices of connectivity. As media theorist Juan Llamas-Rodriguez argues, while legitimized control infrastructure such as bridges "function[s] . . . to sort populations [and] to categorize users," tunnels reorganize "geographies of control for a stretch of time" around hierarchies of users who seek to "'hack' their way around" biopolitical infrastructure (32–33). Llamas-Rodriguez's analysis shows that as networked forms bridges and tunnels can still be distinguished in terms of their medial temporality and their social effects.

By the time transborder tunnels are mentioned in *Sicario*, the movie's narrative agenda has already deterritorialized the bridge as a border symbol; the tunnel, however, remains as an object of cultural power, a border space that always already exists beyond the borders drawn by states and negated by war, a place that is not the absence of order, but rather a site of secret order, with its own localized cultural practices. The middle arc of the movie's narrative concerns what Sorrensen calls "tunnel surveillance and investigation," during which Matt and Alejandro, ambivalently accompanied by Kate, seek information on a transborder tunnel rumored to exist near Sasabe, Arizona (331). While *The Bridge* introduces tunnels as a concern of underground migration economies, *Sicario* immediately qualifies them as the infrastructure of narco economies; a tunnel is "rumor[ed]" to be Sonora cartel leader Fausto Alarcon's "main road into Arizona." As a system of underground crossing, this tunnel has symbolic value beyond its ability to move drugs beneath national borders. As Matt, Alejandro, and Kate find out, it also demarcates an alternate sovereignty that is understood and obeyed by migrants, who, in informal interrogations with the protagonists, advise, "never cross where there are tunnels," since they indicate "drug land." Furthermore, as one migrant with a bruised face carefully explains, tunnels mark cartels' territorial co-option by of well-worn migration routes. "For years," the man recounts, "[the area where Fausto's tunnel is] was the best place to cross," as it was close to the highways, with water and shade. Alejandro is less interested in this cultural history of the region than he is in the specific geography of the tunnel. "Can you mark the trail to the tunnel?" he asks the man, gesturing to a map on his smart phone.

These informal interrogations, during which government operatives exploit the cultural knowledge of migrants in order to strategize a covert military maneuver through a transborder tunnel, exemplify the tunnel's association, as Llamas-Rodriguez argues, with localized hierarchies and the hacking of control systems (32–33). Matt and Alejandro cannot access the tunnel without the intelligence provided by migrant informants who must be briefly repurposed from the control of the state—that is to say, stayed from deportation. The entire arrangement functions as a "reorganiz[ation] of geographies of control for a stretch of time," during which the special-ops force will again cross the border, this time without binational cooperation, or the explicit oversight of law enforcement, through a narcotics tunnel, in order to clandestinely "[place] an agent" into Mexico (Llamas-Rodriguez 33). Once in Mexico, the agent, Alejandro, will utilize an already-corrupted officer of the Policía Estatal to exploit the control geography of highways, kidnap a drug mule, and locate narco boss Fausto Alarcon at his place of residence.

As depicted in *Sicario* the cultural practice of tunneling is overdetermined by temporality; the mission undertaken by the special-ops force underground is choreographed to coincide with a series of other habitual and unique events involving the Sonora cartel's distribution network. Most importantly, the tunnel must be accessed while it is still in use; as one Mexican government liaison warns Alejandro regarding locating the tunnel, "Time is against you. In three days, nobody will be where they are today." Llamas-Rodriguez argues that the "stretch of time that tunnels occupy . . . becomes a crucial aspect to their successful implementation," and that this principle has two meanings, referring both "to the span of time that the tunnel is active before it is found and shut down [and to] to the spatial stretch, that is, to the time it takes to cross the tunnel" (38). While these factors would conventionally articulate between legitimized cultures of law enforcement, who seek to find tunnels and shut them down quickly, and illicit cultures of criminal organizations, which seek to manage the space and efficiency of tunnels, these distinctions are blurred in *Sicario*, wherein the special-ops team seeks both to find and to use the tunnel efficiently and expediently.

In using the tunnel, the film's protagonists, including Matt, Alejandro, the army's Delta Force unit, Kate, and her FBI partner Reggie Wayne (Daniel Kaluuya) encounter another necessary characteristic of tunneling, namely its suppression of visibility. As the squad enters the tunnel, four different types of visualization are used on film, simulating the characters' points of view: natural light, which mediates the darkness of the night outside the tunnel, and the deeper darkness inside the tunnel; night vision, with its spectrum of greenish hues; thermal vision, with glowing white to gray tones. Additionally, drone shots monitor the squad from above until they enter the tunnel fully. Upon reaching the interior of the tunnel, incandescent bulbs light the hallways, revealing the structure to be a so-called super tunnel, with multiple electrified, reinforced passageways (Llamas-Rodriguez 35). Although the tunnel subverts the political border between the United States and Mexico, the characters' movement from the darkness of the desert and the tunnel mouth into the interior spaces of the tunnel, with its electrically lit corridors, represents its own kind of border crossing, a movement through "reorganize[d] . . . cultural and political geographies," where cartels control the infrastructure and mark their own borders (Llamas-Rodriguez 38). However, although the alternate cultural space of the tunnel "bypass[es] borders" it does not "permanently erase . . . geopolitically enforced boundaries." As Llamas-Rodriguez asserts, as a reaction to the structural restrictions of legitimate borders, tunnels can only leave dominant cultural and political geographies "disturbed but not disrupted"; because tunnels must be made visible, however briefly or furtively, to be used, their existence is always dependent on stable cultural signs at some level (38).

Conclusion

Roughly one minute into the pilot of *The Bridge*, after a series of shots depicting the extensive bridge and highway infrastructure of El Paso–Juárez, the camera cuts to the U.S. Customs and Border Protection control center, where a bank of video monitors has suddenly gone static. "What the hell's going on?" one officer asks, while another taps a screen to get it to work. As the screens come back to life, flashing scenes of vehicular traffic, the officers express relief, until one of them notices the body left behind on the borderline. "Holy shit," the officer says, "shut the border." The cold open cuts here, giving way to the title sequence of the show ("Pilot").

With this efficient sequence, *The Bridge* establishes its technological borderscape of highways and bridges, customs and traffic, all interconnecting over the channeled Rio Grande as it divides El Paso–Juárez, and by extension the

United States and Mexico. As the screens in the control center turn static, the techniques by which the state constructs identity and disciplines bodies are flipped against themselves; the ability to make the other visible is blocked by a wave of signal traffic, and the officers are themselves rendered subjects prone to forces beyond their control. At the customs stations, the officers are likewise powerless—the lights on the bridge were extinguished along with the video surveillance—and as brightness returns, the agents of the state move their bodies as if waking from slumber. Darkness and video traffic—invisible and illegible symbols—the show's cold open asserts, are all it takes to disrupt the system of identity construction that undergirds the border. The infrastructure of identity construction can be turned against itself, or even turned off.

However, the television screens at the center of this technological network are an early cue to viewers that they are themselves implicit in and connected to the cultural practices that underlie border enforcement. As they stare into the mise en abyme represented by their screen representing another screen, representing static, viewers are themselves interpellated as border subjects, initiated into a symbolic chain of categorization along lines of race and gender, prone to television's structural discipline, and given the ability to self-identify with the characters and events unfolding before them. In this context, *The Bridge*'s viewers become "a political and social necessity," border subjects given the ability to include or exclude "a large diverse Latino cast of major recurring characters, one . . . not likely to [be] encounter[ed] again anytime soon" (Populistacademic).

As a film, and not a serial television show, *Sicario* presents audiences with a more concise, albeit more sonically and visually imposing, expression of the border. In its presentation, however, *Sicario* is also self-referential; by regularly drawing attention to the camerawork of state power, whether as simulations of helicopter or drone video, or splices of surveillance cameras, the movie also interpellates viewers as border subjects, citizens with implicit access to the "images and symbols" of the border, and the ability to interpret these visual expressions as cultural formations. In this regard, both *Sicario* and *The Bridge* function as nodes in a borderlands network that make other parts of that network, like bridges and tunnels, visible as cultural techniques. In this role, both productions perform what Andreas would call "image management" of the borderlands (9). Although, with their predicates of policing and crime and/or military set-pieces, *The Bridge* and *Sicario* could both be interpreted as exemplars of the "loss-of-control narrative" of the U.S.–Mexico border, I argue that these filmic productions are better understood as expressions of the borderlands as a processual space, distributed among technological objects, such as bridges and tunnels, and deeply informed by the cultural crossings mediated by this infrastructure (Andreas 8). Indexed amid the symbolic border architecture glimpsed in *The Bridge* and *Sicario*, and the real technologies managing every-day cultural life in the United States and Mexico, are cultural histories of the borderlands that deconstruct slogans about the border.

Works Cited

Alambrista! Dir. Robert M. Young. Filmhaus, 1977. Film.

Amaya, Hector. *Citizenship Excess: Latino/as, Media, and the Nation.* New York: NYU P, 2013. Print.

Andreas, Peter. *Border Games: Policing the U.S.–Mexico Divide.* 2nd edition. Ithaca: Cornell UP, 2009. Print.

Anzaldúa, Gloria E. *The Gloria Anzaldúa Reader.* Ed. AnaLouise Keating. Durham: Duke UP, 2009. Print.

Bowen, Diana I. "Voices from the Archive: Family Names, Official Documents, and Unofficial Ideologies in the Gloria Anzaldúa Papers." *Journal of Multimodal Rhetorics* 1 (2017): 26–41. Print.

"The Bridge." *www.yuco.com.* yU+co. 2016. Web. February 28, 2017.

"Calaca." *The Bridge.* FX. 17 July 2013. Television.

Campbell, Howard. *Drug War Zone: Frontline Dispatches from the Streets of El Paso and Juárez.* Austin: U of Texas P, 2009. Print.

Carbado, Devon W. "Racial naturalization." *American Quarterly* 57.3 (2005): 633–658. Print.

El Norte. Dir. Gregory Nava. American Playhouse, Channel Four Films, Independent Productions, Island Alive, Public Broadcasting Service, 1983. Film.

Farrar, Nancy. *The Chinese in El Paso.* El Paso: Texas Western P, 1972. Print.

"Goliath." *The Bridge.* FX. August 27, 2014. Television.

Gonyea, Don. "Trump's Plan To 'Make Mexico Pay' For The Wall." *NPR.* April 5, 2016. Web.

Hernández, Kelly Lytle. *Migra!: A History of the U.S. Border Patrol.* Berkeley: U of California P, 2010. Print.

"Hillary Clinton: 'We build bridges not walls.'" *BBC News.* November 8, 2016. Web.

"Jubilex." *The Bridge.* FX. 1 October 2014. Television.

"Lamia." *The Bridge.* FX. 20 August 2014. Television.

Llamas-Rodriguez, Juan. "Tunneling Media: Geoblocking and Online Border Resistance." *Geoblocking and Global Video Culture.* Eds. Ramon Lobato and James Meese. Amsterdam: Institute of Network Cultures, 2016. Print.

"Maria of the Desert." *The Bridge.* FX. July 31, 2013. Television.

Marshall, Kate. *Corridor: Media Architectures in American Fiction.* Minneapolis: U of Minnesota P, 2013. Print.

"Pilot." *The Bridge.* FX. July 10, 2013. Television.

Populistacademic. "'The Bridge' Troubles Waters, Future Uncertain." elitistacademic .wordpress.com. September 19, 2014. Web.

"Quetzalcoatl." *The Bridge.* FX. 24 Sep. 2014. Television.

Romo, David Dorado. *Ringside Seat to a Revolution: An Underground Cultural History of El Paso and Juárez: 1893–1923.* El Paso: Cinco Puntos Press, 2005. Print.

San Diego Union-Tribune. "Border Tunnels: Complete List of Those Found." *San Diego Union-Tribune.* October 22, 2015. Web.

Serres, Michel. *The Parasite.* Trans. Lawrence R. Schehr. Baltimore: Johns Hopkins UP, 1982. Print.

Sicario. Dir. Denis Villeneuve. Screenplay by Taylor Sheridan. Black Label Media, Lionsgate, Thunder Road Pictures, 2015. Film.

Siegert, Bernhard. *Cultural Techniques: Grids, Filters, Doors, and Other Articulations of the Real.* Trans. Geoffrey Winthrop-Young. New York: Fordham UP, 2015. Print.

———. "Doors: On the Materiality of the Symbolic." Trans. John Durham Peters. *Grey Room* 47 (2012): 6–23. Print.

———. "Fictitious Identities: On the interrogatorios and registros de pasajeros a Indias in the Archivo General de Indias (Seville) (16th century)." Ficciones de los medios en la periferia. Técnicas de comunicación en la literatura hispanoamericana moderna. *Kölner elektronische Schriftenreihe* 1 (2008): 19–30. Web.

———. "The Map *Is* the Territory." *Radical Philosophy* 169 (2011): 13–16. Print.

Simmel, Georg. "Bridge and Door." Trans. Mark Ritter. *Theory, Culture, and Society* 11.1 (February 1994): 5–10. Print.

Sorrensen, Cynthia. "Making the Subterranean Visible: Security, Tunnels, and the United States–Mexico Border." *Geographical Review* 104.3 (July 2014): 328–345. Print.

Sowards, Stacey K., and Richard D. Pineda. "Immigrant Narratives and Popular Culture in the United States: Border Spectacle, Unmotivated Sympathies, and Individualized Responsibilities." *Western Journal of Communication* 77.1 (January 2013): 72–91.

Texas Department of Transportation. *Texas–Mexico International Bridges and Border Crossings.* Austin: TX DOT, 2015. Print.

Torpey, John. *The Invention of the Passport: Surveillance, Citizenship, and the State.* Cambridge: Cambridge UP, 2000. Print.

Touch of Evil. Dir. Orson Welles. Universal Pictures, 1958. Film.

Traffic. Dir. Steven Soderbergh. Bedford Falls Productions, Laura Bickford Productions, Initial Entertainment Group, 2000. Film.

Vismann, Cornelia. "Starting from Scratch: Concepts of Order in No-Man's Land." *War, Violence, and the Modern Condition.* Ed. Bernd Hüppauf. Berlin: Walter de Gruyter, 1997. Print.

"Yankee." *The Bridge.* FX. July 9, 2014. Television.

13

Red Land, White Power, Blue Sky

• •

Settler Colonialism and
Indigeneity in *Breaking Bad*[1]

JAMES H. COX

In alignment with the enduring trend on network and cable television in the United States, indigenous characters exclusively occupy the margins of the main narrative arc of AMC's *Breaking Bad* (2008–2013).[2] The series, however, does not surrender entirely to what indigenous and critical media studies scholar Dustin Tahmahkera (Comanche Nation) calls "the dominant media tradition of colonizing representations of the Indian" (*Tribal Television* 3). In its production of Native characters, *Breaking Bad* does not oversimplify (see Adam Beach's casino manager Tommy Flute in *Big Love*) or caricature (see Jonathan Joss's casino owner Ken Hotate in *Parks and Recreation* and Randolph Mantooth's Chief Charlie Horse in *Sons of Anarchy*) contemporary Native life, culture, and politics.[3] On the series' commendable depiction of indigenous people, Blackfeet writer Gyasi Ross observes in *Indian Country Today*:

> It was historical because here was this MAJOR big ticket show that had a backdrop of Indian Country and Native characters in a lot of the episodes. Almost as amazingly, . . . nobody on the show REALLY CARED about them being Native or not. No, those poor Native saps on *Breaking Bad* were just another person on

the show who died a horrible death (because everybody died a horrible death on the show), not because they were Native, but just because. Imagine that—Native people who were just "people." ("Native Influences"; uppercase letters in original)

To use Tahmahkera's terminology, *Breaking Bad* works against "*recognizably Indian*" representations—"one-dimensional, trite, stereotypical, or otherwise problematic discursive and visual constructions of Indians"—and takes tentative steps toward "*recognizably Native*" ones—"those informed by and attuned to, even if conflicting and perplexing, Native individual and tribal recognition of what constitutes indigenous identities and what it means to be indigenous" (8).[4] As Ross suggests, the series creators produce representations of Native characters that earn his praise by assiduously avoiding most of the familiar cultural and political markers of indigeneity. Instead, the series defines them either by occupation or by the prominent place that they occupy in contemporary Native cinematic and visual culture.

More dramatically, the presence of Native characters and images throughout the series and the frequency of scenes set at Tohajiilee, part of the Navajo Nation, contribute to a robust condemnation of settler colonialism.[5] Political scientist Glen Coulthard (Yellowknives Dene First Nation) defines a settler-colonial relationship as

> one characterized by a particular form of *domination*; that is, it is a relationship where power—in this case, interrelated discursive and nondiscursive facets of economic, gendered, racial, and state power—has been structured into a relatively secure or sedimented set of hierarchical social relations that continue to facilitate the *dispossession* of Indigenous peoples of their lands and self-determining authority. (6–7)

Drawing upon discursive as well as economic and racial facets of settler-colonial state power, Walter Hartwell White (Bryan Cranston)—always Mr. White to his sidekick, Jesse Pinkman (Aaron Paul)—claims a privileged place within the settler-colonial structure of the southwestern United States. Indeed, *Breaking Bad* exhibits many features of the settler-colonial narrative as described by Lorenzo Veracini in his instructive overview of settler-colonial studies: with no possible return to a home country, "the settler coloniser moves forward along a story line that cannot be turned back"; "settlers do not discover: they carry their sovereignty and lifestyles with them"; "they settle another place without really moving" (98); "settlers construe their very movement forward as a 'return' to something that was irretrievably lost: a return to the land, but also a return to an Edenic condition . . . , to a Golden Age of unsurrendered freedoms" (98–99); "settler colonialism mobilises peoples in the teleological expectation of irreversible transformation" (99). Walter White, as he moves onto indigenous land and irreversibly transforms from unassuming high school teacher to the drug lord Heisenberg, carries his sovereignty and lifestyle with him.

This line of inquiry touches upon the topics of but diverges from both Cordelia Barrera's study of *Breaking Bad*'s challenge to dominant national myths "that have often romanticized the cruel realities of Euro-American conquest" (17) and Timothy Dansdill's analysis of Walter White's imperial selfhood as made legible through associations with the "unrepentant, but always evolving, imperialist" poet, Walt Whitman (186). Barrera observes, for example, that "Native Americans in the US Southwest signify a ruined and conquered past," and she focuses on "Native ghosts and demons that yet menace the landscape" (20; 21). This chapter, as guided by a Native American and indigenous studies approach, considers the indigenous land and people of the Native present that play such a central role in the series.

White responds to a cancer diagnosis and struggles with the lingering bitterness of romantic and professional betrayal by claiming settler-colonial authority and several settler-colonial privileges, especially freedom from suspicion by state and federal authorities and freedom of access to indigenous land.[6] He becomes a producer of methamphetamine and moves gradually and, within the context of the carefully plotted narrative arc, logically toward a gang of neo-Nazis as his final partners in crime. White's nom de guerre, Heisenberg, aligns him with the Nobel Prize–winning physicist who helped to develop Nazi Germany's nuclear program in the 1940s, as scientists worked simultaneously on the Manhattan Project at many places throughout the United States, including Los Alamos, approximately 100 miles northeast by car from Albuquerque.[7] Much of the uranium mining in the United States occurs on Native land, including within the borders of the Navajo Nation, and as writers Leslie Marmon Silko (Laguna Pueblo) in her novel *Ceremony* (1977) and Gloria Bird (Spokane) in the essay "Breaking the Silence: Writing as Witness" demonstrate, the extraction process poisons the environment and its residents. White works at the Science Research Center in Los Alamos, and Skyler suggests that "all those chemicals they had you working around" at the lab in Los Alamos caused his cancer ("Cancer Man"). *Breaking Bad* thus closely links White, the master chef of various toxic substances and a highly addictive drug, to white supremacy and nuclear power, which form two components or ingredients of his settler-colonial identity.

The Empire Business: Walter White's Settler-Colonial Supremacy

Although White's cancer diagnosis and the danger that it poses to the family's finances appear as the primary motivation for his criminal enterprise, which he calls "the empire business" in the season five episode "Buyout," the cancer represents to him only a stage in a series of indignities and disappointments.

When White was a child, his father developed Huntington's disease and, after the inherited illness ravaged his body, died. After abruptly ending a romance with his lab assistant, Gretchen (Jessica Hecht), White sells his interest in Gray Matter Technologies for five thousand dollars to Elliott Schwartz (Adam Godley), their mutual friend and the company cofounder. Elliott and Gretchen later marry, and the value of Gray Matter rises into the billions, giving the couple national recognition, as evidenced by their interview with Charlie Rose in the penultimate episode of the series. In stark contrast, White lives in a middle-class Albuquerque neighborhood and teaches high school chemistry to a room full of disengaged students. The cancer, therefore, threatens to foreclose on White's efforts to fulfill the promise of the Nobel Prize for which he earned recognition as part of a research team at the lab in Los Alamos.[8] He makes a desperate, even ferocious attempt to rehabilitate his position in the White family and in affluent white settler-colonial society by producing and widely distributing a highly addictive, toxic stimulant.

The repeated use of powerful and dangerous chemicals by a white man named Mr. White to injure, poison, or kill people of color and, in several cases, destroy their bodies, establishes White's settler-colonial practice as distinctly toxic and highlights the deep racial antagonism that circulates through the series. In an act of self-defense in the pilot, he uses red phosphorus to kill a drug dealer, Emilio Koyama (John Koyama), who has forced Pinkman to bring him and his cousin, Domingo "Krazy 8" Molina (Max Arciniega), to the cooksite on Navajo land. Molina survives the explosion and poisonous phosphine gas cloud, but White eventually kills him two episodes later in a more ambiguous act of self-defense. He uses hydrofluoric acid to dispose of both corpses. In episode six of season one, "Crazy Handful of Nothin'," White makes fulminated mercury from mercury, nitric acid, and ethanol to create an explosion at meth distributor Tuco Salamanca's (Raymond Cruz) hideout. Ricin, a poison found in a castor oil plant's beans, and toxic cardiac glycosides, derived from lily of the valley and used to poison Pinkman's girlfriend Andrea Cantillo's (Emily Rios) son in season four's "End Times," also appear on White's menu of poisonous substances. White's ability to create toxins and chemical weapons facilitates the expansion of his settler-colonial authority and illicit drug empire in the region at the expense of American Indians and Latinos.

To make explicit White's status as a latent and then emergent settler-colonial force, the show exploits the similarities between discourses of drug dealing and colonial exploration and expansion. As he views a map of Albuquerque, White points to several neighborhoods and asks Pinkman, "Why aren't we exploiting that?" Pinkman responds, "Cuz it's not our territory" ("Negro y Azul"). White persists, though, by explaining that a rumor about Jesse killing a man gives them the opportunity to expand their territory. Later in the episode, Pinkman adopts White's language during a meeting that White held with his dealers, Brandon "Badger" Mayhew (Matt Jones), Skinny Pete (Charles Baker), and Christian "Combo" Ortega (Rodney Rush), earlier in the same episode at the National Museum of Nuclear Science & History. Pinkman first walks in front of a picture of a nuclear bomb explosion, then says to his dealers as they gather around him: "This is our city. All right. All of it. The whole damn place. Our territory. We're staking our claim" ("Negro y Azul"). Pinkman's ambitions are reinforced by the map of Russia's vast national territory in the background, and, from another camera angle, the photograph of Vladimir Lenin. When Pinkman joins White in his vehicle following the meeting, a missile in the background appears to emerge from the trunk of the car. In episode ten of season two, "Over," Walt recognizes the materials for a meth cook in another customer's cart during his own shopping excursion at a hardware store. After first giving the young man advice, White confronts him and his partner in the parking lot by their RV and growls, "Stay out of my territory." Both "Negro y Azul" and "Over" position Walt as radioactive, most explicitly in the meetings at the museum but also in the reference in the latter episode to Walt's radiation pneumonitis. A product of the chemotherapy, the radiation pneumonitis also conveys Walt's connection to Heisenberg and Nazi Germany, on one hand, and the U.S. nuclear program in the southwest, on the other. He has become literally toxic. By episode thirteen of season two, we learn, as D.E.A. Agent Hank Schrader (Dean Norris), White's brother-in-law, and his colleagues view a map of the Southwest (Texas, New Mexico, Arizona, Colorado, Utah, and Nevada) that White has "gone regional" ("ABQ"). His business, and the toxic settler colonialism that it represents, has metastasized.

Even as he expands his business internationally, with the help of a German company named Madrigal Electromotive GmbH, the series continues a pattern of linking White as a settler colonial to Indian Country. In the pilot, White attacks a young man mocking his son, Walt Jr. (R. J. Mitte). As he stands on the young man's leg and pins him to the floor, he asks, "What's wrong, chief? Having a little trouble walking?" ("Pilot"). After Saul Goodman (Bob Odenkirk), White's attorney, tells White that Skyler "snuck off the reservation" in episode three of season four, Mike Ehrmantraut (Jonathan Banks) says the same of White: he has "gone off the rez" ("Green Light"). The show also uses White's choice of vehicle—the Pontiac Aztek—to establish him as a settler colonial. The car's name, taken from the eighteenth-century Odawa leader Pontiac or Obwandiyag and the indigenous people that dominated central Mexico from 1428 to 1521, doubles the common appropriation of indigeneity by U.S. corporations. In a running gag, the car sustains damage, especially to its windshield, by falling debris ("Over") and a piece of cement thrown by Jesse ("Más"). White also damages the car when he runs over two drug dealers who killed Pinkman's girlfriend Andrea's brother ("Half Measures"), and when he intentionally crashes it to avoid aiding Schrader's investigation of Giancarlo Esposito's Gustavo "Gus" Fring ("Crawl Space"). He finally sells the car for fifty dollars in the fourth episode of the final season. By the time White asserts to Skyler, "I am the danger—I am the one who knocks" in the sixth episode of season four ("Cornered"), he has left a bloody trail in his wake. The serial destruction of the Pontiac Aztek suggests the danger that men like White present to indigenous people. The series claims a Native space (the literal reservation and the figurative "rez"; the Pontiac Aztek) for White, and this appropriation manifests in an actual physical threat to American Indians from White and his emergent empire.

Who Are Those Masked Men?

The series establishes the indigenous and settler colonial contexts of this threat in the first two episodes. The pilot opens on Navajo land at Tohajiilee, where White and Pinkman have been cooking the methamphetamine with the street name "Blue Sky" that will eventually make them infamous. After White crashes the RV, their mobile meth lab, he stands in the dirt road with his pistol drawn as sirens from emergency vehicles grow louder. At the end of the episode, viewers learn that the RV might contain two dead bodies and that the sirens announce the arrival of fire engines rather than police cars. The scene draws on several important contexts that shape the entire narrative arc of the series: similarly to many non-Natives before them, White and Pinkman have entered a reservation to engage in criminal activity; White's wild desperation, evidenced by the decision to cook meth despite having a D.E.A. agent as a brother-in-law and his failed suicide attempt at the end of the episode, situates him in a long history in the United States of "thinking of the West as madness" or even "regarding madness as the true West" (Fiedler 185); and the almost but not quite total absence of indigenous people, and, throughout the series, indigenous communities, which establishes their secondary status in Heisenberg's origin story.[9]

Yet the series includes enough Native characters to confirm Walt's position as a settler colonial who threatens, within the narrative borders of the show, to complete the settler-colonial "progress" from "displacement" to "ultimate erasure" (Veracini 101). The second episode, "Cat's in the Bag . . .," introduces the first Native character to appear in the series: the backhoe operator that White hires to pull the RV out of a ditch. While the show defines the man, played by Anthony Wamego, by his job, rather than by either indigenous political or cultural markers, he plays a role familiar to viewers of conventional Westerns: he stands skeptically and stoically and does not speak throughout the scene. White lies to him about the circumstances that led to the accident, after which Pinkman hands him a few bills, wet from the chemical spill inside the RV, to pay for his services. White, reading the driver's frown as displeasure with the payment, grabs more chemical-soaked cash and hands it to him. Two more Native characters appear at the end of the episode: while kicking a rubber ball, a young boy and girl find the gas mask apparently thrown from the RV as it crashed. The girl puts it on, fixes her hair, adjusts the mask, walks a few steps, and looks up into the sky; the mask ominously engulfs her head.[10] White and Pinkman use masks throughout the series to protect themselves from the toxic chemicals used to make meth, and the masks, in a reversal of Lone Ranger mythology, become iconic markers of settler-colonial criminality rather than vigilante justice. To emphasize the significance of the mask to White's identity as Heisenberg, one appears in the final scene in the series finale, "Felina." The soundtrack begins to play Badfinger's 1972 single "Baby Blue" at the precise moment that White sees the mask as he walks through the neo-Nazi gang's meth lab. He picks it up and holds the marker of settler-colonial criminality, now imbued with the white power that was always latent in White's desire to dominate, as he drops dead on the floor.

A conventional Lone Ranger figure appears in episode three, "And the Bag's in the River," but, even as a law enforcement official, he poses a threat to indigenous people within the settler-colonial frame of the series. As Schrader and his partner, Steven Gomez (Steven Michael Quezada), investigate the cook site, Schrader makes one of his frequent bigoted, demeaning comments to Gomez: "You people used to be conquistadors for Christ's sake." Schrader's disrespect for Gomez, the Tonto to his Lone Ranger, and his apparent respect for the conquistadors, position him as another settler-colonial antagonist to the Native children and their mother. The mother hands the gas mask to the police officer, who calls to Schrader and Gomez while holding the gas mask high above his head so that they can see it.[11] As Schrader and Gomez approach, the camera frames the policeman and the family between their bodies, with D.E.A. featured in large white letters on their jackets, before moving to a close-up of the policeman, mother, and son. The mother glances first at the mask, then the agents, then the mask again, as if assessing the relative danger to indigenous people of either a drug dealer or a federal agent. White fills the role of conventional villain of the wild West, even donning a black hat at the end of season one, but the indigenous presence in the show reminds viewers of the settler-colonial dynamic that makes Schrader and other federal authorities as dangerous to them as White. The show emphasizes the settler-colonial family connection between the brothers-in-law and, drawing on the pattern of references to Germany, hints at their shared sense of white superiority.[12]

Native characters continue to come into contact with White's dangerous toxicity—the poison of settler colonialism. In episode six, the series introduces the third Native character, and the first with a name, to clean up one of White's messes. When White leaves his classroom to go to the bathroom to vomit, a response to his chemotherapy, the janitor, a Native man named Hugo Archuleta, tells Walt that he will clean it up. Hugo, played by Klamath/ Lakota actor Pierre Barrera, interrupts White in the act of getting some paper towels and says, "I got it, Mr. White. Don't worry. You got kids to teach" ("Crazy Handful of Nothin'"). Later in the episode, Hugo hands White a stick of gum after he once again gets sick in the bathroom. At this point in the series, a Native man has pulled White's meth lab out of a reservation ditch and accepted chemical-soaked cash, and a young Native girl has recovered a gas mask used in a meth cook. Hugo, following the pattern, cleans up the product of White's radiation treatments.

In a settler-colonial context, Hugo, not White, fits the profile of a criminal, and Hugo's kindness does not protect him from becoming the first Native character to fall victim to White's criminal enterprise. The scene that follows has Schrader visiting White's classroom with the gas mask, pulling the mask from his bag, and asking if White recognizes it. When White says no, Schrader explains, "Well that was used to cook meth. Found it out on some Indian land about 40 miles from here." Schrader tells White that the mask came from the locked storeroom attached to his classroom. The next morning, as Hugo raises the American flag at the school, Schrader approaches and arrests him. Over a card game at the White's, Schrader explains to Walt Jr. that Hugo "has a record, yeah, a couple of possession beefs. We figured he was the guy that was stealing your school's chemistry gear." He "fit the profile," Schrader adds, and they searched his truck and "found a big old fat blunt." White protests that "Hugo just doesn't strike me as a thief," but Schrader says, "We got a search warrant, and we tore old Hugo's house apart. Turns out he's a major league pot head." As the card game continues, White asks, "What's going to happen to him? Hugo?" Schrader explains, "He's going to lose his job. Like he should. Probably spend a couple months in county cause it's not his first rap." White's expression of sympathy for Hugo lasts only briefly. When Schrader taunts him to "man up or puss out," White bluffs his way to a win by getting Schrader to fold with "an ace and a cowboy," or a king. White's successful attempt to "cowboy up," or to out-cowboy his more hypermasculine brother-in-law, permanently and callously shifts the focus of the conversation from the racial profiling of Hugo.

The series brings into sharper relief, at the beginning of the next episode, the white, settler-colonial privilege that protects White. In a meeting between the D.E.A. and a group of parents, one parent inquires about Hugo, "the janitor that was dealing drugs at the school." Carmen Molina (Carmen Serano), the assistant principal, tells the gathered parents that "there is no indication that this individual was selling drugs" ("A No-Rough-Stuff-Type Deal"). As the parents continue to focus their outrage and suspicions on Hugo, White starts touching Skyler's leg under the table. After the meeting, the scene cuts to White and Skyler having sex in his Pontiac Aztek, which White parked next to a police car. Skyler remarks breathlessly, "Where did that come from? And why was it so damn good?" White says, "Cause it was illegal." The scene carefully juxtaposes the continued condemnation in the meeting of Hugo, even after he has already lost his job and his freedom, and White's flaunting of the ease with which he escapes punishment.

White continues to establish and assert his dominance over Native land, people, and culture later in the same episode by using them as an alibi for his criminal activities. He settles on a trip to a "Navajo sweat lodge up by Farmington, a healing ceremony" as cover for the theft of an ingredient for his meth. He adds, "I'm not saying that I believe in it, but it might be an experience." Similarly to Hugo, who took the fall if not the explicit blame for the theft of lab equipment, the Navajos become White's alibi. When White returns from the theft, Skyler kisses him and smells the chemicals from a cook in Pinkman's basement. He tells her that the smell comes from "sacred Navajo herbs." As the first season ends, White and Pinkman make a sale to Tuco Salamanca. Pinkman sports a jacket with a picture of a skull wearing a headdress and a wolf or coyote head emerging from the feathers.[13] The image of a dead, decomposed, and commodified indigenous person displayed on his body confirms White's and Pinkman's ascendance within the settler-colonial order.

The skull on Pinkman's jacket foreshadows the fate of Native people in the series, as they regularly become casualties of Walt's empire building. After addicts steal some meth from Skinny Pete in "Peekaboo," the sixth episode of season two, Pinkman tries to recover the product. The thief, an addict named Spooge (David Ury), tells Pinkman that he can pay for the meth with money from a stolen ATM machine. When Pinkman protests that the ATM comes from his bank, Spooge tells him, "It's FIDC insured, yo. It's a victimless crime."[14] He describes the theft, insists that there were no witnesses, and repeats, "I'm telling you. Victimless crime." Simultaneously with his repetition of this assertion, the camera pans up the body of a dead Native man sitting in a large pool of blood. A bat near his left hand suggests that he was an employee of the convenience store and attempted to stop the robbery. His bloody torso and the two streaks of blood on the wall behind him convey the horror of the final moments of his life. In Spooge's narrative, however, an indigenous person does not count as a victim.

Three of the four Native characters in season three—a cashier, tribal cop, mother, and druglord henchman—face the same fate as Spooge's unnamed murder victim. The sole survivor of the four characters appears in episode four, "Green Light," which opens with a sharply angled shot of the head of a Native man in a headdress, a variation of the image on Pinkman's jacket in the last episode of season one and the first episode of season two, painted on a wall beneath a "Big Chief/Dr. Pepper" sign. The scene cuts to a cigarette vending machine next to an ATM from the same bank as the one stolen by Spooge in season two. The ATM even appears to have either red paint or blood at its base. These opening images also link the episode to the anti-Native violence in "Peek-aboo." As Pinkman pulls into the gas station in the RV, the camera reveals the name: Big Chief Gas Station and Market. The camera angle shifts to include the painting of the Native man and the RV rolling in front of and hiding it from view as Pinkman cuts the engine. Pinkman fills the tank but does not have money to pay for it, so he offers the cashier, Cara (Jolene Purdy), a young Native woman, meth as payment: "Maybe we could trade." After acknowledging that she smokes pot, Cara asks, "But that stuff's really addictive, right?" Pinkman replies, "Not really. It's just a media thing, ya know?" In response to her question about the experience of using meth, Jesse says, "It's awesome. Everything's maximum interesting." He finishes his sales pitch by urging Cara to accept it: "Come on. What do you say?" As a New Mexico state cop gets in line behind Pinkman, Cara takes it. The scene resonates with the history of unequal and coerced trades between non-Natives and American Indians, and it reminds viewers that in a settler-colonial context, white crime often occurs in full public view.

While the encounter with Pinkman does not end tragically for Cara, she still faces, like Hugo, abuse from an intimidating agent of the federal government. When Schrader follows a lead to the gas station, he interrogates Cara. Displeased with her attempt to evade his questions, Schrader says, "You're a bad liar, Cara," then raises the level of aggression by shouting at her and slamming his hand on the counter ("Green Light"). Cara breaks, tells Schrader the truth, and provides him with a description of Pinkman: "He looked pretty normal. You know, um, white. Um, I think his hair was lightish brown. He had really blue eyes. You know, really, really blue" ("Green Light"). After Cara confirms the settler-colonial physical norm—white skin, brown hair, blue eyes—she begins to cry. Schrader insists that she think harder, but she cannot give him any more useful information. After he leaves the building, Schrader notices the ATM and decides to check the camera in it to identify the man who gave the meth to Cara. She does not appear again in the series.

The violence that White sets in motion threatens indigenous peace officers and villains equally. In "Sunset," episode six of season three, the series introduces a Native character with at least some authority in a settler-colonial context: a tribal police officer, Deputy Bobby Kee, played by Jose Avila.[15] His badge identifies him as a member of the Pueblo of Santa Ana police department. The episode opens with a shot of a small sign reading "Homeland Security" hanging from a rearview mirror. As it turns, a photo of Geronimo and three other Apache men with rifles comes into view above the caption "Fighting Terrorism Since 1492." The same photo also appears on other consumer items, such as shirts, with the words "Homeland Security." The terrorism in this case is settler-colonial, both U.S. and, as the result of the involvement of a cartel,

Mexican. Kee takes a call from the dispatcher, who tells him that a woman has called from California to say that she has not heard from her mother, Mrs. Peyketewa, recently.[16] As Kee looks into a window, the camera faces him from inside the house and reveals a drawing of Walter White as Heisenberg. Kee walks the property and hears flies by the outhouse. The sound leads him to Mrs. Peyketewa's corpse. Kee calls to report the homicide and request backup. As one cartel hitman emerges from the house and stares at Kee, the other, his twin brother, approaches him from behind and kills him with an axe. Two additional swings of the axe emphasize the brutality of the murder.[17]

Gus Fring's right-hand man, Victor, played by Navajo and Omaha actor Jeremiah Bitsui, has the only recurring role for a Native character in the series. Bitsui came to *Breaking Bad* as an established young actor with roles in *Natural Born Killers* (1994) and *Flags of Our Fathers* (2006). More significantly for his visibility in Native cinematic culture, he played Johnny Chee, a young Navajo "trying to become a man by playing gangster" on the streets of Albuquerque, in *A Thousand Roads* (2005). Chris Eyre (Cheyenne and Arapahoe) directed *A Thousand Roads*, advertised as the "Signature Film of the Smithsonian's National Museum of the American Indian," from a script cowritten by Scott Garen and Joy Harjo (Mvskoke or Muscogee Creek). Although the narrative establishes Victor as an antagonist to White and Pinkman, the latter are far more dangerous than any imagined Native threat. After a brief introduction in "Mandala," episode eleven of season two, Victor appears in six episodes in season three and one episode in season four. He has few speaking lines and primarily hovers around and watches first White and Pinkman and then White and his new lab partner, Gale Boetticher (David Costabile). In the context of his own violent acts, including homicide, Pinkman's observation, "that guy's got dead eyes," deflects suspicion from him and positions Victor as more dangerous ("I See You"). In anticipation of replacing White with Boetticher, Fring orders Victor to bring White to the lab to kill him. After White calls Pinkman and frantically urges him to kill Boetticher, Victor runs from the lab with plans to stop him. In "Box Cutter," however, Victor appears too late at Boetticher's house. Victor has the "dead eyes," according to Pinkman, but Victor tries to stop Pinkman from committing murder.

The expression "dead eyes" takes on a different though familiar meaning in the following episode within the show's settler-colonial context. Back at the lab, Victor, concerned that he failed to save Boetticher, turns on the equipment, puts on a gas mask, and starts to cook: "That's right, genius, watch me," he says. "We ain't missing no cook" ("Box Cutter"). By showcasing his skills, Victor attempts to position himself as indispensable to Fring, and he insists that he knows how to produce Blue Sky, despite White's objections. Fring apparently decides, though, that he cannot run his business without White, and he cuts Victor's throat with a box cutter. The blood sprays over White and Pinkman, and Fring throws the body at their feet. As his blood runs across the floor, Pinkman and White begin to dispose of the body in a barrel filled with hydrofluoric acid. After a man puts a corrosive sticker on the barrel, the episode cuts to the lab, where Pinkman and White mop the blood from the floor. The gruesome murder of Victor recalls the murder of Deputy Kee and includes the postmortem desecration: an acid bath for Victor, with the additional insult of having his corpse identified as toxic waste, and the extra swings of the axe for Deputy Kee.

From "Box Cutter" until the final few episodes of the series, Native characters and images occur with less frequency and, when they do, as when Navajo actor Ryan Begay appears as "Good Samaritan" in "Dead Freight," fleetingly.[18] However, White, now a more powerful but also more desperate settler colonial in alliance with neo-Nazis, returns to indigenous land in episodes thirteen and fourteen, "To'hajiilee" and "Ozymandias," of season five. "To'hajiilee" finds White at the site of his first cook with Pinkman on Navajo land, where he has buried seven barrels full of cash; the barrels of cash on American Indian land evoke the fantasies of buried treasure that drove some of the Spanish colonization of the Southwest. White and his hoard draw Schrader and Gomez, with the help of Pinkman, to the reservation. After they arrest White, Schrader says, "We'll call the tribal police on my way out, let them know we're here." But White, by asking them to execute Pinkman then withdrawing the request, has also drawn the neo-Nazis to the reservation. When they arrive, Gomez thinks at first that they are the tribal police. Gomez's mistake clarifies the secondary and threatened status of Native people and the Navajo Nation's jurisdiction over its land.

Within the context of the show's depiction of toxic settler colonialism, the neo-Nazi gang functions as the cavalry. In the following episode, titled after a Percy Shelley sonnet about a mighty pharaoh, Ramses II, whose empire long ago disappeared, viewers see the result of the shootout: Gomez's dead body and an injured Schrader contradicting White and telling the gang leader, Jack Welker (Michael Bowen), "You bet your ass the cavalry's coming." In the most conventional sense, Schrader's statement is only wishful thinking: he has kept his investigation secret, and the U.S. cavalry in the form of the D.E.A. or any other police force will not appear. However, the neo-Nazi gang arrives to save White and defeat his enemies, including Pinkman. They take most of White's money, bury Schrader and Gomez, capture Pinkman, and set White free with one barrel of cash.[19]

The appearance of revered Sac and Fox actor Saginaw Grant as "Native American Man" in "Ozymandias" brings to a conclusion the series's explicit commentary on settler colonialism. "Ozymandias" opens with a scene from the beginning of the series with White and Pinkman cooking on the reservation in the RV. After White, Pinkman, and the RV fade out, the sound of gunfire returns viewers to the present and the scene fades in. White starts to leave the reservation, but his car runs out of gas: a bullet fired during the shootout punctured the gas tank. As he rolls the single barrel of cash over reservation land, the melancholy folksong "Take My True Love By the Hand" by the Limeliters plays. A wide-angle shot reveals White and his barrel as tiny specks on the landscape surrounded by dirt and cactus. The camera cuts to a small stone home and pans along the wall to Native American Man looking through a glassless pane. When the pan stops, the camera focuses on the glass next to the man's face. White, reflected in the pane, comes into view. The man exits his home, and the camera pans back along the landscape past the fence that marks the boundary of his land and stops as White walks into the frame. A wide-angle shot shows Native American Man and White greeting each other over the fence, as if some balance has been established between the two: an elderly Native American man on a small piece of land and the nearly defeated drug kingpin with one barrel of earnings remaining. White says he would like to buy the man's truck. After Native American Man says, "It's not for sale," White, partially framed by a steer's skull hanging on the fence, approaches the fence while reaching into his inside jacket pocket. He hands Native American Man a stack of bills through the barbed wire. The narrative skips the actual sale and cuts to White putting the barrel into the bed of the truck as Native American Man watches. While Native American Man has money to buy a new truck, the sale of his old one reads as coerced. Like Pinkman's trade of a small bag of Blue Sky for gas at Big Chief Gas Station and Market, White's purchase of the truck evokes a long history of negotiations between Natives and non-Natives that favored the latter. White, once again in an "indigenous" ride, drives the truck home, parks it in his driveway, and later uses it as he flees with his infant daughter, Holly. After Native American Man's truck enables this bleak parody of conventional captivity narratives, White abandons it.

In one of the most memorable scenes in Silko's novel *Ceremony*, the character Old Grandmother comments on witnessing the Trinity Test on July 16, 1945, at Alamogordo in southern New Mexico: "You know, I have never understood that thing I saw. Later on there was something about it in the newspaper. Strongest thing on this earth. . . . Now I only wonder why, grandson. Why did they make a thing like that?" (245). Silko situates the release of such malign power in "witchery" that drives the world toward death and destruction. White's laboratory skills, which both he and Boetticher imply make them magicians, would register within Silko's narrative as colonial and settler-colonial witchery.[20] Indeed, methamphetamine is a destructive force in the Navajo Nation, as the documentary *G: Methamphetamine on the Navajo Nation* (2004) makes so painfully clear.[21] Contrary to Pinkman's assertion to Cara, the young Native cashier at the Big Chief Station, meth addiction is not a media creation. His self-serving and menacing lie captures as dramatically as the deaths of Deputy Kee and Victor the kind of threat that White and Pinkman pose to indigenous people. At least the series leaves viewers with the characters Good

Samaritan and Native American Man, along with the Native mother and her two children, as survivors of White's empire building. White tells Skyler, "I did it for me. I liked it. I was good at it. And . . . I was . . . really . . . I was alive" ("Felina"). The settler-colonial structure that allows White to find or regenerate himself but imprisons Native people like Hugo, however, also remains.[22] When White gets his revenge on the neo-Nazis in a hail of bullets in the series finale, he also fatally shoots himself. He is, this fate suggests, more like Welker and the members of his gang than his Ph.D. and khakis might indicate. Irreversibly transformed by the full effect of white and White power, he falls victim to his own settler-colonial plot.

Notes

1   The title plays on Vine Deloria Jr.'s *Red Earth, White Lies: Native Americans and the Myth of Scientific Fact*, in which Deloria Jr. describes his loss of faith in a "science gone mad" (7). He explains further: "This book deals with some of the problems created for American Indians by science" (22).

2   Recent exceptions include *Law and Order: SVU* (twenty-one episodes from 2007 to 2008 with Adam Beach as Mohawk police officer Chester Lake), *Longmire* (forty-nine episodes from 2012 to 2016 with Lou Diamond Phillips as bar owner Henry Standing Bear, twenty-one episodes with A. Martinez as casino owner Jacob Nighthorse, and several more Native characters with less frequently recurring roles) and *The Red Road* (twelve episodes from 2014 to 2015 with various Native roles including star Jason Momoa as Phillip Kopus).

3   Q'orianka Kilcher, of Quechua-Huachipaeri ancestry through her father, plays a nonindigenous American character, Kerrianne Telford, in four episodes of *Sons of Anarchy*. In an interview with Dustin Tahmahkera, Joss says of Hotate, "If there's a joke with Ken, the joke involves him and is not about him" ("Actor Jonathan Joss"). While the series conveys self-awareness of the jokes, the comedy nevertheless rests on caricatures of American Indian culture and politics (opossums as Wamapoke currency, ceremonial peace pipes, sacred burial ground curses, sacred artifacts, etc.). Professor Del Redclay (Larry Sellers) and Chief Doug Smith (Nick Chinlund) from the "Christopher" episode of *The Sopranos* fit into this pattern of caricatured American Indian characters.

4   Tahmahkera observes that the "'casino Indian' and Indian casino" are "a dominant representation of and setting for the recognizably Indian," not the "recognizably Native" (19).

5   The series spells "Tohajiilee" as "To'hajiilee."

6   See Bradley for more insight from *Breaking Bad* creator Vince Gilligan into Walt's motivations for leaving Gretchen and Gray Matter.

7   Leonard Engel focuses on Heisenberg's "uncertainty principle," rather than on his position within the German science community during Nazi Party rule, in his study of *Breaking Bad* as a contemporary morality tale.

8   In the pilot, as Walt exercises, the camera pans to a plaque on the wall that reads "Science Research Center, Los Alamos, New Mexico, Hereby recognizes Walter H. White, Crystallography Project Leader for Proton Radiography, 1985, Contributor to Research Awarded the Nobel Prize."

9   One can reach this "true West," Fiedler suggests, by going on a "trip," that is, "an excursion into the unknown with the aid of drugs" (186).

10 The image of the young girl in the gas mask might have inspired Jeff Barnaby, director of *Rhymes for Young Ghouls* (2013). In the film, Mohawk actress Kawennáhere Devery Jacobs plays Alia, the weed princess of Red Crow. She wears a gas mask as she prepares the product for her customers.

11 The officer with the Native family might be a tribal policeman, though the show does not make it clear.

12 Schrader is a German surname that means tailor, and Hank brews his own German beer, Schraderbräu.

13 Beneath the skull, the jacket reads, "Beyond the Possibility of Defeat."

14 Spooge says FIDC but means FDIC.

15 Kee/Kii is a common Navajo surname.

16 Peyketewa is a Hopi surname.

17 The twins, Leonel and Marco Salamanca (played by Daniel and Luis Moncada), are Hector Salamanca's nephews and Tuco Salamanca's cousin.

18 Skyler visits the Four Corners Monument, for example, a park run by the Navajo Nation Department of Parks and Recreation, where she passes a Navajo frybread stand ("Cornered"). Viewers could read other characters as American Indian too, including Cynthia, played by Ashley Kajiki, at Los Pollos Hermanos and another restaurant employee in "Hermanos." See Davis for Kajiki's thoughts on playing characters of various ethnicities. Begay as the character "Good Samaritan" appears when White and Pinkman rob a train with the help of Ehrmantraut, Todd Alquist (Jesse Plemons), and Patrick Kuby (Bill Burr), in a scene reminiscent of the train robberies so central to Westerns. "Good Samaritan" interrupts the crime by offering to help push Kuby's truck off the railroad tracks ("Dead Freight").

19 The shootout in "Ozymandias" might evoke for some viewers the gun battle at the Pine Ridge Reservation on June 26, 1975, that culminated in the deaths of F.B.I. agents Jack Coler and Ronald Williams and the incarceration of Leonard Peltier. If the creators of *Breaking Bad* had this event in mind, they produced a provocative reimagining of it.

20 See "Sunset" for White's and Boetticher's references to the "magic" that they do.

21 Poet Natalie Diaz (Mojave; enrolled Gila River Indian Community) provides an intimate and painful look at the ravages of meth in *When My Brother Was an Aztec* (2012), while Cherokee author Sara Sue Hoklotubbe includes a raid on a meth lab in her mystery novel *The American Café* (2011).

22 See Richard Slotkin, *Regeneration through Violence*, in which he argues, "The first colonists saw in America an opportunity to regenerate their fortunes, their spirits, and the power of their church and nation; but the means to that regeneration ultimately became the means of violence, and the myth of regeneration through violence became the structuring metaphor of the American experience" (5).

Works Cited

"ABQ." *Breaking Bad.* AMC. 31 May 2009. Television.

"And the Bag's in the River." *Breaking Bad.* AMC. February 10, 2008. Television.

Barrera, Cordelia. "'Negro y Azul': The Narcocorrido Goes Gothic." *Breaking Down*

Breaking Bad: Critical Perspectives. Eds. Matt Wanant and Leonard Engel. Albuquerque: U of New Mexico P, 2016. 15–32.

Bird, Gloria. "Breaking the Silence: Writing as Witness." In *Speaking for the Generations: Native Writers on Writing*. Ed. Simon J. Ortiz. Tucson: U of Arizona P, 1997.

"Box Cutter." *Breaking Bad*. AMC. July 17, 2011. Television.

Bradley, Bill. "Vince Gilligan Finally Reveals Why Walter White Left Gray Matter." *The Huffington Post*, March 17, 2016. Web. July 28, 2016.

"Buyout." *Breaking Bad*. AMC. August 19, 2012. Television.

"Cancer Man." *Breaking Bad*. AMC. February 17, 2008. Television.

"Cat's in the Bag. . . ." *Breaking Bad*. AMC. January 27, 2008. Television.

"Cornered." *Breaking Bad*. AMC. August 21, 2011. Television.

Coulthard, Glen. *Red Skin, White Masks: Rejecting the Colonial Politics of Recognition*. Minneapolis: U of Minnesota P, 2014. Print.

"Crawl Space." *Breaking Bad*. AMC. 25 Sep. 2011. Television.

"Crazy Handful of Nothin'." *Breaking Bad*. AMC. Television.

Dansdill, Timothy. "The Arc of W. W.: Imperial Selfhood and Metastatic Poetry in *Breaking Bad*." In *Breaking Down* Breaking Bad: *Critical Perspectives*. Eds. Matt Wanant and Leonard Engel. Albuquerque: U of New Mexico P, 2016. 173–195. Print.

Davis, Stella. "'Breaking Bad': Actress Ashley Kajiki Has Fond Memories of Role on Show." *Daily Freeman News*. August 12, 2013. http://www.dailyfreeman.com/article/DF /20130812/NEWS/308129991. Web. August 4, 2016.

"Dead Freight." *Breaking Bad*. AMC. August 12, 2012. Television.

Deloria, Vine, Jr. *Red Earth, White Lies: Native Americans and the Myth of Scientific Fact*. Golden, CO: Fulcrum, 1997. Print.

"End Times." *Breaking Bad*. AMC. October 2, 2011. Television.

Engel, Leonard. "*Breaking Bad*—Morality Play Meets Heisenberg's Uncertainty Principle." *Breaking Down* Breaking Bad: *Critical Perspectives*. Eds. Matt Wanant and Leonard Engel. Albuquerque: U of New Mexico P, 2016. 1–14. Print.

Fiedler, Leslie A. *The Return of the Vanishing American*. New York: Stein and Day, 1968.

G: Methamphetamine on the Navajo Nation. Directed by Shonie de la Rosa. Shenandoah Films, 2004. Film.

"Green Light." *Breaking Bad*. AMC. April 11, 2010. Television.

"Half Measures." *Breaking Bad*. AMC. June 6, 2010. Television.

"I See You." *Breaking Bad*. AMC. May 9, 2010. Television.

"Más." *Breaking Bad*. AMC. April 18, 2010. Television.

"Negro y Azul." *Breaking Bad*. AMC. April 19, 2009. Television.

"A No-Rough-Stuff-Type of Deal." *Breaking Bad*. AMC. 9 Mar. 2008. Television.

"Over." *Breaking Bad*. AMC. May 10, 2009. Television.

"Ozymandias." *Breaking Bad*. AMC. September 15, 2013. Television.

"Peekaboo." *Breaking Bad*. AMC. April 12, 2009. Television.

"Pilot." *Breaking Bad*. AMC. January 20, 2008. Television.

Ross, Gyasi. "Native Influences on 'Breaking Bad': Murdered on the Best Show Ever." *Indian Country Today*, April 4, 2014. Web. July 28, 2016.

Silko, Leslie Marmon. *Ceremony*. New York: Penguin, 1977. Print.

Slotkin, Richard. *Regeneration through Violence: The Mythology of the American Frontier, 1600–1860*. 1973. Norman: U of Oklahoma P, 2000. Print.

"Sunset." *Breaking Bad*. AMC. April 25, 2010. Television.

Tahmahkera, Dustin. "Actor Jonathan Joss Talks 'Parks and Rec,' 'King of the Hill,' and
His NAMA Nomination." *Indian Country Today*, April 3, 2013. Web. July 28, 2016.
———. *Tribal Television: Viewing Native People in Sitcoms*. Chapel Hill: U of North
Carolina P, 2014. Print.
A Thousand Roads. Directed by Chris Eyre. Seven Arrows/Telenova, 2005.
"To'hajiilee." *Breaking Bad*. AMC. September 8, 2013. Television.
Veracini, Lorenzo. *Settler Colonialism: A Theoretical Overview*. New York: Palgrave
Macmillan, 2010.

Acknowledgments

Race and Cultural Practice in Popular Culture is the result of sustained collaboration, and more than a little tenacity and patience. We are incredibly grateful to the volume's contributors and believe that their combined efforts have resulted in a collection that will shape conversations across disciplines. We would also like to extend our thanks to those early contributors who for various reasons could not be with us at the finish line. Your initial insights were critical to the shaping of this volume.

We would like to thank Rutgers Press for their support of the project from its inception. Associate Director/Editor in Chief Leslie Mitchner immediately saw the value in what we wanted to accomplish, even before it was fully formed. Her enthusiasm and flexibility helped to sustain us throughout this process.

Thank you Jazmine Ja'nicole Wells and Megan McKeon, our graduate assistants on the project, who at different stages, helped in the initial preparation of the manuscript and kept us organized.

This volume is also indebted to the support of Frederick Luis Aldama, who generously offered insights and revisions on early versions of our manuscript.

The professional support we received from the University of Texas at Austin proved vital to the realization of *Race and Cultural Practice*. We are particularly appreciative of the resources the Department of Mexican American and Latina/o Studies and the Center for Mexican American Studies devoted to our work. Through this volume, we are proud to continue their intellectual missions.

Rachel would like to extend her gratitude to the Woodrow Wilson Early Career Fellowship and Mellon-Mays Program that helped support a semester of research leave during which our manuscript was completed.

We would like to thank our families for their patience and good humor as we dedicated days and nights to completing this manuscript.

And finally, to Maria Elsa Ortiz Perez, who influenced our work but passed on before seeing its realization, your stories, music, dancing, pageants, novelas, cooking, and spirituality demonstrated daily the intersections of cultural practice and community enactment. May our efforts do justice to the richness of your life.

Notes on Contributors

RAISA ALVARADO UCHIMA earned a PhD in communication and cultural studies at the University of Denver. Dr. Alvarado's most recent work explores the intersectional implications of girl-oriented social movements and activism. Broadly, her research focuses on the rhetoric of social movements, Chicana feminism, identity assemblages, and postcolonial studies.

JOSÉ G. ANGUIANO is an assistant professor in Chicana/o and Latina/o Studies and The Honors College at California State University, Los Angeles. Dr. Anguiano is a cultural studies scholar with a primary focus on listeners and audiences of popular music and on sound cultures of Southern California. Dr. Anguiano's research documents how popular music links communities of listeners across time and space, and how listening can be an active and creative form of claiming space, citizenship, and respect.

MARCEL BROUSSEAU is a Carlos E. Castañeda Postdoctoral Fellow in the Center for Mexican American Studies at the University of Texas at Austin. He has a PhD in comparative literature from the University of California, Santa Barbara. He is at work on a book manuscript, "Over the Line: Cultural Techniques of the Trans-American Hyperborder," which examines the U.S.–Mexico border as a network of interconnected literary, cartographic, and infrastructural objects. He also produces critical cartography and has adapted Óscar Martínez's migration account *Los migrantes que no importan* into a "moralized road map." His essays about Kiowa literary and digital mapping, about teaching the work of author Jovita González, and about sports media and augmented reality are forthcoming.

OLIVIA CADAVAL is curator and chair of Cultural Research and Education at the Smithsonian Institution, Center for Folklife and Cultural Heritage. She holds a PhD in American studies and folklife from George Washington University. She has curated numerous festival programs, websites, and exhibitions and produced curriculum-enrichment materials. She has worked extensively on documentation, public programs, and education projects in the Latino community of Washington, D.C. She has published books, articles, book reviews, and a catalog and produced the bilingual website "Assembling the Festival Program: Colombia."

JAMES H. COX is a professor of English and Distinguished Teaching Professor at the University of Texas at Austin. He is the author of *Muting White Noise: Native American and European American Novel Traditions* (Oklahoma, 2006) and *The Red Land to the South: American Indian Writers and Indigenous Mexico* (Minnesota, 2012). He also co-edited *The Oxford Handbook of Indigenous American Literature* (Oxford, 2014) with Daniel Heath Justice of the University of British Columbia. His book *The Politics of American Indian Literature* is forthcoming from the University of Minnesota Press.

K. ANGELIQUE DWYER is an associate professor of Spanish and chair of Latin American, Latina/o and Caribbean Studies (LALACS) in the Department of Modern Languages, Literatures and Cultures at Gustavus Adolphus College. She specializes in Mexico/U.S. intercultural studies, Chicana/Latina cultural production, performance art, and film. Dwyer was a recipient of the President's Civic Engagement Steward Award in 2016 and a nominee for the Earnest A. Lynton Award for the Scholarship of Engagement. Her current research is tripartite, focusing on her areas of specialization: interdisciplinary teaching pedagogy, and creative nonfiction.

RACHEL GONZÁLEZ-MARTIN is an assistant professor of Mexican American and Latina/o studies at the University of Texas at Austin. She holds a PhD in the field of folklore and ethnomusicology from Indiana University–Bloomington. Her areas of specialty include Latina/o cultural studies and American folkloristics. Her forthcoming book, *Coming Out Latina: Quinceañera Style and Latina Consumer Identities*, investigates contemporary cultural practices that link conceptions of racialized capitalism and class performativity to the staging of Latina coming-of-age rituals known as quinceañeras.

NICOLE M. GUIDOTTI-HERNÁNDEZ is an associate professor of American studies and Mexican American and Latina/o studies at the University of Texas at Austin. She was the inaugural chair of the Department of Mexican American and Latin/o Studies and the founding director of the Mellon Mays Undergraduate Fellowship program from 2014 to 2016 at the University of Texas at

Austin. She has published articles in *RHR, Latino Studies, The Latin Americanist, ELN,* and *Social Text.* Her 2001 book *Unspeakable Violence: Reimagining U.S. and Mexican National Imaginaries,* won the 2011–2012 MLA Book Award for Chicano/a and Latino/a Literary and Cultural Studies and was a finalist for the Berkshire Women's History First Book Prize.

DANIELA GUTIÉRREZ LÓPEZ is a PhD candidate in gender studies at Indiana University-Bloomington. She was born in Bogotá, Colombia, where she completed a BA in literature in 2012. Daniela moved to the United States to pursue a master's degree in women's and gender studies at Rutgers University-New Brunswick. Her thesis was titled: "The Displays, Silences, and Aesthetic Possibilities of Museum Fashion's Gendered Geopolitics" (2014). Her current research focuses on decolonial onto-epistemologies. It is aimed at understanding the ways queer students of color use performance within activist practices in order to challenge the oppressive political economy the U.S. imperial university sustains.

JAIME GUZMÁN is a lecturer at California State University, Los Angeles and at Long Beach City College. He received his PhD in Communication Studies with an emphasis in communication and culture from the University of Denver. His areas of research include critical geography, whiteness studies, and latinidad. His current research is situated in the neighborhood of Boyle Heights, California, which is the site of current gentrification initiatives.

RUTH Y. HSU is an associate professor of English at the University of Hawai'i at Manoa, in Honolulu, Hawai'i. Her teaching and research focus on the issues of racial, ethnic, and gender categories, especially as these groupings intersect with ideas of nationality, class, and geographic and political space and time. Her main areas of specialty reside in Asian American and Asian diaspora literary and cultural production within the concept of North American literature and culture and the enduring configurations of racialist tropes. She is co-editor of a new Modern Language Association volume on teaching the works of Karen Tei Yamashita. Other works in progress include a monograph on recent novels by Yamashita and essays on recent formulations of race and ethnic discourse of the United States.

MINTZI AUANDA MARTÍNEZ-RIVERA is a visiting assistant professor and the interim associate director of the Latino Studies Program at Indiana University–Bloomington. During twenty-four months of fieldwork research in the P'urhépecha community of Santo Santiago de Angahuan in the state of Michoacán, México, she documented the community's life-cycle rituals and the full social-religious calendar of events. In her work, she argues that cultural transformations are integral to the continuity and survival of indigenous culture and identity. By focusing on young adults in the community and their active participation in celebrations like the *tembuchakua* (the wedding), she demonstrates how transformations in celebrations contribute to the continuation and survival of the P'urhépecha culture.

DOMINO RENEE PEREZ is an associate professor in the Department of English and the Center for Mexican American Studies at the University of Texas at Austin. Her book *There Was a Woman: La Llorona from Folklore to Popular Culture* (2008) examines one of the most famous figures in U.S./Mexican folklore. She has published numerous book chapters and articles on topics ranging from film and indigeneity in Mexican American studies to young adult fiction and folklore.

CHANNETTE ROMERO is an associate professor of English and Native American studies at the University of Georgia. She is the author of *Activism and the American Novel: Religion and Resistance in Fiction by Women of Color* (2012). Professor Romero has published essays on literature and film in *American Indian Quarterly, Studies in American Indian Literatures, The Oxford Handbook of Indigenous American Literatures, African American Review,* and *ELN.* Her current book-in-progress, *In-forming Native Film: Genre and American Indian Cinema,* explores Indigenous American filmmakers' growing fascination and experimentation with genre films.

GERALD VIZENOR is a professor emeritus of American studies at the University of California, Berkeley. He is a citizen of the White Earth Nation and has published more than thirty books, including *Shrouds of White Earth* (2011), *Native Liberty: Natural Reason and Cultural Survivance* (2009); *Survivance: Narratives of Native Presence* (2008); *Father Meme* (2008), and *Fugitive Poses: Native American Indian Scenes of Absence and Presence* (1998), along with many others influential works. His most recent publications are *Blue Ravens* (2014), a historical novel about Native American Indians who served in the First World War in France, and *Treaty Shirts* (2016), seven narratives about constitutional and totemic liberty. Vizenor has received numerous awards, such as the Pen Excellence Award, American Book Award, Western Literature Association Distinguished Achievement Award, and Lifetime Literary Achievement Award from the Native Writer's Circle of the Americas.

JAMES WILKEY is a PhD student at Louisiana State University, where he specializes in Cuban historical memory and the history of Cuban migration. His interests also include Latin American film and pop-culture expression. James received his MA at Queen's University Belfast in 2011 and his bachelor's degree from the University of Florida in 2010.

Index

Aageson, Thomas H., 5
Acosta, Oscar Zeta, 178–179
African American Music: An Introduction
(Burnim and Maultsby), 8–9
African Americans. *See* race and diversity,
in United States
Alba, Jessica, 220
Aldama, Frederick, 6–7
algorithm culture, 30n5
Alla en el rancho grande (*Out on the Big
Ranch*), 65
Allen, Woody, 77
alt-left, 30n3
alt-right, 16, 30n3
Alzate, Gastón, 141–142
American Indians. *See* Native Americans
Anderson, Benedict, 133
antifa, 30n3
Anzaldúa, Gloria, 115, 155; on borderlands,
112, 243; bridge and, 248; language for,
122; nepantla and, 245
Autobiography of a Brown Buffalo (Acosta),
178–179
Avilés, Quique, 129, 129n1; academic
racism and, 119; African Americans and,
118; on art and social change, 115; art
genre of, 113–114; audience of, 114, 117,
126, 128; Banks and, 119–121; *el barrio*
for, 117–118; on borderlands, 112, 123;
*Caminata: A Walk through Immigrant
America* by, 127; Carroll and, 120–121;

"Crazy: Loco Culebra's Monologue" by,
123; at DCWritersCorps, 120; on
dignity, 124; DuBois and, 121–122;
education of, 118–119; on El Salvador,
115–116; family of, 116; identity for,
124–126; language for, 115, 122, 125–126;
LatiNegro and, 119–120; new American
identity and, 113, 123, 128; pluralism and,
126; pluriculturalism and, 124; on race
and diversity, 110–113; Salvadoran
immigrant imaginary for, 121–122;
spoken resistance of, 113–115, 121, 127;
stereotypes and, 126–127; theater for,
119; third space for, 125, 128; Third World
imaginary for, 121; translocal discourses
of, 122–123; verbal art and, 114, 128

Badger, Tom, 85–86
Banks, Michelle, 119–121
Barnouw, Victor, 85–86
Barnum, P.T., 68
Barrera, Cordelia, 264
barrio, el (Washington D.C. neighbor-
hood), 116; Avilés and, 117–118;
gentrification and, 117–118
Bartra, Roger, 133–134
Bats'i Fest: Festival de Rock Indígena,
101–102
Bauman, Richard, 114
Berger, Harris M., 6
Beyoncé, 139

285